MW01622980

MEATBALLS

The Ultimate Cookbook

Meatballs

13-Digit ISBN: 978-1-64643-014-7
10-Digit ISBN: 1-64643-014-X

This book may be ordered by mail from the publisher. Please include $5.99 for postage and handling. Please support your local bookseller first!

Books published by Cider Mill Press Book Publishers are available at special discounts for bulk purchases in the United States by corporations, institutions, and other organizations. For more information, please contact the publisher.

Cider Mill Press Book Publishers
"Where good books are ready for press"
PO Box 454
12 Spring Street
Kennebunkport, Maine 04046
Visit us online
cidermillpress.com

Typography: Adobe Garamond, Brandon Grotesque, Lastra, Sackers English Script
Front cover image: Meatballs with Olives & Sun-Dried Tomatoes, see page 190
Back cover image: Italian Escarole & Meatball Soup, see page 54
Front endpaper image: Chicken Tsukune, see page 280
Back endpaper image: Sweet & Sour Meatballs, see page 255

Printed in China

1 2 3 4 5 6 7 8 9 0

First Edition

MEATBALLS

The Ultimate Cookbook

ELLEN BROWN

CONTENTS

INTRODUCTION

For centuries, meatballs were a peasant dish. This is because a small amount of meat from the less luxurious parts of animals could be stretched to feed a large number of people through the addition of vegetables and cereal grains. They were made with leftover meat, traditionally beef and lamb, which was shredded by hand, with ingredients added to give the mixture the ability to be formed into a small ball. Today, meatballs remain inexpensive to make and easy to eat, and they represent multicultural culinary masterpieces that appeal to generations the world over as a quintessential comfort food.

What constitutes a meatball is loosely defined. In the 1800s, the *Oxford English Dictionary* defined one as "any combination of raw or cooked meat shaped into a ball." That's certainly broad enough to leave plenty of room for personal interpretation. Every cuisine includes a variety of options, and the character and seasoning of the meatball reflect its country of origin, as well as the ingredients commonly used in that specific geographic enclave. The oldest meatballs were grilled, fried in oil, or poached in broth; they were served alone, floating in soup, or blanketed by a sauce. As meatballs evolved they were also skewered as kebabs, piled into sandwiches, or used to crown bowls of pasta or tossed salad greens.

Meatballs seem to have developed along the same geographic route followed by the spice

trade. For that reason, even though its origin remains mysterious, most food historians accept Persia as the birthplace of the meatball. In Farsi, *kofta*—the generic word for meatballs—literally means "pounded meat." You see derivations of the word in many cultures to this day, from Turkish *koftë* to Israeli *ktzitzot*. From the Persians, meatballs went to the Arabs, who proceeded to take them everywhere they went. From the 2nd to the 9th centuries, the Arabs dominated a huge expanse spanning from the Far East to the Mediterranean Sea, and as Islam spread so did its traditional foods, including the meatball. And the Mughals, who learned about meatballs from their Persian cousins, brought them to India and Central Asia.

Meatballs then traveled around the world via oceanic exploration starting in the late 15th century. While meatballs can be viewed as an Arabic addition to the cuisines of Spain and Portugal, the Spanish and Portuguese then shipped the form to the New World. When "Columbus sailed the ocean blue" he was searching for gold, but it's a safe bet that his crew got fed *albóndigas*, Spanish meatballs made with both beef and pork.

While all those meatballs were faithful to historic prototypes, meatballs came to occupy their own special niche in American cuisine when brought by waves of immigrants from Europe—particularly from Italy—in the late 19th and early 20th centuries.

Today, cooks plunk packages of ground, raw meats into their shopping carts from a refrigerated supermarket case. But for thousands of years the meat destined for meatballs would be laboriously chopped by hand, either raw or cooked. The shift to the current state began in the early part of the 19th century, when industrious inventors began submitting plans, and being awarded patents, for meat grinders. They contained a spiral feed tube that was animated by a handle, and rotating cutting knives. This innovation made it possible for the average person to buy ground meat, preventing them from having to mince it themselves or use cooked leftovers. And butchers would grind meat to order, accommodating a home cook's personal preferences.

While a meat grinder is a piece of durable physical equipment, it also has a place as time-honored slang. One definition is to participate in a draining physical activity or military battle, such as "the last few miles of the marathon were a real meat grinder, and almost a third of the participants dropped out." But a variation on that meaning is that a situation can be injurious in a nonphysical way, such as "Confirmation hearings before the Senate are such a meat grinder that it discourages worthy candidates from moving forward."

WHEN KOFTA RULED THE WORLD

According to *The Oxford Companion to Food*, kofta appears in some of the earliest Arabic cookbooks, in recipes that called for ground lamb to be rolled into meatballs the size of oranges, which were then glazed with egg yolk and saffron. This early leg up for lamb has proven to be extremely difficult to overcome—today, even in countries with small Muslim populations, it's rare to find meatballs made with the then-verboten pork.

Turkish cuisine features more than 80 types of kofta, and most of them are named for their village of origin. You'll find references to Izmir and Trabzon, all regions of Turkey, and in Turkish the name changes from kofta to köfte.

In North Africa, meatballs represented a melding of ancient traditions and the Arab influence that came later. Moroccan *kefta mkaouara*, a stew of meatballs and eggs in a spicy tomato sauce, is cooked in a clay tajine, a vestige of the region's Berber heritage.

Not all forms of kofta are cooked. The best known of these Middle Eastern versions of steak tartare is *kibbeh*, native to the Levantine region occupied by modern-day Syria, Lebanon, Jordan, and Israel. Kibbeh is so popular it approaches the status of a national dish in many of these countries. The finely ground and spicy lamb—or occasionally beef or camel—is mixed with bulgur wheat and served garnished with mint leaves and scallions. In nearby Turkey, *cig köfte* is another variation on the dish, and the lamb-and-ground wheat mixture is shaped by hand. Due to immigration patterns in the late 19th and early 20th centuries, kibbeh is also found in some parts of Latin America, including the coastline of Colombia and Mexico's Yucatan Peninsula.

Not only can kofta be raw, it doesn't have to be made with meat at all. Balls made from paneer cheese cooked in a curry sauce are part of Indian cuisine, as are some crafted from mashed cooked vegetables. In Mughlai cuisine, a result of Central Asian and Iranian culinary traditions melding with those of India during the Mughal Empire, a dish known as *malai kofta* features deep-fried balls of potato and paneer that are simmered in spicy tomato sauce. And in nearby Bangladesh, a Muslim country with hundreds of miles of rivers and a small coastline, fish is a popular grist for kofta. *Chitol macher kofta* is made from finely ground fish mixed with cumin, coriander, ginger, turmeric, hot chilies, and onion; the balls are first fried and then added to a thick curry sauce.

EUROPEAN ENTICEMENT

Meatballs have a place in all European cuisines. While some national versions are tied to the spread of Muslim culture, many are tied to the practice of sausage-making, which has been part of European cuisines for centuries.

Meatballs in France, called *boulettes*, have one foot in the Muslim world. Morocco, Tunisia, and Algeria were all French colonies at one point, and the spicing and aromatic aspects of those cuisines moved across the Mediterranean Sea with traders and immigrants. They are still called boulettes in those countries, although they have other names in local dialects. One can smell the aromatic spices drifting from North African restaurants in Paris, where the meatballs are frequently served with couscous or stewed tagine-style with saffron. Many French recipes also incorporate both parsley and cilantro into the meat mixture, and other recipes add additional spice to the meat by utilizing North African merguez, a sausage made from lamb. With the exception of these North African transplants, meatballs are insignificant in regional French cooking.

Across the English Channel, sausages were common, served as a key component in the popular meal of bangers and mash, as well as sausage rolls in pubs. English cuisine includes an unusual meatball, dating to 1842 and popular in South and Central Wales as well as in the English Midlands. It's called a *faggot.* Made primarily of pork, they traditionally included a large percentage of pork liver and heart, and they were wrapped in caul (the fat surrounding the abdominal organs) before cooking. Due to the food rationing required during World War II, faggots were very popular and often served with onion gravy, mashed potatoes, and peas. They declined in popularity after the war, but they've experienced a renaissance in the 21st century as part of the "nose-to-tail" eating trend. The commercial ones sold frozen in supermarkets vary from the homemade ones, which tend to have a coarser texture.

Faggots have an international cousin in South Africa, *skilpadjies.* While brought by English settlers, the cuisine in South Africa was also greatly influenced both by Dutch colonists as well as its indigenous traditions. In the South African version, the pork is replaced with beef, sometimes with venison and ostrich added. More highly seasoned than the English version, the cakes are flavored with nutmeg and gain some sweetness from chopped dried fruit. Liver remains an important ingredient in these meatballs, which are also called *muise*, *vlermuise*, and *pofadder*.

In the Netherlands, you're most likely to encounter meatballs billed as *bitterballen.* They were traditionally less time-consuming for home cooks because the meat started out by being braised, which made it much easier to chop. The chopped meat was then folded into its broth, which was stiffened with gelatin. The chilled mixture was then made into small balls

that were coated with bread crumbs and deep-fried. The interior of the bitterballen was succulent and creamy while the outside was crunchy. The method is similar to how croquettes, or *croquetas* in Spanish, are made. Bitterballen continue to be a popular bar food in the Netherlands, although they are now washed down with beer far more often than bitters.

Just as is true with the myriad versions of kofta named for Turkish cities, the most unusual meatball that remains beloved in German cuisine is also named for its place of origin. *Königsberger klopse*, literally "meatballs in the style of Königsberg," was named for a region in eastern Prussia. They include ingredients that are rarely associated with German cooking, such as capers, anchovies, and lemon zest. The city became part of what is now Poland after World War II, and it was renamed Kaliningrad after Mikhail Kalinin, who was a close ally of Joseph Stalin in the Soviet leadership. While they've lost their geographic anchor, the meatballs live on in their country of origin, and are popular in all parts of Germany today.

Meatballs are beloved in all the Scandinavian countries. The dishes are similar in feel across the region, and vary according to the locally preferred meat, as well as the language used to name them.

In Sweden they're called *köttbullar*. They are traditionally made with a combination of beef and pork scented with allspice and nutmeg, and they're served in brown gravy with lingonberry jam.

IKEA, of course, has brought Swedish meatballs to the world, thanks to Ingvar Kamprad, who founded the company in 1943 at the age of 17. He maintained that "it's difficult to do business with someone on an empty stomach." Working from this premise, he started to sell authentic Swedish meatballs in the 1980s, and the 340 stores worldwide now sell 2 million meatballs a day.

We may think of köttbullar as authentic to Sweden, and as much a part of the culture as IKEA and ABBA. But they, too, have a connection to Middle Eastern kofta. And through European history, we even have insights into the parentage of this food that's ubiquitous both in American public school cafeterias and on an authentic Swedish *smörgasbord*. King Charles XII, who ruled Sweden from 1697 to 1718, took refuge in the Ottoman Empire for four years in the early 1700s after being defeated in a war with Russia. He was introduced to meatballs while in exile, and brought them, along with coffee, back to Sweden.

In nearby Denmark, meatballs are dubbed *frikadeller*, and they're customarily made with both pork and veal and modestly seasoned with salt and pepper. They are frequently panfried, so they are slightly flattened into an oval instead of a round ball. They are also served on the famous Danish open-faced sandwiches.

Moving around the Baltic Sea, the Norwegian name for meatballs is *kjøttkaker*, which translates to "meat cakes." They resemble their Danish cousins, but are usually made with beef and served, as in Sweden, with gravy and lingonberry jam. Also reliant on beef as the main source of protein are the *lihapullat* of Finland, although some versions feature ground reindeer meat. They are also served with jam, but sometimes pickled cucumbers are served alongside as a textural foil.

While Italian American meatballs rule on the New World side of the Atlantic Ocean, meatballs, called *polpette*, are rather insignificant in authentic Italian cuisine. Although we know from Apicius that they were made in early Rome, meatballs today are made with some combination of beef and veal. They are rarely put in any sauce, and are most often served as part of an antipasto spread or as a second course. Authentic Italian meatballs are much smaller than their American cousins. In the Abruzzo region they can be as small as marbles, and they're named with the diminutive *polpettines*. The only Italian meatballs touching a tomato sauce come from the southern part of the country, and it is these that serve as the prototypes for American meatballs. There are a few interesting meatballs remaining in Venetian cuisine that date to when Venice was important in the spice trade and dealt extensively with Arab countries. Some of these recipes for *polpette di carne* include sweet candied citron and toasted pine nuts, and can even be dusted with sugar. There is another Italian first cousin of meatballs, called *crocchette*, that is made from a wide variety of ingredients, ranging from cheese and vegetables to fish and potatoes. Similar to croquettes, crocchette are almost always fried.

Across the Adriatic Sea in Greece, *keftedes* are a popular appetizer. Made from lamb and occasionally beef, they are flavored with garlic and oregano and then fried until crisp. They are usually accompanied by a bowl of dill-laced tzatziki, or they can be served alongside rice or a tomato sauce as a meal.

Food writing hardly began with James Beard, M. F. K. Fisher, or Craig Claiborne. In the 1st century CE there was a Roman gourmet named Marcus Gavius Apicius, whose name has become synonymous with a luxurious life and diet. In *De Re Coquinaria Libria Decem*, he mentions several types of *isicia*, which are patties comprised of different types of animal proteins (aka meatballs), and ranks them in order of personal preference. His favorites were made from peacock, then the list descends to pheasant, rabbit, and chicken with suckling pig pegged last.

EASTERN EUROPEAN VARIATIONS

While the physical map of this part of the world has been extensively redrawn, a process that began following the end of World War I, the culinary traditions—including some variations on meatballs—have been entrenched for centuries. There are some vestiges of Persian and Muslim influence, but then there are other unique forms fashioned from ground meat.

In Poland they're called *pulpety*, and they're served in a variety of sauces, ranging from tomato and wild mushroom to a flour-thickened white gravy. In addition to serving them with potatoes, as is true in all of the nearby Scandinavian countries, they are frequently accompanied by buckwheat groats, called *kasha*. Sometimes these meatballs are flattened and fried, so they can resemble a hamburger, at least outwardly. In some parts of the country this iteration is named *mielony*, which means "minced cutlet."

In nearby Romania, the popular form of meatballs is called *mici*, which translates to "little ones." According to legend, the father of mici was Iorache Ionescu, a cook who worked in a popular pub in Bucharest that was famous for its sausages. One day he ran out of casings, and came up with the idea of grilling just the filling. The dish was first mentioned in 1870 by French Romanian journalist Ulysse de Marsillac. These grilled meatballs are rolled into a cylindrical shape similar to a sausage. The base is a mixture of beef, lamb, and pork, with seasonings such as garlic, pepper, thyme, coriander, savory, and, sometimes, paprika. An unusual addition to the mixture is sodium bicarbonate, a leavening agent. It gives the mici a light

texture. They are most often served with mustard, french fries, and pickled vegetables. There are some regional variations that include caraway seeds and allspice, too.

While mici are related to European sausage-making traditions, another Romanian meatball, *chiftele*, is tied to the country's proximity to Turkey. These meatballs combine pork with mashed potatoes, and they're traditionally fried. While not sauced, they are usually accompanied by either a sour cream dip containing dill or a mustard sauce.

Due to the cold winters, many Eastern European cuisines simmer meatballs in a flavorful broth and serve the pair as dinner. In Latvia, a favorite soup is *frikadelu zupa*. The actual meatballs are made from a combination of beef and pork flavored with onion and bound with eggs and bread crumbs. The meatballs are then cooked in water flavored with bay leaves and peppercorns along with diced vegetables, including carrots, celery, and potatoes. All the ingredients are simmered together so the meat and vegetables flavor the stock. Typically the soup is enriched with dill-laced sour cream just prior to serving.

Bulgarian cuisine also includes a rich and delicious meatball soup, called *supa topcheta*. The beef-and-pork meatballs are flavored with paprika and garlic, and bound together with bread and eggs. The beef broth base is filled with chunks of carrot, celery, leeks, and potatoes. The soup is then thickened with egg yolks and spiked with lemon juice-laced yogurt. The resulting soup is creamy without being overly heavy, and it's served with additional yogurt and—as is standard with any soup served in Eastern Europe—a loaf of crusty bread.

FROM ARAB-INFLUENCED SPAIN TO THE NEW WORLD

The Muslim takeover of the Iberian Peninsula was a seven-year campaign that began in 711 CE, and the reign lasted until 1492, when the last stronghold, Granada, fell. The capital of the region was in the south; it was called Al-Andalus, and centuries of this rule coincided with the Abassid period, which is also known as the Golden Age of Baghdad. This was a time of refined cooking in the Muslim world, and Spanish tables reflected this as well.

The Spanish word for meatballs is albóndigas, and it's derived from the Arabic word for hazelnut, *al-bunduq*. Food historians assume that these early meatballs were very small, although that is not the case today. Two of the most common preparations for albóndigas are in a spicy tomato sauce emboldened with hot paprika and garlic, and also a very delicate one. *Albóndigas en salsa de almendras*, which sees meatballs that are frequently a combination of beef and pork being served in a sauce scented and colored with saffron, and thickened with ground almonds. These meatballs spread through the Spanish-speaking world, from Mazatlán to Manila. In the Philippines they're called *almondigas*, and they're most often served in broth with rice noodles.

Similar dishes are found on the Portuguese side of the peninsula, where the name is *almôndegas*. A few of those authentic recipes include the region's famed Port wine, as well as chopped sausage. These are the meatballs that arrived in Brazil, where they are frequently paired with black beans.

ASIAN ADAPTATIONS

Meatballs made with a variety of meats as well as fish hold a place in many Asian cuisines. Just think of steamed meatballs on small plates wending their way around a room via dim sum carts, or a huge meatball the size of a fist, intended to represent a lion's head, presented with a steamed cabbage mane in restaurants and homes.

In addition to seasonings, it is texture that distinguishes the majority of Asian meatballs from their European counterparts. In Europe the ingredients, including the meat, are finely minced. In Asia the meat is almost pulverized, which gives meatballs a smooth and springy texture. It's akin to the process used to make *surimi* from pollock and other fish. The pulverizing renders them into an almost gelatinous consistency when cooked because it uncoils the protein strands in the meat.

As is true with many foods, China can claim some of the oldest known preparations of meatballs. There are records describing meatballs as early as 200 BCE. Many were part of Lunar New Year celebrations. The large meatballs originated in Yangzhou and Zhenjiang, and became part of Shanghai cuisine in the 19th century when large waves of immigrants arrived. While made with fatty pork, the meatballs are given textural variety with the inclusion of toothy ingredients like water chestnuts and bamboo shoots. The plain variety is usually steamed with napa cabbage, while ones known as "red cooked" are also flavored with soy sauce. Smaller varieties of pork meatballs are served floating in soups, and in Cantonese cuisine beef is swapped for the ubiquitous pork in small meatballs that are steamed and served as part of a common dim sum presentation.

In addition to meatballs, there's a long tradition in Chinese cuisine for fishballs, especially in southern China. They are best known in Hong Kong, and are categorized by their colors: yellow, golden, or white. The yellow fishballs are sold primarily by street vendors and are made from inexpensive fish. Sold on bamboo skewers that hold anywhere from five to seven, the fishballs get their name from the curry satay dipping sauces created by the vendors, each one offering their own personal take. The golden fishballs are a snack in Cheung Chau, an island about six miles from Hong Kong. They are larger in size than yellow fishballs, although they are also served with curry sauce. White fishballs are on restaurant menus, and they keep their pristine color because only egg whites or cornstarch are added to the fish paste before they are boiled. Another reason for the pale color is that the balls are made from more expensive fish, such as Spanish mackerel.

In Indonesia, *bakso* is the generic term for meatballs and it is unclear whether they came to the islands from China, or with the Dutch settlers who colonized the nation. They are most often served in soup, and in modern times the meat mixture gets an extensive whirring in a food processor because the desired texture is almost rubbery. Bakso is sold on the street and in small mom-and-pop cafes, as well as at traditional restaurants.

Another country in which meatballs in broth are the most common preparation is Vietnam, and chances are those meatballs were influenced by Chinese cuisine. *Bò viên* are springy spheres, and most often they're eaten as part of *pho*. Typically, the meatballs are made from beef, but in some parts of the country they're crafted from chicken and pork. There's also a place on the meatball roster in Vietnam for grilled varieties similar to sausages. Called *nem nướng*, that's what you'll find on the menu at Slanted Door, Charles Phan's famous San

Francisco restaurant. The grilled meatballs are flavored with fish sauce, garlic, sugar, black pepper, and scallions; they're served with a julienne of vegetables and rice noodles.

Meatballs were never really a part of traditional Japanese cooking, but some have found their way into Japanese cuisine. *Tsukune* are skewers of chicken meatballs brushed with a sweet glaze and grilled like traditional yakitori.

THE ALL-AMERICAN MEATBALL

Spaghetti topped with meatballs in a red sauce is emblematic of how America's cooking pot came to resemble the international melting pot of its population. It's an entirely native-born dish, with few connections to Italian polpette. Like all ethnic populations, the 4 million Italians who emigrated to America between 1880 and 1920 had to make do with the ingredients they could find and afford.

More than 80 percent of those Italians moved from the very poor regions of southern Italy, including Sicily, Calabria, Campania, Abruzzi, and Molise. In the States, meat became a central part of the meal rather than a rare luxury. In Italy, more than three-quarters of a family's income would be devoted to putting food on the table, and that number plummeted to 25 percent in the New World. While they could afford meat, it was far from a Sunday roast or filet mignon. They used chopped meat and other economical cuts that they could have ground, and stretched it with vegetables and bread soaked in milk. In Italy the ratio of meat to bread in polpette was 1-to-1, but as the Italians gained financial security in the United States, the bread's share decreased, meat's increased, and the meatballs became much denser.

While meatballs reach back into ancient history, we know that the classic marinara sauce with which they're served couldn't have been invented before the mid-16th century, when Spaniards brought the tomato from the New World back to Europe. There are claims by both Naples and Sicily of its parentage, so it's safe to assume it can be pegged geographically to the same southern Italian regions from which the majority of Italian immigrants came to North America.

In his book *How Italian Food Conquered the World*, published in 2011, John Mariani explained that the sauce was quick to make,

Perhaps the most iconic movie scene featuring meatballs is from Disney's 1955 animated classic, *Lady and the Tramp*. While the plot revolves around the romance of the purebred cocker spaniel and a lovable mutt, everyone remembers their "date" at Tony's restaurant, sharing a plate of spaghetti and meatballs, and eventually a kiss, as the owner and cook serenade them by singing the romantic tune, "Bella Notte." But that's not the only cinematic role meatballs have landed. In 1979, Bill Murray got his first starring role in *Meatballs*, playing a misfit camp counselor herding misfit kids, branded "meatballs." And in 1998, Adam Sandler had the title role in *The Wedding Singer*. He gives singing lessons to an elderly lady in return for her famous meatballs.

so that the sailors' wives could start it when they saw their husbands' fleet of fishing boats on the distant horizon. For home cooks in the United States in the 20th century, canned tomatoes and spaghetti are two foods that could easily be found in markets, leading to the further popularization of their ancestors' sauce.

Now that the protein and the sauce have been pinned down, the question remains as to how pasta became the center of the dish. Most food historians concur that it is because Americans were accustomed to eating one course instead of the multi-course meal favored in Italy—both in homes and restaurants—and they wanted a starch to match the protein on the plate. While spuds were supreme on America's plates, rice and various forms of pasta—from egg noodles to macaroni and cheese—were also common. So Italian restaurants married the main course with the pasta course in order to meet demand.

But this resulting dish was clearly as American as the chop suey served at Chinese restaurants. Mariani includes in his book some quotations from the 1950s writings of a Sicilian restaurateur, Niccoló de Quattrociocchi. He reported that he'd dined at an Italian restaurant where "I was introduced to two very fine, traditional American specialties called 'spaghetti with meatballs' and 'cotoletta parmigiana',"

which he thought were "just for fun called Italian." But he added: "as a matter of fact I found them both extremely satisfying and I think someone in Italy should invent them for Italians over there."

Meatballs in red sauce not only top plates of pasta, Americans also cut them up as a pizza topping and stuff them into rolls to make sandwiches. The late 20th century and this century saw the rise of meatball variations of other beloved American dishes. It's now common to find Philly cheesesteak meatballs on menus in a sauce made with American cheese along with some sautéed onions and bell peppers. Meatballs are also stuffed inside packaged refrigerated dough with a slice of cheese and served as cheeseburger meatballs.

Clearly, meatballs make the world go round. Daniel Handler, the American author who penned the children's book series "A Series of Unfortunate Events" under the pseudonym Lemony Snicket, wrote that "miracles are like meatballs, because nobody can exactly agree on what they are made of, where they come from, or how often they should appear." That may be true, but at least we know that they're beloved.

Ellen

When you think of the 1960s, visions of *Mad Men* come to mind. For those who lived it, entertaining in that decade can be summarized by one piece of equipment: the chafing dish. Set over a basin of simmering water, the chafing dish was the inevitable holder of food for "fancy dinner parties." And a preparation that often found its way into one was Sweet and Sour Meatballs. This recipe was a signature item from *Elegant but Easy*, a cookbook by Marian Burros and Lois Levine first published in 1962. The sauce joined bottled chili sauce and grape jelly with a hit of lemon juice, and the meatballs simmered in it for almost 2 hours before being transferred to the chafing dish.

THE ANATOMY OF A MEATBALL

Meatballs are good news for home cooks. Why? Meatballs are one of the easiest foods to pull off successfully. It's almost impossible to mess them up. They reside at the opposite end of the spectrum from the soufflé that can turn into a flat pancake instead of reaching great heights. In other words, you don't need to be a professional chef with a battery of culinary skills.

My definition of "meatball" is a broad one; anything made from a mixture that is ground and takes on a round form is a meatball. A number of the recipes that follow don't even use meat. There are meatballs made with poultry, fish, and vegetables (and there are even recipes for ball-shaped desserts).

Each ingredient in the mixture has a purpose—to produce a flavorful meatball with an appealing soft texture. While many meatballs are the size of golf balls, no one wants them to taste like one. The ideal texture for a meatball is a soft interior; the exterior can be hard or soft, depending on how they are cooked. Some of the ingredients play more than one role. For example, using rye bread for moisture adds flavor from the caraway seeds, and adding ketchup to enhance the flavor will also add moisture to the mix. Here are the various categories of ingredients that comprise a meatball, with some variations given:

The Primary Ingredient: This is usually meat, but that can mean beef, veal, lamb, pork, poultry, or some combination of these. Meatballs can also be made with fish and shellfish. Grains, legumes, and vegetables can also take on the starring role, but lend a different touch than meat or seafood.

The Flavor Boosters: This category includes herbs, spices, cheeses, vegetables, sauces, and condiments. These ingredients vary in proportion by recipe; there are no hard and fast rules. If the meatball is intended to be eaten in a sauce, there will be fewer flavoring ingredients in the meatball itself, compared with those that are eaten off a toothpick as a stand-alone item. In addition to the flavor they provide, cheeses and condiments such as ketchup, mustard, or soy sauce also add moisture to meatballs. The vegetables in the meatball mixture can be either raw or cooked. Onions, celery, garlic, and carrots are the most frequently used, but chopped mushrooms or mashed potatoes can be added as well.

The Seasonings: Specific amounts of salt and pepper aren't listed in the recipes, because I believe this to be a personal matter. First, make the meatball mixture without salt and pepper; some of the secondary ingredients—such as seasoned bread crumbs or a condiment—may already include salt and pepper. Season the mixture after all other ingredients have been incorporated and a small bit of the mix has been cooked and tasted.

The Texture Enhancers: Most meatball recipes include at least one whole egg, and sometimes an additional egg yolk or egg white. The egg serves as a binding agent for the other

ingredients, allowing a meatball to hold its shape as it cooks. The egg also offers a bit of fat and liquid to give the meatball a satisfying mouth feel. Some vegetables, such as cooked chopped spinach or shredded cooked carrots, also add texture to meatballs.

The Moisture Magnets: In addition to preferring meatballs with a soft interior, we also like meatballs that have a moist interior. That's where the need for some sort of carbohydrate enters the picture. It can be anything from torn bread, fluffy Japanese panko, crushed crackers, plain bread crumbs, or grains such as rice (raw or cooked), oatmeal, or bulgur. The purpose of the carbohydrate is to absorb moisture as the meat cooks and releases liquid. Depending on what ingredient is used, the moisture magnet can also add flavor and texture to the meatball. As some recipes have a low moisture content, the moisture magnet is occasionally soaked in a liquid before adding it to the mixture. In recipes with a high moisture content the carbohydrate is added dry. The liquid in which it soaks can be as simple as water, which will add moisture only, or wine, stock, fruit juice, or tomato sauce to add flavor. While the various recipes in this book will specify a particular carbohydrate, feel free to use whatever is on hand. Experiment. The only caveat is to determine if the moisture magnet will also contribute to the flavor of the meatball and adjust accordingly. For example, preseasoned Italian bread crumbs are one of the great convenience foods on the market, but if all you have are plain bread crumbs, add ½ teaspoon of Italian seasoning (or some combination of dried basil, oregano, and thyme) to the mixture for every ½ cup of bread crumbs used.

If you buy loaves of crusty bread on a regular basis, you can save money by making your own bread crumbs. Once a loaf is a day old and the texture is no longer optimal, cut some of it into 1-inch cubes and let them sit at room temperature for a day or so. Then place the rock-hard cubes in a food processor and blitz until you have fine bread crumbs. Store the bread crumbs in an airtight container for up to 1 week.

THE DAILY GRIND

The quality and type of ground meat makes an enormous difference when cooking beef meatballs, as some cuts of beef are more flavorful than others. The best beef meatballs are made with ground chuck that is 80 percent lean and comes from a very well marbled and flavorful cut. Should you want a leaner cut, look for ground sirloin. Avoid any packages generically labeled "ground beef."

The same distinctions are not made with other ground meats, such as pork or lamb. But in most supermarkets you do have the choice between ground turkey and all-white meat ground turkey. The all-white meat is a bit leaner and not as flavorful as the mixture that includes dark meat. For meatballs made with a mixture of meats—usually beef, pork, and veal—many supermarkets carry a product called "meatloaf mix" containing all three meats in an equal proportion. I use this same proportion in many recipes that call for different types of meat.

Almost no one actually grinds meat at home these days; my meat grinder lives in a box in the basement along with other culinary antiques such as my fish poacher and waffle iron. But chopping fish and seafood at home is necessary for some recipes, and there is no better friend than the food processor to accomplish this task.

For salmon, tuna, or cod, start by cutting the fish into 1-inch cubes and arrange the cubes on a baking sheet lined with a sheet of plastic wrap. For shrimp, remove and discard the shell, and then devein the shrimp. Place the baking sheet in the freezer for 20 to 30 minutes, or until the fish/shrimp is partially frozen. Then transfer to the work bowl of the food processor and pulse until either fine or coarse, according to the directions in the specific recipe. In some recipes, part of the chopped fish or shellfish is removed from the work bowl to add texture to the mixture, and the remainder is pureed with eggs to become the mousse-like base for the fishballs.

MEATBALL MIXTURES

There is an order in which the various categories of ingredients are combined to create the best meatballs, although this may change to some extent from recipe to recipe. But, remember, this isn't rocket science. It's meatballs. And if you combine ingredients in an order other than the one specified in the recipe, your results will still be delicious.

Most recipes start by combining the ancillary ingredients, and then adding the meat last.

If bread crumbs or another carbohydrate are to soak in liquid, then that will be the first step. In a few recipes any liquid remaining is discarded after the initial soaking time. If you don't have to drain excess moisture, the recipe will begin by beating the egg with liquid, and then adding the carbohydrate.

While the crumbs soak, the vegetables can be chopped and sautéed, if necessary, and the other ingredients can be assembled. If the vegetables are sautéed, they are then allowed to cool briefly so that they don't cook the egg when added to the mixing bowl. The last thing added is the meat itself, and then the mixture is formed.

The secret to achieving meatballs with lots of texture is to create a mixture with your fingertips—either wearing disposable plastic gloves or using your well-washed hands. The ancillary ingredients are either chopped by hand or in a food processor, using the pulse function so that the mixture is combined as quickly as possible and individual ingredients retain their characteristics.

For a smooth and satiny texture, the mixture should be beaten either in a food processor or in a stand mixer using the paddle attachment; handheld mixers do not have enough power to beat a meat mixture into a smooth paste.

I use both accessories, switching between them depending on the recipe. But if you like smooth meatballs above all else, use the food processor.

Once the mixture is combined, it's time to taste for seasoning and add salt and pepper, if necessary. Because almost all mixtures contain raw eggs and meat, do not sample it from the bowl. You can fry up a small amount in a skillet, but I hate to dirty a pan for that task. I prefer to cook a few teaspoons, uncovered, in a microwave for 20 to 25 seconds. It will be pale and not very visually appealing, but it will be cooked through and safe to sample.

If time permits, the flavor of meatballs is vastly improved if the mixture is refrigerated for at least 1 hour. In fact, it can be refrigerated for up to 12 hours, but after that should be cooked because it contains raw ingredients that can be carriers of foodborne illnesses.

If you don't want to cook a meatball until it's well done, then make the mixture without an egg. There are some recipes in this book made without eggs because their flavors and textures are improved if the meat is slightly rare. If that's your general preference, you can omit the egg from the recipe and add more liquid to the mixture to replace its role in providing moisture.

SIZING UP THE SITUATION

Each recipe in this book tells you what size to make your meatballs, but you can make your meatballs any size you wish. Here is some guidance for measuring the mixture:

- The large side of a melon baller produces a 1-inch meatball.
- A level tablespoon produces a 1½-inch meatball.
- A heaping tablespoon produces a 2-inch meatball.
- A ¼ cup dry measuring cup produces a 2½- to 3-inch meatball.

Perhaps you want to try a recipe that yields 2-inch balls, but you want to serve them at a cocktail party. Look for a similar recipe that makes 1-inch balls, which are a perfect size for a single bite, and follow the cooking time of that recipe. Here are some other tips:

- Cut back on cooking time by one-third when reducing the size of a meatball by half. There is not a direct proportion because of the density of most meat mixtures.
- If you want to make a dipping sauce out of a sauce you typically use for simmering meatballs, add 5 minutes of cooking time to the meatballs to compensate for the time they would have simmered.
- If you are planning on freezing meatballs, undercook them by a few minutes so that they will not become too dry when reheated. The reheating should complete the cooking.

FROM MIXTURE TO MEATBALL

Whether your meatballs are the size of an egg yolk, the size of an egg, or the size of an orange, what's important is that the meatballs in each batch are all the same size so that they cook at the same rate. That might seem obvious, but it's actually harder to control than you think. Over the course of forming meatballs, they have a tendency to grow larger and larger unless you're careful when portioning the meat.

It is faster to make meatballs—and forming them can take far more time than making the mixture from which they are formed—if you follow an assembly line process.

First, measure out your mixture with an implement of a specific size, and then turn the individual portions into balls. For very small, appetizer-sized meatballs you can use the large side of a melon baller, and for slightly larger meatballs use a tablespoon. Large meatballs can be formed using a ¼-cup dry measuring cup, and there are specialized cookie dough scoops that come in a variety of sizes. Another benefit of these scoops is that they are spring-loaded, which allows them to quickly discharge the mixture.

Once all of the mixture has been portioned, it's time to form these amorphous blobs into meatballs. The easiest way is to gently roll the meat between the palms of your hands. If you like meatballs with a lot of texture, the mixture should not be over-handled or it will negate all the good work you've done to give them

texture. If you like meatballs with a smooth texture, roll the mixture into a Platonic orb, but you will still have to do it gently, because you are working with such a soft mixture.

COOKING METHODS

In addition to being made from various ingredients, meatballs are cooked in myriad ways. Some are fried; others are steamed. Some are grilled over very high heat while others are gently poached in barely simmering liquid.

Most meatballs are browned initially to create a crispy exterior, and this can be done in the oven or in a skillet on top of the stove. Some meatballs are coated with crumbs or a batter before they are cooked, while others are cooked as they are.

The kind of mixture that makes up the meatball often informs how it should be eaten. Sometimes they are served without a sauce, so all the flavor is in the meatball itself. Other times they are simmered in a sauce (like the ubiquitous spaghetti and meatballs), or dunked into a dipping sauce.

One factor that remains constant is that meatballs are intended to be cooked through and not eaten rare, even those made from ground red meats that many people would eat rare as a steak or even as a burger. Since most meatballs are made with eggs, eating uncooked or undercooked eggs can be dangerous from a health standpoint because eggs can be carriers of salmonella.

I am a firm believer that if one method requires constant attention while another method requires none of my attention, I'll always opt for the latter. I'd much rather be reading a book than turning meatballs in a skillet, and that's why the recipes in this book specify browning them in a hot oven. It happens all at once, and you're done with that step. If the meatballs are coated with crumbs, a light coating of cooking spray will accomplish the same browning as the fat you would have in a skillet, and the crumbs absorb less fat. But if you like to be more involved with your meatballs, brown them (or cook them completely) in a skillet. Use a 12-inch skillet, or larger, and begin by adding enough cooking oil to coat the bottom. Heat it over medium-high heat until a meatball sizzles loudly when placed in the pan. Then add the meatballs in a clockwise fashion starting at the top of the pan, being careful to leave at least 1½ to 2 inches between each one; if they are too close together in the skillet they won't brown, they'll steam.

Adjust the heat so that there is a merry sizzling sound and turn the meatballs gently every few minutes so that all sides brown. The best implement to use is either a soup spoon or a pair of soup spoons, and not a spatula, which is too large to maneuver gracefully around the skillet. Do not turn the meatballs until a dark brown crust has formed on the side touching the pan. Because meatballs are round and the pan is flat, it is not easy to brown all sides evenly. Toward the end of the process, use one meatball as a prop for a neighboring meatball to keep it in the proper position.

Now you're ready to make some meatballs!

MEATBALLS IN BROTH

There's an old Spanish proverb: "Of soup and love, the first is best." Nourishing soups exist in every culture—from rustic to haute cuisine—and you'll find a wide range of recipes in this chapter. These hearty, healthful soups are meals in a bowl. Most of them can be made up to 2 days in advance and refrigerated, tightly covered; reheat over low heat, covered. One last thing: be sure to enjoy all the emotional satisfaction that goes along with preparing—and eating—them.

CHICKEN & VEGETABLE SOUP WITH MATZO BALLS

YIELD: 6 TO 8 SERVINGS / **ACTIVE TIME:** 15 MINUTES / **TOTAL TIME:** 1 HOUR AND 30 MINUTES

Sometimes dubbed "Jewish penicillin," a hearty bowl of chicken soup with light and fluffy dumplings made from eggs and ground matzo crackers doesn't need a reason like a cold to enjoy.

INGREDIENTS:

FOR THE MATZO BALLS

- 4 LARGE EGGS
- ¼ CUP CHICKEN STOCK (SEE PAGE 660)
- ¼ CUP OLIVE OIL
- 1 CUP MATZO MEAL
- SALT AND PEPPER, TO TASTE

FOR THE SOUP

- 8 CUPS CHICKEN STOCK
- 2 CARROTS, SLICED
- 1 CELERY STALK, SLICED
- SALT AND PEPPER, TO TASTE
- FRESH PARSLEY, FOR GARNISH

1. To begin preparations for the matzo balls, place the eggs in a mixing bowl with the stock and oil and whisk to combine. Stir in matzo meal and season with salt and pepper. Refrigerate the mixture for at least 30 minutes.

2. Bring a large pot of salted water to a boil. Using wet hands, form the matzo dough into 1-inch balls and drop them into the boiling water. Cover the pot, reduce the heat to low, and simmer the matzo balls for 35 minutes without removing the cover from the pot.

3. While matzo balls simmer, begin preparations for the soup. Place the stock in a large saucepan and bring it to a boil. Add the carrots and celery, reduce the heat to low, and cook the vegetables until the carrots are tender, about 10 minutes.

4. Transfer the matzo balls to the soup, season with salt and pepper, garnish with parsley, and ladle into warmed bowls.

CHICKEN SOUP WITH CHICKEN LIVER MATZO BALLS

YIELD: 4 SERVINGS / **ACTIVE TIME:** 30 MINUTES / **TOTAL TIME:** 1 HOUR AND 50 MINUTES

These are not your grandmother's matzo balls. The chicken liver filling adds a rich and earthy component that elevates this comfort food.

INGREDIENTS:

- 1 TABLESPOON OLIVE OIL
- ½ ONION, MINCED
- 1 CARROT, PEELED AND MINCED
- 1 CELERY STALK, FINELY CHOPPED
- 1 TABLESPOON FINELY CHOPPED FRESH THYME
- 4 CUPS CHICKEN STOCK (SEE PAGE 660)
- SALT AND PEPPER, TO TASTE
- CHICKEN LIVER MATZO BALLS (SEE RECIPE)
- FRESH PARSLEY, CHOPPED, FOR GARNISH

CHICKEN LIVER MATZO BALLS

- ⅔ CUP MATZO MEAL
- 1 LARGE EGG
- 2 TABLESPOONS FINELY CHOPPED FRESH PARSLEY
- 5 TABLESPOONS CHICKEN OR DUCK FAT
- 4 TEASPOONS WATER
- SALT AND PEPPER, TO TASTE
- 1 SMALL ONION, MINCED
- 2 OZ. CHICKEN LIVER, MINCED

1. Place the oil in a large saucepan and cook over medium heat until warm. Add the onion and cook for 5 minutes, or until soft. Add the remaining vegetables and cook until tender.

2. Add the thyme and stock, bring to a boil, and then reduce heat so that the soup simmers. Cook for 20 minutes.

3. Season with salt and pepper, bring to a boil, and add the prepared Chicken Liver Matzo Balls. Cook for 12 minutes.

4. Place 2 balls in a bowl and pour the broth over the top. Garnish with parsley and serve.

CHICKEN LIVER MATZO BALLS

1. In a mixing bowl, add the matzo meal, egg, parsley, and 1 tablespoon of the chicken or duck fat. Stir to combine, add water to form a soft dough, and season with salt and pepper.

2. Cover with plastic wrap and refrigerate for 1 hour.

3. In a sauté pan, add 1 tablespoon of chicken or duck fat and the onion. Cook over medium heat for 5 minutes, or until soft.

4. Season with salt and pepper, add the chicken liver, and cook for another 3 minutes, or until the liver is cooked through.

5. Remove the pan from heat and let cool.

6. Spoon the liver mixture into eight piles, place the piles on a plate, and freeze for 10 minutes. Remove and form into balls. Return to the freezer for 10 minutes.

7. Divide the matzo mixture into eight portions and wrap them around the liver-and-onion balls.

8. In a medium saucepan, add the remaining chicken or duck fat and warm over medium heat. Add the matzo balls and cook until golden brown. Remove and set aside until ready to add to simmering soup.

WRAPPING THE MATZO BALL AROUND A FILLING

Place the matzo mix in the palm of your non-dominant hand and spread it so it's about an ⅛ inch thick. Place the ball of liver in the middle of the matzo and slowly make your hand into a ball shape. Seal the edges together with your dominant hand, and then roll the mixture into a smooth ball.

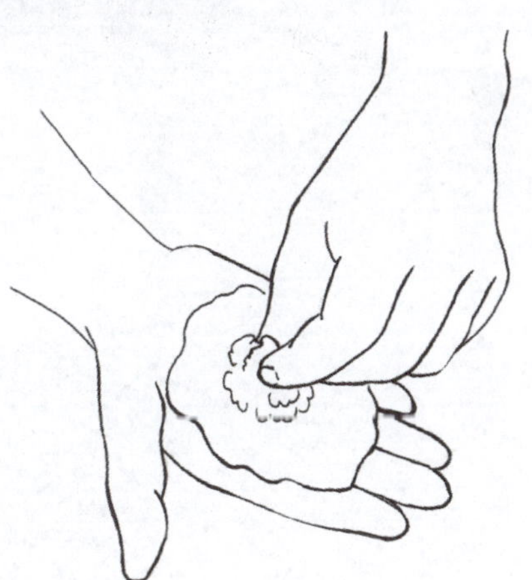

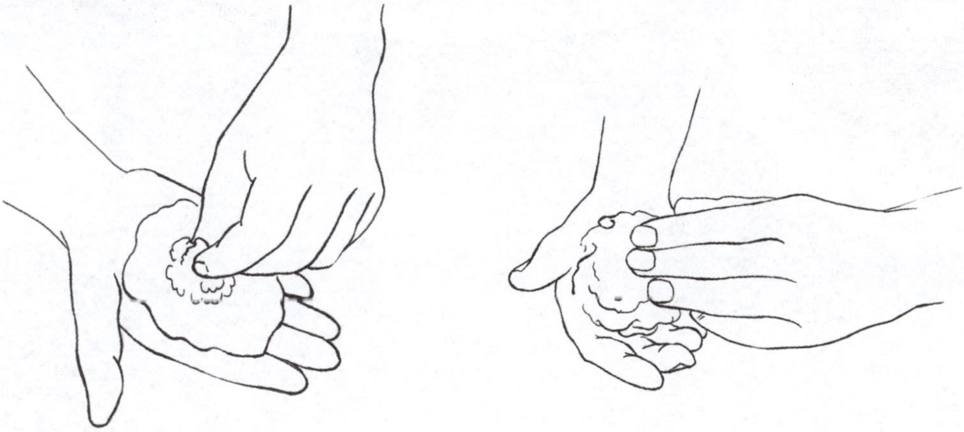

SPICY THAI CHICKEN MEATBALL SOUP

YIELD: 4 TO 6 SERVINGS / **ACTIVE TIME:** 20 MINUTES / **TOTAL TIME:** 40 MINUTES

Soups that can serve as the main course are part of every Asian cuisine. This broth is laced with assertive flavors like ginger and chilies, and the delicate meatballs are cooked right in the soup.

INGREDIENTS:

FOR THE SOUP

- 1 CUP DRIED SHIITAKE MUSHROOMS
- 1 (1 OZ.) PACKAGE CELLOPHANE NOODLES
- 1 CUP FRESH CILANTRO LEAVES, PLUS MORE FOR GARNISH
- 1-INCH PIECE FRESH GINGER, PEELED AND MINCED
- 3 GARLIC CLOVES, MINCED
- 1 JALAPEÑO OR SERRANO PEPPER, STEMMED, SEEDS AND RIBS REMOVED, AND CHOPPED
- 2 TABLESPOONS FISH SAUCE
- 1 TABLESPOON FIRMLY PACKED LIGHT BROWN SUGAR
- 7 CUPS CHICKEN STOCK (SEE PAGE 660)
- SALT AND PEPPER, TO TASTE
- SCALLIONS, TRIMMED AND MINCED, FOR GARNISH

FOR THE MEATBALLS

- 3 TABLESPOONS FISH SAUCE
- 3 TABLESPOONS CORNSTARCH
- 1¼ LBS. GROUND CHICKEN
- 3 GARLIC CLOVES, GRATED
- 1 TABLESPOON SESAME OIL

1. To begin preparations for the soup, cover the shiitake mushrooms with boiling water and let them soak for 10 minutes. Place the noodles in a baking dish, cover with boiling water, and let them soak until tender. Drain the noodles and cut them into 2-inch pieces. Drain the mushrooms and reserve the soaking liquid. Remove the stems from the mushrooms, chop the caps, and set them aside. Strain the soaking liquid through a piece of cheesecloth and set it aside.

2. While the mushrooms and noodles are soaking, prepare the meatballs. Place the fish sauce and cornstarch in a mixing bowl and stir until combined. Add the chicken, garlic, and sesame oil and stir to combine. Form the mixture into ¾-inch balls and set them aside.

3. Place the cilantro, ginger, garlic, chili pepper, fish sauce, and brown sugar in a food processor and puree until smooth. Place the mixture in a large saucepan, stir in the stock and reserved soaking liquid, and bring to a boil over medium-high heat, while stirring occasionally.

4. Add the meatballs to the broth, reduce the heat to low, and cook the soup until the meatballs are cooked through, 6 to 8 minutes. Stir in the noodles and mushrooms, simmer for 2 more minutes, and season with salt and pepper. Ladle the soup into warmed bowls and garnish each portion with scallions and additional cilantro.

VARIATIONS

- Use a combination of ground shrimp and cod for a lighter flavor.
- To add more protein, incorporate 1 cup diced extra-firm tofu into the soup.
- Add sliced bok choy to the soup at the same time as the meatballs to increase the vegetable content without diluting the flavor.

MEXICAN TURKEY MEATBALL SOUP

YIELD: 4 TO 6 SERVINGS / **ACTIVE TIME:** 20 MINUTES / **TOTAL TIME:** 45 MINUTES

A fun take on the traditional tortilla soup, with a cornucopia of vegetables to make it into a meal, and meatballs featuring the unique texture supplied by the crunchy corn chips.

INGREDIENTS:

FOR THE MEATBALLS

- 1 LARGE EGG
- ¼ CUP TOMATO JUICE
- 2 GARLIC CLOVES, MINCED
- 2 TEASPOONS CUMIN
- 1 TEASPOON DRIED OREGANO
- 1¼ LBS. GROUND TURKEY
- ½ CUP CRUSHED TORTILLA CHIPS
- SALT AND PEPPER, TO TASTE

FOR THE SOUP

- ¼ CUP OLIVE OIL
- 1 LARGE ONION, CHOPPED
- 2 GARLIC CLOVES, MINCED
- 2 TABLESPOONS CHILI POWDER
- 6 CUPS CHICKEN STOCK (SEE PAGE 660)
- 2 (14 OZ.) CANS DICED TOMATOES
- 2 CELERY STALKS, SLICED
- 2 CARROTS, PEELED AND SLICED
- 1 (14 OZ.) CAN KIDNEY BEANS, DRAINED AND RINSED
- 1 CUP CORN KERNELS
- SALT AND PEPPER, TO TASTE
- FRESH CILANTRO, FOR GARNISH (OPTIONAL)

1. Preheat the oven to 450°F and line a rimmed baking sheet with aluminum foil. To prepare the meatballs, place the egg, tomato juice, garlic, cumin, and oregano in a mixing bowl and stir until combined. Add the turkey and tortilla chips, season with salt and pepper, and stir until thoroughly combined. Form the mixture into 1-inch meatballs and arrange them on the baking sheet. Spray the tops of meatballs with nonstick cooking spray, place them in the oven, and bake for 12 to 15 minutes, until cooked through. Remove from the oven and set aside.

2. While the meatballs are baking, begin preparations for the soup. Place the olive oil in a large saucepan and warm over medium-high heat. When the oil starts to shimmer, add the onion and garlic and cook, stirring frequently, until the onion is translucent, about 3 minutes. Stir in the chili powder and cook for 1 minute, while stirring constantly.

3. Stir in the stock, tomatoes, celery, and carrots, bring the soup to a boil, and then reduce the heat so that it simmers. Simmer until vegetables are tender, about 20 minutes.

4. Stir in the meatballs, kidney beans, and corn and simmer for 5 minutes. Season with salt and pepper and ladle into warmed bowls. Garnish with cilantro, if desired.

VARIATIONS

- Make the meatballs from beef or a combination of beef and pork.
- Use any sort of canned bean readily available; there's no reason to purchase kidney beans if you have others around.

MEATBALL & CONCHIGLIE PASTA SOUP

YIELD: 4 SERVINGS / **ACTIVE TIME:** 45 MINUTES / **TOTAL TIME:** 1 HOUR AND 15 MINUTES

With orange-scented meatballs and a hearty sauce thickened by cannellini beans, this is a surefire Italian classic.

INGREDIENTS:

FOR THE MEATBALLS

- 2 SLICES WHITE BREAD, CRUST REMOVED AND TORN INTO SMALL PIECES
- 6 TABLESPOONS MILK
- ¾ LB. GROUND VEAL
- ½ ONION, CHOPPED
- 3 TABLESPOONS PARSLEY, LEAVES REMOVED AND CHOPPED
- 1 TABLESPOON ORANGE ZEST
- 2 GARLIC CLOVES, MINCED
- 1 EGG, BEATEN
- SALT AND PEPPER, TO TASTE
- 2 TABLESPOONS EXTRA VIRGIN OLIVE OIL

FOR THE SOUP

- 1 (14 OZ.) CAN CANNELLINI BEANS, RINSED AND DRAINED
- 4 CUPS CHICKEN STOCK (SEE PAGE 660)
- 2 TABLESPOONS OLIVE OIL
- 1 ONION, CHOPPED
- 1 GARLIC CLOVE, MINCED
- 1 THAI CHILI PEPPER, STEMMED, SEEDS AND RIBS REMOVED, AND CHOPPED
- 1 CELERY STALK, CHOPPED
- 1 CARROT, PEELED AND CHOPPED
- 1 TABLESPOON TOMATO PASTE
- ½ LB. CONCHIGLIE PASTA
- SALT AND PEPPER, TO TASTE
- PECORINO CHEESE, FOR GARNISH
- FRESH BASIL, FINELY CHOPPED, FOR GARNISH

1. To begin preparations for the meatballs, place the bread and milk in a bowl and let stand for 10 minutes.

2. Add the veal, onion, parsley, orange zest, garlic, and egg. Mix with your hands until well-combined.

3. Season with salt and pepper and roll the mixture into ½-inch balls.

4. In a large sauté pan, add the oil and cook over medium heat until warm. Add the meatballs and cook for 5 minutes, or until browned all over.

5. Remove from pan with a slotted spoon and set on paper towels to drain.

6. To begin preparations for the soup, place the cannellini beans and 1 cup of the stock in a food processor, puree until smooth, and set aside.

7. In a medium saucepan, add the olive oil, onion, garlic, Thai chili, celery, and carrot and sauté for 5 minutes, or until the vegetables are soft.

8. Add the tomato paste, the cannellini puree, and the remaining stock and bring to a boil.

9. Reduce heat so that the soup simmers and cook for 10 minutes.

10. Add the pasta and cook for 8 minutes, until tender. Add the meatballs, cook for 5 minutes until heated through, and then season with salt and pepper.

11. Serve in warm bowls and garnish with pecorino and basil.

ITALIAN WEDDING SOUP

YIELD: 4 SERVINGS / **ACTIVE TIME:** 30 MINUTES / **TOTAL TIME:** 1 HOUR AND 15 MINUTES

The term wedding soup comes from the phrase *minestra maritata*, which means "married soup," a reference to the combination of leafy greens and meat.

INGREDIENTS:

FOR THE MEATBALLS

- ¾ LB. GROUND CHICKEN
- ⅓ CUP PANKO
- 1 GARLIC CLOVE, MINCED
- 2 TABLESPOONS FINELY CHOPPED FRESH PARSLEY
- ¼ CUP GRATED PARMESAN CHEESE
- 1 TABLESPOON MILK
- 1 EGG, BEATEN
- ⅛ TEASPOON FENNEL SEEDS
- ⅛ TEASPOON RED PEPPER FLAKES
- ½ TEASPOON PAPRIKA
- SALT AND PEPPER, TO TASTE

FOR THE SOUP

- 2 TABLESPOONS OLIVE OIL
- 1 ONION, CHOPPED
- 2 CARROTS, PEELED AND CHOPPED
- 1 CELERY STALK, MINCED
- 6 CUPS CHICKEN STOCK (SEE PAGE 660)
- ¼ CUP WHITE WINE
- ½ CUP TUBETINI PASTA
- 2 TABLESPOONS FINELY CHOPPED FRESH DILL
- 6 OZ. BABY SPINACH
- SALT AND PEPPER, TO TASTE
- PARMESAN CHEESE, GRATED, FOR GARNISH

1. To begin preparations for the meatballs, preheat oven to 450°F and line a rimmed baking sheet with aluminum foil.

2. In a bowl, add all the ingredients and mix with a fork until well-combined.

3. Divide the mixture into 16 portions, form them into 1-inch balls, and then place them on the baking sheet.

4. Place the meatballs in the oven and bake for 12 to 15 minutes, until browned and cooked through. Remove from oven and set aside.

5. To begin preparations for the soup, place the olive oil in a saucepan and warm over medium heat. When the oil starts to shimmer, add the onion, carrots, and celery and sauté until they start to soften, about 5 minutes.

6. Add the stock and the wine and bring to a boil.

7. Reduce heat so that the soup simmers, add the pasta, and cook for 8 minutes.

8. Add the cooked meatballs and simmer for 5 minutes. Add the dill and the spinach and cook for 2 minutes, or until the spinach has wilted.

9. Ladle into warm bowls and garnish with Parmesan.

ITALIAN EGG DROP SOUP WITH TURKEY MEATBALLS

YIELD: 6 TO 8 SERVINGS / **ACTIVE TIME:** 20 MINUTES / **TOTAL TIME:** 1 HOUR

Tasty greens, swirls of creamy egg, lots of heady Parmesan, and flavorful turkey meatballs are what awaits in this effortless soup. Flank it with a loaf of garlic bread and your meal is complete.

INGREDIENTS:

FOR THE MEATBALLS

1 LARGE EGG

½ CUP ITALIAN BREAD CRUMBS

¼ CUP WHOLE MILK

1 SMALL ONION, GRATED

2 GARLIC CLOVES, MINCED

¼ CUP FINELY CHOPPED FRESH PARSLEY

½ CUP GRATED PARMESAN CHEESE

1½ LBS. GROUND TURKEY

SALT AND PEPPER, TO TASTE

FOR THE SOUP

8 CUPS CHICKEN STOCK (SEE PAGE 660)

1 LB. CURLY ENDIVE, RINSED, CORED, AND CHOPPED

2 LARGE EGGS

½ CUP GRATED PARMESAN CHEESE

SALT AND PEPPER, TO TASTE

1. To begin preparations for the meatballs, place the egg, bread crumbs, milk, onion, garlic, parsley, and Parmesan in a mixing bowl and stir until thoroughly combined. Stir in the turkey and season with salt and pepper.

2. To begin preparations for the soup, place the stock and endive in a large saucepan and bring to a boil. Reduce the heat to low and simmer the soup for 10 minutes.

3. Working with wet hands, form the meatball mixture into 1-inch balls and drop them into simmering soup. Cook the meatballs until cooked through, 7 to 10 minutes.

4. Place the eggs and 2 tablespoons of the Parmesan cheese in a bowl and whisk to combine. Gradually add the mixture to the soup, while stirring constantly to form thin strands. Season with salt and pepper, ladle into warmed bowls, and serve with the remaining Parmesan.

VARIATIONS

- Substitute escarole for the curly endive.
- Ground pork, or a combination of pork and veal, is equally delicious for the meatballs.

RED LENTIL SOUP WITH TURKEY MEATBALLS

YIELD: 4 TO 6 SERVINGS / **ACTIVE TIME:** 20 MINUTES / **TOTAL TIME:** 50 MINUTES

While Americans are most familiar with brown lentils, those with vibrant color play a more prominent role in many of the world's cuisines, such as the red lentils in this rich soup flavored with Middle Eastern spices.

INGREDIENTS:

FOR THE SOUP

- 3 TABLESPOONS OLIVE OIL
- 1 SMALL ONION, MINCED
- 1 CARROT, PEELED AND MINCED
- 1 CELERY STALK, MINCED
- 3 GARLIC CLOVES, MINCED
- 1 TABLESPOON TURMERIC
- 2 TEASPOONS CUMIN
- 1 TEASPOON CORIANDER
- 6 CUPS CHICKEN STOCK (SEE PAGE 660)
- 1 LB. RED LENTILS, RINSED
- 3 TABLESPOONS FINELY CHOPPED FRESH PARSLEY
- SALT AND PEPPER, TO TASTE

FOR THE MEATBALLS

- 2 TABLESPOONS OLIVE OIL
- 1 ONION, MINCED
- 2 GARLIC CLOVES, MINCED
- 1 LARGE EGG
- ½ CUP BREAD CRUMBS
- ¼ CUP MILK
- 1¼ LBS. GROUND TURKEY
- ⅓ CUP DRIED CURRANTS
- 3 TABLESPOONS FINELY CHOPPED FRESH PARSLEY
- SALT AND PEPPER, TO TASTE

1. To begin preparations for the soup, place the olive oil in a large saucepan and warm over medium-high heat. When the oil starts to shimmer, add the onion, carrot, celery, and garlic and sauté until the onion is translucent, about 3 minutes. Stir in the turmeric, cumin, and coriander and cook for 1 minute, while stirring constantly.

2. Stir in the stock, lentils, and parsley and bring to a boil, while stirring occasionally. Reduce the heat to low and simmer until the lentils are tender, about 20 minutes. Remove the soup from heat and set it aside.

3. While the soup is simmering, begin preparations for the meatballs. Preheat the oven to 450°F and line a rimmed baking sheet with aluminum foil. Place the oil in a large skillet and warm over medium-high heat. When the oil starts to shimmer, add the onion and garlic and sauté, until the onion is translucent, about 3 minutes. Remove the pan from heat and let it cool.

4. Place the egg in a mixing bowl and add the bread crumbs and milk. Allow the mixture to sit for 5 minutes and then stir in the turkey, dried currants, and parsley. Add the onion mixture to the mixing bowl, season with salt and pepper, and stir until well combined. Working with wet hands, form the mixture into 1-inch meatballs and place them on the baking sheet. Spray the tops of the meatballs with nonstick cooking spray.

5. Place the meatballs in the oven and bake for 10 to 12 minutes, until they are cooked through.

6. Transfer the soup to a food processor and puree until smooth, working in batches if necessary. Return the soup to the saucepan and stir in the meatballs. Season with salt and pepper and ladle the soup into warmed bowls.

VARIATIONS

- Use green, brown, or yellow lentils in place of red ones.
- Try dried cranberries or finely chopped dried apricots in the meatballs instead of dried currants.
- Substituting ground lamb, ground beef, or a combination of the two will make for a heartier soup.

ONION SOUP WITH GRUYÈRE & BEEF MEATBALLS

YIELD: 6 TO 8 SERVINGS / **ACTIVE TIME:** 25 MINUTES / **TOTAL TIME:** 1 HOUR AND 15 MINUTES

There's nothing like a steaming bowl of onion soup to warm you up on a winter night, and the addition of meatballs made with Gruyère cheese makes for a memorable meal.

1. To begin preparations for the soup, place the butter and oil in a large saucepan and warm over low heat. When the butter starts to foam, stir in the onions, cover the pan, and cook for 10 minutes, stirring occasionally. Remove the cover, raise the heat to medium-low, and stir in the sugar. Cook, stirring frequently, until the onions are dark brown, about 35 minutes.

2. Reduce heat to low, stir in the flour, and cook for 2 minutes, while stirring constantly. Stir in the stock, wine, parsley, thyme, and bay leaf and bring the soup to a boil over medium heat. Reduce heat to low, partially cover the pan, and simmer for 40 minutes. Season with salt and pepper, remove the bay leaf, and discard it.

3. While soup is simmering, begin preparations for the meatballs. Preheat the oven to 450°F and line a rimmed baking sheet with aluminum foil. Tear bread into small pieces, place them in a bowl, add the milk, and stir to combine.

4. Place the butter in a small skillet and melt over medium-high heat. Add the onion and garlic and sauté until the onion is translucent, about 3 minutes. Place the egg in a mixing bowl, whisk it until scrambled, and then stir in the bread mixture, beef, parsley, and cheese. Add onion mixture to the mixing bowl, season with salt and pepper, and stir until thoroughly combined.

5. Working with wet hands, form the mixture into 1-inch meatballs and place them on the baking sheet. Spray the tops of meatballs with cooking spray, place them in the oven, and bake for 8 to 10 minutes, until cooked through. Remove the pan from the oven and stir the meatballs into soup. Season with salt and pepper and ladle into warmed bowls.

VARIATIONS

- Although not traditional, red onions will impart a sweeter flavor.
- Instead of Gruyère, try provolone or cheddar cheese in the meatballs.

INGREDIENTS:

FOR THE SOUP

- 3 TABLESPOONS UNSALTED BUTTER
- 1 TABLESPOON OLIVE OIL
- 3 LBS. YELLOW ONIONS, SLICED THIN
- 1 TEASPOON SUGAR
- 3 TABLESPOONS ALL-PURPOSE FLOUR
- 8 CUPS BEEF STOCK (SEE PAGE 663)
- ¾ CUP DRY RED WINE
- 3 TABLESPOONS FINELY CHOPPED FRESH PARSLEY
- 1 TABLESPOON FINELY CHOPPED FRESH THYME
- 1 BAY LEAF
- SALT AND PEPPER, TO TASTE

FOR THE MEATBALLS

- 3 SLICES WHITE BREAD
- 2 TABLESPOONS MILK
- 2 TABLESPOONS UNSALTED BUTTER
- 1 SMALL ONION, MINCED
- 2 GARLIC CLOVES, MINCED
- 1 LARGE EGG
- 1½ LBS. GROUND CHUCK
- 2 TABLESPOONS FINELY CHOPPED FRESH PARSLEY
- ¾ CUP GRATED GRUYÈRE CHEESE
- SALT AND PEPPER, TO TASTE

ITALIAN ESCAROLE & MEATBALL SOUP

YIELD: 6 TO 8 SERVINGS / **ACTIVE TIME:** 20 MINUTES / **TOTAL TIME:** 45 MINUTES

Similar to the Italian Egg Drop Soup with Turkey Meatballs (see page 49), this soup combines meatballs and hearty greens, but forgoes the eggs.

INGREDIENTS:

FOR THE MEATBALLS

- 3 TABLESPOONS OLIVE OIL
- 1 LARGE ONION, CHOPPED
- 2 GARLIC CLOVES, MINCED
- 1 LARGE EGG
- ½ CUP ITALIAN BREAD CRUMBS
- ¼ CUP MILK
- 1½ LBS. MEATLOAF MIX
- ½ CUP GRATED PARMESAN CHEESE
- ¼ CUP CHOPPED FRESH PARSLEY
- SALT AND PEPPER, TO TASTE

FOR THE SOUP

- 1 LB. ESCAROLE, SLICED THIN
- 3 TABLESPOONS OLIVE OIL
- 2 LARGE ONIONS, DICED
- 2 GARLIC CLOVES, MINCED
- 8 CUPS CHICKEN STOCK (SEE PAGE 660)
- SALT AND PEPPER, TO TASTE
- ½ CUP GRATED PARMESAN CHEESE, FOR SERVING

1. Preheat the oven to 450°F and line a rimmed baking sheet with aluminum foil. To begin preparations for the meatballs, place the oil in a small skillet and warm over medium-high heat. When the oil starts to shimmer, add the onion and garlic and sauté until the onion is translucent, about 3 minutes. Remove the pan from heat and let cool.

2. Place the egg in a mixing bowl, briefly whisk, and then stir in the bread crumbs and milk. Add the meat, Parmesan, and parsley and stir until thoroughly combined. Stir in the onion mixture and season with salt and pepper. Working with wet hands, form the mixture into 1-inch meatballs, arrange them on the baking sheet, and spray the tops of the meatballs with cooking spray. Place them in the oven and bake for 10 to 12 minutes, until cooked through. Remove the pan from the oven and set it aside.

3. While the meatballs are in the oven, begin preparations for the soup. Bring a large pot of salted water to a boil and prepare an ice bath. Add the escarole to the boiling water and cook for 1 minute. Transfer to the ice bath and let it sit for 2 minutes. Drain, pat dry with paper towels, and set it aside.

4. Place the oil in a large saucepan and warm over medium-high heat. Add the onion and garlic and sauté until the onion is translucent, about 3 minutes. Add the stock and escarole and bring to a boil. Reduce heat to low and simmer the soup for 10 minutes. Add the meatballs, season the soup with salt and pepper, and ladle into warmed bowls. Serve alongside the Parmesan.

VARIATIONS

- For a more assertive flavor, use collard greens instead of escarole.
- For a more delicate flavor and prettier color, use rainbow chard.

Blanching is a preliminary cooking of green vegetables and some fruits. The food is briefly cooked in boiling salted water and then quickly plunged into ice water before being drained. For vegetables, the process either removes bitterness or sets a dark green color. For fruits such as peaches and tomatoes, it makes the skins easy to remove.

MUSHROOM, BARLEY & BEEF MEATBALL SOUP

YIELD: 6 TO 8 SERVINGS / **ACTIVE TIME:** 20 MINUTES / **TOTAL TIME:** 1 HOUR AND 30 MINUTES

While mushrooms grow everywhere, this filling soup is most closely identified with Eastern European countries such as Poland and Russia. The combination of aromatic and flavorful dried mushrooms with the delicate flavor and texture of fresh mushrooms makes it a winner.

1. To begin preparations for the soup, cover the porcini mushrooms with boiling water and soak for 10 minutes. Drain, reserve the soaking liquid, chop the mushrooms, and set them aside. Strain soaking liquid through a piece of cheesecloth and set it aside.

2. Place the oil in a large saucepan and warm over medium-high heat. When it starts to shimmer, add the onion and sauté until translucent, about 3 minutes. Stir in the carrots, celery, button mushrooms, stock, barley, parsley, thyme, chopped porcini, and reserved soaking liquid and bring to a boil. Reduce heat to low, cover the pan, and simmer until the barley is tender, about 1 hour.

3. While the soup is simmering, begin preparations for the meatballs. Preheat the oven to 450°F and line a baking sheet with aluminum foil. Tear the bread into small pieces, place it in a bowl with the milk, and stir to combine.

4. Place the oil in a small skillet and warm over medium-high heat. When it starts to shimmer, add the onion and garlic and sauté until the onion is translucent, about 3 minutes. Remove from heat and set side.

5. Place the egg in a mixing bowl and whisk until scrambled. Stir in the bread mixture, beef, and parsley. Add the onion mixture, season with salt and pepper, and stir until thoroughly combined. Working with wet hands, form the mixture into 1-inch meatballs, arrange them on the baking sheet, and spray the tops of the meatballs with nonstick cooking spray.

6. Bake meatballs for 10 to 12 minutes, or until cooked through. Remove the pan from the oven and add meatballs to soup, season with salt and pepper, and serve immediately.

VARIATIONS

- The mushroom flavor will be more pronounced if you use Mushroom Stock (see page 668) and make the meatballs from ground turkey rather than beef.
- For a stronger flavor, substitute fresh portobello mushrooms for the button mushrooms.

INGREDIENTS:

FOR THE SOUP

¼ CUP DRIED PORCINI MUSHROOMS

2 TABLESPOONS OLIVE OIL

1 LARGE ONION, CHOPPED

2 CARROTS, PEELED AND SLICED

2 CELERY STALKS, SLICED

1 LB. BUTTON MUSHROOMS, STEMMED AND SLICED

8 CUPS BEEF STOCK (SEE PAGE 663)

1 CUP WHOLE BARLEY, RINSED WELL

3 TABLESPOONS FINELY CHOPPED FRESH PARSLEY

1 TABLESPOON FINELY CHOPPED FRESH THYME

SALT AND PEPPER, TO TASTE

FOR THE MEATBALLS

4 SLICES WHITE BREAD

⅓ CUP MILK

2 TABLESPOONS OLIVE OIL

1 SMALL ONION, MINCED

2 GARLIC CLOVES, MINCED

1 LARGE EGG

1½ LBS. GROUND CHUCK

2 TABLESPOONS FINELY CHOPPED FRESH PARSLEY

SALT AND PEPPER, TO TASTE

CHINESE HOT & SOUR SOUP WITH PORK MEATBALLS

YIELD: 4 TO 6 SERVINGS / **ACTIVE TIME:** 20 MINUTES / **TOTAL TIME:** 40 MINUTES

Unlike many dishes found on Chinese restaurant menus in North America, hot and sour soup is authentically Chinese—it comes from Sichuan province. The thick and hearty broth and flavor-packed meatballs are joined by wholesome tofu in this satisfying dish.

1. Preheat the oven to 450°F and line a rimmed baking sheet with aluminum foil. To begin preparations for the meatballs, cover the shiitake mushrooms with boiling water and soak for 10 minutes. Drain the mushrooms, reserve the soaking liquid, remove the stems from the mushrooms, and chop the caps. Strain the soaking liquid through a piece of cheesecloth. Set the mushrooms and the liquid aside.

2. Place the egg, soy sauce, scallions, and garlic in a mixing bowl and stir to combine. Stir in the pork, rice, and reconstituted mushrooms and season with salt and pepper. Working with wet hands, form the mixture into 1-inch meatballs, arrange them on the baking sheet, and spray the tops of the meatballs with cooking spray. Place the meatballs in the oven and bake for about 10 minutes, until cooked through. Remove from the oven and set aside.

3. To begin preparations for the soup, place the olive oil and sesame oil in a large saucepan and warm over medium-high heat. When the oils start to shimmer, add the scallions and garlic and cook, stirring constantly, until fragrant, about 1 minute. Stir in the stock, rice vinegar, soy sauce, sherry, and reserved soaking liquid. Bring the soup to a boil and then reduce the heat so that the mixture simmers. Simmer for 10 minutes, stir in the tofu and the meatballs, and then simmer for another 10 minutes.

4. Place the cornstarch and water in a small bowl and stir until combined. Stir the slurry into the soup and simmer until the soup thickens slightly. While stirring constantly, gradually incorporate the eggs. Simmer for another minute, season with salt and white pepper, and ladle into warmed bowls.

VARIATIONS

- Make the meatballs from shrimp or a combination of shrimp and pork.
- Add some fresh shiitake mushrooms to the broth.

INGREDIENTS:

FOR THE MEATBALLS

- ½ CUP DRIED SHIITAKE MUSHROOMS
- 1 LARGE EGG
- 2 TABLESPOONS SOY SAUCE
- 4 SCALLIONS, TRIMMED AND CHOPPED
- 2 GARLIC CLOVES, MINCED
- 1¼ LBS. GROUND PORK
- 1 CUP COOKED WHITE RICE
- SALT AND PEPPER, TO TASTE

FOR THE SOUP

- 2 TABLESPOONS OLIVE OIL
- 2 TABLESPOONS SESAME OIL
- 6 SCALLIONS, TRIMMED AND SLICED THIN
- 3 GARLIC CLOVES, MINCED
- 6 CUPS CHICKEN STOCK (SEE PAGE 660)
- ⅓ CUP RICE VINEGAR
- ¼ CUP SOY SAUCE
- 2 TABLESPOONS SHERRY
- ½ LB. FIRM TOFU, DRAINED, RINSED, AND CHOPPED
- 2 TABLESPOONS CORNSTARCH
- 2 TABLESPOONS WATER
- 3 LARGE EGGS, LIGHTLY BEATEN
- SALT AND WHITE PEPPER, TO TASTE

AVGOLEMONO WITH LAMB MEATBALLS

YIELD: 4 TO 6 SERVINGS / **ACTIVE TIME:** 20 MINUTES / **TOTAL TIME:** 30 MINUTES

This is a cornerstone of Greek cuisine. It's thick while not too rich, and the keys to its flavor are good chicken stock and subtly seasoned meatballs made from lamb and rice.

INGREDIENTS:

FOR THE MEATBALLS

2 TABLESPOONS OLIVE OIL

1 ONION, MINCED

1 GARLIC CLOVE, MINCED

1 LARGE EGG

1¼ LBS. GROUND LAMB

1 CUP COOKED WHITE RICE

3 TABLESPOONS FINELY CHOPPED FRESH PARSLEY

1 TABLESPOON FINELY CHOPPED FRESH ROSEMARY

SALT AND PEPPER, TO TASTE

FOR THE SOUP

7 CUPS CHICKEN STOCK (SEE PAGE 660)

4 LARGE EGGS

⅓ CUP FRESH LEMON JUICE

½ TEASPOON LEMON ZEST

SALT AND PEPPER, TO TASTE

1. Preheat the oven to 450°F and line a rimmed baking sheet with aluminum foil. To begin preparations for the meatballs, place the oil in a small skillet and warm over medium-high heat. When it starts to shimmer, add the onion and garlic and sauté until the onion is translucent, about 3 minutes. Remove the pan from heat and let cool.

2. Place the egg in a mixing bowl, beat until scrambled, and then stir in the lamb, rice, parsley, and rosemary. Add the onion mixture, season with salt and pepper, and stir until thoroughly combined. Working with wet hands, form the mixture into 1-inch meatballs, arrange them on the baking sheet, and spray the tops with cooking spray. Place in the oven and bake for 10 to 12 minutes, until cooked through. Remove from the oven and set aside.

3. To begin preparations for the soup, place the stock in a saucepan and bring it to a boil over medium-high heat. Place the eggs, lemon juice, and lemon zest in a mixing bowl and stir until combined. Remove the stock from heat and stir for 45 seconds to cool. The stock should not be bubbling at all. Stir in the egg mixture, cover the pan, and let the soup sit for 5 minutes.

4. Season with salt and pepper, stir in the meatballs, and ladle into warmed bowls.

VARIATIONS

- Make the meatballs from beef or a combination of beef and veal.
- Orzo, a rice-shaped pasta, can be used instead of rice. Any chopped cooked pasta will work as well.

ALBONDIGAS SOUP WITH CHORIZO MEATBALLS

YIELD: 6 TO 8 SERVINGS / **ACTIVE TIME:** 25 MINUTES / **TOTAL TIME:** 50 MINUTES

Filled with healthful vegetables and legumes, this soup is enriched by the earthy and spicy chorizo sausage. Serve with Corn Tortillas (see page 535).

INGREDIENTS:

FOR THE SOUP

2 TABLESPOONS OLIVE OIL

1 LARGE ONION, CHOPPED

2 GARLIC CLOVES, MINCED

1 JALAPEÑO OR SERRANO PEPPER, STEMMED, SEEDS AND RIBS REMOVED, AND MINCED

2 CARROTS, PEELED AND CHOPPED

1 POTATO, PEELED AND CHOPPED

2 CELERY STALKS, SLICED

8 CUPS CHICKEN STOCK (SEE PAGE 660)

1 (14 OZ.) CAN DICED TOMATOES

2 SMALL ZUCCHINI, CHOPPED

1 (14 OZ.) CAN CHICKPEAS, DRAINED AND RINSED

SALT AND PEPPER, TO TASTE

FOR THE MEATBALLS

¼ CUP OLIVE OIL

3 GARLIC CLOVES, MINCED

1 CUP FIRMLY PACKED FRESH CILANTRO LEAVES

1 LB. GROUND PORK

½ LB. CHORIZO, CHOPPED

1 LARGE EGG, LIGHTLY BEATEN

½ CUP BREAD CRUMBS

SALT AND PEPPER, TO TASTE

1. Preheat the oven to 450°F and line a rimmed baking sheet with aluminum foil. To begin preparations for the soup, place the oil in a large saucepan and warm over medium-high heat. When it starts to shimmer, add the onion, garlic, and pepper and sauté until the onion is translucent, about 3 minutes. Add the carrots, potato, celery, stock, and tomatoes and bring to a boil over medium-high heat. Reduce the heat to low, cover the pan, and simmer for 15 minutes. Stir in the zucchini and chickpeas and simmer until the vegetables are tender, about 10 minutes.

2. While the soup is simmering, prepare the meatballs. Place the oil, garlic, and cilantro in a food processor and puree until smooth. Place the puree, pork, chorizo, egg, and bread crumbs in a mixing bowl, season with salt and pepper, and stir until thoroughly combined. Working with wet hands, form the mixture into 1-inch meatballs, arrange them on the baking sheet, and spray the tops with cooking spray. Place the meatballs in the oven and bake for 10 to 12 minutes, until cooked through.

3. Stir the meatballs into soup, season with salt and pepper, and ladle into warmed bowls.

VARIATIONS

- Add some sautéed bell pepper to the mix.
- Instead of chickpeas, use pinto or kidney beans.

CHINESE VEGETABLE SOUP WITH SHRIMP & PORK MEATBALLS

YIELD: 6 TO 8 SERVINGS / **ACTIVE TIME:** 25 MINUTES / **TOTAL TIME:** 55 MINUTES

This is one of my favorite meals to eat when I'm counting calories; the vegetables are crunchy, so there is some textural variation, and the broth makes it very filling—as well as delicious.

INGREDIENTS:

FOR THE MEATBALLS

- 2 TABLESPOONS SOY SAUCE
- 2 TABLESPOONS CORNSTARCH
- 3 LARGE EGG WHITES
- 1 TABLESPOON SESAME OIL
- 3 SCALLIONS, TRIMMED AND CHOPPED
- 3 TABLESPOONS FINELY CHOPPED FRESH CILANTRO
- 1-INCH PIECE FRESH GINGER, PEELED AND GRATED
- 2 GARLIC CLOVES, MINCED
- 1 LB. GROUND PORK
- ½ LB. SHRIMP, PEELED, DEVEINED, AND MINCED
- ½ CUP MINCED WATER CHESTNUTS
- SALT AND PEPPER, TO TASTE

FOR THE SOUP

- 7 CUPS CHICKEN STOCK (SEE PAGE 660)
- 6 SCALLIONS, TRIMMED AND CHOPPED, PLUS MORE FOR GARNISH
- 2 GARLIC CLOVES, MINCED
- 1-INCH PIECE FRESH GINGER, PEELED AND GRATED
- 2 TABLESPOONS SOY SAUCE
- 1 LARGE CARROT, PEELED AND JULIENNED
- 2 CUPS CHOPPED BOK CHOY
- 1 CUP SLICED SNOW PEAS
- SALT AND PEPPER, TO TASTE

1. To begin preparations for the meatballs, place the soy sauce and cornstarch in a bowl and stir to combine. Place the mixture in a large mixing bowl, add the egg whites, sesame oil, scallions, cilantro, ginger, and garlic and stir until combined. Stir in the pork, shrimp, and water chestnuts, season with salt and pepper, and stir until the mixture is a smooth paste. Refrigerate for 30 minutes.

2. To begin preparations for the soup, place the stock, scallions, garlic, ginger, soy sauce, and carrot in a large saucepan and bring to a boil over medium-high heat. Reduce the heat to low and simmer for 10 minutes.

3. Working with wet hands, form the meatball mixture into 1-inch balls and drop them into the simmering soup. Cook for about 10 minutes, until the meatballs are completely cooked through. Stir the bok choy and snow peas into the soup and simmer for 2 minutes. Season with salt and pepper, ladle into warmed bowls, and garnish with additional scallions.

VARIATIONS

- Incorporate some reconstituted dried shiitake mushrooms or baby spinach.
- Use ground turkey instead of the pork and shrimp as the protein in the meatballs.

RAMEN WITH CHICKEN MEATBALLS

YIELD: 4 SERVINGS / **ACTIVE TIME:** 20 MINUTES / **TOTAL TIME:** 45 MINUTES

The constantly shifting flavor of miso and a refreshing bean sprout salad sever any connections to the dreaded college standby.

1. To begin preparations for the meatballs, place the oil in a skillet and warm over medium-high heat. When the oil starts to shimmer, add the scallions, garlic, ginger, and black bean paste and stir-fry for 1 minute. Stir in the carrot and celery and stir-fry for 3 minutes, until the carrot just starts to soften. Remove the pan from heat and set it aside.

2. Place the egg, hoisin sauce, soy sauce, chili garlic sauce, and rice in a mixing bowl and stir until thoroughly combined. Add the chicken and the vegetable mixture and stir until thoroughly combined. Working with wet hands, form the mixture into 1½-inch meatballs and set them aside.

3. To begin preparations for the soup, place the sesame seeds in a dry skillet and toast over medium heat until browned, about 2 minutes. Remove from the pan and use a mortar and pestle to grind them into a paste, adding water as needed.

4. Place the sesame oil in a large saucepan and warm over medium heat. When the oil starts to shimmer, add the garlic, ginger, and shallots and cook until fragrant, about 2 minutes.

5. Raise the heat to medium-high and add the chili garlic sauce, miso, toasted sesame paste, sugar, sake, and stock and stir to combine. Bring to a boil, reduce heat so that the soup simmers, stir in the meatballs, and season with salt and pepper. Simmer until the meatballs are cooked through, about 10 minutes, and then remove the pan from heat.

6. While the soup is simmering, cook the noodles according to manufacturer's instructions. Drain the noodles and place them in warmed bowls. Pour the soup over the noodles and divide the meatballs between the bowls.

INGREDIENTS:

FOR THE MEATBALLS

2 TABLESPOONS SESAME OIL

3 SCALLIONS, TRIMMED AND CHOPPED

3 GARLIC CLOVES, MINCED

1-INCH PIECE FRESH GINGER, PEELED AND GRATED

1 TABLESPOON FERMENTED BLACK BEAN PASTE

1 CARROT, MINCED

1 CELERY STALK, MINCED

1 LARGE EGG

3 TABLESPOONS HOISIN SAUCE

1 TABLESPOON SOY SAUCE

1 TABLESPOON CHILI GARLIC SAUCE

½ CUP COOKED WHITE RICE

1¼ LBS. GROUND CHICKEN

FOR THE RAMEN

¼ CUP SESAME SEEDS

2 TABLESPOONS SESAME OIL

4 GARLIC CLOVES, MINCED

2-INCH PIECE FRESH GINGER, PEELED AND MINCED

2 SHALLOTS, MINCED

2 TEASPOONS CHILI GARLIC SAUCE

6 TABLESPOONS WHITE MISO PASTE

2 TABLESPOONS SUGAR

2 TABLESPOONS SAKE

8 CUPS CHICKEN OR VEGETABLE STOCK (SEE PAGES 660 OR 664, RESPECTIVELY)

NOODLES FROM 2 PACKETS RAMEN

SALT AND PEPPER, TO TASTE

The official start of
tree lighting
The second tree lighting
December 8, at 5:30 PM.

CREAM OF TOMATO WITH FONTINA JALAPEÑO HUSH PUPPIES

YIELD: 4 SERVINGS / **ACTIVE TIME:** 30 MINUTES / **TOTAL TIME:** 1 HOUR AND 15 MINUTES

This revitalizing classic is a favorite with diners of all ages.

INGREDIENTS:

- 2 TABLESPOONS UNSALTED BUTTER
- 1 ONION, CHOPPED
- 2 LBS. TOMATOES, CHOPPED
- 2 CARROTS, PEELED AND CHOPPED
- 5 CUPS CHICKEN STOCK (SEE PAGE 660)
- 2 TABLESPOONS FINELY CHOPPED FRESH PARSLEY
- ½ TEASPOON FINELY CHOPPED FRESH THYME
- 6 TABLESPOONS HEAVY CREAM
- SALT AND PEPPER, TO TASTE
- FONTINA JALAPEÑO HUSH PUPPIES (SEE RECIPE), FOR SERVING

1. Place the butter in a large saucepan and cook over medium heat until melted. Add the onion and sauté until it starts to soften, about 5 minutes.

2. Add the tomatoes, chopped carrots, chicken stock, parsley, and thyme. Reduce heat to low and simmer for 20 minutes, or until the vegetables are tender.

3. Transfer the soup to a food processor, puree until smooth, and strain through a fine sieve.

4. Return the soup to the pan and add the cream. Reheat gently and season with salt and pepper. Ladle the soup into bowls and serve with Fontina Jalapeño Hush Puppies.

FONTINA JALAPEÑO HUSH PUPPIES

FONTINA JALAPEÑO HUSH PUPPIES

- 2 CUPS VEGETABLE OIL
- ½ CUP CORNMEAL
- 3 TABLESPOONS ALL-PURPOSE FLOUR, PLUS 1½ TEASPOONS
- 4½ TABLESPOONS SUGAR
- ¾ TEASPOON KOSHER SALT
- ¼ TEASPOON BAKING POWDER
- ⅛ TEASPOON BAKING SODA
- ⅛ TEASPOON CAYENNE PEPPER
- ¼ CUP BUTTERMILK
- 1 EGG, BEATEN
- 2 TABLESPOONS CHOPPED JALAPEÑO PEPPER
- ¾ CUP GRATED FONTINA CHEESE

1. Place the oil in a Dutch oven and warm it to 320°F.

2. Add the cornmeal, flour, sugar, salt, baking powder, baking soda, and cayenne pepper to a small bowl and whisk until combined.

3. In a separate bowl, add the buttermilk, egg, and jalapeño. Whisk to combine.

4. Combine the buttermilk mixture and the dry mixture.

5. Add the cheese and stir until combined.

6. Drop spoonfuls of the batter into the hot oil and fry until golden brown.

7. Remove from oil with a slotted spoon and place on paper towels to drain.

IRISH LEEK & CASHEL BLUE CHEESE SOUP WITH BLUE CHEESE FRITTERS

YIELD: 6 SERVINGS / **ACTIVE TIME:** 30 MINUTES / **TOTAL TIME:** 1 HOUR

If you like blue cheese and haven't tried Cashel blue, remedy that immediately. If you have, you know that it is perfect for this traditional Irish soup.

1. In a medium saucepan, add the butter and oil and warm over low heat. When the butter starts to foam, add the leeks and sauté until they start to soften, about 5 minutes.

2. Break the Cashel blue into small pieces and add to the saucepan. Cook, while stirring, until the cheese is melted.

3. Add the flour and cook for 2 minutes, while stirring constantly, then stir in the mustard.

4. Slowly add the stock, stirring to prevent any lumps from forming. Bring to a boil, reduce heat so that the soup simmers, and cook for 10 minutes.

5. Season with pepper and ladle into warmed bowls. Garnish with Blue Cheese Fritters, chives, and additional mustard.

INGREDIENTS:

- 4 TABLESPOONS UNSALTED BUTTER
- 2 TABLESPOONS OLIVE OIL
- 3 LARGE LEEKS, SLICED THIN
- ½ LB. CASHEL BLUE CHEESE
- 2 TABLESPOONS ALL-PURPOSE FLOUR
- 1 TABLESPOON WHOLE GRAIN MUSTARD, PLUS MORE FOR GARNISH
- 6 CUPS CHICKEN STOCK (SEE PAGE 660)
- BLACK PEPPER, TO TASTE
- BLUE CHEESE FRITTERS (SEE RECIPE), FOR GARNISH
- FRESH CHIVES, FINELY CHOPPED, FOR GARNISH

BLUE CHEESE FRITTERS

1. Place the oil in a medium saucepan and warm to 350°F.

2. Place the eggs in a bowl and beat with a fork. Place the flour and bread crumbs in separate bowls.

3. Dredge the cheese in the flour, remove, and shake to remove any excess. Place the floured blue cheese in the egg wash and coat evenly. Remove from egg wash, shake to remove any excess egg, and gently coat with the panko.

4. Repeat with the egg wash and panko.

5. Place the cheese in the hot oil and fry until golden brown. Use a slotted spoon to remove the fritters from the oil, set on paper towels to drain, and season with salt.

BLUE CHEESE FRITTERS

- 2 CUPS VEGETABLE OIL
- 3 EGGS
- ¼ CUP ALL-PURPOSE FLOUR
- 1 CUP PANKO, FINELY GROUND
- 6 OZ. CASHEL BLUE, CUT INTO 12 CUBES
- SALT, TO TASTE

NEW ENGLAND CHOWDER WITH CLAM FRITTERS

YIELD: 4 TO 6 SERVINGS / **ACTIVE TIME:** 25 MINUTES / **TOTAL TIME:** 50 MINUTES

Early chowder recipes call for everything from beer to ketchup, but not milk. What we now know as New England chowder dates from the mid-19th century. One of the greatest convenience foods on the market are shucked and minced quahog or cherrystone clams; you'll find them in the seafood department.

1. To begin preparations for the fritters, place the clams in a sieve and let them drain over a bowl. Press down on the clams with the back of a spoon to extract as much liquid as possible from them. Reserve the liquid and store the clams in the refrigerator.

2. To begin preparations for the chowder, place half of the butter in a large saucepan and melt over medium heat. Add the onions and celery and sauté until the onions are translucent, about 3 minutes. Add the bottled clam juice, reserved liquid, potatoes, parsley, bay leaf, and thyme to the pan. Bring to a boil, reduce the heat to low, and simmer until the potatoes are tender, about 12 minutes.

3. Place the remaining butter in a small saucepan and melt over low heat. Stir in the flour and cook, stirring constantly, for 2 minutes. Raise the heat to medium and whisk in milk. Bring to a boil, while stirring frequently, and simmer for 2 minutes. Stir the mixture into the chowder and add the cream. Bring to a boil, reduce the heat to low, and simmer for 3 minutes. Remove and discard the bay leaf, season the chowder with salt and pepper, and cover the pan.

4. To resume preparations for the clam fritters, place the egg and milk in a mixing bowl and stir until combined. Stir in the flour, baking powder, clams, and scallions and season with salt and pepper.

5. Line a baking sheet with paper towels and add oil to a Dutch oven until it is about 2 inches deep. Warm it to 375°F over medium-high heat. Drop tablespoons of the fritter batter into the hot oil and fry them until golden brown, 2 to 3 minutes. Place the cooked fritters on the paper towels to drain.

6. When all of the fritters have been cooked, ladle the chowder into warmed bowls and top each portion with some of the fritters.

VARIATIONS

- Cook ½ lb. bacon in a skillet until crisp. Remove bacon from the pan with a slotted spoon, and discard all but ¼ cup of the bacon fat. Cook the vegetables in bacon fat rather than the butter. Chop the bacon and add it to the chowder along with the clam fritters.
- Add ½ cup cooked corn kernels to the chowder, along with ¼ cup chopped and sautéed red bell pepper.

INGREDIENTS:

FOR THE FRITTERS

2 CUPS CHOPPED FRESH CLAMS

1 LARGE EGG

¾ CUP WHOLE MILK

1½ CUPS ALL-PURPOSE FLOUR

1½ TEASPOONS BAKING POWDER

2 SCALLION WHITES, MINCED

SALT AND PEPPER, TO TASTE

VEGETABLE OIL, AS NEEDED

FOR THE CHOWDER

4 TABLESPOONS UNSALTED BUTTER

2 ONIONS, CHOPPED

2 CELERY STALKS, SLICED

1 CUP CLAM JUICE

2 RED POTATOES, CHOPPED

2 TABLESPOONS FINELY CHOPPED FRESH PARSLEY

1 BAY LEAF

1 TABLESPOON FINELY CHOPPED FRESH THYME

SALT AND PEPPER, TO TASTE

3 TABLESPOONS ALL-PURPOSE FLOUR

2 CUPS WHOLE MILK

1 CUP HEAVY CREAM

MANHATTAN CHOWDER WITH CLAM FRITTERS

YIELD: 4 TO 6 SERVINGS / **ACTIVE TIME:** 30 MINUTES / **TOTAL TIME:** 45 MINUTES

Adding tomatoes and other vegetables to chowder is considered heretical in New England, but this version is popular in the Mid-Atlantic and further south. While named for New York, legend has it that the chowder was actually developed by Portuguese settlers in Rhode Island in the late 18th century.

1. To begin preparations for the fritters, place the clams in a sieve and let them drain over a bowl. Press down on the clams with the back of a spoon to extract as much liquid as possible from them. Reserve the liquid and store the clams in the refrigerator.

2. To begin preparations for the chowder, place the oil in a large saucepan and warm over medium-high heat. When it starts to shimmer, add the onion, bell pepper, and celery and sauté until the onion is translucent, about 3 minutes. Add the potatoes, reserved liquid, clam juice, tomatoes, parsley, and thyme and bring the chowder to a boil. Reduce the heat to low and simmer, stirring occasionally, until the potatoes are tender, about 10 minutes. Season with salt and pepper, remove the pan from heat, and cover it to keep warm.

3. To resume preparations for the clam fritters, place the egg and milk in a mixing bowl and stir until combined. Stir in the flour, baking powder, clams, and scallions and season with salt and pepper.

4. Line a baking sheet with paper towels and add oil to a Dutch oven until it is about 2 inches deep. Warm it to 375°F over medium-high heat. Drop tablespoons of the fritter batter into the hot oil and fry them until golden brown, 2 to 3 minutes. Place the cooked fritters on the paper towels to drain.

5. When all of the fritters have been cooked, ladle the chowder into warmed bowls and top each portion with some of the fritters.

VARIATIONS

- For some Southwestern flavor, add 2 tablespoons chili powder and 1 tablespoon cumin to the vegetables while they are sautéing. Cook over low heat, stirring constantly, for 1 minute. Then add ½ cup corn kernels to the soup.
- For an Italian take on the chowder, add ¼ cup finely chopped fresh basil along with the other herbs.

INGREDIENTS:

FOR THE FRITTERS

- 2 CUPS CHOPPED FRESH CLAMS
- 1 LARGE EGG
- ¾ CUP WHOLE MILK
- 1½ CUPS ALL-PURPOSE FLOUR
- 1½ TEASPOONS BAKING POWDER
- 2 SCALLION WHITES, MINCED
- SALT AND PEPPER, TO TASTE
- VEGETABLE OIL, AS NEEDED

FOR THE CHOWDER

- 2 TABLESPOONS OLIVE OIL
- 1 ONION, CHOPPED
- ½ BELL PEPPER, STEMMED, SEEDED, AND CHOPPED
- 2 CELERY STALKS, SLICED
- 2 RED POTATOES, CHOPPED
- 2 CUPS CLAM JUICE
- 1 (14 OZ.) CAN DICED TOMATOES
- 3 TABLESPOONS FINELY CHOPPED FRESH PARSLEY
- 1 TABLESPOON FINELY CHOPPED FRESH THYME
- SALT AND PEPPER, TO TASTE

SWEDISH MEATBALL SOUP

YIELD: 4 TO 6 SERVINGS / **ACTIVE TIME:** 30 MINUTES / **TOTAL TIME:** 1 HOUR AND 15 MINUTES

Swedish meatballs are a meal on their own. Cook them in a nice seasoned broth and they become an ideal dinner option.

1. To begin preparations for the meatballs, place the panko and cream in a mixing bowl and stir to combine. Let soak for 10 minutes.

2. In a small sauté pan, add 1 tablespoon of the oil and warm over medium heat. Add the onion and sauté until it starts to soften, about 5 minutes. Remove the pan from heat and let the onion cool.

3. Once cool, add the cooked onion to the mixing bowl. Add the remaining ingredients and stir until thoroughly combined.

4. Place a small amount of the mixture in the microwave or cook a small amount on the stove. Taste and adjust seasoning accordingly.

5. Divide the mixture into 24 portions and roll each one into a nice, round ball.

6. In a large saucepan, add the remaining oil and warm over medium-high heat.

7. When the oil starts to shimmer, add the meatballs to the pan and cook for 5 minutes, while stirring constantly. When they are golden brown all over, remove and set aside.

8. To begin preparations for the soup, place the butter in a saucepan and melt it over medium heat.

9. Add the carrots and celery and sauté for 3 minutes. Add the mushrooms and garlic and sauté until the carrots start to soften, about 3 minutes.

10. Add the flour and cook for 3 minutes. Slowly add the stock to the pan, stirring constantly to prevent any lumps from forming.

11. Bring to a boil, reduce the heat to medium-low, add the meatballs, and simmer for 15 minutes, or until the meatballs are cooked through.

12. Add the cream, Worcestershire sauce, paprika, and red pepper flakes. Cook for 5 minutes, season with salt and pepper, ladle into bowls, and garnish with fresh parsley.

INGREDIENTS:

FOR THE MEATBALLS

- 1 CUP PANKO
- ½ CUP HEAVY CREAM
- 2 TABLESPOONS OLIVE OIL
- 1 ONION, CHOPPED
- ½ LB. GROUND BEEF
- ½ LB. GROUND PORK
- 1 EGG
- ⅛ TEASPOON ALLSPICE
- SALT AND PEPPER, TO TASTE

FOR THE SOUP

- 4 TABLESPOONS UNSALTED BUTTER
- 2 CARROTS, PEELED AND CHOPPED
- 2 CELERY STALKS, CHOPPED
- ½ LB. BUTTON MUSHROOMS, SLICED THIN
- 2 GARLIC CLOVES, MINCED
- ⅓ CUP ALL-PURPOSE FLOUR
- 6 CUPS BEEF STOCK (SEE PAGE 663)
- ¾ CUP HEAVY CREAM
- 1 TEASPOON WORCESTERSHIRE SAUCE
- ½ TEASPOON PAPRIKA
- ½ TEASPOON RED PEPPER FLAKES
- SALT AND PEPPER, TO TASTE
- FRESH PARSLEY, FINELY CHOPPED, FOR GARNISH

OLD FASHIONED CHICKEN DUMPLING SOUP

YIELD: 4 SERVINGS / **ACTIVE TIME:** 30 MINUTES / **TOTAL TIME:** 1 HOUR AND 15 MINUTES

This one may be "old fashioned," but for comfort food, it can't be beat.

INGREDIENTS:

FOR THE DUMPLINGS

- 4 SLICES BREAD, CHOPPED
- ½ CUP FRESH PARSLEY, CHOPPED
- 1¼ CUPS ALL-PURPOSE FLOUR
- 1 TEASPOON BAKING POWDER
- ½ CUP MILK
- 1 EGG
- 4 TABLESPONS UNSALTED BUTTER, MELTED
- 1 CUP COOKED CHICKEN LEG MEAT, CHOPPED
- SALT AND PEPPER, TO TASTE
- 4 CUPS CHICKEN STOCK

FOR THE BROTH

- 1 TABLESPOON OLIVE OIL
- ½ ONION, MINCED
- 1 CARROT, PEELED AND MINCED
- 1 CELERY STALK, MINCED
- 1 TABLESPOON FINELY CHOPPED FRESH THYME
- 4 CUPS CHICKEN STOCK (SEE PAGE 660)
- SALT AND PEPPER, TO TASTE
- PARSLEY, CHOPPED, FOR GARNISH

1. To begin preparations for the dumplings, place the bread and parsley in a food processor and pulse until combined. Add the flour and the baking powder, pulse, then slowly add the milk, egg, and butter. Pulse until a smooth paste forms and transfer to a mixing bowl.

2. Fold in the chicken meat and season with salt and pepper. Refrigerate for 1 hour.

3. To begin preparations for the broth, place the oil in a saucepan and warm it over medium heat. Add the onion and sauté until it starts to soften, about 5 minutes. Add the remaining vegetables and cook until tender.

4. Add the thyme and the stock and bring to a boil. Reduce the heat so that the soup simmers and cook for 20 minutes.

5. Drop tablespoon-sized balls of the dumpling dough into the simmering broth. Cover and cook for 12 minutes. Season with salt and pepper, ladle into warmed bowls, and garnish with the parsley.

SIMPLE DUMPLING SOUP

YIELD: 4 SERVINGS / **ACTIVE TIME:** 30 MINUTES / **TOTAL TIME:** 1 HOUR

The bacon ties everything together in this simple yet satisfying soup.

INGREDIENTS:

FOR THE DUMPLINGS

- 1 CUP ALL-PURPOSE FLOUR
- ½ TEASPOON BAKING POWDER
- ½ TEASPOON KOSHER SALT
- ½ TABLESPOON OLIVE OIL
- 1 EGG
- 6 TABLESPOONS WATER
- 1 TABLESPOON FINELY CHOPPED FRESH CHIVES

FOR THE SOUP

- 2 TABLESPOONS UNSALTED BUTTER
- 4 SLICES THICK-CUT BACON, CHOPPED
- 1 ONION, CHOPPED
- 4 CUPS PEELED AND CHOPPED POTATOES
- 6 CUPS CHICKEN STOCK (SEE PAGE 660)
- SALT AND PEPPER, TO TASTE

1. To begin preparations for the dumplings, place the flour, baking powder, and salt in a mixing bowl and stir until combined.

2. Add the oil, egg, water, and chives and stir with a fork until a loose dough forms. Cover the dough and set aside.

3. To begin preparations for the soup, place the butter in a saucepan and melt it over medium heat.

4. Add the bacon and onion and cook until the bacon is crispy and the onion starts to soften, about 5 minutes.

5. Add the potatoes and cook for 3 minutes. Add the stock and bring to a boil.

6. Reduce heat so that the soup simmers and cook for 10 minutes, or until the potatoes are tender.

7. Season with salt and pepper. Drop tablespoons of the dough into the broth.

8. Once all of the dumplings have been incorporated, simmer for 3 minutes and then turn off the heat.

9. Let stand for a few minutes, then ladle into warmed bowls and serve.

VARIATIONS

- Add spinach to make the soup heartier.
- Replace the potatoes with cooked cannellini beans.

CREAMED VEGETABLE SOUP WITH TURKEY DUMPLINGS

YIELD: 4 SERVINGS / **ACTIVE TIME:** 45 MINUTES / **TOTAL TIME:** 4 HOURS AND 15 MINUTES

Got lots of leftover turkey from your Thanksgiving dinner? Here's a great way to use it up. Feel free to adjust what vegetables are used: this soup is very accommodating.

INGREDIENTS:

- 2 TABLESPOONS OLIVE OIL
- 1 ONION, CHOPPED
- 2 CELERY STALKS, CHOPPED
- 1 CELERIAC, PEELED AND CHOPPED
- 2 PARSNIPS, PEELED AND CHOPPED
- 1 TABLESPOON FINELY CHOPPED FRESH ROSEMARY
- ½ CUP WHITE WINE
- 4 CUPS TURKEY STOCK (SEE RECIPE)
- 1 CUP HEAVY CREAM
- SALT AND PEPPER, TO TASTE
- TURKEY DUMPLINGS (SEE RECIPE), FOR SERVING

TURKEY STOCK

- 1 LEFTOVER TURKEY CARCASS
- 16 CUPS WATER
- 2 CELERY STALKS, CHOPPED
- 2 CARROTS, PEELED AND CHOPPED
- 1 ONION, CHOPPED
- 2 THYME SPRIGS
- 2 BAY LEAVES
- 6 WHOLE BLACK PEPPERCORNS

1. In a medium saucepan, warm the oil over medium heat. When it starts to shimmer, add the onion, celery, celeriac, and parsnips and sauté until tender, about 10 minutes.

2. Add the rosemary and cook for 2 minutes. Add the white wine and stock and bring to a boil.

3. Reduce heat so that the soup simmers and cook until the vegetables are very tender, about 30 minutes.

4. Transfer the soup to a food processor, puree until smooth, and then strain through a fine sieve.

5. Place the soup in a clean pan and bring to a simmer. Stir in the heavy cream and season with salt and pepper.

6. Serve in warm bowls with the Turkey Dumplings.

TURKEY STOCK

1. Place all of the ingredients in a large stockpot. Bring to a boil, reduce heat so that stock simmers, and cook for 3½ hours, or until the flavor has developed to your liking.

2. Skim the surface to remove impurities from the stock. Strain through a fine sieve and use as desired.

TURKEY DUMPLINGS

1. Place the bread and parsley in a food processor and pulse until combined. Add the flour and baking powder and blitz until combined.

2. Slowly add the milk, egg, and butter to the food processor. Pulse until a paste forms.

3. Fold in the turkey and season with salt and pepper. Refrigerate for 1 hour.

4. Place the turkey stock in a medium saucepan and bring to a simmer over medium heat.

5. Drop tablespoons of the turkey mixture into the stock. Cover and cook for 12 minutes. Remove the dumplings from the broth and set aside.

TURKEY DUMPLINGS

- 4 SLICES BREAD, CHOPPED
- ½ CUP FRESH PARSLEY, CHOPPED
- 1¼ CUP ALL-PURPOSE FLOUR
- 1 TEASPOON BAKING POWDER
- ½ CUP MILK
- 1 EGG
- 4 TABLESPOONS UNSALTED BUTTER, MELTED
- 1 CUP COOKED TURKEY LEG MEAT, CHOPPED
- SALT AND PEPPER, TO TASTE
- 4 CUPS TURKEY STOCK

BROKEN PASTA SOUP

YIELD: 4 SERVINGS / **ACTIVE TIME:** 20 MINUTES / **TOTAL TIME:** 45 MINUTES

This is a great healthy soup, which becomes much easier to eat with the broken pasta.

INGREDIENTS:

- 2 TEASPOONS OLIVE OIL
- 1 ONION, CHOPPED
- 2 GARLIC CLOVES, MINCED
- 2 CARROTS, PEELED AND CHOPPED
- 1 ZUCCHINI, CHOPPED
- 4 CELERY STALKS, CHOPPED
- 2 (14 OZ.) CANS STEWED TOMATOES
- 4 CUPS VEGETABLE STOCK (SEE PAGE 664)
- 2 OZ. SPAGHETTI, BROKEN INTO 2-INCH PIECES
- CLASSIC ITALIAN MEATBALLS (SEE PAGE 158)
- 2 TABLESPOONS FINELY CHOPPED FRESH PARSLEY
- SALT AND PEPPER, TO TASTE

1. Place the oil in a saucepan and warm over medium heat. When the oil starts to shimmer, add the onion and sauté until it starts to soften, about 5 minutes. Add the garlic, carrots, zucchini, and celery, and cook until they start to soften, about 5 minutes. Stir in the tomatoes and stock and bring to a boil.

2. Reduce heat so that the soup simmers and cook for 15 minutes.

3. Add the spaghetti and cook until it is tender, 8 to 10 minutes.

4. Stir in the meatballs and parsley and cook until the meatballs are warmed through. Season with salt and ladle into warmed bowls.

TOMATO SOUP WITH SMOKED CHEDDAR MEATBALLS

YIELD: 4 SERVINGS / **ACTIVE TIME:** 30 MINUTES / **TOTAL TIME:** 1 HOUR

Do you like tomato soup and grilled cheese? Then you are certain to love this soup that puts a meaty twist on this classic.

INGREDIENTS:

- 2 TABLESPOONS UNSALTED BUTTER
- 1 ONION, CHOPPED
- 2 LBS. TOMATOES, CHOPPED
- 2 CARROTS, PEELED AND CHOPPED
- 5 CUPS CHICKEN STOCK (SEE PAGE 660)
- 2 TABLESPOONS FINELY CHOPPED FRESH PARSLEY, PLUS MORE FOR GARNISH
- ½ TEASPOON FINELY CHOPPED FRESH THYME
- 6 TABLESPOONS HEAVY CREAM, PLUS MORE FOR GARNISH
- SALT AND PEPPER, TO TASTE
- MEXICAN SMOKED CHEDDAR MEATBALLS (SEE PAGE 162)
- PARMESAN CHEESE, SHAVED, FOR GARNISH

1. Place the butter in a large saucepan and melt it over medium heat.

2. Add the onion and sauté until it starts to soften, about 4 minutes.

3. Stir in the tomatoes, carrots, stock, parsley, and thyme, reduce heat to low, and simmer for 20 minutes, until the vegetables are tender.

4. Transfer the soup to a food processor, blitz until smooth, and then strain through a fine sieve.

5. Return the soup to the pan and add the cream. Season with salt and pepper and bring to a simmer over medium-low heat. Drop the meatballs into the soup and simmer until cooked through, about 10 minutes.

6. Ladle into warmed bowls and garnish with the shaved Parmesan.

KHAO SOI GAI

YIELD: 4 SERVINGS / **ACTIVE TIME:** 30 MINUTES / **TOTAL TIME:** 1 HOUR

Enjoy this classic from Northern Thailand. Don't let the exotic name intimidate you: it's delicious!

INGREDIENTS:

- 1 THAI CHILI PEPPER, STEMMED, SEEDS AND RIBS REMOVED, AND CHOPPED
- 2 SHALLOTS, PEELED AND CUT INTO QUARTERS, PLUS MORE FOR GARNISH
- 4 GARLIC CLOVES, MINCED
- 1 LEMONGRASS STALK, CRUSHED
- 1 TEASPOON LIME ZEST
- 1-INCH PIECE GALANGAL ROOT, PEELED AND MINCED
- 1-INCH PIECE FRESH GINGER, PEELED AND MINCED
- SMALL BUNCH FRESH CILANTRO, LEAVES REMOVED, STEMS RESERVED
- 1 TEASPOON CORIANDER SEEDS
- SEEDS OF 1 CARDAMOM POD
- SALT AND PEPPER, TO TASTE
- 1½ TABLESPOONS SHRIMP PASTE
- 1 CUP VEGETABLE OIL
- 4 OZ. RICE NOODLES
- 2 (14 OZ.) CANS COCONUT MILK
- 1 CUP CHICKEN STOCK (SEE PAGE 660)
- 2 TABLESPOONS SUGAR
- 4 CHICKEN LEGS, SPLIT INTO DRUMSTICKS AND THIGHS
- STEAMED STICKY RICE MEATBALLS (SEE PAGE 256)
- FISH SAUCE, TO TASTE
- LIME WEDGES, FOR GARNISH

1. In a nonstick sauté pan, add the chili, shallots, garlic, lemongrass, lime zest, galangal root, ginger, cilantro stalks, coriander seeds, and cardamom seeds and cook over low heat for 5 minutes, or until the mixture becomes fragrant.

2. Transfer the contents of the saucepan to a mortar. Add a pinch of salt and the shrimp paste and grind with a pestle until a very fine paste is formed. Set aside.

3. Place the oil in a Dutch oven and cook over medium-high heat until it reaches 325°F.

4. Place 1 oz. of rice noodles into the oil and cook until nice and crispy. Remove with a slotted spoon, set to drain on a paper towel, and season with salt. Reserve for garnish.

5. In a medium saucepan, add 1 tablespoon of the hot vegetable oil and 2 tablespoons of the cream from the top of the coconut milk. Cook over high heat until the coconut fat breaks up and begins to smoke. Add the paste and cook for 45 seconds, while stirring constantly.

6. Reduce heat and whisk in the remaining coconut milk, stock, and sugar.

7. Add the chicken pieces and simmer, while turning the chicken occasionally, for 30 minutes, or until the chicken is tender.

8. In the meantime, bring a pot of salted water to a boil and add the remaining rice noodles. Turn off heat, cover, and let stand for 3 minutes.

9. Place the noodles in warm bowls. Stir the meatballs into the soup and cook until warmed through. Season the soup with fish sauce, salt, and pepper and ladle the soup over the noodles. Garnish with the additional shallot, the lime wedges, and crispy rice noodles.

CORN & PLANTAIN SOUP WITH MANGO MEATBALLS

YIELD: 4 SERVINGS / **ACTIVE TIME:** 15 MINUTES / **TOTAL TIME:** 40 MINUTES

A common combination in both Caribbean and African cooking, corn and plantain packs enough sweetness and creaminess to accommodate a wide array of meatballs.

1. To begin preparations for the meatballs, place the oil in a saucepan and melt over medium heat. Add the onion and garlic and sauté until the onion starts to soften, about 5 minutes.

2. Place the egg and milk in a mixing bowl and stir to combine. Tear the bread into tiny pieces and stir them into the mixture along with the ginger and nutmeg. Add the pork and the onion mixture, season with salt and pepper, and stir until thoroughly combined. Working with wet hands, form the mixture into 1½-inch meatballs and set them aside.

3. To begin preparations for the soup, place the butter in a saucepan and melt it over medium heat. Add the onion and garlic and sauté until the onion starts to soften, about 5 minutes.

4. Stir in the plantains, tomatoes, corn kernels, and tarragon and cook for 5 minutes.

5. Add the stock, jalapeño, and nutmeg, and bring to a boil.

6. Add the meatballs, reduce the heat to medium-low, and simmer until the meatballs are cooked through and the plantains are tender, about 10 minutes.

7. Season with salt and pepper and ladle into warmed bowls.

INGREDIENTS:

FOR THE MEATBALLS

2 TABLESPOONS OLIVE OIL

1 LARGE ONION, CHOPPED

3 GARLIC CLOVES, MINCED

1 LARGE EGG

2 TABLESPOONS WHOLE MILK

3 SLICES WHITE BREAD

½ TEASPOON GROUND GINGER

¼ TEASPOON GROUND NUTMEG

1¼ LBS. GROUND PORK

SALT AND PEPPER, TO TASTE

1 TABLESPOON CURRY POWDER

1 CUP CHOPPED MANGO

FOR THE SOUP

4 TABLESPOONS UNSALTED BUTTER

1 ONION, CHOPPED

2 GARLIC CLOVES, MINCED

2 RIPE YELLOW PLANTAINS, PEELED AND SLICED

2 PLUM TOMATOES, CHOPPED

4 EARS OF CORN, KERNELS REMOVED

1 TABLESPOON FINELY CHOPPED FRESH TARRAGON

4 CUPS CHICKEN STOCK (SEE PAGE 660)

1 TABLESPOON MINCED JALAPEÑO PEPPER

⅛ TEASPOON GRATED FRESH NUTMEG

SALT AND PEPPER, TO TASTE

ASPARAGUS, PEA & GREEK MEATBALL SOUP

YIELD: 6 SERVINGS / **ACTIVE TIME:** 25 MINUTES / **TOTAL TIME:** 1 HOUR AND 20 MINUTES

Asparagus is sold year-round. However, there is nothing better than buying it from your local farm stand when it's in season in the spring. The lemon zest is key here, as it lightens the whole soup.

INGREDIENTS:

- ¾ LB. GREEN ASPARAGUS
- 2 TABLESPOONS UNSALTED BUTTER
- 1 LEEK, TRIMMED, CHOPPED, AND RINSED WELL
- 1¼ CUPS FRESH OR FROZEN PEAS, ¼ CUP RESERVED FOR GARNISH
- 1 TABLESPOON FINELY CHOPPED FRESH PARSLEY
- 5 CUPS VEGETABLE STOCK (SEE PAGE 664)
- ½ CUP HEAVY CREAM
- ZEST OF 2 LEMONS, 1 TABLESPOON RESERVED FOR GARNISH
- SALT AND PEPPER, TO TASTE
- GREEK MEATBALLS (SEE PAGE 201)
- PARMESAN CHEESE, SHAVED, FOR GARNISH

1. Remove the woody ends of the asparagus and discard. Separate the spears, remove the tips and reserve, and chop the remaining pieces.

2. In a medium saucepan, add the butter and melt over medium heat. Add the leek and sauté until it has softened, about 5 minutes.

3. Add the chopped asparagus, 1 cup of the peas, and the parsley. Cook for 3 minutes, add the stock, and bring to a boil. Reduce heat so that the soup simmers and cook for 6 to 8 minutes, or until the vegetables are tender.

4. Transfer the soup to a food processor, puree until smooth, and strain through a fine sieve.

5. Place soup in a clean pan. Stir in the cream and lemon zest, season with salt and pepper, and bring to a simmer. Stir in the meatballs, cook until warmed through, and remove the pan from heat.

6. Bring a small pan of salted water to a boil. Place the asparagus tips in the pan and cook for 3 to 4 minutes, or until tender. Remove tips, submerge in ice water, dry, and set aside.

7. Ladle the soup into warmed bowls and garnish with the asparagus tips, reserved peas, reserved lemon zest, and Parmesan.

COCONUT & SPINACH SOUP WITH CARIBBEAN CHUTNEY MEATBALLS

YIELD: 4 SERVINGS / **ACTIVE TIME:** 20 MINUTES / **TOTAL TIME:** 45 MINUTES

Dip into the islands with the tropical ingredients that give this soup its unforgettable flavor.

INGREDIENTS:

- 3 TABLESPOONS UNSALTED BUTTER
- 1 ONION, CHOPPED
- 16 CUPS SPINACH, CHOPPED
- 4 CUPS VEGETABLE STOCK (SEE PAGE 664)
- 1 TABLESPOON ALL-PURPOSE FLOUR
- 2 CUPS COCONUT MILK
- CARIBBEAN CHUTNEY MEATBALLS (SEE PAGE 178)
- SALT AND PEPPER, TO TASTE
- ¼ TEASPOON GROUND NUTMEG, PLUS MORE FOR GARNISH
- FRESH CHIVES, CHOPPED, FOR GARNISH
- ALMONDS, SLICED AND TOASTED, FOR GARNISH
- UNSWEETENED SHREDDED COCONUT, FOR GARNISH

1. Place 2 tablespoons of the butter in a medium saucepan and melt over medium heat. Add the onion and sauté until it starts to soften, about 5 minutes.

2. Add the spinach, cover the pan, and cook over low heat for 5 minutes, or until wilted.

3. Add the stock and bring to a boil.

4. Transfer the soup to a food processor, blend until creamy, and strain through a fine sieve.

5. In a clean saucepan, add the remaining butter and melt. Stir in the flour and cook for 2 minutes. Add the coconut milk, meatballs, and soup to the pan with the butter and flour. Cook until everything is warmed through, about 5 minutes. Season with salt, pepper, and nutmeg, ladle into warmed bowls, and garnish with additional nutmeg, chives, toasted sliced almonds, and coconut.

ROASTED PUMPKIN & MOLE SOUP WITH SOUTHWESTERN MEATBALLS

YIELD: 4 SERVINGS / **ACTIVE TIME:** 20 MINUTES / **TOTAL TIME:** 1 HOUR AND 30 MINUTES

Mole is a traditional Mexican sauce, with the flavor of chocolate and chili. Mole paste is a mixture of rehydrated chilies, nuts, bread, garlic, and raisins. I have opted to remove the chocolate, but if you prefer, add a small amount of dark chocolate at the very end of your preparation.

1. Preheat the oven to 450°F.

2. Sprinkle 1 tablespoon of the olive oil on a baking sheet. Place the two pumpkin halves on the pan, cut-side down, and roast for 30 minutes, or until the flesh is tender.

3. Remove from the oven and let stand for 30 minutes.

4. Meanwhile, reduce the oven temperature to 325°F.

5. Place the pumpkin seeds, brown sugar, cumin, salt, and remaining olive oil in a bowl. Toss until the seeds are coated, place on a baking sheet, and bake for 8 minutes. Remove from the oven and set aside.

6. Scoop the flesh out of the cooked pumpkin and place in a food processor with the ancho chili. Puree until smooth.

7. In a small saucepan, add the mole paste and water. Cook over low heat and whisk until it forms a thick paste. Remove from heat and set aside.

8. In a large saucepan, add the pumpkin puree, the mole sauce, and buttermilk. Bring to a simmer over medium heat, stirring constantly. Reduce the heat to medium-low, stir in the meatballs, and cook until warmed through.

9. Season with salt and pepper and ladle into warmed bowls. Garnish with the Lime Sour Cream, chives, and toasted pumpkin seeds.

INGREDIENTS:

- 1½ TABLESPOONS OLIVE OIL
- 1 3-LB. PUMPKIN, HALVED, SEEDS REMOVED
- ½ CUP PUMPKIN SEEDS
- 1 TEASPOON BROWN SUGAR
- ½ TEASPOON CUMIN
- ¼ TEASPOON KOSHER SALT
- 1 DRIED ANCHO CHILI PEPPER, RECONSTITUTED
- 1 TABLESPOON MOLE PASTE
- ¼ CUP WATER
- 2 CUPS BUTTERMILK
- CRUNCHY SOUTHWESTERN MEATBALLS (SEE PAGE 228)
- SALT AND PEPPER, TO TASTE
- LIME SOUR CREAM (SEE RECIPE), FOR GARNISH
- FRESH CHIVES, CHOPPED, FOR GARNISH

LIME SOUR CREAM

- 1 CUP SOUR CREAM
- ZEST AND JUICE OF 1 LIME
- SALT AND PEPPER, TO TASTE

LIME SOUR CREAM

1. Place all of the ingredients in a bowl and stir until combined. Refrigerate until ready to use.

SWEET POTATO SOUP WITH SOUTH AFRICAN MEATBALLS

YIELD: 4 TO 6 SERVINGS / **ACTIVE TIME:** 25 MINUTES / **TOTAL TIME:** 55 MINUTES

Do you love sweet potatoes? Then you are certain to love this soup. The curry is very subtle, but it adds a nice bit of flavor.

INGREDIENTS:

- 1½ TABLESPOONS UNSALTED BUTTER
- 1 SMALL ONION, CHOPPED
- 5 CUPS CHICKEN STOCK (SEE PAGE 660)
- ½ TEASPOON CURRY POWDER
- 10 CUPS PEELED AND CHOPPED SWEET POTATOES
- 2 TABLESPOONS MAPLE SYRUP
- 2 TABLESPOONS FINELY CHOPPED FRESH THYME
- PINCH OF CAYENNE PEPPER
- SOUTH AFRICAN MEATBALLS (SEE PAGE 206), FORMED AND UNCOOKED
- 2 CUPS HEAVY CREAM
- 2 PINCHES OF GROUND NUTMEG
- SALT AND PEPPER, TO TASTE
- FRESH CILANTRO, FINELY CHOPPED, FOR GARNISH

1. In a medium saucepan, add the butter and melt over medium heat. Add the onion and sauté until it starts to soften, about 5 minutes.

2. Add the stock, curry powder, sweet potato, maple syrup, thyme, and cayenne pepper. Bring to a boil, reduce heat so that the soup simmers, and cook for 25 minutes, or until the sweet potatoes are tender.

3. Transfer the soup to a food processor. Puree until creamy and then strain through a fine sieve.

4. Return the soup to the pan and bring to a simmer. Stir in the meatballs and simmer until they are cooked through, about 10 minutes. Add the cream, nutmeg, salt, and pepper and cook until the soup is warmed through.

5. Ladle into warmed bowls and garnish with the cilantro.

BEEF & SAUSAGE MEATBALL AND BARLEY SOUP

YIELD: 4 SERVINGS / **ACTIVE TIME:** 20 MINUTES / **TOTAL TIME:** 1 HOUR AND 30 MINUTES

Any soup that includes barley is hearty, but adding meatballs makes it a filling, well-rounded meal.

1. In a medium saucepan, add the olive oil and warm over medium-high heat.

2. Add the onion and garlic and sauté until the onion starts to soften, about 5 minutes. Stir in the herbs and stock and bring the soup to a boil.

3. Add the carrot and barley, turn the heat down to its lowest setting, and cover the saucepan. Cook for 1 hour, or until the barley is tender.

4. Add the meatballs and cook for 5 minutes, or until the meatballs are warmed through.

5. Season with salt and pepper and ladle into warmed bowls

INGREDIENTS:

2 TABLESPOONS OLIVE OIL

1 ONION, DICED

2 GARLIC CLOVES, MINCED

1 TEASPOON FINELY CHOPPED FRESH BASIL

1 TEASPOON FINELY CHOPPED FRESH OREGANO

1 TEASPOON FINELY CHOPPED FRESH THYME

8 CUPS CHICKEN STOCK (SEE PAGE 660)

1 CARROT, SLICED

¼ CUP PEARL BARLEY

BEEF & SAUSAGE MEATBALLS (SEE PAGE 330)

SALT AND PEPPER, TO TASTE

LEMONY GREEK MEATBALL & LENTIL SOUP

YIELD: 4 SERVINGS / **ACTIVE TIME:** 20 MINUTES / **TOTAL TIME:** 1 HOUR AND 30 MINUTES

I'm almost certain that lamb and lentils were created for each other. After you try this quick, easy, and delicious soup, I'm certain you'll feel the same way.

1. In a large saucepan, add the stock, onion, garlic, bay leaves, cloves, and thyme. Bring to a boil, then reduce the heat so that the soup simmers. Cook until the flavor has developed to your liking, about 30 minutes.

2. Remove the bay leaves, cloves, and thyme, add the potato, lentils, and meatballs, cover the pan, and cook for 15 minutes, or until the lentils and potatoes are tender and the meatballs are cooked through.

3. Season with salt and pepper, add the parsley, and ladle the soup into warmed bowls.

INGREDIENTS:

- 4 CUPS VEGETABLE STOCK (SEE PAGE 664)
- 1 ONION, MINCED
- 2 GARLIC CLOVES, MINCED
- 2 BAY LEAVES
- 4 WHOLE CLOVES
- 4 SPRIGS FRESH THYME
- 1 POTATO, PEELED AND CUT INTO ½-INCH PIECES
- ½ CUP BROWN LENTILS
- LEMONY GREEK MEATBALLS (SEE PAGE 337), FORMED AND UNCOOKED
- SALT AND PEPPER, TO TASTE
- 2 TABLESPOONS FINELY CHOPPED FRESH PARSLEY

MOROCCAN MEATBALL & LENTIL STEW

YIELD: 6 TO 8 SERVINGS / **ACTIVE TIME:** 10 MINUTES / **TOTAL TIME:** 8 HOURS

Set this incredibly filling stew on before you head out the door in the morning and you'll have a delicious dinner waiting for you when you come home.

1. Place the lentils in a fine sieve and rinse to remove any impurities. Place all of the ingredients, save the cannellini beans, meatballs, and the garnishes, in a slow cooker. Cover and cook on low for 7½ hours.

2. After 7½ hours, stir in the cannellini beans and the meatballs. Cover the slow cooker and cook for another 30 minutes. Ladle the stew into warmed bowls and garnish each portion with fresh mint and goat cheese.

INGREDIENTS:

1 CUP BROWN LENTILS

½ CUP FRENCH LENTILS

4 CUPS VEGETABLE STOCK (SEE PAGE 664)

3 CARROTS, PEELED AND CHOPPED

1 LARGE WHITE ONION, CHOPPED

3 GARLIC CLOVES, MINCED

3-INCH PIECE FRESH GINGER, PEELED AND MINCED

ZEST AND JUICE OF 1 LEMON

3 TABLESPOONS SMOKED PAPRIKA

2 TABLESPOONS CINNAMON

1 TABLESPOON CORIANDER

1 TABLESPOON TURMERIC

1 TABLESPOON CUMIN

1½ TEASPOONS ALLSPICE

2-3 BAY LEAVES

SALT AND PEPPER, TO TASTE

1 (14 OZ.) CAN CANNELLINI BEANS

MOROCCAN MEATBALLS (SEE PAGE 166), FORMED AND UNCOOKED

FRESH MINT, FINELY CHOPPED, FOR GARNISH

GOAT CHEESE, CRUMBLED, FOR GARNISH

SPICY BABY SPINACH & RICE SOUP WITH MEATBALLS

YIELD: 4 SERVINGS / **ACTIVE TIME:** 15 MINUTES / **TOTAL TIME:** 45 MINUTES

This is perfect for a spring or summer day. Feel free to toss in whatever vegetables you like.

1. In a saucepan, add the water and the spinach and cook over medium-high heat for 5 minutes, or until the spinach has wilted. Drain, let the spinach cool, and chop.

2. Add the oil to a large saucepan and warm over medium heat. Add the onion, garlic, and chili and sauté until the onion is translucent, about 3 minutes.

3. Add the stock and stir in the rice. Bring to a boil, reduce the heat so that the soup simmers, and cook for 15 minutes.

4. Add the meatballs and spinach and cook until the rice is tender and the meatballs are warmed through, about 5 minutes. Ladle into warmed bowls and garnish each portion with Romano cheese.

INGREDIENTS:

- 2 TABLESPOONS WATER
- 12 CUPS BABY SPINACH
- 3 TABLESPOONS OLIVE OIL
- 1 SMALL ONION, MINCED
- 2 GARLIC CLOVES, MINCED
- 1 SMALL RED CHILI PEPPER, STEMMED, SEEDS AND RIBS REMOVED, AND MINCED
- 4 CUPS VEGETABLE STOCK (SEE PAGE 664)
- ⅓ CUP ARBORIO RICE
- LEMON & ROSEMARY MEATBALLS (SEE PAGE 247)
- SALT AND PEPPER, TO TASTE
- ROMANO CHEESE, GRATED, FOR GARNISH

CANNELLINI BEAN SOUP WITH SICILIAN MEATBALLS

YIELD: 4 TO 6 SERVINGS / **ACTIVE TIME:** 30 MINUTES / **TOTAL TIME:** 1 HOUR

This hearty Italian soup is sure to warm up your insides!

INGREDIENTS:

- 1 TABLESPOON OLIVE OIL
- 1 ONION, CHOPPED
- ¼ CUP CHOPPED LEEK
- 1 CARROT, PEELED AND CHOPPED
- 1 CELERY STALK, CHOPPED
- 1 GARLIC CLOVE, MINCED
- 1 (14 OZ.) CAN DICED TOMATOES
- 4 CUPS CHICKEN STOCK (SEE PAGE 660)
- 2 TABLESPOONS MEDITERRANEAN HERBS (SEE RECIPE)
- 2 CUPS SAVOY CABBAGE, FINELY SLICED
- 1 (14 OZ.) CAN CANNELLINI BEANS, DRAINED AND RINSED
- SICILIAN MEATBALLS (SEE PAGE 333), FORMED AND UNCOOKED
- SALT AND PEPPER, TO TASTE
- PESTO, FOR SERVING (SEE STEP 2 ON PAGE 442 FOR HOMEMADE)

1. In a medium saucepan, add the oil and warm over medium heat.

2. Add the onion, leek, carrot, celery, and garlic and sauté for 5 minutes, or until vegetables are soft.

3. Add the tomatoes, stock, and Mediterranean Herbs and bring to a boil.

4. Reduce heat so that the soup simmers. Add the cabbage and cook for 15 minutes, or until the cabbage is tender.

5. Add the cannellini beans and the meatballs and simmer until the meatballs are cooked through, about 10 minutes. Season with salt and pepper, ladle into warmed bowls, and serve with the Basil Pesto.

MEDITERRANEAN HERBS

MEDITERRANEAN HERBS

- 1 TABLESPOON DRIED ROSEMARY
- 2 TEASPOONS CUMIN
- 2 TEASPOONS CORIANDER
- 1 TEASPOON DRIED OREGANO
- ⅛ TEASPOON KOSHER SALT

1. Place all of the ingredients in a bowl, stir until thoroughly combined, and use as desired.

CHICKEN MEATBALL CHILI

YIELD: 4 TO 6 SERVINGS / **ACTIVE TIME:** 30 MINUTES / **TOTAL TIME:** 1 HOUR AND 30 MINUTES

This is a great recipe to warm up with on a snowy winter day. Feel free to adjust the chili powder according to your spice threshold.

INGREDIENTS:

1 TABLESPOON OLIVE OIL

1 ONION, CHOPPED

2 GARLIC CLOVES, MINCED

1 TABLESPOON CHILI POWDER

4 TOMATOES, DICED

2 CUPS MEXICAN TOMATO SAUCE (SEE PAGE 678)

½ CUP TOMATO PASTE

1 (14 OZ.) CAN KIDNEY BEANS

1 (14 OZ.) CAN WHITE BEANS

1 (14 OZ.) CAN BLACK BEANS

SANTA FE CHICKEN MEATBALLS (SEE PAGE 276), FORMED AND UNCOOKED

SALT AND PEPPER, TO TASTE

CHEDDAR CHEESE, SHREDDED, FOR GARNISH

SOUR CREAM, FOR GARNISH

FRESH CHIVES, CHOPPED, FOR GARNISH

CORN BREAD (SEE PAGE 524), FOR SERVING

1. In a large saucepan, add the olive oil and warm over medium-high heat.

2. Add the onion and sauté until it starts to soften, about 5 minutes.

3. Add the garlic and cook for 2 minutes, then add the chili powder, tomatoes, tomato sauce, tomato paste, and beans. Bring to a boil, reduce heat so that the chili simmers, and cook for 20 minutes.

4. When the flavor has developed to your liking, stir the meatballs into the chili and simmer until they are cooked through, about 10 minutes. Season with salt and pepper, ladle into warmed bowls, and garnish with the cheddar cheese, sour cream, and chives. Serve with the Corn Bread.

SOUTHWESTERN BARBECUE MEATBALL STEW

YIELD: 6 SERVINGS / **ACTIVE TIME:** 30 MINUTES / **TOTAL TIME:** 3 HOURS AND 30 MINUTES

Save this for a Sunday during football season: it's so good, it won't even matter if your team ends up losing.

INGREDIENTS:

- 1 (28 OZ.) CAN CRUSHED SAN MARZANO TOMATOES
- 1 RED BELL PEPPER, CHOPPED
- 2 SMALL YELLOW ONIONS, CHOPPED, PLUS MORE FOR GARNISH
- 4 GARLIC CLOVES, MINCED
- 1 JALAPEÑO PEPPER, STEMMED, SEEDS AND RIBS REMOVED, AND MINCED
- 1 LB. PINK BEANS, SOAKED OVERNIGHT AND DRAINED
- ¼ CUP FRESH CILANTRO, CHOPPED, PLUS MORE FOR GARNISH
- ¼ CUP HOT SAUCE
- 2 TABLESPOONS CHILI POWDER
- 1 TABLESPOON BLACK PEPPER
- 1 TABLESPOON KOSHER SALT
- 2 TABLESPOONS GRANULATED GARLIC
- ⅓ CUP CUMIN
- 1 TABLESPOON MADRAS CURRY POWDER
- 1 TABLESPOON DRIED OREGANO
- SOUTHWESTERN BARBECUE MEATBALLS (SEE PAGE 161), FORMED AND UNCOOKED
- CHEDDAR CHEESE, GRATED, FOR GARNISH

1. Place all of the ingredients, except for the meatballs and the cheese, in a large saucepan, stir to combine, and bring to a boil over medium-high heat. Reduce the heat to low and simmer until the beans are fork-tender and the flavor is to your liking, about 3 hours.

2. Stir in the meatballs and cook until they are very tender and cooked through, about 30 minutes. Ladle into warmed bowls and garnish with the cheddar cheese, and the additional onion and cilantro.

POZOLE

YIELD: 6 SERVINGS / **ACTIVE TIME:** 30 MINUTES / **TOTAL TIME:** 24 HOURS

In Spanish, pozole means "hominy," a key ingredient in this traditional Mexican soup.

INGREDIENTS:

FOR THE MEATBALLS

- 3 TABLESPOONS OLIVE OIL
- 1 ONION, CHOPPED
- 1 SMALL ZUCCHINI, MINCED
- 3 GARLIC CLOVES, MINCED
- 1 LARGE EGG
- 2 TABLESPOONS WHOLE MILK
- ½ CUP BREAD CRUMBS
- 1 TABLESPOON DRIED OREGANO
- 1 TEASPOON CUMIN
- 1¼ LBS. GROUND PORK
- SALT AND PEPPER, TO TASTE

FOR THE SOUP

- 2 CUPS DRIED HOMINY, SOAKED OVERNIGHT
- 2 TABLESPOONS OLIVE OIL
- 1 LARGE YELLOW ONION, CHOPPED
- SALT AND PEPPER, TO TASTE
- 4 DRIED CHIPOTLE PEPPERS, SEEDED AND CHOPPED
- 2 TABLESPOONS FINELY CHOPPED FRESH THYME
- 2 TABLESPOONS CUMIN
- 3 GARLIC CLOVES, MINCED
- FRESH CILANTRO, FINELY CHOPPED, FOR GARNISH
- LIME WEDGES, FOR SERVING

1. To begin preparations for the meatballs, place the oil in a skillet and warm over medium-high heat. When it starts to shimmer, add the onion, zucchini, and garlic and sauté until the onion is translucent, about 3 minutes. Remove the pan from heat and set it aside.

2. Place the egg, milk, bread crumbs, oregano, and cumin in a mixing bowl and stir until combined. Add the pork and onion mixture, season with salt and pepper, and stir until thoroughly combined. Working with wet hands, form the mixture into 1½-inch meatballs and set them aside.

3. To begin preparations for the soup, drain the hominy and set it aside. Place the oil in a Dutch oven and warm over medium-high heat. When the oil starts to shimmer, add the onion, season with salt and pepper, and cook, while stirring occasionally, until the onion is well browned, about 12 minutes.

4. Stir in the chipotles, thyme, and cumin, meatballs, and hominy, cover the mixture with water, and bring to a boil. Reduce the heat to medium-low and simmer, stirring occasionally, until the meatballs are cooked through and the hominy is tender, about 1½ hours.

5. Stir in the garlic, cook for 5 minutes, and taste. Adjust seasoning if necessary, ladle the soup into warmed bowls, garnish with cilantro, and serve with the lime wedges.

SPICY EGGPLANT & MEATBALL SOUP

YIELD: 4 SERVINGS / **ACTIVE TIME:** 45 MINUTES / **TOTAL TIME:** 2 HOURS AND 30 MINUTES

This is based off a popular Cambodian dish, and its sweet, spicy, and tangy flavor comes from the Tuk Trey and the jaggery.

INGREDIENTS:

- 2 DRIED NEW MEXICO CHILIES
- 8 CUPS BEEF STOCK (SEE PAGE 663)
- 3-INCH PIECE FRESH GINGER, SLICED
- 1 CINNAMON STICK
- 2 STAR ANISE
- ½ TEASPOON BLACK PEPPERCORNS
- SEEDS OF 4 CARDAMOM PODS, CRUSHED
- 1 LIME LEAF
- 1 LEMONGRASS STALK, BRUISED
- 1-INCH PIECE FRESH GALANGAL ROOT, PEELED AND CHOPPED
- 1 TABLESPOON SOY SAUCE
- 3 TABLESPOONS TUK TREY (SEE RECIPE)
- 1 TABLESPOON VEGETABLE OIL
- 1 SHALLOT, MINCED
- 2 TABLESPOONS TAMARIND EXTRACT
- 1 TABLESPOON JAGGERY
- 8 THAI EGGPLANTS, TRIMMED AND CUT INTO ¼-INCH SLICES
- SALT AND PEPPER, TO TASTE
- CRYING TIGER MEATBALLS (SEE PAGE 177)
- 1 TEASPOON CURRY LEAVES, CHOPPED
- ½ BUNCH FRESH WATERCRESS
- FRESH RED CHILI PEPPERS, STEMMED, SEEDS AND RIBS REMOVED, AND SLICED, FOR GARNISH
- TOASTED PEANUTS, FOR GARNISH

1. Soak the dried chilies in water for 30 minutes.

2. In a large saucepan, add the stock, ginger, cinnamon, star anise, peppercorns, cardamom, lime leaf, lemongrass, and galangal root. Bring to a boil, reduce the heat so that the soup simmers, cover the pan, cook until the broth is very flavorful, about 1 hour.

3. Remove the lid and stir in the soy sauce and Tuk Trey.

4. Simmer until the broth has reduced by half, about 45 minutes. Strain the broth through a fine sieve and set aside.

5. Drain the soaked chilies, mince, and discard the seeds.

6. In a medium saucepan, add the oil and cook over medium heat until warm. Add the shallot and chopped chilies and cook for 5 minutes.

7. Add the strained broth to the saucepan and bring to a simmer.

8. Add the tamarind extract, jaggery, and eggplant. Cook for an additional 20 minutes.

9. Season the soup to taste. Stir in the meatballs, curry leaves, and watercress and cook until warmed through.

10. Ladle into warmed bowls, garnish with fresh chilies and peanuts, and serve.

TUK TREY

1. Place all of the ingredients in a bowl, stir to combine, and use as desired.

TUK TREY

- 1 TEASPOON SUGAR
- 1½ TABLESPOONS FISH SAUCE
- JUICE OF ½ LIME
- 2 TABLESPOONS WATER
- 1 GARLIC CLOVE, MINCED
- ¼ CUP ROASTED PEANUTS, CHOPPED
- 2 TABLESPOONS MINCED RED CHILI PEPPER

MEATBALL CHAMIN

YIELD: 4 SERVINGS / **ACTIVE TIME:** 30 MINUTES / **TOTAL TIME:** 14 HOURS AND 30 MINUTES

This stew based off of a traditional Jewish dish served at the Shabbat morning meal in Sephardi homes.

1. Preheat oven to 250°F. To begin preparations for the meatballs, place the beef, lamb, garlic, onion, parsley, coriander, cumin, and cinnamon in a mixing bowl, season with salt and pepper, and stir until thoroughly combined. Working with wet hands, form the mixture into 1-inch meatballs and set them aside.

2. To begin preparations for the soup, drain the chickpeas. Place the oil in a Dutch oven and warm over medium heat.

3. When the oil starts to shimmer, add the onion, garlic, parsnip, carrots, cumin, turmeric, and ginger and sauté for 2 minutes.

4. Add the stock and bring to a simmer.

5. Add the potato, zucchini, tomatoes, lentils, bay leaf, meatballs, cilantro, and chickpeas.

6. Cover the Dutch oven, place it in the oven, and bake for 1 hour and 15 minutes, or until the meatballs are cooked through and the chickpeas are tender.

7. Remove from the oven, discard the bay leaf, and skim the fat from the top of the stew. Season with salt and pepper and ladle into warmed bowls. Serve with rice and lemon wedges and garnish with the chilies.

INGREDIENTS:

FOR THE MEATBALLS

- ¾ LB. GROUND CHUCK
- ½ LB. GROUND LAMB
- 4 GARLIC CLOVES, MINCED
- ¼ CUP GRATED RED ONION
- ¼ CUP CHOPPED FRESH PARSLEY
- 1 TABLESPOON CORIANDER
- 2 TEASPOONS CUMIN
- ½ TEASPOON CINNAMON
- SALT AND PEPPER, TO TASTE

FOR THE SOUP

- ½ CUP DRIED CHICKPEAS, SOAKED OVERNIGHT
- 1½ TABLESPOONS OLIVE OIL
- 1 SMALL ONION, CHOPPED
- 5 GARLIC CLOVES, MINCED
- ¾ CUP CHOPPED PARSNIP
- 2 CARROTS, PEELED AND SLICED
- 1 TEASPOON CUMIN
- ¼ TEASPOON TURMERIC
- 1½-INCH PIECE FRESH GINGER, PEELED AND MINCED
- 4 CUPS BEEF STOCK (SEE PAGE 663)
- 1 SMALL POTATO, PEELED AND CHOPPED
- 1 SMALL ZUCCHINI, SLICED
- ½ LB. FRESH TOMATOES, DICED
- 2 TABLESPOONS BROWN LENTILS
- 1 BAY LEAF
- ½ BUNCH FRESH CILANTRO, CHOPPED
- SALT AND PEPPER, TO TASTE
- LONG-GRAIN RICE, COOKED, FOR SERVING
- LEMON WEDGES, FOR SERVING
- RED CHILI PEPPERS, STEMMED, SEEDS AND RIBS REMOVED, AND CHOPPED, FOR GARNISH

SWEET & SOUR SOUP WITH PORK MEATBALLS

YIELD: 4 SERVINGS / **ACTIVE TIME:** 30 MINUTES / **TOTAL TIME:** 50 MINUTES

The sour comes from the tamarind and lime and the sweet comes from the honey—this is a perfect flavor profile for pork.

INGREDIENTS:

- 2 SHALLOTS, MINCED
- 2 GARLIC CLOVES, MINCED
- ½ TEASPOON BLACK PEPPERCORNS
- 2 TEASPOONS SHRIMP PASTE
- 1-INCH PIECE FRESH GINGER, PEELED AND MINCED
- ½ CUP WATER
- 1 TEASPOON SUGAR
- 1 TEASPOON TAMARIND CONCENTRATE
- 1 TABLESPOON OLIVE OIL
- 4 CUPS CHICKEN STOCK (SEE PAGE 660)
- BEIJING MEATBALLS (SEE PAGE 259), FORMED AND UNCOOKED
- 3 CUPS CHOPPED RIPE PAPAYA
- 1 TEASPOON HONEY
- JUICE OF 1 LIME
- 1 SMALL THAI CHILI PEPPER, STEMMED, SEEDS AND RIBS REMOVED, AND SLICED, PLUS MORE FOR GARNISH
- 2 SCALLION WHITES, SLICED, PLUS MORE FOR GARNISH
- SALT AND PEPPER, TO TASTE

1. In a food processor, add the shallots, garlic, peppercorns, shrimp paste, ginger, water, sugar, and tamarind concentrate. Blitz until the mixture is a smooth paste.

2. Place the oil in a medium saucepan and warm over medium heat. Add the paste and cook for 2 minutes. Add the stock and bring to a boil.

3. Reduce the heat so that the soup simmers. Add the meatballs and papaya and simmer for about 10 minutes, until the meatballs are cooked through.

4. Stir in the honey, lime juice, Thai chili, and the scallions. Season with salt and pepper, ladle into warmed bowls, and garnish with additional chilies and scallions.

ITALIAN MEATBALL SOUP

YIELD: 4 SERVINGS / **ACTIVE TIME:** 20 MINUTES / **TOTAL TIME:** 1 HOUR

This winter favorite is very easy to prepare and makes for a beautiful, filling main course.

1. In a medium saucepan, add the olive oil and warm over medium heat.

2. When the oil starts to shimmer, add the onion, carrots, celery, and garlic to the pan and sauté until the onion starts to soften, about 5 minutes.

3. Add the stock and bring to a boil. Reduce heat so that the soup simmers and cook for 10 minutes.

4. Add the meatballs, zucchini, tomatoes, and beans and cook until the meatballs are cooked through and the vegetables are tender, about 15 minutes.

5. Season with salt and pepper and ladle into warmed bowls.

INGREDIENTS:

2 TABLESPOONS OLIVE OIL

1 ONION, CHOPPED

2 CARROTS, PEELED AND CHOPPED

1 CELERY STALK, CHOPPED

2 GARLIC CLOVES, MINCED

6 CUPS BEEF STOCK (SEE PAGE 663)

BEEF & SAUSAGE MEATBALLS (SEE PAGE 330), FORMED AND UNCOOKED

1 ZUCCHINI, CHOPPED

1 (14 OZ.) CAN STEWED TOMATOES

1 (14 OZ.) CAN CANNELLINI BEANS

SALT AND PEPPER, TO TASTE

SUMMER VEGETABLE STEW WITH BEEF & SAUSAGE MEATBALLS

YIELD: 6 TO 8 SERVINGS / **ACTIVE TIME:** 15 MINUTES / **TOTAL TIME:** 50 MINUTES

A quick-and-easy stew that helps you make the most of the summer's bounty without much effort.

1. Place the butter in a saucepan and melt it over medium-high heat. Add the onion and garlic and sauté until the onion starts to soften, about 5 minutes.

2. Stir in the remaining ingredients, except for the parsley, reduce the heat to medium-low, cover the pan, and simmer until the flavor has developed to your liking, about 30 minutes, removing the cover to stir the stew occasionally.

3. Ladle into warmed bowls, garnish with the parsley, and serve.

INGREDIENTS:

2 TABLESPOONS UNSALTED BUTTER

1 ONION, DICED

2 GARLIC CLOVES, MINCED

BEEF & SAUSAGE MEATBALLS (SEE PAGE 330), FORMED AND UNCOOKED

2 TEASPOONS CHILI POWDER

½ TEASPOON CAYENNE PEPPER

2 RED BELL PEPPERS, STEMMED, SEEDS AND RIBS REMOVED, AND CHOPPED

3 CUPS FRESH CORN KERNELS

1 SMALL ZUCCHINI, CHOPPED

4 TOMATOES, SEEDED AND CHOPPED

SALT AND PEPPER, TO TASTE

FRESH PARSLEY, FINELY CHOPPED, FOR GARNISH

SAUERKRAUT & CHORIZO SOUP

YIELD: 4 SERVINGS / **ACTIVE TIME:** 25 MINUTES / **TOTAL TIME:** 1 HOUR AND 10 MINUTES

This soup comes to us from Slovakia, where many of the households make and smoke their own chorizo. Another way to enjoy these flavors is to remove the potato from the soup and serve it with a baked potato.

1. To begin preparations for the meatballs, place the egg, milk, bread crumbs, paprika, cumin, and oregano in a mixing bowl and stir until combined. Add the chorizo, season with salt and cayenne, and stir until thoroughly combined. Working with wet hands, form the mixture into 1½-inch meatballs and set them aside.

2. To begin preparations for the soup, place the oil in a saucepan and warm over medium heat. Add the potato and onion and sauté until they start to soften, about 5 minutes.

3. Add the garlic and cook for 3 minutes. Add the bay leaf and caraway seeds and cook for 2 minutes.

4. Add the paprika, cayenne pepper, water, sauerkraut, and meatballs. Reduce heat to low, cover the pan, and simmer for 45 minutes.

5. Season with salt and pepper, ladle into warmed bowls, and garnish each portion with a spoonful of sour cream.

INGREDIENTS:

FOR THE MEATBALLS

- 1 LARGE EGG
- 2 TABLESPOONS WHOLE MILK
- ¼ CUP BREAD CRUMBS
- 1 TABLESPOON PAPRIKA
- 2 TEASPOON CUMIN
- 1 TEASPOON DRIED OREGANO
- 1½ LBS. CHORIZO, CHOPPED AND CASING REMOVED
- SALT AND CAYENNE PEPPER, TO TASTE

FOR THE SOUP

- 1 TABLESPOON OLIVE OIL
- 1 LARGE POTATO, PEELED AND CHOPPED
- 1 SMALL ONION, FINELY CHOPPED
- 3 GARLIC CLOVES, MINCED
- 1 BAY LEAF
- 1 TEASPOON CARAWAY SEEDS
- 2 TABLESPOONS SWEET PAPRIKA
- LARGE PINCH OF CAYENNE PEPPER
- 4 CUPS WATER
- 1 LB. SAUERKRAUT
- SALT AND PEPPER, TO TASTE
- SOUR CREAM, FOR GARNISH

LAMB MEATBALL & CANNELLINI SOUP

YIELD: 4 TO 6 SERVINGS / **ACTIVE TIME:** 20 MINUTES / **TOTAL TIME:** 13 HOURS AND 30 MINUTES

The flavors of Greece are showcased in this lively soup.

INGREDIENTS:

FOR THE MEATBALLS

- 2 TABLESPOONS OLIVE OIL
- 1 ONION, MINCED
- 1 GARLIC CLOVE, MINCED
- 1 LARGE EGG
- 1¼ LBS. GROUND LAMB
- 1 CUP COOKED WHITE RICE
- 3 TABLESPOONS FINELY CHOPPED FRESH PARSLEY
- 1 TABLESPOON FINELY CHOPPED FRESH ROSEMARY
- SALT AND PEPPER, TO TASTE

FOR THE SOUP

- 2 TABLESPOONS OLIVE OIL
- 1 ONION, CHOPPED
- 2 GARLIC CLOVES, MINCED
- 3 CARROTS, PEELED AND CHOPPED
- 3 CELERY STALKS, CHOPPED
- 1 (14 OZ.) CAN STEWED TOMATOES
- ¼ CUP FRESH PARSLEY, AND CHOPPED
- 2 TABLESPOONS FINELY CHOPPED FRESH THYME
- ½ LB. CANNELLINI BEANS, SOAKED OVERNIGHT AND DRAINED
- 6 CUPS CHICKEN STOCK (SEE PAGE 660)
- ½ LB. BABY SPINACH
- ¼ CUP KALAMATA OLIVES, PITTED AND SLICED
- SALT AND PEPPER, TO TASTE
- FETA CHEESE, FOR GARNISH

1. To begin preparations for the meatballs, place the oil in a small skillet and warm over medium-high heat. When it starts to shimmer, add the onion and garlic and sauté until the onion is translucent, about 3 minutes. Remove the pan from heat and set it aside.

2. Place the egg in a mixing bowl, beat until scrambled, and then stir in the lamb, rice, parsley, and rosemary. Add the onion mixture, season with salt and pepper, and stir until thoroughly combined. Working with wet hands, form the mixture into 1-inch meatballs and set them aside.

3. To begin preparations for the soup, place the olive oil in a saucepan and warm over medium heat.

4. When the oil starts to shimmer, add the onion and sauté until it starts to soften, about 5 minutes.

5. Add the garlic and cook for an additional 2 minutes.

6. Add the carrots and celery and cook for an additional 5 minutes.

7. Stir in the tomatoes, herbs, cannellini beans, and chicken stock. Bring to a boil, reduce heat so that the soup simmers, cover, and cook for 1 hour, or until the beans are tender.

8. Add the meatballs, spinach, and olives and cook until the meatballs are cooked through and the spinach is wilted, about 10 minutes.

9. Season with salt and pepper, ladle into warmed bowls, and sprinkle some feta cheese over each portion.

LASAGNA SOUP

YIELD: 4 SERVINGS / **ACTIVE TIME:** 20 MINUTES / **TOTAL TIME:** 45 MINUTES

This warm, rich soup is great for a birthday party, or when your childrens' friends come over to play.

INGREDIENTS:

- 12 LASAGNA NOODLES, BROKEN INTO PIECES
- 2 TABLESPOONS OLIVE OIL
- 1 ONION, CHOPPED
- 2 GARLIC CLOVES, MINCED
- 2 TEASPOONS DRIED OREGANO
- 2 TABLESPOONS TOMATO PASTE
- 4 CUPS BEEF STOCK (SEE PAGE 663)
- 2 (14 OZ.) CANS CRUSHED TOMATOES
- CLASSIC ITALIAN AMERICAN MEATBALLS (SEE PAGE 326), FORMED AND UNCOOKED
- ½ CUP FRESH BASIL, CHOPPED, PLUS MORE FOR GARNISH
- ¼ CUP GRATED PARMESAN CHEESE
- ¼ CUP HEAVY CREAM
- 1 CUP RICOTTA CHEESE, FOR GARNISH

1. Cook the lasagna noodles according to the manufacturer's instructions. Drain and set aside.

2. In a medium saucepan, add the olive oil and warm over medium heat.

3. When the oil starts to shimmer, add the onion and sauté until it starts to soften, about 5 minutes

4. Add the garlic and oregano and sauté for 2 minutes.

5. Add the tomato paste, stock, and tomatoes and bring to a boil.

6. Stir in the meatballs, reduce the heat to medium-low, and simmer until the meatballs are cooked through, about 10 minutes.

7. Stir in the noodles, basil, Parmesan, and heavy cream. Simmer until the cheese is melted, about 2 minutes.

8. Ladle into warmed bowls and garnish with the ricotta and additional basil.

LEMON, ASPARAGUS & LAMB MEATBALL SOUP

YIELD: 4 SERVINGS / **ACTIVE TIME:** 15 MINUTES / **TOTAL TIME:** 30 MINUTES

An almost impossibly bright-tasting broth allows the savory meatballs to make an outsized impression.

1. To begin preparations for the meatballs, place the oil in a small skillet and warm over medium-high heat. When it starts to shimmer, add the onion and garlic and sauté until the onion is translucent, about 3 minutes. Remove the pan from heat and set it aside.

2. Place the egg in a mixing bowl, beat until scrambled, and then stir in the lamb, rice, parsley, and rosemary. Add the onion mixture, season with salt and pepper, and stir until thoroughly combined. Working with wet hands, form the mixture into 1-inch meatballs and set them aside.

3. To begin preparations for the soup, place the butter in a saucepan and melt it over medium heat. Add the leek and sauté until it starts to soften, about 5 minutes.

4. Add the chopped asparagus and stock and bring to a boil. Reduce the heat so that the soup simmers and cook for 6 to 8 minutes, or until the vegetables are tender.

5. Remove the pan from heat and transfer the soup to a food processor. Blitz until smooth and then strain through a fine sieve.

6. Return soup to a clean pan and stir in the meatballs, cream, and lemon zest. Season with salt and pepper and bring to a simmer. Simmer until the meatballs are cooked through, about 10 minutes.

7. Ladle into warmed bowls and garnish with the parsley, Parmesan, and additional lemon zest.

INGREDIENTS:

FOR THE MEATBALLS

2 TABLESPOONS OLIVE OIL

1 ONION, MINCED

1 GARLIC CLOVE, MINCED

1 LARGE EGG

1¼ LBS. GROUND LAMB

1 CUP COOKED WHITE RICE

3 TABLESPOONS FINELY CHOPPED FRESH PARSLEY

1 TABLESPOON FINELY CHOPPED FRESH ROSEMARY

SALT AND PEPPER, TO TASTE

FOR THE SOUP

2 TABLESPOONS UNSALTED BUTTER

1 LEEK, TRIMMED, CHOPPED, AND RINSED WELL

1½ LBS. GREEN ASPARAGUS, TRIMMED AND CHOPPED

5 CUPS VEGETABLE STOCK (SEE PAGE 664)

½ CUP HEAVY CREAM

ZEST OF 2 LEMONS, PLUS MORE FOR GARNISH

SALT AND PEPPER, TO TASTE

FRESH PARSLEY, FINELY CHOPPED, FOR GARNISH

PARMESAN CHEESE, GRATED, FOR GARNISH

BEEF, VEAL & LAMB MEATBALLS

Meatballs made from ground beef are an essential part of every American cook's repertoire; in fact, a meatball recipe featuring ground chuck was probably the first dish many learned to cook.

While ground beef and lamb are world travelers that have been embraced by cuisines all over the globe, veal features prominently in just one: Italian. As such, many of the preparations featuring veal in this chapter will have an Italian tinge to them. That said, you shouldn't be afraid to experiment with veal in other preparations, as its mild flavor can fit into a surprising number of meatballs.

BLUE CHEESE MEATBALLS

YIELD: 4 TO 6 SERVINGS / **ACTIVE TIME:** 15 MINUTES / **TOTAL TIME:** 30 MINUTES

Blue cheese is a natural pairing with hearty beef and this recipe takes full advantage of that inclination.

1. Preheat the oven to 450°F and line a rimmed baking sheet with aluminum foil. Tear the bread into small pieces, place the bread in a mixing bowl, add the milk, and stir to combine.

2. Place the butter in a small skillet and melt over medium-high heat. Add the onion and garlic and sauté until the onion is translucent, about 3 minutes. Remove the pan from heat and set it aside.

3. Place the egg in a mixing bowl and whisk until scrambled. Stir in the bread mixture, parsley, cheese, and thyme and then add the onion mixture and beef. Season with salt and pepper and stir until thoroughly combined again. Working with wet hands, form the mixture into 1½-inch meatballs, arrange them on the baking sheet, and spray with cooking spray.

4. Place the meatballs in the oven and bake for 12 to 15 minutes, until cooked through. Remove from the oven and serve with the Patatas Bravas.

VARIATIONS

- Ground turkey can be substituted for the beef. Cook the turkey meatballs until the internal temperature is 160°F on an instant-read thermometer.
- Any blue cheese—from Italian Gorgonzola to English Stilton—works well in this recipe.

INGREDIENTS:

3 SLICES WHITE BREAD

⅓ CUP WHOLE MILK

2 TABLESPOONS UNSALTED BUTTER

1 SMALL ONION, MINCED

2 GARLIC CLOVES, MINCED

1 LARGE EGG

2 TABLESPOONS FINELY CHOPPED FRESH PARSLEY

¾ CUP CRUMBLED BLUE CHEESE

1 TABLESPOON FINELY CHOPPED FRESH THYME

1¼ LBS. GROUND CHUCK

SALT AND PEPPER, TO TASTE

PATATAS BRAVAS (SEE PAGE 623), FOR SERVING

MEATBALL STROGANOFF

YIELD: 4 TO 6 SERVINGS / **ACTIVE TIME:** 20 MINUTES / **TOTAL TIME:** 45 MINUTES

Beef Stroganoff, supposedly named for a Russian prince, was the epitome of elegant dinner party fare in the 1960s. It, like quiche, eventually got a bad rap as cliché, but it's really delicious.

INGREDIENTS:

- 2 TABLESPOONS OLIVE OIL
- 2 LARGE ONIONS, CHOPPED
- 3 GARLIC CLOVES, MINCED
- 1 LARGE EGG
- 2 TABLESPOONS WHOLE MILK
- ½ CUP BREAD CRUMBS
- 1¼ LBS. GROUND CHUCK
- SALT AND PEPPER, TO TASTE
- 2 TABLESPOONS UNSALTED BUTTER
- 3 TABLESPOONS ALL-PURPOSE FLOUR
- 1½ CUPS BEEF STOCK (SEE PAGE 663)
- 2 TABLESPOONS TOMATO PASTE
- 1 TABLESPOON DIJON MUSTARD
- ½ CUP SOUR CREAM
- 2 TABLESPOONS FINELY CHOPPED FRESH PARSLEY
- EGG NOODLES, FOR SERVING

1. Preheat the broiler to high, position a rack so the tops of the meatballs will be approximately 6 inches below the broiler, and line a rimmed baking sheet with aluminum foil.

2. Place the oil in a skillet and warm over medium-high heat. When it starts to shimmer, add the onions and garlic and sauté until the onions are translucent, about 3 minutes. Remove the pan from heat and set it aside.

3. Place the egg and milk in a mixing bowl and stir to combine. Add the bread crumbs, half of the onion mixture, and the beef, season with salt and pepper, and stir until thoroughly combined again. Working with wet hands, form the mixture into 2-inch meatballs, arrange them on the baking sheet, and spray the tops with cooking spray.

4. Place the meatballs in the oven and broil until browned all over, turning them as they cook. Remove the meatballs from the oven and set aside.

5. Place the butter in a skillet and melt over medium-low heat. Add the remaining onion mixture and the flour and cook for 2 minutes, while stirring constantly. Gradually add the stock while stirring and bring the sauce to a boil. Stir in the tomato paste and mustard, reduce the heat to low, and simmer for 3 minutes. Remove the pan from heat.

6. Add the meatballs to the sauce, reduce the heat to low, cover the pan, and simmer, turning the meatballs occasionally, until they are cooked through, about 15 minutes. Stir the sour cream and parsley into the sauce and serve over egg noodles.

VARIATIONS

- Make the meatballs from ground turkey or ground veal, and then substitute Chicken Stock (see page 660) for the Beef Stock.
- Add ½ lb. sautéed mushrooms to the sauce along with the meatballs.

MEATBALLS AU POIVRE

YIELD: 4 TO 6 SERVINGS / **ACTIVE TIME:** 15 MINUTES / **TOTAL TIME:** 30 MINUTES

A touch of heady red wine, some herbs, and piquant capers lend these meatballs a flavor similar to the classic French dish steak au poivre.

INGREDIENTS:

- 1 LARGE EGG
- ¼ CUP DRY RED WINE
- ½ CUP BREAD CRUMBS
- 2 TABLESPOONS WHOLE-GRAIN DIJON MUSTARD, PLUS MORE FOR SERVING
- 2 SHALLOTS, MINCED
- 2 GARLIC CLOVES, MINCED
- 2 TABLESPOONS CAPERS, DRAINED, RINSED, AND CHOPPED
- 1 TABLESPOON FINELY CHOPPED FRESH THYME
- 1¼ LBS. GROUND CHUCK
- SALT, TO TASTE
- 3 TABLESPOONS BLACK PEPPER
- BLUE CHEESE POLENTA (SEE PAGE 595)

1. Preheat the oven to 450°F and line a rimmed baking sheet with aluminum foil. Place the egg and wine in a mixing bowl and stir until combined. Add ¼ cup of the bread crumbs, the mustard, shallots, garlic, capers, and thyme and stir until thoroughly combined. Stir in the beef and season with salt.

2. Place the remaining bread crumbs in a small bowl and stir in the pepper. Form the meat mixture into 1½-inch meatballs and roll them in the seasoned bread crumbs. Arrange the meatballs on the baking sheet and spray the tops with cooking spray.

3. Place the meatballs in the oven and bake for 12 to 15 minutes, until cooked through. Remove and serve immediately with the Blue Cheese Polenta and additional Dijon mustard.

VARIATIONS

- Use lamb in place of the beef.
- Omit the capers and in their place add 2 tablespoons finely chopped fresh rosemary to the meat mixture.

COTTAGE PIE WITH MEATBALLS

YIELD: 6 TO 8 SERVINGS / **ACTIVE TIME:** 25 MINUTES / **TOTAL TIME:** 1 HOUR AND 15 MINUTES

Flavorful meatballs and vegetables in a rich, brown gravy are crowned with a layer of cheddar mashed potatoes, making this the perfect meal to warm you up on a chilly night.

INGREDIENTS:

- 2 LBS. RED POTATOES, PEELED AND DICED
- ½ CUP HEAVY CREAM
- 4 TABLESPOONS UNSALTED BUTTER, PLUS MORE AS NEEDED
- 1½ CUPS GRATED SHARP CHEDDAR CHEESE
- SALT AND PEPPER, TO TASTE
- ¼ CUP OLIVE OIL
- 1 LARGE ONION, MINCED
- 2 GARLIC CLOVES, MINCED
- 4 OZ. FRESH MUSHROOMS, CHOPPED
- 1 LARGE EGG
- 2 TABLESPOONS WHOLE MILK
- ½ CUP BREAD CRUMBS
- 1½ LBS. GROUND CHUCK
- 2 CUPS DRY RED WINE
- 2 TABLESPOONS MUSHROOM GRAVY (SEE RECIPE)
- 2 TABLESPOONS FINELY CHOPPED FRESH PARSLEY
- 1 TABLESPOON FINELY CHOPPED FRESH THYME
- 1 (10 OZ.) PACKAGE FROZEN MIXED VEGETABLES, THAWED

1. Bring a pot of salted water to a boil and add the potatoes. Reduce the heat to medium and cook the potatoes until they are fork-tender, about 20 minutes. Drain and set the potatoes aside.

2. Place the cream, butter, and 1 cup of the cheese in the saucepan and cook over medium heat until the cheese has melted, while stirring occasionally. Return the potatoes to saucepan and mash until the mixture is smooth. Season with salt and pepper and set aside.

3. Preheat the broiler to high, position a rack so that the tops of the meatballs will be approximately 6 inches below the broiler, and line a rimmed baking sheet with aluminum foil. Place the oil in a large skillet and warm over medium-high heat. When it starts to shimmer, add the onion and garlic and sauté until the onion is translucent, about 3 minutes. Stir in the mushrooms and cook for another three minutes. Remove the pan from heat and let it cool slightly.

4. Place the egg, milk, and bread crumbs in a mixing bowl and stir until thoroughly combined. Add the beef and the sautéed vegetables, season with salt and pepper, and stir until thoroughly combined. Working with wet hands, form the mixture into 1½-inch meatballs, arrange them on the baking sheet, and spray the tops with cooking spray.

5. Place the meatballs under the broiler and broil until browned all over, turning them as they cook. Remove the meatballs from the oven and set aside. Preheat the oven to 400°F and grease a 9 x 13–inch baking pan with butter.

6. Place the wine, gravy, parsley, and thyme in a saucepan and stir to combine. Bring to a boil over medium-high heat, stirring frequently, reduce the heat to low, and simmer for 2 minutes.

7. Arrange the meatballs in the baking pan and pour the sauce over them. Cover the pan with aluminum foil, place in the oven, and bake for 15 minutes.

8. Remove from the oven, stir in the frozen vegetables, and bake for another 10 minutes.

9. Raise the oven temperature to 450°F. Spread the mashed potatoes evenly over the meatballs and vegetables and sprinkle the remaining cheese on top. Place in the oven and bake for about 15 minutes, until the cheese is melted and golden brown. Remove and let cool slightly before serving.

MUSHROOM GRAVY

MUSHROOM GRAVY

- 2 TABLESPOONS UNSALTED BUTTER
- ½ LB. MUSHROOMS, SLICED
- SALT AND PEPPER, TO TASTE
- 2 TABLESPOONS ALL-PURPOSE FLOUR
- 2 CUPS BEEF STOCK (SEE PAGE 663)
- FRESH THYME, TO TASTE

1. Place the butter in a skillet and melt over medium heat. Add the mushrooms, season with salt, and cook until all of the liquid the mushrooms release has evaporated, about 20 minutes.

2. Add the flour and cook, while stirring constantly, for 5 minutes. Incorporate the stock 1 cup at a time, season with salt, pepper, and thyme, and reduce the heat to medium-low. Simmer until the gravy has reduced to the desired consistency, about 30 minutes.

VARIATION

- Use lamb in place of beef and add 1 tablespoon chopped fresh rosemary to the gravy.

PROVENÇAL MEATBALLS

YIELD: 4 TO 6 SERVINGS / **ACTIVE TIME:** 20 MINUTES / **TOTAL TIME:** 1 HOUR AND 15 MINUTES

Think of this dish as a meatball version of the French classic, beef bourguignon, where the meatballs are cooked in a mixture of red wine and herbs. Serve over buttered egg noodles or mashed potatoes and flank it with a solid Burgundy.

INGREDIENTS:

- 3 TABLESPOONS UNSALTED BUTTER
- 1 ONION, CHOPPED
- 2 GARLIC CLOVES, MINCED
- 1 LARGE EGG
- ¼ CUP WHOLE MILK
- ½ CUP BREAD CRUMBS
- 3 TABLESPOONS FINELY CHOPPED FRESH PARSLEY
- 1 TABLESPOON FINELY CHOPPED FRESH THYME
- 1¼ LBS. GROUND CHUCK
- SALT AND PEPPER, TO TASTE
- 1¼ CUPS DRY RED WINE
- 1 CUP BEEF STOCK (SEE PAGE 663)
- 3 TABLESPOONS TOMATO PASTE
- 1 TABLESPOON HERBES DE PROVENCE
- 1 CUP GRATED GRUYÈRE CHEESE
- EGG NOODLES OR MASHED POTATOES, FOR SERVING

1. Preheat the broiler to high, position a rack so that the tops of the meatballs will be approximately 6 inches below the broiler, and line a rimmed baking sheet with aluminum foil.

2. Place the butter in a small skillet and melt over medium-high heat. Add the onion and garlic and sauté until the onion is translucent, about 3 minutes. Remove the pan from heat and set it aside.

3. Place the egg and milk in a mixing bowl and stir until combined. Stir in the bread crumbs, parsley, and thyme and then add the beef and the onion mixture. Season with salt and pepper and stir until thoroughly combined. Working with wet hands, form the mixture into 2-inch meatballs, arrange them on the baking sheet, and spray the tops with cooking spray.

4. Place the meatballs in the oven and broil until browned all over, turning them as they cook. Remove the meatballs from the oven and transfer them to a 9 x 13–inch baking pan. Preheat the oven to 375°F.

5. Place the wine, stock, tomato paste, and Herbes de Provence in a mixing bowl, season with salt and pepper, and stir to combine. Pour the mixture over the meatballs, cover the pan with aluminum foil, and bake for 30 minutes. Remove the pan from the oven, remove the aluminum foil, and sprinkle cheese over the meatballs. Return to the oven and bake for an additional 15 minutes, until cheese is melted and bubbling. Remove and let cool briefly before serving with egg noodles or mashed potatoes.

VARIATIONS

- Add ½ lb. sautéed mushrooms to the sauce.
- Cut red potatoes into 1-inch cubes and bake them along with the meatballs and sauce.

WILD MUSHROOM & CARAMELIZED ONION MEATBALLS

YIELD: 4 TO 6 SERVINGS / **ACTIVE TIME:** 30 MINUTES / **TOTAL TIME:** 1 HOUR AND 15 MINUTES

Between the sweet onions, woodsy mushrooms, and pungent cheese there is so much flavor in these meatballs that they need no additional sauce for dipping or topping. Instead, serve with mashed potatoes and a green salad.

INGREDIENTS:

- 3 TABLESPOONS OLIVE OIL
- 2 TABLESPOONS UNSALTED BUTTER
- 2 LARGE ONIONS, CHOPPED
- SALT AND PEPPER, TO TASTE
- 2 TEASPOONS GRANULATED SUGAR
- ½ LB. SHIITAKE MUSHROOMS, STEMMED AND CHOPPED
- 2 GARLIC CLOVES, MINCED
- 1 LARGE EGG
- ½ CUP BREAD CRUMBS
- 3 TABLESPOONS WHOLE MILK
- ½ CUP GRATED GRUYÈRE CHEESE
- 2 TEASPOONS FINELY CHOPPED FRESH THYME
- 1¼ LBS. GROUND CHUCK

1. Place the oil and butter in a large skillet and warm over medium heat. When the butter has melted, stir in the onions, cover the pan, and cook for 10 minutes, while stirring occasionally. Sprinkle salt, pepper, and the sugar over the onions, reduce the heat to medium-low, and cook until the onions start to caramelize, 30 to 35 minutes.

2. Preheat the oven to 450°F and line a rimmed baking sheet with aluminum foil. Add the mushrooms and garlic to the skillet and cook, stirring frequently, for 5 to 7 minutes, until mushrooms are starting to brown. Remove the skillet from heat and set it aside.

3. Place the egg, bread crumbs, milk, cheese, and thyme in a mixing bowl and stir until combined. Add the beef and sautéed vegetables, season with salt and pepper, and stir until thoroughly combined. Working with wet hands, form the mixture into 1½-inch meatballs, arrange them on the baking sheet, and spray the tops with cooking spray.

4. Place the meatballs in the oven and bake for 12 to 15 minutes, until cooked through. Remove from the oven and serve immediately.

VARIATION

- Ground lamb can be substituted for the beef.

The word "dill" comes from the Norse *dilla*, meaning "to lull," a definition that is derived from the practice of drinking dill tea to help with insomnia. The ancient Greeks and Romans also knew dill as a medicinal herb, as soldiers placed charred dill seeds on their wounds to promote healing.

MUSTARD & DILL MEATBALLS

YIELD: 4 TO 6 SERVINGS / **ACTIVE TIME:** 15 MINUTES / **TOTAL TIME:** 30 MINUTES

The freshness of the dill serves as a wonderful counterpoint to the sharpness of the mustard.

1. Preheat the oven to 450°F and line a rimmed baking sheet with aluminum foil. Place the butter in a small skillet and melt over medium-high heat. Add the onion and garlic and sauté until the onion is translucent, about 3 minutes. Remove the pan from heat and set it aside.

2. Place the stock, egg, and mustard in a mixing bowl and stir until combined. Tear the bread into small pieces and add it and the dill to the bowl. Stir in the beef and onion mixture, season with salt and pepper, and stir until thoroughly combined. Working with wet hands, form the mixture into 1½-inch meatballs, arrange them on the baking sheet, and spray the tops with cooking spray.

3. Place the meatballs in the oven and bake for 12 to 15 minutes, until cooked through. Remove from the oven and serve alongside the Dill & Scallion Sauce.

VARIATION

- For a lighter dish, replace the beef with ground turkey or ground pork.

INGREDIENTS:

2 TABLESPOONS UNSALTED BUTTER

1 SMALL ONION, CHOPPED

2 GARLIC CLOVES, MINCED

½ CUP BEEF STOCK (SEE PAGE 663)

1 LARGE EGG

2 TABLESPOONS DIJON MUSTARD

3 SLICES CARAWAY RYE BREAD

¼ CUP FINELY CHOPPED FRESH DILL

1¼ LBS. GROUND CHUCK

SALT AND PEPPER, TO TASTE

1 CUP DILL & SCALLION SAUCE (SEE PAGE 718)

MEATBALLS WITH MUSTARD & DRIED APRICOTS

YIELD: 4 TO 6 SERVINGS / **ACTIVE TIME:** 15 MINUTES / **TOTAL TIME:** 30 MINUTES

These are one of my favorite hors d'oeuvre to serve at a cocktail party; the dried apricots and the potent kick of mustard make each bite a memorable one.

INGREDIENTS:

- 3 TABLESPOONS OLIVE OIL
- 2 LARGE SHALLOTS, CHOPPED
- 2 GARLIC CLOVES, MINCED
- 1 LARGE EGG
- ⅓ CUP DIJON MUSTARD
- 3 TABLESPOONS WHOLE MILK
- ¾ CUP PANKO
- ½ CUP MINCED DRIED APRICOTS
- 2 TABLESPOONS FINELY CHOPPED FRESH SAGE
- 2 TABLESPOONS FINELY CHOPPED FRESH CILANTRO
- 1¼ LBS. GROUND CHUCK
- SALT AND PEPPER, TO TASTE
- ½ CUP APRICOT PRESERVES
- ½ TEASPOON HOT SAUCE

1. Preheat the oven to 450°F and line a rimmed baking sheet with aluminum foil. Place the oil in a small skillet and warm over medium-high heat. When the oil starts to shimmer, add the shallots and garlic and sauté until shallots start to soften, about 5 minutes. Remove the pan from heat and set it aside.

2. Place the egg, ¼ cup of the mustard, and milk in a mixing bowl and stir until combined. Stir in the panko, dried apricots, sage, and cilantro and then add the beef and shallot mixture. Season with salt and pepper and stir until thoroughly combined. Working with wet hands, form the mixture into 1½-inch meatballs, arrange them on the baking sheet, and spray the tops with cooking spray.

3. Place the meatballs in the oven and bake for 12 to 15 minutes, until cooked through.

4. While the meatballs are in the oven, place the remaining mustard, the apricot preserves, and the hot sauce in a bowl and stir to combine. Set the sauce aside.

5. Remove the meatballs from the oven and serve alongside the sauce.

VARIATION

• Make these meatballs with ground pork or ground turkey.

MEATBALLS IN SOUR CHERRY SAUCE

YIELD: 4 TO 6 SERVINGS / **ACTIVE TIME:** 25 MINUTES / **TOTAL TIME:** 50 MINUTES

Northern European cuisines, such as those hailing from Scandinavia as well as Germany and Austria, frequently use fruit in savory dishes. After a taste of this, you'll begin to understand the appeal.

INGREDIENTS:

- 1½ CUPS DRIED SOUR CHERRIES
- 2 CUPS BEEF STOCK (SEE PAGE 663)
- ¼ CUP OLIVE OIL
- 2 ONIONS, CHOPPED
- 1 CARROT, PEELED AND CHOPPED
- 1 LARGE EGG
- ½ CUP BREAD CRUMBS
- 2 GARLIC CLOVES, MINCED
- ¾ TEASPOON CINNAMON
- ½ TEASPOON GROUND GINGER
- PINCH OF ALLSPICE
- 1¼ LBS. GROUND CHUCK
- SALT AND PEPPER, TO TASTE
- 1 TABLESPOON CORNSTARCH
- 1 TABLESPOON KIRSCH

1. Place the dried cherries and 1¾ cups of the stock in a saucepan and bring to a boil over medium-high heat. Remove the pan from the heat and let the cherries steep.

2. Place the oil in a large skillet and warm over medium-high heat. When it starts to shimmer, add the onions and carrot and sauté until the onions are translucent, about 3 minutes. Add the cherries and stock, bring to a boil, and then reduce the heat to medium-low. Cover the pan and simmer the sauce for 15 minutes.

3. Preheat the broiler to high, position a rack so that the tops of the meatballs will be approximately 6 inches below the broiler, and line a rimmed baking sheet with aluminum foil. Place the egg and remaining stock in a mixing bowl and stir until combined. Stir in the bread crumbs, garlic, cinnamon, ginger, and allspice and then add the beef. Season with salt and pepper and stir until thoroughly combined. Working with wet hands, form the mixture into 1½-inch meatballs, arrange them on the baking sheet, and spray the tops with cooking spray.

4. Place the meatballs in the oven and broil until browned all over, turning them as they cook. Remove from the oven, add the meatballs to the sauce, raise the heat to medium, and bring to a boil. Reduce heat to low, cover the pan, and simmer the meatballs, turning them occasionally, until they are cooked through, about 15 minutes.

5. Place the cornstarch and kirsch in a small bowl and stir to combine. Stir the slurry into the sauce and simmer until it thickens slightly, about 2 minutes. Serve immediately.

VARIATION

- Make the meatballs from a combination of ground pork and ground beef; they will be lighter and the fruit flavor will seem more intense.

MEATBALLS WITH APPLES & RAISINS

YIELD: 4 TO 6 SERVINGS / **ACTIVE TIME:** 25 MINUTES / **TOTAL TIME:** 1 HOUR AND 30 MINUTES

This is one of my favorite dishes, and both my sister and I fondly remember it from childhood as a delicious filling for blanched cabbage leaves. I dispensed with the cabbage many years ago, and now just revel in the sweet tang of the sauce.

INGREDIENTS:

- 1¼ LBS. GROUND CHUCK
- 1 CUP COOKED WHITE RICE
- 1 SMALL ONION, GRATED
- 2 GARLIC CLOVES, MINCED
- SALT AND PEPPER, TO TASTE
- UNSALTED BUTTER, AS NEEDED
- 3 GOLDEN DELICIOUS APPLES, PEELED, CORED, AND DICED
- ¾ CUP RAISINS
- 1¾ CUPS TOMATO SAUCE
- ¾ CUP APPLE CIDER VINEGAR
- ¾ CUP FIRMLY PACKED DARK BROWN SUGAR

1. Preheat the broiler to high, position a rack so that the tops of the meatballs will be approximately 6 inches below the broiler, and line a rimmed baking sheet with aluminum foil.

2. Place the beef, rice, onion, garlic, salt, and pepper in a mixing bowl and stir until thoroughly combined. Working with wet hands, form the mixture into 2-inch meatballs, arrange them on the baking sheet, and spray the tops with cooking spray.

3. Place the meatballs in the oven and broil until browned all over, turning them as they cook. Remove the pan from the oven and set the meatballs aside.

4. Preheat the oven to 375°F and grease a 9 x 13–inch baking pan with butter. Distribute the apples and raisins in the pan and place the meatballs on top. Place the tomato sauce, vinegar, and brown sugar in a mixing bowl and stir until thoroughly combined. Pour the sauce over the meatballs and cover the pan with aluminum foil.

5. Place the meatballs in the oven and bake for 30 minutes. Remove from the oven, remove the foil, and bake for another 30 minutes, until the apples are very tender. Remove and let cool briefly before serving.

VARIATIONS

- Instead of raisins, use chopped dried apricots, dried cranberries, or a combination of various dried fruits.
- Instead of beef, make the dish with ground turkey, ground veal, or some combination of the two.

MEATBALL GOULASH

YIELD: 4 TO 6 SERVINGS / **ACTIVE TIME:** 25 MINUTES / **TOTAL TIME:** 45 MINUTES

Goulash is a traditional Hungarian stew that can accommodate a number of alterations. Serve over some buttered egg noodles with a steamed green vegetable.

INGREDIENTS:

- 2 TABLESPOONS OLIVE OIL
- 2 LARGE ONIONS, CHOPPED
- 3 GARLIC CLOVES, MINCED
- 1 LARGE EGG
- 2 TABLESPOONS WHOLE MILK
- 2 SLICES CARAWAY RYE BREAD
- 1¼ LBS. GROUND CHUCK
- SALT AND PEPPER, TO TASTE
- 5 TABLESPOONS HUNGARIAN PAPRIKA
- 2 TABLESPOONS TOMATO PASTE
- 2 CUPS BEEF STOCK (SEE PAGE 663)
- 2 TEASPOONS CRUSHED CARAWAY SEEDS
- ¾ CUP SOUR CREAM
- EGG NOODLES, FOR SERVING

1. Preheat the broiler to high, position a rack so the tops of the meatballs will be approximately 6 inches below the broiler, and line a rimmed baking sheet with aluminum foil.

2. Place the oil in a skillet and warm over medium-high heat. When it starts to shimmer, add the onions and garlic and sauté until the onions are translucent, about 3 minutes. Remove the pan from heat and set it aside.

3. Place the egg and milk in a mixing bowl and stir to combine. Tear the bread into small pieces, add them to the mixing bowl, and then stir in half of the onion mixture and the beef. Season the mixture with salt and pepper. Working with wet hands, form the mixture into 2-inch meatballs, arrange them on the baking sheet, and spray the tops with cooking spray.

4. Place the meatballs in the oven and broil until browned all over, turning them as they cook. Remove from the oven and set the meatballs aside.

5. While the meatballs are in the oven, add the paprika to the skillet containing the remaining onion mixture and warm over low heat for 1 minute, stirring constantly. Stir in the tomato paste, stock, and caraway seeds, raise the heat to medium-high, and bring the mixture to a boil.

6. Add the meatballs to the sauce, reduce the heat to low, cover the skillet, and simmer for 15 minutes, occasionally turning the meatballs as they cook. Stir in sour cream and serve over the egg noodles.

VARIATION

- Make the meatballs from ground turkey or ground pork.

CLASSIC ITALIAN MEATBALLS

YIELD: 4 TO 6 SERVINGS / **ACTIVE TIME:** 20 MINUTES / **TOTAL TIME:** 35 MINUTES

The combination of different herbs, various vegetables, and two cheeses gives these simple meatballs tremendous flavor. They make a great hors d'oeuvre, or you can keep them in the freezer to use on pizza (see page 532) or to top pasta.

1. Preheat the oven to 450°F and line a rimmed baking sheet with aluminum foil. Tear the bread into small pieces, place them in a bowl with the milk, and stir to combine.

2. Place the oil in a small skillet and warm over medium-high heat. When it starts to shimmer, add the onion, garlic, and carrot and sauté until the onion is translucent, about 3 minutes. Remove the pan from heat and set it aside.

3. Place the egg in a mixing bowl and stir in the bread mixture, parsley, basil, oregano, mozzarella, and Parmesan. Add the beef and the onion mixture, season with salt and pepper, and stir until thoroughly combined. Working with wet hands, form the mixture into 1½-inch meatballs, arrange them on the baking sheet, and spray the tops with cooking spray.

4. Place the meatballs in the oven and bake for 12 to 15 minutes, until cooked through. Remove the pan from the oven and serve alongside the Marinara Sauce.

VARIATIONS

- Make the meatballs with a combination of ground beef, ground pork, and ground Italian sausage.
- Use ground turkey instead of ground chuck.

INGREDIENTS:

- 3 SLICES WHITE BREAD
- 3 TABLESPOONS WHOLE MILK
- 3 TABLESPOONS OLIVE OIL
- 1 SMALL ONION, MINCED
- 2 GARLIC CLOVES, MINCED
- 1 SMALL CARROT, PEELED AND GRATED
- 1 LARGE EGG
- 3 TABLESPOONS FINELY CHOPPED FRESH PARSLEY
- 2 TABLESPOONS FINELY CHOPPED FRESH BASIL
- 1 TABLESPOON FINELY CHOPPED FRESH OREGANO
- ½ CUP GRATED WHOLE-MILK MOZZARELLA CHEESE
- ¼ CUP GRATED PARMESAN CHEESE
- 1¼ LBS. GROUND CHUCK
- SALT AND PEPPER, TO TASTE
- 1 CUP MARINARA SAUCE (SEE PAGE 674), WARMED, FOR SERVING

SOUTHWESTERN BARBECUE MEATBALLS

YIELD: 4 TO 6 SERVINGS / **ACTIVE TIME:** 20 MINUTES / **TOTAL TIME:** 35 MINUTES

These easy-to-make meatballs contain a wide range of popular Southwestern flavors—from fiery chilies, creamy cheese, and lots of herbs and spices. Serve with a basket of warm Corn Tortillas (see page 535).

INGREDIENTS:

- 1 LARGE EGG
- 2 CHIPOTLES IN ADOBO
- 2 TABLESPOONS WHOLE MILK
- ½ CUP BREAD CRUMBS
- ½ CUP GRATED JALAPEÑO JACK CHEESE
- 3 TABLESPOONS FINELY CHOPPED FRESH CILANTRO
- 3 TABLESPOONS CANNED DICED GREEN CHILIES, DRAINED
- 4 GARLIC CLOVES, MINCED
- 1 TABLESPOON DRIED OREGANO
- 1 TABLESPOON SMOKED PAPRIKA
- 2 TEASPOONS CUMIN
- 1¼ LBS. GROUND CHUCK
- SALT AND PEPPER, TO TASTE
- 1 CUP SOUTHWESTERN BARBECUE SAUCE (SEE PAGE 684), WARMED, FOR SERVING

1. Preheat the oven to 450°F and line a rimmed baking sheet with aluminum foil. Place the egg, chipotles, milk, and bread crumbs in a food processor and puree until smooth. Place the mixture in a mixing bowl, add the cheese, cilantro, green chilies, garlic, oregano, paprika, and cumin and stir until thoroughly combined.

2. Stir in the beef and season the mixture with salt and pepper. Working with wet hands, form the mixture into 1½-inch meatballs, arrange them on the baking sheet, and spray the tops with cooking spray.

3. Place the meatballs in the oven and bake for 12 to 15 minutes, or until cooked through. Remove the pan from the oven and serve immediately, accompanied by a bowl of Southwestern Barbecue Sauce.

VARIATIONS

- Make lighter meatballs by using ground turkey in place of the beef.
- Adjust the spice level by using plain Monterey Jack cheese instead of the jalapeño version and serve with a more mild barbecue sauce, such as the Coffee & Bourbon Barbecue Sauce (see page 687).

MEXICAN SMOKED CHEDDAR MEATBALLS

YIELD: 4 TO 6 SERVINGS / **ACTIVE TIME:** 25 MINUTES / **TOTAL TIME:** 40 MINUTES

Bacon adds a smoky nuance to these spicy meatballs. Beer, by far, is the best beverage to accompany them.

INGREDIENTS:

- 6 STRIPS BACON
- 1 ONION, CHOPPED
- 3 GARLIC CLOVES, MINCED
- 2 LARGE JALAPEÑO OR SERRANO PEPPERS, STEMMED, SEEDS AND RIBS REMOVED, AND MINCED
- 1 LARGE EGG
- ¼ CUP WHOLE MILK
- ½ CUP BREAD CRUMBS
- ½ CUP GRATED SMOKED CHEDDAR CHEESE
- 2 TABLESPOONS FINELY CHOPPED FRESH CILANTRO
- 1 TABLESPOON DRIED OREGANO
- 2 TEASPOONS GROUND CUMIN
- 1¼ LBS. GROUND CHUCK
- SALT AND PEPPER, TO TASTE
- SPANISH RICE (SEE PAGE 552), FOR SERVING

1. Preheat the oven to 450°F and line a rimmed baking sheet with aluminum foil. Place the bacon in a large skillet and cook over medium-high heat until it is crispy, about 6 minutes. Transfer the bacon to a paper towel–lined plate to drain and remove all but 2 tablespoons of the rendered fat from the skillet. When the bacon is cool enough to handle, chop it into small pieces.

2. Add the onion, garlic, and peppers to the skillet and sauté until the onion is translucent, about 3 minutes. Remove the pan from heat and set it aside.

3. Place the egg and milk in a mixing bowl and stir to combine. Add the bread crumbs, cheddar, cilantro, oregano, and cumin and stir until thoroughly combined.

4. Stir in the beef, bacon, and the onion mixture and season with salt and pepper. Working with wet hands, form the mixture into 1½-inch meatballs, arrange them on the baking sheet, and spray the tops with cooking spray.

5. Place the meatballs in the oven and bake for 12 to 15 minutes, until cooked through. Remove the pan from the oven and serve with the Spanish Rice.

VARIATION

- Use a combination of ground pork and ground veal for a lighter flavor.

CARNE ASADA MEATBALLS

YIELD: 6 SERVINGS / **ACTIVE TIME:** 15 MINUTES / **TOTAL TIME:** 30 MINUTES

These can also be prepared in the oven, but for the famously mouthwatering flavor, the grill is a necessity.

INGREDIENTS:

- 1¼ LBS. GROUND CHUCK
- 1 JALAPEÑO PEPPER, STEMMED, SEEDS AND RIBS REMOVED, AND MINCED
- 3 GARLIC CLOVES, MINCED
- ¼ CUP FINELY CHOPPED FRESH CILANTRO
- JUICE OF 1 SMALL ORANGE
- 2 TABLESPOONS APPLE CIDER VINEGAR
- 2 TEASPOONS CAYENNE PEPPER
- 1 TEASPOON ANCHO CHILI POWDER
- 1 TEASPOON GARLIC POWDER
- 1 TEASPOON PAPRIKA
- 1 TEASPOON KOSHER SALT
- 1 TEASPOON CUMIN
- 1 TEASPOON DRIED OREGANO
- ¼ TEASPOON BLACK PEPPER
- GUACAMOLE (SEE PAGE 765), FOR SERVING
- CORN TORTILLAS (SEE PAGE 535), FOR SERVING

1. If using bamboo skewers, soak them in cold water. Preheat your gas or charcoal grill to medium-high (450°F).

2. Place all of the ingredients, except for the Guacamole and Corn Tortillas, in a mixing bowl and stir until thoroughly combined. Working with wet hands, form the mixture into 1-inch balls and thread three on each of the skewers.

3. Place the meatballs on the grill and cook, while turning, until browned all over and medium-rare, 6 to 8 minutes. Make sure to leave the grill uncovered if using a charcoal grill. Serve with the Guacamole and Corn Tortillas.

MOROCCAN MEATBALLS IN TOMATO SAUCE

YIELD: 4 TO 6 SERVINGS / **ACTIVE TIME:** 20 MINUTES / **TOTAL TIME:** 45 MINUTES

Aromatic cinnamon and earthy cumin are the dominant flavors in these Moroccan-inspired meatballs. Serve them over couscous in order to salvage every last drop of the sauce.

INGREDIENTS:

- ¼ CUP OLIVE OIL
- 2 LARGE ONIONS, CHOPPED
- 4 GARLIC CLOVES, MINCED
- 1 LARGE EGG
- 2 TABLESPOONS WHOLE MILK
- ½ CUP PANKO
- ⅔ CUP CHOPPED FRESH PARSLEY
- 1 TABLESPOON CHILI POWDER
- ½ TEASPOON CINNAMON
- 1¼ LBS. GROUND CHUCK
- SALT AND CAYENNE PEPPER, TO TASTE
- 2 CUPS TOMATO SAUCE
- 2 TEASPOONS CUMIN

1. Preheat the broiler to high, position a rack so that the tops of the meatballs will be approximately 6 inches below the broiler, and line a rimmed baking sheet with aluminum foil.

2. Place the oil in a skillet and warm over medium-high heat. When it starts to shimmer, add the onions and garlic and sauté until the onions are translucent, about 3 minutes. Remove the pan from heat and set it aside.

3. Place the egg and milk in a mixing bowl and stir to combine. Stir in the bread crumbs, half of the parsley, the chili powder, and cinnamon and then add the beef and half of the onion mixture.

4. Season the mixture with salt and cayenne pepper and stir until thoroughly combined. Working with wet hands, form the mixture into 2-inch meatballs, arrange them on the baking sheet, and spray the tops with cooking spray.

5. Place the meatballs in the oven and broil until browned all over, turning them as they cook. Remove the meatballs from the oven and set them aside.

6. Place the tomato sauce, cumin, and remaining parsley in the skillet containing the remaining onion mixture and bring to a boil over medium-high heat, stirring occasionally.

7. Add the meatballs to the sauce, reduce the heat to low, cover the pan, and simmer the meatballs, turning them occasionally, until cooked through, about 15 minutes. Serve immediately.

VARIATION

- Use ground lamb instead of beef for the meatballs.

BERBERE MEATBALLS

YIELD: 6 TO 8 SERVINGS / **ACTIVE TIME:** 20 MINUTES / **TOTAL TIME:** 45 MINUTES

Berbere is an Ethiopian spice mix that carries an incredible amount of versatility. Serving these meatballs alongside the Injera makes for an authentic experience.

INGREDIENTS:

- 1 TABLESPOON OLIVE OIL
- 1 SMALL YELLOW ONION, MINCED
- 3 GARLIC CLOVES, MINCED
- 1 TEASPOON GROUND FENUGREEK
- 1 TEASPOON RED PEPPER FLAKES
- 2 TABLESPOONS SWEET PAPRIKA
- ½ TEASPOON CARDAMOM
- 1 TEASPOON GROUND NUTMEG
- ⅛ TEASPOON GARLIC POWDER
- ⅛ TEASPOON GROUND CLOVES
- ⅛ TEASPOON CINNAMON
- ⅛ TEASPOON ALLSPICE
- 1¼ LBS. GROUND CHUCK
- SALT AND PEPPER, TO TASTE
- INJERA (SEE PAGE 544), FOR SERVING

1. Preheat the oven to 450°F and line a rimmed baking sheet with aluminum foil. Place the oil in a small skillet and warm over medium-high heat. When it starts to shimmer, add the onion and garlic and sauté until the onion is translucent, about 3 minutes. Remove the pan from heat and set it aside.

2. Place the fenugreek, red pepper flakes, sweet paprika, cardamom, nutmeg, garlic powder, cloves, cinnamon, and allspice in a mixing bowl and stir to combine. Add the beef and the onion mixture, season with salt and pepper, and stir until thoroughly combined. Working with wet hands, form the mixture into 1½-inch meatballs, arrange them on the baking sheet, and spray the tops with cooking spray.

3. Place the meatballs in the oven and bake for 12 to 15 minutes, until cooked through. Remove the pan from the oven and serve immediately, accompanied by the Injera.

VARIATION

- Use lamb instead of the ground beef.

GRILLED MIDDLE EASTERN MEATBALLS

YIELD: 4 TO 6 SERVINGS / **ACTIVE TIME:** 15 MINUTES / **TOTAL TIME:** 30 MINUTES

Grilling ground meat on skewers is ubiquitous in cuisines throughout the Middle East, and because these kebabs contain no egg they can be seared on the outside and enjoyed slightly rare on the inside.

INGREDIENTS:

- 1¼ LBS. GROUND CHUCK
- 4 GARLIC CLOVES, MINCED
- ¼ CUP GRATED RED ONION
- ¼ CUP CHOPPED FRESH PARSLEY
- 1 TABLESPOON CORIANDER
- 2 TEASPOONS CUMIN
- ½ TEASPOON CINNAMON
- SALT AND PEPPER, TO TASTE
- 1 CUP MIDDLE EASTERN YOGURT SAUCE OR TRADITIONAL HUMMUS (SEE PAGES 734 OR 710, RESPECTIVELY)
- PITA BREAD (SEE PAGE 539), FOR SERVING

1. If using bamboo skewers, soak them in cold water. Preheat your gas or charcoal grill to medium-high (450°F).

2. Place the beef, garlic, onion, parsley, coriander, cumin, cinnamon, salt, and pepper in a mixing bowl and stir until thoroughly combined. Divide the mixture into 8 to 12 portions and form each portion into a sausage shape. Skewer each sausage so that the tip of the skewer just pokes through the top end of the meatball.

3. Place the meatballs on the grill and cook, while turning, until browned all over and medium-rare, about 6 minutes. Make sure to leave the grill uncovered if using a charcoal grill. Serve immediately alongside Middle Eastern Yogurt Sauce or Traditional Hummus and Pita Bread.

VARIATION

- Make the meatballs from turkey, ground lamb, or a combination of ground lamb and ground chuck.

To add additional flavor to grilled meatballs, use large rosemary branches as skewers. Make sure to soak them in water as you would bamboo skewers. Once heated, they add aroma to the fire and the food.

CARIBBEAN MEATBALLS IN SPICED RUM SAUCE

YIELD: 4 TO 6 SERVINGS / **ACTIVE TIME:** 20 MINUTES / **TOTAL TIME:** 55 MINUTES

The foods of the Caribbean often include ingredients associated with both Asian cooking (ginger and lime) and Western cooking (olives and tomatoes), as the islands were once instrumental in various trade routes. The rum adds its own special flavor to this spicy sauce.

INGREDIENTS:

- 1¼ LBS. GROUND CHUCK
- 1 CUP COOKED RICE
- 1 YELLOW ONION, GRATED
- 6 GARLIC CLOVES, MINCED
- SALT AND PEPPER, TO TASTE
- 2 TABLESPOONS OLIVE OIL
- 1 RED ONION, CHOPPED
- 1 GREEN BELL PEPPER, STEMMED, SEEDS AND RIBS REMOVED, AND CHOPPED
- 1 LARGE JALAPEÑO OR SERRANO PEPPER, STEMMED, SEEDS AND RIBS REMOVED, AND MINCED
- 2 CUPS BEEF STOCK (SEE PAGE 663)
- ¼ CUP DARK RUM
- ¼ CUP SLICED PIMENTO-STUFFED OLIVES
- 3 TOMATOES, CORED, SEEDED, AND CHOPPED
- 2-INCH PIECE FRESH GINGER, PEELED AND GRATED
- 2 TABLESPOONS TOMATO PASTE
- 2 TABLESPOONS MOLASSES
- 2 TABLESPOONS FRESH LIME JUICE
- ¼ CUP CHOPPED FRESH CILANTRO
- 1 TABLESPOON CORNSTARCH
- 1 TABLESPOON WATER
- ½ CUP CHOPPED SALTED PEANUTS, FOR GARNISH

1. Preheat the broiler to high, position a rack so that the tops of the meatballs will be approximately 6 inches below the broiler, and line a rimmed baking sheet with aluminum foil.

2. Place the beef, rice, yellow onion, two of the garlic cloves, salt, and pepper in a mixing bowl and stir until thoroughly combined. Working with wet hands, form the mixture into 2-inch meatballs, arrange them on the baking sheet, and spray the tops with cooking spray.

3. Place the meatballs in the oven and broil until browned all over, turning them as they cook. Remove from the oven and set aside.

4. Place the oil in a large skillet and warm over medium-high heat. When it starts to shimmer, add the red onion, remaining garlic, the bell pepper, and chili pepper and sauté until the onion is translucent, about 3 minutes. Stir in the stock, rum, olives, tomatoes, ginger, tomato paste, molasses, and lime juice and bring to a boil, while stirring frequently. Reduce the heat to low and simmer the sauce for 10 minutes.

5. Stir the meatballs and cilantro into the sauce, cover the pan, and simmer the meatballs, turning them occasionally, until they are cooked through, about 15 minutes.

6. Combine the cornstarch and water and then stir the slurry into the sauce. Cook until the sauce thickens slightly, about 2 minutes. Sprinkle the peanuts on top and serve immediately.

VARIATIONS

- Make the meatballs from chopped fish such as cod, and cook them in the sauce without broiling.
- Make the meatballs with ground chicken or turkey.

CHINESE MEATBALLS WITH PEPPERS & ONIONS

YIELD: 4 TO 6 SERVINGS / **ACTIVE TIME:** 25 MINUTES / **TOTAL TIME:** 50 MINUTES

This hearty dish is a variation on the pepper steak that is popular in Chinese American restaurants.

INGREDIENTS:

- 1¼ LBS. GROUND CHUCK
- 1 CUP COOKED WHITE RICE
- 4 SCALLIONS, TRIMMED AND CHOPPED
- 4 GARLIC CLOVES, MINCED
- ¼ CUP SOY SAUCE
- 2 TABLESPOONS DRY SHERRY
- 2 TABLESPOONS SESAME OIL
- BLACK PEPPER, TO TASTE
- 1½ CUPS BEEF STOCK (SEE PAGE 663)
- 3 TABLESPOONS FERMENTED BLACK BEAN PASTE
- 2 TABLESPOONS CORNSTARCH
- 2 TEASPOONS SUGAR
- 3 TABLESPOONS OLIVE OIL
- 2-INCH PIECE FRESH GINGER, PEELED AND GRATED
- ½ TEASPOON RED PEPPER FLAKES, OR TO TASTE
- 1 LARGE RED ONION, SLICED THIN
- 2 BELL PEPPERS, STEMMED, SEEDS AND RIBS REMOVED, AND SLICED THIN
- 3 TABLESPOONS FINELY CHOPPED FRESH CILANTRO, FOR GARNISH

1. Preheat the oven to 450°F and line a rimmed baking sheet with aluminum foil. Place the beef, rice, scallions, two of the garlic cloves, 2 tablespoons of the soy sauce, sherry, sesame oil, and pepper in a mixing bowl and stir until thoroughly combined. Working with wet hands, form the mixture into 1½-inch meatballs, arrange them on the baking sheet, and spray the tops with cooking spray.

2. Place the meatballs in the oven and bake for 12 to 15 minutes, until cooked through. Remove the pan from the oven and set aside. While the meatballs are in the oven, place the stock, black bean paste, remaining soy sauce, the cornstarch, and sugar in a bowl and stir until thoroughly combined and the sugar is dissolved. Set aside.

3. Place the olive oil in a large skillet and warm over medium-high heat. When the oil starts to shimmer, add the remaining garlic, the ginger, and the red pepper flakes and stir-fry until fragrant, about 15 seconds. Add the onion and bell peppers, stir-fry for 2 minutes, and then stir in the sauce. Cook until it thickens slightly, about 2 minutes.

4. Stir the meatballs into the skillet and cook for 1 minute. Garnish with the cilantro and serve immediately.

VARIATION

- Substitute pork or chicken in place of the beef, and use Chicken Stock (see page 660) instead of Beef Stock.

CRYING TIGER MEATBALLS

YIELD: 6 TO 8 SERVINGS / **ACTIVE TIME:** 15 MINUTES / **TOTAL TIME:** 30 MINUTES

Don't be thrown by the name—the only tears resulting from these fried meatballs are those of joy.

INGREDIENTS:

- 1¼ LBS. GROUND CHUCK
- 2 TABLESPOONS SOY SAUCE
- 1 TABLESPOON OYSTER SAUCE
- 1 TABLESPOON BROWN SUGAR, PLUS 1 TEASPOON
- ⅓ CUP FRESH LIME JUICE
- ¼ CUP FISH SAUCE
- 2 TABLESPOONS FINELY CHOPPED FRESH CILANTRO
- 1½ TABLESPOONS TOASTED RICE POWDER (SEE RECIPE)
- 1 TABLESPOON RED PEPPER FLAKES
- VEGETABLE OIL, AS NEEDED
- 2 TABLESPOONS FINELY CHOPPED FRESH MINT
- 2 TABLESPOONS FINELY CHOPPED FRESH BASIL
- THAI FRIED RICE (SEE PAGE 604), FOR SERVING

TOASTED RICE POWDER

- ½ CUP JASMINE RICE

1. Place all of the ingredients, except for the oil, mint, basil, and fried rice, in a large bowl and stir until thoroughly combined. Working with wet hands, form the mixture into 1-inch balls, place them on a parchment-lined baking sheet, and firm the meatballs up in the freezer for 15 minutes.

2. Add vegetable oil to a Dutch oven until it is approximately 2 inches deep and warm to 375°F over medium-high heat. Working in batches, add the meatballs to the oil and fry until crispy and cooked through, about 5 minutes. Transfer the cooked meatballs to a paper towel–lined plate to drain. When all of the meatballs have been cooked, sprinkle the mint and basil over the top and serve with the Thai Fried Rice.

TOASTED RICE POWDER

1. Warm a cast-iron skillet over medium-high heat. Add the rice and toast until it starts to brown. Remove and grind into a fine powder using a mortar and pestle.

CARIBBEAN CHUTNEY MEATBALLS

YIELD: 4 TO 6 SERVINGS / **ACTIVE TIME:** 15 MINUTES / **TOTAL TIME:** 30 MINUTES

These meatballs include the assertive flavors the Caribbean is known for, but the heat is tempered by the sweet chutney.

INGREDIENTS:

- 1 LARGE EGG
- ½ CUP MANGO CHUTNEY
- 2 TABLESPOONS WHOLE MILK
- ½ CUP BREAD CRUMBS
- 2 TABLESPOONS FINELY CHOPPED FRESH CILANTRO
- 4 GARLIC CLOVES, MINCED
- 1 TABLESPOON FRESH LIME JUICE
- 1 TABLESPOON CURRY POWDER
- 2 TEASPOONS CUMIN
- ¼ TEASPOON ALLSPICE
- 3-5 DASHES HOT SAUCE
- 1¼ LBS. GROUND CHUCK
- SALT AND PEPPER, TO TASTE

1. Preheat the oven to 450°F and line a rimmed baking sheet with aluminum foil. Place the egg, chutney, milk, and bread crumbs in a food processor and puree until smooth. Place the mixture in a mixing bowl and stir in the cilantro, garlic, lime juice, curry powder, cumin, allspice, and hot sauce.

2. Add the beef, season with salt and pepper, and stir until thoroughly combined. Working with wet hands, form the mixture into 1½-inch meatballs, arrange them on the baking sheet, and spray the tops with cooking spray.

3. Place the meatballs in the oven and bake for 12 to 15 minutes, until cooked through. Remove the pan from the oven and serve immediately.

VARIATION

- Make the meatballs from ground turkey or ground chicken.

JAPANESE SCALLION MEATBALLS

YIELD: 4 TO 6 SERVINGS / **ACTIVE TIME:** 15 MINUTES / **TOTAL TIME:** 30 MINUTES

Negimaki are thin slices of beef that are wrapped around scallions and then grilled. These meatballs include all of the flavors of that Japanese classic, and make for a perfect hors d'oeuvre.

INGREDIENTS:

- 1¼ LBS. GROUND CHUCK
- 1 CUP COOKED WHITE RICE
- 6 SCALLIONS, TRIMMED AND CHOPPED
- 3 GARLIC CLOVES, MINCED
- ¼ CUP SOY SAUCE
- 2 TABLESPOONS SESAME OIL
- 1-INCH PIECE FRESH GINGER, PEELED AND GRATED
- ¼ TEASPOON FIVE-SPICE POWDER
- BLACK PEPPER, TO TASTE
- 1 CUP SESAME & HONEY MUSTARD SAUCE (SEE PAGE 738), FOR SERVING

1. Preheat the oven to 450°F and line a rimmed baking sheet with aluminum foil. Place the beef, rice, scallions, garlic, soy sauce, sesame oil, ginger, five-spice powder, and pepper in a mixing bowl and stir until combined. Working with wet hands, form the mixture into 1½-inch meatballs, arrange them on the baking sheet, and spray the tops with cooking spray.

2. Place the meatballs in the oven and bake for 12 to 15 minutes, until cooked through. Remove the pan from the oven and serve alongside the Sesame & Honey Mustard Sauce.

VARIATION

- Make the meatballs from ground pork and serve with the Sweet & Sour Dipping Sauce (see page 746).

MEATBALL PARMIGIANA

YIELD: 4 TO 6 SERVINGS / **ACTIVE TIME:** 25 MINUTES / **TOTAL TIME:** 1 HOUR

Veal parmigiana is an Italian American invention, and you'd be hard-pressed to find it on a menu in Italy. This meatball version is easy to make, and ideal for a potluck dinner.

INGREDIENTS:

- 3 TABLESPOONS OLIVE OIL
- 1 ONION, CHOPPED
- 3 GARLIC CLOVES, MINCED
- 1 LARGE EGG
- 2 TABLESPOONS WHOLE MILK
- 3 SLICES WHITE BREAD
- 2 TABLESPOONS FINELY CHOPPED FRESH PARSLEY
- 1¼ LBS. GROUND VEAL
- SALT AND PEPPER, TO TASTE
- 2 CUPS MARINARA SAUCE (SEE PAGE 674)
- 2 CUPS GRATED FRESH MOZZARELLA CHEESE
- ¼ CUP GRATED PARMESAN CHEESE

1. Preheat the broiler to high, position a rack so that the tops of the meatballs will be approximately 6 inches below the broiler, and line a rimmed baking sheet with aluminum foil.

2. Place the oil in a large skillet and warm over medium-high heat. When it starts to shimmer, add the onion and garlic and sauté until the onion is translucent, about 3 minutes. Remove the pan from heat and set it aside.

3. Place the egg and milk in a mixing bowl and stir until combined. Tear the bread into small pieces and stir them into the mixing bowl. Add the parsley, veal, and the onion mixture, season with salt and pepper, and stir until thoroughly combined. Working with wet hands, form the mixture into 1½-inch meatballs, arrange them on the baking sheet, and spray the tops with cooking spray.

4. Place the meatballs in the oven and broil until browned all over, turning them as they cook. Remove the meatballs from the oven and set them aside.

5. While the meatballs are in the oven, place the sauce in a large skillet and warm over medium heat, stirring occasionally.

6. Transfer the meatballs to the sauce, reduce the heat to low, cover the pan, and simmer, stirring occasionally, until the meatballs are cooked through, about 15 minutes.

7. Set the broiler to high. Transfer the meatballs and sauce to a 9 x 13–inch baking dish, season with salt and pepper, and sprinkle the mozzarella and Parmesan over the top. Place in the oven and broil for about 2 minutes, until cheese is browned and bubbling. Remove from the oven and serve immediately.

VARIATION

- Substitute ground chicken or turkey for the veal.

MEATBALL MARSALA

YIELD: 4 TO 6 SERVINGS / **ACTIVE TIME:** 25 MINUTES / **TOTAL TIME:** 50 MINUTES

Veal, like chicken and pork, carries a mild flavor and takes to a wide variety of seasonings and sauces. Marsala wine, mushrooms, and herbs create a delicious mélange for these meatballs. Serve this over pasta.

INGREDIENTS:

- 3 TABLESPOONS OLIVE OIL
- 1 ONION, CHOPPED
- 6 GARLIC CLOVES, MINCED
- 1 LARGE EGG
- 2 TABLESPOONS WHOLE MILK
- 3 SLICES WHITE BREAD
- ⅓ CUP FINELY CHOPPED FRESH PARSLEY
- 1¼ LBS. GROUND VEAL
- SALT AND PEPPER, TO TASTE
- 3 TABLESPOONS UNSALTED BUTTER
- ½ LB. MUSHROOMS, STEMMED AND DICED
- 3 TABLESPOONS ALL-PURPOSE FLOUR
- 1 TABLESPOON FINELY CHOPPED FRESH OREGANO
- 2 TEASPOONS FINELY CHOPPED FRESH THYME
- 1 CUP CHICKEN STOCK (SEE PAGE 660)
- ⅔ CUP SWEET MARSALA WINE

1. Preheat the broiler to high, position a rack so that the tops of the meatballs will be approximately 6 inches below the broiler, and line a rimmed baking sheet with aluminum foil.

2. Place the oil in a large skillet and warm over medium-high heat. When it starts to shimmer, add the onion and garlic and sauté until the onion is translucent, about 3 minutes. Remove the pan from heat and set it aside.

3. Place the egg and milk in a mixing bowl and stir until combined. Tear the bread into small pieces and stir them into the mixing bowl. Add the parsley, veal, and one-quarter of the onion mixture, season with salt and pepper, and stir until thoroughly combined. Working with wet hands, form the mixture into 1½-inch meatballs, arrange them on the baking sheet, and spray the tops with cooking spray.

4. Place the meatballs in the oven and broil until they are browned all over, turning them as they cook. Remove the meatballs from the oven and set aside.

5. Place the butter in a skillet and melt over medium-high heat. Add the mushrooms and cook until the mushrooms start to soften, about 5 minutes. Add the flour, oregano, and thyme and cook over low heat for 1 minute while stirring constantly. Stir in the remaining onion mixture, stock, and Marsala wine. Bring the sauce to a boil, reduce the heat to medium, and simmer for 10 minutes.

6. Add the meatballs to the sauce, reduce the heat to low, cover the pan, and simmer, turning the meatballs occasionally, until they are cooked through, about 15 minutes. Season with salt and pepper and serve immediately.

VARIATION

- Substitute ground chicken or turkey for the veal.

MEATBALLS CORDON BLEU

YIELD: 4 TO 6 SERVINGS / **ACTIVE TIME:** 25 MINUTES / **TOTAL TIME:** 40 MINUTES

A twist on the French classic, with the sharp and pungent blue cheese getting mixed in with the veal and balanced by the sweet leeks.

INGREDIENTS:

- 3 TABLESPOONS UNSALTED BUTTER
- 3 LARGE LEEKS, TRIMMED, CHOPPED, AND RINSED WELL
- 2 GARLIC CLOVES, MINCED
- ½ CUP CHICKEN STOCK (SEE PAGE 660)
- 1 LARGE EGG
- ½ CUP BREAD CRUMBS
- ½ CUP CRUMBLED BLUE CHEESE
- 2 TABLESPOONS FINELY CHOPPED FRESH PARSLEY
- 1 TABLESPOON FINELY CHOPPED FRESH THYME
- 1¼ LBS. GROUND VEAL
- SALT AND PEPPER, TO TASTE
- 1 CUP BLUE CHEESE SAUCE (SEE PAGE 717), FOR SERVING

1. Preheat the oven to 450°F and line a rimmed baking sheet with aluminum foil. Place the butter in a skillet and melt over medium-high heat. Add the leeks and garlic and sauté until leeks start to soften, about 5 minutes. Stir in the stock and cook, while stirring frequently, until half of the liquid has been reduced, about 5 minutes. Remove the pan from heat and set it aside.

2. Place the egg in a mixing bowl, beat until scrambled, and then stir in the bread crumbs, blue cheese, parsley, and thyme. Add the veal and the vegetable mixture, season with salt and pepper, and stir until thoroughly combined. Working with wet hands, form the mixture into 1½-inch meatballs, arrange them on the baking sheet, and spray the tops with cooking spray.

3. Place the meatballs in the oven and bake for 12 to 15 minutes, until cooked through. Remove the pan from the oven and serve with the Blue Cheese Sauce.

VARIATION

- Substitute ground chicken or turkey for the veal.

SPINACH & GRUYÈRE MEATBALLS

YIELD: 4 TO 6 SERVINGS / **ACTIVE TIME:** 25 MINUTES / **TOTAL TIME:** 40 MINUTES

Fresh-tasting spinach, mellow Gruyère cheese, and delicate veal make these meatballs so flavorful they can be served plain, though the Marinara Sauce is splendid company.

INGREDIENTS:

- 2 TABLESPOONS UNSALTED BUTTER
- 2 SHALLOTS, CHOPPED
- 2 CUPS FIRMLY PACKED BABY SPINACH
- 1 LARGE EGG
- 2 TABLESPOONS DRY VERMOUTH
- ½ CUP PANKO
- 1 CUP GRATED GRUYÈRE CHEESE
- 2 TABLESPOONS FINELY CHOPPED FRESH PARSLEY
- 1¼ LBS. GROUND VEAL
- SALT AND PEPPER, TO TASTE
- 1 CUP MARINARA SAUCE (SEE PAGE 674), FOR SERVING

1. Preheat the oven to 450°F and line a rimmed baking sheet with aluminum foil. Place the butter in a small skillet and melt it over medium-high heat. Add the shallots and sauté until they are translucent, about 3 minutes. Stir in the spinach and cook until it has wilted, about 2 minutes. Remove the pan from heat and set it aside.

2. Place the egg and vermouth in a mixing bowl and stir until combined. Stir in the panko, cheese, and parsley, and then add the veal and the vegetable mixture. Season with salt and pepper and stir until thoroughly combined. Working with wet hands, form the mixture into 1½-inch meatballs, arrange them on the baking sheet, and spray the tops with cooking spray.

3. Place the meatballs in the oven and bake for 12 to 15 minutes, until cooked through. Remove from the oven and serve with the Marinara Sauce.

TIP: A dry white wine can be substituted for the dry vermouth.

VARIATION

- Substitute ground pork, chicken, or turkey for the veal.

MEATBALLS WITH OLIVES & SUN-DRIED TOMATOES

YIELD: 4 TO 6 SERVINGS / **ACTIVE TIME:** 25 MINUTES / **TOTAL TIME:** 40 MINUTES

Dehydrating foods intensifies their natural sweetness, especially in tomatoes. That sweetness contrasts beautifully with the savory olives here, an opposition that is bridged by the subtle flavor of veal.

1. Preheat the oven to 450°F and line a rimmed baking sheet with aluminum foil. Place the reserved oil in a small skillet and warm over medium-high heat. When the oil starts to shimmer, add the shallots and garlic and sauté until the shallots are translucent, about 3 minutes. Remove the pan from heat and set it aside.

2. Place the egg and milk in a mixing bowl, stir to combine, and then stir in the bread crumbs, olives, cheese, parsley, oregano, and sun-dried tomatoes. Add the veal and the shallot mixture, season with salt and pepper, and stir until thoroughly combined. Working with wet hands, form the mixture into 1½-inch meatballs, arrange them on the baking sheet, and spray the tops with cooking spray.

3. Place the meatballs in the oven and bake for 12 to 15 minutes, until cooked through. Remove from the oven and serve with the Sun-Dried Tomato Sauce.

VARIATIONS

- Substitute ground pork, chicken, or turkey for the veal.
- For a heartier dish, substitute ½ lb. chopped Italian sausage for ½ lb. of the veal.

INGREDIENTS:

- ½ CUP SUN-DRIED TOMATOES IN OLIVE OIL, CHOPPED, OIL RESERVED
- 2 SHALLOTS, CHOPPED
- 3 GARLIC CLOVES, MINCED
- 1 LARGE EGG
- 2 TABLESPOONS WHOLE MILK
- ½ CUP ITALIAN BREAD CRUMBS
- ¼ CUP CHOPPED OIL-CURED BLACK OLIVES
- ¼ CUP GRATED PARMESAN CHEESE
- 2 TABLESPOONS FINELY CHOPPED FRESH PARSLEY
- 1 TABLESPOON FINELY CHOPPED FRESH OREGANO
- 1¼ LBS. GROUND VEAL
- SALT AND PEPPER, TO TASTE
- 1 CUP SUN-DRIED TOMATO SAUCE (SEE PAGE 679)

MEATBALLS IN CREAMY DILL SAUCE

YIELD: 4 TO 6 SERVINGS / **ACTIVE TIME:** 25 MINUTES / **TOTAL TIME:** 50 MINUTES

A dish inspired by Scandinavian cuisine, where veal is used on rare occasions. To turn this into a meal, serve with some buttered egg noodles.

1. Preheat the broiler to high, position a rack so that the tops of the meatballs will be approximately 6 inches below the broiler, and line a rimmed baking sheet with aluminum foil.

2. Place 2 tablespoons of the butter in a large skillet and melt over medium-high heat. When it starts to shimmer, add the onion and sauté until the onion is translucent, about 3 minutes. Remove the pan from heat and set it aside.

3. Place the egg and milk in a mixing bowl and stir until combined. Tear the bread into small pieces and stir them in along with the nutmeg, allspice, and ginger. Add the veal and sautéed onion, season with salt and pepper, and stir until thoroughly combined. Working with wet hands, form the mixture into 1½-inch meatballs, arrange them on the baking sheet, and spray the tops with cooking spray.

4. Place the meatballs in the oven and broil until they are browned all over, turning them as they cook. Remove the meatballs from the oven and set aside.

5. Place the remaining butter in the skillet and melt over low heat. Add the flour and cook for 2 minutes, while stirring constantly. Stir in the stock, cream, and dill, raise the heat to medium-high, and bring to a boil. Reduce the heat to medium and simmer the sauce for 10 minutes.

6. Transfer the meatballs to the sauce, reduce the heat to low, cover the pan, and simmer the meatballs, turning them occasionally, until cooked through, about 15 minutes. Season with salt and pepper and serve immediately.

VARIATION

- Substitute ground pork, chicken, or turkey for the veal.

INGREDIENTS:

- 4 TABLESPOONS UNSALTED BUTTER
- 1 SMALL ONION, CHOPPED
- 1 LARGE EGG
- 2 TABLESPOONS WHOLE MILK
- 3 SLICES WHITE BREAD
- PINCH OF GROUND NUTMEG
- PINCH OF ALLSPICE
- PINCH OF GROUND GINGER
- 1¼ LBS. GROUND VEAL
- SALT AND PEPPER, TO TASTE
- 3 TABLESPOONS ALL-PURPOSE FLOUR
- 1 CUP CHICKEN STOCK (SEE PAGE 660)
- ⅔ CUP LIGHT CREAM
- ¼ CUP CHOPPED FRESH DILL

GRILLED VEAL MEATBALLS

YIELD: 4 TO 6 SERVINGS / **ACTIVE TIME:** 20 MINUTES / **TOTAL TIME:** 35 MINUTES

Veal is not used in Asian cuisines, but it's delicious when grilled, especially when flavors common to those cuisines are incorporated into the mix. Some rice and stir-fried vegetables would round out your plate nicely.

1. If using bamboo skewers, soak them in cold water. Preheat your gas or charcoal grill to medium-high (450°F). Place the egg, soy sauce, sherry, panko, water chestnuts, scallions, ginger, cilantro, and garlic in a mixing bowl and stir until combined. Add the veal, season with pepper, and stir until thoroughly combined.

2. Divide the mixture into 8 to 12 portions and form each portion into a sausage shape. Insert a skewer into each sausage until the tip of the skewer is just clear of the top end of the meatball.

3. Place the meatballs on the grill and cook, turning them as they brown, until they are cooked through, 6 to 8 minutes. If using a charcoal grill, leave it uncovered. Remove the meatballs from the grill and serve immediately, accompanied by the Musaengchae.

VARIATION

- Substitute ground pork, chicken, or turkey for the veal.

INGREDIENTS:

- 1 LARGE EGG
- 3 TABLESPOONS SOY SAUCE
- 2 TABLESPOONS DRY SHERRY
- ½ CUP PANKO
- ½ CUP FINELY CHOPPED WATER CHESTNUTS
- 6 SCALLIONS, TRIMMED AND SLICED THIN
- 2-INCH PIECE FRESH GINGER, PEELED AND GRATED
- ¼ CUP CHOPPED FRESH CILANTRO
- 4 GARLIC CLOVES, MINCED
- 1¼ LBS. GROUND VEAL
- BLACK PEPPER, TO TASTE
- MUSAENGCHAE (SEE PAGE 583), FOR SERVING

MEATBALL CURRY

YIELDS: 4 TO 6 SERVINGS / **ACTIVE TIME:** 25 MINUTES / **TOTAL TIME:** 55 MINUTES

Creamy coconut, succulent dried fruit, and curry powder create a sauce that positively transforms these lamb meatballs.

INGREDIENTS:

- 2 TABLESPOONS SESAME OIL
- 8 SCALLIONS, TRIMMED AND CHOPPED
- 6 GARLIC CLOVES, MINCED
- 2-INCH PIECE FRESH GINGER, PEELED AND GRATED
- 1 LARGE EGG
- 2 TABLESPOONS SOY SAUCE
- ½ CUP PANKO
- 2 TABLESPOONS FINELY CHOPPED FRESH CILANTRO
- 1¼ LBS. GROUND LAMB
- SALT AND PEPPER, TO TASTE
- 3 TABLESPOONS CURRY POWDER
- 1 (14 OZ.) CAN COCONUT MILK
- ½ CUP CHICKEN STOCK (SEE PAGE 660)
- ½ CUP CHOPPED DRIED APRICOTS
- 3 TABLESPOONS DRIED CURRANTS
- 1 TABLESPOON CORNSTARCH
- 1 TABLESPOON WATER
- SAAG ALOO (SEE PAGE 620), FOR SERVING

1. Preheat the broiler to high, position a rack so that the tops of the meatballs will be approximately 6 inches below the broiler, and line a rimmed baking sheet with aluminum foil.

2. Place the oil in a large skillet and warm over medium-high heat. When the oil starts to shimmer, add the scallions, garlic, and ginger and sauté until the scallions are translucent, about 3 minutes. Remove the pan from heat and set it aside.

3. Place the egg and soy sauce in a mixing bowl and stir until combined. Stir in the bread crumbs, cilantro, lamb, and half of the scallion mixture, season with salt and pepper, and stir until thoroughly combined. Working with wet hands, form the mixture into 1½-inch meatballs, arrange them on the baking sheet, and spray the tops with cooking spray.

4. Place the meatballs in the oven and broil until browned all over, turning them as they cook. Remove the meatballs from the oven and set them aside.

5. Add the curry powder to the remaining scallion mixture in the skillet and cook over low heat, stirring constantly, for 1 minute. Stir in the coconut milk, stock, apricots, and currants, raise the heat to medium-high, and bring to a boil over medium-high heat. Reduce the heat to medium and simmer the sauce for 10 minutes.

6. Add the meatballs to the sauce, reduce the heat to low, cover the pan, and simmer the meatballs, turning them occasionally, until they are cooked through, about 15 minutes.

7. Combine the cornstarch and water in a small bowl and then stir the slurry into the sauce. Cook until it has thickened slightly, about 2 minutes, season with salt and pepper, and serve alongside the Saag Aloo.

VARIATIONS

- Substitute ground chuck for the lamb.
- Use chopped prunes, raisins, or dried cranberries for the dried fruit.

GRILLED TANDOORI MEATBALLS

YIELD: 4 TO 6 SERVINGS / **ACTIVE TIME:** 15 MINUTES / **TOTAL TIME:** 30 MINUTES

The "tandoori" appellation means that a dish is cooked over high heat in a traditional round *tandoor*, or oven. Many traditional Indian breads such as naan are also cooked in these ovens. But, as you'll see, an outdoor grill does just as good a job.

INGREDIENTS:

- ½ CUP PLAIN YOGURT
- 1 LARGE EGG
- 3 GARLIC CLOVES, MINCED
- 3 SCALLIONS, CHOPPED
- 1-INCH PIECE FRESH GINGER, PEELED AND GRATED
- 2 TABLESPOONS PAPRIKA
- 2 TEASPOONS CORIANDER
- 2 TEASPOONS CUMIN
- 1 TEASPOON SUGAR
- 1 TEASPOON GROUND GINGER
- ⅛ TEASPOON CINNAMON
- ½ CUP BREAD CRUMBS
- 1¼ LBS. GROUND LAMB
- SALT AND CAYENNE PEPPER, TO TASTE
- NAAN (SEE PAGE 540), FOR SERVING
- 1 CUP RAITA (SEE PAGE 712), FOR SERVING

1. If using bamboo skewers, soak them in cold water. Preheat your gas or charcoal grill to medium-high (450°F). Place the yogurt, egg, garlic, scallions, fresh ginger, paprika, coriander, cumin, sugar, ground ginger, cinnamon, and bread crumbs in a mixing bowl and stir until thoroughly combined. Stir in the lamb, season with salt and cayenne, and divide mixture into 8 to 12 portions. Form each portion into a sausage shape and insert a skewer into each one so that the tip of the skewer just clears the top end of the meatball.

2. Place the meatballs on the grill and cook, turning them as they brown, until cooked through, 6 to 8 minutes. If using a charcoal grill, leave it uncovered, Serve immediately alongside the Naan and Raita.

VARIATION

- Substitute ground chuck, chicken, or turkey for the lamb.

GREEK MEATBALLS

YIELD: 4 TO 6 SERVINGS / **ACTIVE TIME:** 20 MINUTES / **TOTAL TIME:** 45 MINUTES

In Greek cooking, mint is used in savory dishes rather than in desserts. When used judiciously, as in this recipe, the flavor enlivens the other herbs.

1. Preheat the oven to 450°F and line a rimmed baking sheet with aluminum foil. Place the oil in a small skillet and warm over medium-high heat. When it starts to shimmer, add the onion and garlic and sauté until the onion is translucent, about 3 minutes. Remove the pan from heat and set it aside.

2. Place the egg, milk, lemon juice, bread crumbs, oregano, parsley, and mint in a mixing bowl and stir until combined. Add the lamb and onion mixture, season with salt and pepper, and stir until thoroughly combined. Working with wet hands, form the mixture into 1½-inch meatballs, arrange them on the baking sheet, and spray the tops with cooking spray.

3. Place the meatballs in the oven and bake for 12 to 15 minutes, until cooked through. Remove the pan from the oven and serve with the Middle Eastern Yogurt Sauce or Traditional Hummus and Pita Bread.

VARIATION

- Substitute ground chuck for the lamb.

INGREDIENTS:

- 3 TABLESPOONS OLIVE OIL
- 1 SMALL ONION, CHOPPED
- 3 GARLIC CLOVES, MINCED
- 1 LARGE EGG
- 2 TABLESPOONS WHOLE MILK
- 1 TABLESPOON FRESH LEMON JUICE
- ½ CUP ITALIAN BREAD CRUMBS
- 3 TABLESPOONS FINELY CHOPPED FRESH OREGANO
- 2 TABLESPOONS FINELY CHOPPED FRESH PARSLEY
- 1 TABLESPOON FINELY CHOPPED FRESH MINT
- 1¼ LBS. GROUND LAMB
- SALT AND PEPPER, TO TASTE
- 1 CUP MIDDLE EASTERN YOGURT SAUCE OR TRADITIONAL HUMMUS (SEE PAGES 734 OR 710, RESPECTIVELY), FOR SERVING
- PITA BREAD (SEE PAGE 539), FOR SERVING

ROSEMARY & GARLIC MEATBALLS IN TOMATO SAUCE

YIELD: 4 TO 6 SERVINGS / **ACTIVE TIME:** 20 MINUTES / **TOTAL TIME:** 45 MINUTES

Rosemary and garlic are my favorite seasonings for lamb, and here they manage to flavor both the meatballs and the red wine sauce in which they're cooked.

INGREDIENTS:

- ¼ CUP OLIVE OIL
- 2 LARGE ONIONS, CHOPPED
- 5 GARLIC CLOVES, MINCED
- 1 LARGE EGG
- 2 TABLESPOONS WHOLE MILK
- 1 TABLESPOON FRESH LEMON JUICE
- ½ CUP BREAD CRUMBS
- ¼ CUP CHOPPED FRESH ROSEMARY
- 2 TABLESPOONS FINELY CHOPPED FRESH PARSLEY
- 1 TABLESPOON LEMON ZEST
- 1¼ LBS. GROUND LAMB
- SALT AND PEPPER, TO TASTE
- 1¾ CUPS TOMATO SAUCE
- ¾ CUP DRY RED WINE

1. Preheat the broiler to high, position a rack so that the tops of the meatballs will be approximately 6 inches below the broiler, and line a rimmed baking sheet with aluminum foil.

2. Place the oil in a large skillet and warm over medium-high heat. When it starts to shimmer, add the onions and garlic and sauté until the onions are translucent, about 3 minutes. Remove the pan from heat and set aside.

3. Place the egg, milk, and lemon juice in a mixing bowl and stir until combined. Stir in the bread crumbs, 2 tablespoons of the rosemary, the parsley, and lemon zest and then add the lamb and half of the onion mixture. Season with salt and pepper and stir until thoroughly combined. Working with wet hands, form the mixture into 1½-inch meatballs, arrange them on the baking sheet, and spray the tops with cooking spray.

4. Place the meatballs in the oven and broil until browned all over, turning them as they cook. Remove the meatballs from the oven and set aside.

5. Add the tomato sauce, wine, and remaining rosemary to the skillet containing remaining onion mixture. Bring the sauce to a boil over medium-high heat, stirring occasionally.

6. Add the meatballs to the sauce, reduce the heat to low, cover the pan, and simmer, turning the meatballs occasionally, until they are cooked through, about 15 minutes. Serve immediately.

VARIATION

- Substitute ground chuck for the lamb.

SPANISH MEATBALLS IN ALMOND SAUCE

YIELD: 4 TO 6 SERVINGS / **ACTIVE TIME:** 20 MINUTES / **TOTAL TIME:** 45 MINUTES

Spanish and Middle Eastern cooking feature many of the same ingredients, stemming from the period of Moorish rule over Spain. One of those ingredients is almonds. Here, they add a toothsome quality to the sauce.

INGREDIENTS:

- ¼ CUP OLIVE OIL
- 1 LARGE ONION, CHOPPED
- 3 GARLIC CLOVES, MINCED
- 1 LARGE EGG
- ⅔ CUP DRY RED WINE
- ½ CUP ITALIAN BREAD CRUMBS
- 2 TABLESPOONS FINELY CHOPPED FRESH PARSLEY
- 2 TABLESPOONS SMOKED PAPRIKA
- 1¼ LBS. GROUND LAMB
- SALT AND PEPPER, TO TASTE
- ½ CUP SLIVERED ALMONDS
- 1 CUP BEEF STOCK (SEE PAGE 663)
- SPANISH RICE (SEE PAGE 552), FOR SERVING

1. Preheat the broiler to high, position a rack so that the tops of the meatballs will be approximately 6 inches below the broiler, and line a rimmed baking sheet with aluminum foil.

2. Place the oil in a large skillet and warm over medium-high heat. When it starts to shimmer, add the onion and garlic and sauté until the onion is translucent, about 3 minutes. Remove the pan from heat and set it aside.

3. Place the egg and 2 tablespoons of the wine in a mixing bowl and stir until combined. Stir in the bread crumbs, parsley, and paprika and then add the lamb and half of the onion mixture. Season with salt and pepper and stir until thoroughly combined. Working with wet hands, form the mixture into 1½-inch meatballs, arrange them on the baking sheet, and spray the tops with cooking spray.

4. Place the meatballs in the oven and broil until they are browned all over, turning them as they cook. Remove from the oven and set aside.

5. Place the remaining onion mixture, almonds, remaining wine, and stock in a food processor and puree until smooth. Return mixture to the skillet and bring to a boil over medium-high heat, stirring occasionally. Reduce the heat to low and simmer the sauce for 10 minutes.

6. Add the meatballs to the sauce, reduce the heat to low, cover the pan, and simmer, turning the meatballs occasionally, until they are cooked through, about 15 minutes. Serve over the Spanish Rice.

VARIATION

- Substitute ground chuck for the lamb.

SOUTH AFRICAN MEATBALLS

YIELD: 4 TO 6 SERVINGS / **ACTIVE TIME:** 20 MINUTES / **TOTAL TIME:** 35 MINUTES

These meatballs are based on a meatloaf native to South Africa called *bobotie*, which combines apples, curry, and almonds to achieve its unique flavor.

INGREDIENTS:

- 3 TABLESPOONS UNSALTED BUTTER
- 1 ONION, CHOPPED
- 1 GRANNY SMITH APPLE, PEELED, CORED, AND CHOPPED
- ¼ CUP BLANCHED ALMONDS, FINELY CHOPPED
- 1 LARGE EGG
- 2 TABLESPOONS WHOLE MILK
- ½ CUP BREAD CRUMBS
- ½ CUP CHOPPED RAISINS
- 2 TABLESPOONS FINELY CHOPPED FRESH PARSLEY
- 1 TABLESPOON CURRY POWDER
- 1 TEASPOON SUGAR
- 1¼ LBS. GROUND LAMB
- SALT AND PEPPER, TO TASTE
- 1 CUP MARINARA SAUCE (SEE PAGE 674), FOR SERVING

1. Preheat the oven to 450°F and line a rimmed baking sheet with aluminum foil. Place the butter in a small skillet and warm over medium-high heat. When it starts to shimmer, add the onion, apple, and almonds and sauté until the onion is translucent, about 3 minutes. Remove the pan from heat and set it aside.

2. Place the egg, milk, bread crumbs, raisins, parsley, curry powder, and sugar in a mixing bowl and stir until combined. Add the lamb and the onion mixture, season with salt and pepper, and stir until thoroughly combined. Working with wet hands, form the mixture into 1½-inch meatballs, arrange them on the baking sheet, and spray the tops with cooking spray.

3. Place the meatballs in the oven and bake for 12 to 15 minutes, until cooked through. Remove the pan from the oven and serve immediately, accompanied by the Marinara Sauce.

VARIATIONS

- Substitute ground chuck for the lamb.
- Serve alongside Romesco Sauce (see page 680) instead of the Marinara Sauce.

GOAT CHEESE MEATBALLS

YIELD: 4 TO 6 SERVINGS / **ACTIVE TIME:** 20 MINUTES / **TOTAL TIME:** 35 MINUTES

The sharp flavor of the goat cheese enhances the lamb that encases it in this adaptation of a Provençal dish.

1. Preheat the oven to 450°F and line a rimmed baking sheet with aluminum foil. Place the oil in a small skillet and warm over medium-high heat. When the oil starts to shimmer, add the shallots and garlic and sauté until the shallots are translucent, about 3 minutes. Remove the pan from heat and set it aside.

2. Place the egg and milk in a mixing bowl, stir to combine, and then stir in the bread crumbs, parsley, basil, thyme, and cumin. Add the lamb and shallot mixture, season with salt and pepper, and stir until thoroughly combined. Portion the mixture into heaping tablespoons and place 1 teaspoon goat cheese in the center of each portion. Form 1½-inch meatballs around the cheese, arrange them on the baking sheet, and spray the tops with cooking spray.

3. Place the meatballs in the oven and bake for 12 to 15 minutes, until cooked through. Remove the pan from the oven and serve with the Hollandaise Sauce.

VARIATION

- Substitute ground chuck for the lamb.

INGREDIENTS:

- 2 TABLESPOONS OLIVE OIL
- 2 SHALLOTS, CHOPPED
- 3 GARLIC CLOVES, MINCED
- 1 LARGE EGG
- 2 TABLESPOONS WHOLE MILK
- ½ CUP ITALIAN BREAD CRUMBS
- ¼ CUP CHOPPED FRESH PARSLEY
- 2 TABLESPOONS FINELY CHOPPED FRESH BASIL
- 1 TABLESPOON FINELY CHOPPED FRESH THYME
- 2 TEASPOONS CUMIN
- 1¼ LBS. GROUND LAMB
- SALT AND PEPPER, TO TASTE
- 1 (4 OZ.) LOG GOAT CHEESE
- 1 CUP HOLLANDAISE SAUCE (SEE PAGE 726), FOR SERVING

GRILLED LAMB MEATBALLS WITH PISTACHIOS

YIELD: 4 TO 6 SERVINGS / **ACTIVE TIME:** 20 MINUTES / **TOTAL TIME:** 35 MINUTES

Incorporating nuts, bright green pistachio nuts in particular, into savory dishes is an integral part of Middle Eastern cooking. Grilling these treats adds even more flavor.

INGREDIENTS:

- 3 TABLESPOONS OLIVE OIL
- ½ CUP CHOPPED PISTACHIOS
- 2 SHALLOTS, CHOPPED
- 3 GARLIC CLOVES, CHOPPED
- 1 LARGE EGG
- 2 TABLESPOONS DRY RED WINE
- ½ CUP ITALIAN BREAD CRUMBS
- 2 TABLESPOONS FINELY CHOPPED FRESH PARSLEY
- 1 TABLESPOON FINELY CHOPPED FRESH THYME
- 1 TABLESPOON CUMIN
- 1 TABLESPOON CORIANDER
- 2 TEASPOONS LEMON ZEST
- 1¼ LBS. GROUND LAMB
- SALT AND PEPPER, TO TASTE
- 1 CUP TAHINI (SEE PAGE 733), FOR SERVING

1. If using bamboo skewers, soak them in cold water. Preheat your gas or charcoal grill to medium-high (450°F). Place the oil in a small skillet and warm over medium-high heat. When the oil starts to shimmer, add the pistachios, shallots, and garlic and sauté until the shallots are translucent, about 3 minutes. Remove the pan from heat and set it aside.

2. Place the egg, wine, bread crumbs, parsley, thyme, cumin, coriander, and lemon zest in a mixing bowl and stir to combine. Add the lamb and shallot mixture, season with salt and pepper, and stir until thoroughly combined. Divide mixture into 8 to 12 portions and form each portion into a sausage shape. Insert a skewer into each one so that the tip just clears the top end of the meatball.

3. Place the skewers on the grill and cook, turning them as they brown, until cooked through, 6 to 8 minutes. If using a charcoal grill, leave the grill uncovered. Serve immediately, accompanied by a bowl of Tahini.

VARIATIONS

- Substitute ground chuck for the lamb.
- Should you want something a little creamier to pair with these meatballs, go with Traditional Hummus (see page 710) instead of the Tahini.

PERSIAN MEATBALLS

YIELD: 4 TO 6 SERVINGS / **ACTIVE TIME:** 20 MINUTES / **TOTAL TIME:** 50 MINUTES

Using dried fruits in savory dishes is a hallmark of Persian cooking. Here, the sweet and succulent flavor of the fruit balances the spices and sumptuous lamb.

INGREDIENTS:

- ¼ CUP OLIVE OIL
- 2 LARGE ONIONS, CHOPPED
- 3 GARLIC CLOVES, MINCED
- 2-INCH PIECE FRESH GINGER, PEELED AND GRATED
- 1 LARGE EGG
- 2 CUPS TOMATO SAUCE
- ½ CUP BREAD CRUMBS
- ½ CUP MINCED PRUNES
- 2 TABLESPOONS FINELY CHOPPED FRESH CILANTRO
- 2 TEASPOONS CURRY POWDER
- 1¼ LBS. GROUND LAMB
- SALT AND CAYENNE PEPPER, TO TASTE
- ½ CUP DRY SHERRY
- 2 TABLESPOONS CORIANDER
- 1 BAY LEAF

1. Preheat the broiler to high, position a rack so that the tops of the meatballs will be approximately 6 inches below the broiler, and line a rimmed baking sheet with aluminum foil.

2. Place the oil in a large skillet and warm over medium-high heat. When it starts to shimmer, add the onions, garlic, and ginger and sauté until the onions are translucent, about 3 minutes. Remove the pan from heat and set it aside.

3. Place the egg, 2 tablespoons of the tomato sauce, bread crumbs, prunes, cilantro, and curry powder in a mixing bowl and stir to combine. Add the lamb and half of the onion mixture, season with salt and cayenne, and stir until thoroughly combined. Working with wet hands, form the mixture into 1½ inch meatballs, arrange them on the baking sheet, and spray the tops with cooking spray.

4. Place the meatballs in the oven and broil until browned all over, turning them as they cook. Remove the meatballs from the oven and set aside.

5. Add the remaining tomato sauce, sherry, coriander, and bay leaf to the skillet containing the remaining onion mixture and bring to a boil over medium-high heat, stirring occasionally. Reduce heat to medium and simmer the sauce for 10 minutes.

6. Add the meatballs to the sauce, reduce the heat to low, cover the pan, and simmer, turning the meatballs occasionally, until they are cooked through, about 15 minutes. Serve immediately.

VARIATION

- Substitute ground chuck for the lamb.

LAMB MEATBALLS IN RED WINE SAUCE

YIELD: 4 TO 6 SERVINGS / **ACTIVE TIME:** 25 MINUTES / **TOTAL TIME:** 55 MINUTES

Tender lamb braised in a red wine sauce makes for one of my favorite winter stews, so I decided to create a meatball version.

INGREDIENTS:

- 3 TABLESPOONS UNSALTED BUTTER
- 1 ONION, CHOPPED
- 1 SMALL CARROT, PEELED AND CHOPPED
- 2 GARLIC CLOVES, MINCED
- 1 LARGE EGG
- 2 TABLESPOONS WHOLE MILK
- ½ CUP ITALIAN BREAD CRUMBS
- 3 TABLESPOONS FINELY CHOPPED FRESH ROSEMARY
- 2 TABLESPOONS FINELY CHOPPED FRESH PARSLEY
- 1¼ LBS. GROUND LAMB
- SALT AND PEPPER, TO TASTE
- 3 TABLESPOONS ALL-PURPOSE FLOUR
- 1¼ CUPS DRY RED WINE
- 1 CUP BEEF STOCK (SEE PAGE 663)
- 2 TABLESPOONS TOMATO PASTE
- 1 TABLESPOON HERBES DE PROVENCE

1. Preheat the broiler to high, position a rack so that the tops of the meatballs will be approximately 6 inches below the broiler, and line a rimmed baking sheet with aluminum foil.

2. Place the butter in a large skillet and melt it over medium-high heat. Add the onion, carrot, and garlic and sauté until the onion is translucent, about 3 minutes. Remove the pan from heat and set it aside.

3. Place the egg, milk, bread crumbs, rosemary, and parsley in a mixing bowl and stir to combine. Add the lamb and half of the onion mixture, season with salt and pepper, and stir until thoroughly combined. Working with wet hands, form the mixture into 1½-inch meatballs, arrange them on the baking sheet, and spray the tops with cooking spray.

4. Place the meatballs in the oven and broil until browned all over, turning them as they cook. Remove the meatballs from the oven and set aside.

5. Add the flour to the onion mixture remaining in the skillet and cook over low heat for 2 minutes, stirring constantly. Stir in the wine, stock, tomato paste, and Herbes de Provence, raise the heat to medium-high, and bring the sauce to a boil. Reduce the heat to medium and simmer the sauce for 10 minutes.

6. Add the meatballs to the sauce, reduce the heat to low, cover the pan, and simmer, turning the meatballs occasionally, until they are cooked through, about 15 minutes. Serve immediately.

VARIATION

• Substitute ground chuck for the lamb.

MINT & FETA MEATBALLS

YIELD: 4 TO 6 SERVINGS / **ACTIVE TIME:** 20 MINUTES / **TOTAL TIME:** 35 MINUTES

Crumbly, salty feta is used frequently in Greek and other Mediterranean cuisines. The addition of fresh mint balances the cheese, as well as the cinnamon and allspice.

1. Preheat the oven to 450°F and line a rimmed baking sheet with aluminum foil. Place the oil in a small skillet and warm over medium-high heat. When the oil starts to shimmer, add the shallots and garlic and sauté until the shallots are translucent, about 3 minutes. Remove the pan from heat and set it aside.

2. Place the egg, milk, bread crumbs, feta, mint, cumin, lemon zest, cinnamon, and allspice in a mixing bowl and stir to combine. Add the lamb and shallot mixture, season with salt and pepper, and stir until thoroughly combined. Working with wet hands, form the mixture into 1½-inch meatballs, arrange them on the baking sheet, and spray the tops with cooking spray.

3. Place the meatballs in the oven and bake for 12 to 15 minutes, until cooked through. Remove the pan from the oven and serve with the Middle Eastern Yogurt Sauce for dipping.

VARIATION

- Substitute ground chuck for the lamb.

INGREDIENTS:

2 TABLESPOONS OLIVE OIL

2 SHALLOTS, CHOPPED

3 GARLIC CLOVES, MINCED

1 LARGE EGG

2 TABLESPOONS WHOLE MILK

½ CUP ITALIAN BREAD CRUMBS

½ CUP CRUMBLED FETA CHEESE

3 TABLESPOONS FINELY CHOPPED FRESH MINT

1 TABLESPOON CUMIN

1 TEASPOON LEMON ZEST

PINCH OF CINNAMON

PINCH OF ALLSPICE

1¼ LBS. GROUND LAMB

SALT AND PEPPER, TO TASTE

1 CUP MIDDLE EASTERN YOGURT SAUCE (SEE PAGE 734), FOR SERVING

KEFTA

YIELD: 4 TO 6 SERVINGS / **ACTIVE TIME:** 30 MINUTES / **TOTAL TIME:** 45 MINUTES

Think of kefta as a Moroccan meatball where the lemon zest lends a welcome brightness to the earthy elements.

1. Place all of the ingredients, except for the olive oil and the salad, in a mixing bowl and stir until well combined. Working with wet hands, form the mixture into 18 ovals. Thread three meatballs on a skewer, and repeat until all of them have been skewered.

2. Place the olive oil in a Dutch oven and warm over medium-high heat. Working in two batches, add the skewers to the pot and sear the kefta until browned all over, turning them as they cook, about 8 minutes.

3. Cover the pot and remove it from heat. Let it rest until the kefta are cooked through, about 10 minutes. Remove the kefta from the skewers and serve with the Chickpea Salad.

INGREDIENTS:

- 1¼ LBS. GROUND LAMB
- 1 WHITE ONION, MINCED
- 2 GARLIC CLOVES, ROASTED AND MASHED
- ZEST OF 1 LEMON
- 1 CUP CHOPPED FRESH PARSLEY
- 2 TABLESPOONS FINELY CHOPPED FRESH MINT
- 1 TEASPOON CINNAMON
- 2 TABLESPOONS CUMIN
- 1 TABLESPOON PAPRIKA
- 1 TEASPOON CORIANDER
- SALT AND PEPPER, TO TASTE
- ¼ CUP OLIVE OIL
- CHICKPEA SALAD (SEE PAGE 628), FOR SERVING

PORK MEATBALLS

The versatility of pork constantly amazes me. Because of its naturally subtle flavor and buttery texture, it is somewhat similar to chicken. And like chicken, pork can also be flavored in so many ways, to truly delicious results.

Another advantage to cooking with pork is that it is relatively inexpensive; even the prized tenderloins sell for a fraction of the price of beef tenderloins or racks of lamb. The recipes in this chapter run the gamut of the world's cuisines, providing you with a host of new ways to enjoy the other white meat.

CRUNCHY MEATBALLS IN BOURBON BBQ SAUCE

YIELD: 4 TO 6 SERVINGS / **ACTIVE TIME:** 20 MINUTES / **TOTAL TIME:** 45 MINUTES

Water chestnuts were one of the first ingredients common in Asian cuisines adopted by American cooks; as far back as 50 years ago they were being included in non-Asian dishes. This bourbon and mustard–laced recipe is an updated version of the classic meatballs in BBQ sauce.

INGREDIENTS:

- 2 TABLESPOONS OLIVE OIL
- 1 LARGE ONION, CHOPPED
- 4 GARLIC CLOVES, MINCED
- 1 LARGE EGG
- 2 TABLESPOONS WHOLE MILK
- 3 SLICES WHOLE WHEAT BREAD
- 1 (8 OZ.) CAN WATER CHESTNUTS, DRAINED, RINSED, AND CHOPPED
- 2 TABLESPOONS FINELY CHOPPED FRESH PARSLEY
- 2 TABLESPOONS FINELY CHOPPED FRESH SAGE
- 1¼ LBS. GROUND PORK
- SALT AND PEPPER, TO TASTE
- 1 CUP SOUTHERN BARBECUE SAUCE (SEE PAGE 684)
- ¾ CUP CHICKEN STOCK (SEE PAGE 660)
- ½ CUP BOURBON
- ¼ CUP FIRMLY PACKED LIGHT BROWN SUGAR
- 2 TABLESPOONS GRAINY DIJON MUSTARD
- 2 TEASPOONS CORNSTARCH
- 1 TABLESPOON WATER

1. Preheat the broiler to high, position a rack so that the tops of the meatballs will be approximately 6 inches below the broiler, and line a rimmed baking sheet with aluminum foil.

2. Place the oil in a large skillet and warm over medium-high heat. When it starts to shimmer, add the onion and garlic and sauté until the onion is translucent, about 3 minutes. Remove the pan from heat and set it aside.

3. Place the egg and milk in a mixing bowl and stir to combine. Tear the bread into tiny pieces, add them to the mixing bowl along with the water chestnuts, parsley, and sage, and stir until combined. Add the pork and half of the onion mixture, season with salt and pepper, and stir until thoroughly combined. Working with wet hands, form the mixture into 1½-inch meatballs, arrange them on the baking sheet, and spray the tops with cooking spray.

4. Place the meatballs in the oven and broil until browned all over, turning them as they cook. Remove the meatballs from the oven and set aside.

5. Add the barbecue sauce, stock, bourbon, brown sugar, and mustard to the remaining onion mixture and bring the sauce to a boil over medium-high heat, stirring occasionally. Reduce the heat to low and simmer the sauce for 10 minutes.

6. Add the meatballs to the sauce, reduce the heat to low, cover the pan, and simmer, turning the meatballs occasionally, until they are cooked through, about 15 minutes.

7. Combine the cornstarch and water and stir the slurry into the sauce. Cook until it thickens slightly, about 2 minutes, season with salt and pepper, and serve.

VARIATION

- Use ground turkey in place of the ground pork.

MEATBALLS IN APPLE & MADEIRA SAUCE

YIELD: 4 TO 6 SERVINGS / **ACTIVE TIME:** 20 MINUTES / **TOTAL TIME:** 50 MINUTES

The mellow flavor of baked ham is bound with fresh pork for these meatballs, which are then cooked in a rich sauce for a wonderful dish, and they're a great way to use up leftover ham.

INGREDIENTS:

- 2 TABLESPOONS UNSALTED BUTTER
- 1 LARGE ONION, CHOPPED
- 1 LARGE CARROT, PEELED AND CHOPPED
- 3 GARLIC CLOVES, MINCED
- 1 GRANNY SMITH APPLE, PEELED, CORED, AND CHOPPED
- 1 CUP APPLE CIDER
- ¾ CUP MADEIRA
- ½ CUP RAISINS
- 2 TABLESPOONS FINELY CHOPPED FRESH PARSLEY
- 2 TEASPOONS FINELY CHOPPED FRESH THYME
- ½ TEASPOON CINNAMON
- 1 LARGE EGG
- ½ CUP BREAD CRUMBS
- 1 LB. COOKED HAM, MINCED
- ½ LB. GROUND PORK
- SALT AND PEPPER, TO TASTE
- 1 TABLESPOON CORNSTARCH
- 1 TABLESPOON WATER

1. Place the butter in a large skillet and melt it over medium-high heat. Add the onion, carrot, and garlic and sauté until the onion is translucent, about 3 minutes. Remove half of the vegetable mixture from the pan and set it aside. Add the apple, ¾ cup of the cider, the Madeira, raisins, parsley, thyme, and cinnamon to the skillet and bring the sauce to a boil over medium-high heat, stirring occasionally. Reduce the heat to low and simmer for 15 minutes.

2. While the sauce is simmering, preheat the broiler to high, position a rack so that the tops of the meatballs will be approximately 6 inches below the broiler, and line a rimmed baking sheet with aluminum foil.

3. Place the egg, remaining cider, and the bread crumbs in a mixing bowl and stir to combine. Add the reserved vegetable mixture, ham, and pork, season with salt and pepper, and stir until thoroughly combined. Working with wet hands, form the mixture into 1½-inch meatballs, arrange them on the baking sheet, and spray the tops with cooking spray.

4. Place the meatballs in the oven and broil until browned all over, turning them as they cook. Remove the meatballs from the oven and add them to the simmering sauce. Reduce the heat to low, cover the pan, and simmer, turning the meatballs occasionally, until they are cooked through, about 15 minutes.

5. Combine the cornstarch and water and stir the slurry into the sauce. Cook until it thickens slightly, about 2 minutes, season with salt and pepper, and serve.

VARIATIONS

- Instead of the raisins use a combination of chopped dried apricots and dried cranberries.
- Dry sherry can be used in place of the Madeira.

CRUNCHY SOUTHWESTERN MEATBALLS

YIELD: 4 TO 6 SERVINGS / **ACTIVE TIME:** 20 MINUTES / **TOTAL TIME:** 35 MINUTES

The assertive flavors of Southwestern cooking have always been my favorite among American regional cuisines, and this easy recipe includes many of the flavors associated with it. The crushed tortilla chips not only add flavor, but some texture as well.

INGREDIENTS:

- 2 SLICES WHITE BREAD
- 2 TABLESPOONS WHOLE MILK
- 2 TABLESPOONS OLIVE OIL
- ½ SMALL RED ONION, MINCED
- 2 GARLIC CLOVES, MINCED
- 1 TABLESPOON CHILI POWDER
- 1 TEASPOON CUMIN
- ½ TEASPOON DRIED OREGANO
- 1 LARGE EGG
- ½ CUP CRUSHED TORTILLA CHIPS
- 3 TABLESPOONS FINELY CHOPPED FRESH CILANTRO
- 1¼ LBS. GROUND PORK
- SALT AND PEPPER, TO TASTE
- 1 CUP MEXICAN TOMATO SAUCE (SEE PAGE 678), WARMED, FOR SERVING

1. Preheat the oven to 450°F and line a rimmed baking sheet with aluminum foil. Tear the bread into small pieces, place them in a bowl with the milk, and stir to combine.

2. Place the oil in a small skillet and warm over medium-high heat. When it starts to shimmer, add the onion and garlic and sauté until the onion is translucent, about 3 minutes. Add the chili powder, cumin, and oregano and cook, stirring constantly, for 1 minute. Remove the pan from heat and set it aside.

3. Add the egg, crushed tortilla chips, and cilantro to the bread mixture and stir until thoroughly combined. Add the pork and the onion mixture, season with salt and pepper, and stir until thoroughly combined. Working with wet hands, form the mixture into 1½-inch meatballs, arrange them on the baking sheet, and spray the tops with cooking spray.

4. Place the meatballs in the oven and bake for 12 to 15 minutes, until cooked through. Remove the pan from the oven and serve immediately, accompanied by the Mexican Tomato Sauce.

VARIATIONS

- Make the meatballs from ground chicken or ground turkey.
- Use your favorite salsa in place of the Mexican Tomato Sauce.

BACON BOMBS

YIELD: 6 TO 8 SERVINGS / **ACTIVE TIME:** 5 MINUTES / **TOTAL TIME:** 20 MINUTES

These cheese-stuffed, bacon-wrapped meatballs are as decadent as any in this book.

INGREDIENTS:

- 1¼ LBS. GROUND PORK
- 2 GARLIC CLOVES, MINCED
- 1 TEASPOON FINELY CHOPPED FRESH ROSEMARY
- ½ TEASPOON FIVE-SPICE POWDER
- ½ TEASPOON CAYENNE PEPPER
- SALT AND PEPPER, TO TASTE
- ½ LB. FRESH MOZZARELLA CHEESE, CUBED
- ½ LB. BACON
- PARMESAN CHEESE, GRATED, FOR GARNISH

1. Preheat the oven to 400°F and line a rimmed baking sheet with aluminum foil. Place the pork, garlic, rosemary, five-spice powder, cayenne pepper, salt, and pepper in a bowl and stir to combine. Working with wet hands, form the mixture into 1½-inch balls and make a deep impression in each one with a finger. Insert a piece of cheese in each impression and then cover it with the meatball.

2. Wrap each meatball with a slice of bacon, place them on the baking sheet, and place them in the oven. Bake for about 20 minutes, until the bacon is crispy and the meatballs are cooked through. Remove from the oven, garnish with the Parmesan, and serve.

VARIATION

- Switch out the mozzarella for cubes of cheddar or Monterey Jack.

SAUSAGE, CHEDDAR & RED PEPPER MEATBALLS

YIELD: 4 TO 6 SERVINGS / **ACTIVE TIME:** 20 MINUTES / **TOTAL TIME:** 35 MINUTES

The combination of cheddar and sausage is quintessentially American, and I like to add lots of sweet red bell peppers. These are always a hit when served as a hors d'oeuvre, or at brunch along with scrambled eggs.

1. Preheat the oven to 450°F and line a rimmed baking sheet with aluminum foil.

2. Place the oil in a skillet and warm over medium-high heat. When it starts to shimmer, add the red pepper, scallions, and garlic and sauté for 5 minutes, until the pepper starts to soften. Remove the pan from heat and set it aside.

3. Place the egg, milk, ½ cup of the bread crumbs, cheddar, parsley, and thyme in a mixing bowl and stir until combined. Add the sausage and vegetable mixture, season with salt and pepper, and stir until thoroughly combined. Working with wet hands, form the mixture into 1½-inch meatballs and then roll the meatballs in the remaining bread crumbs. Arrange the meatballs on the baking sheet and spray the tops with cooking spray.

4. Place the meatballs in the oven and bake for 12 to 15 minutes, until cooked through. Remove from the oven and serve immediately, accompanied by a bowl of Marinara Sauce.

VARIATION

- Substitute ground pork, ground veal, or ground turkey for the sausage if you want a milder flavor.

INGREDIENTS:

2 TABLESPOONS OLIVE OIL

1 LARGE RED BELL PEPPER, STEMMED, SEEDS AND RIBS REMOVED, AND CHOPPED

3 SCALLION WHITES, CHOPPED

2 GARLIC CLOVES, MINCED

1 LARGE EGG

2 TABLESPOONS WHOLE MILK

1 CUP ITALIAN BREAD CRUMBS

¾ CUP GRATED CHEDDAR CHEESE

3 TABLESPOONS FINELY CHOPPED FRESH PARSLEY

2 TEASPOONS FINELY CHOPPED FRESH THYME

1¼ LBS. GROUND BREAKFAST SAUSAGE

SALT AND PEPPER, TO TASTE

1 CUP MARINARA SAUCE (SEE PAGE 674), WARMED, FOR SERVING

There's rarely much leftover red wine in my house—my friends and I drink it. If you do have some and you don't want to drink it, here's what to do: boil it down in a saucepan until it has reduced by half, pour it into ice cube trays, and freeze it. When you're making a dish that calls for red wine in the future, just drop in a few cubes.

SAUSAGE MEATBALLS IN PLUM & WINE SAUCE

YIELD: 4 TO 6 SERVINGS / **ACTIVE TIME:** 20 MINUTES / **TOTAL TIME:** 1 HOUR

Cooking sausage with fruit is common in German and other Northern European cuisines, and using flavorful, spicy Italian sausage balances out the sweetness of the fruit here.

INGREDIENTS:

- ¾ CUP SUGAR
- ¾ CUP RED WINE VINEGAR
- ½ CUP DRY RED WINE
- 1 CINNAMON STICK
- 4 WHOLE CLOVES
- 6 PURPLE PLUMS
- 1 LARGE EGG
- 3 TABLESPOONS WATER
- ½ CUP BREAD CRUMBS
- 2 TABLESPOONS FINELY CHOPPED FRESH PARSLEY
- 1¼ LBS. GROUND SWEET ITALIAN SAUSAGE
- SALT AND PEPPER, TO TASTE
- 2 TEASPOONS CORNSTARCH

1. Place the sugar, vinegar, wine, cinnamon stick, and cloves in a saucepan and bring to a boil over medium-high heat, stirring occasionally. Reduce the heat to medium-low and simmer for 5 minutes. Stir in the plums, cover the pan, and simmer for 10 minutes. Remove the plums from the pan with a slotted spoon and reserve the poaching liquid. When cool enough to handle, remove the pits from the plums, slice the plums, place them in a bowl, and set aside.

2. While plums are being poached, preheat the broiler to high, position a rack so that the tops of the meatballs will be approximately 6 inches below the broiler, and line a rimmed baking sheet with aluminum foil.

3. Place the egg, 2 tablespoons of the water, the bread crumbs, and parsley in a mixing bowl and stir to combine. Add the sausage, season with salt and pepper, and stir until thoroughly combined. Working with wet hands, form the mixture into 1½-inch meatballs, arrange them on the baking sheet, and spray the tops with cooking spray.

4. Place the meatballs in the oven and broil until browned all over, turning them as they cook. Remove the meatballs from the oven and add them to the reserved poaching liquid. Bring to a simmer, reduce the heat to low, and cover the pan. Simmer the meatballs, turning them occasionally, until they are cooked through, about 15 minutes. Remove the meatballs from the pan with a slotted spoon and add them to the sliced plums.

5. Raise the heat to medium-high and cook the sauce until it has reduced by half. Combine the cornstarch and remaining water, stir the slurry into the sauce, and cook until it has thickened slightly, about 2 minutes. Stir the meatballs and plums into the sauce, cook until warmed through, and serve.

VARIATIONS

- If you can track down fresh kielbasa sausage, it's great in this recipe.
- Use ground, maple-flavored pork sausage.

ENGLISH MEATBALLS IN CARAMELIZED ONION SAUCE

YIELD: 4 TO 6 SERVINGS / **ACTIVE TIME:** 20 MINUTES / **TOTAL TIME:** 1 HOUR

In English cooking these meatballs are traditionally served with mashed potatoes and peas. While authentic recipes call for using pork innards, I've adapted the recipe to use ground pork.

INGREDIENTS:

- 2 TABLESPOONS OLIVE OIL
- 2 TABLESPOONS UNSALTED BUTTER
- 4 LARGE ONIONS, SLICED THIN
- SALT AND PEPPER, TO TASTE
- 2 TEASPOONS SUGAR
- ½ CUP DRY WHITE WINE
- 2 CUPS CHICKEN STOCK (SEE PAGE 660)
- 2 TABLESPOONS FINELY CHOPPED FRESH PARSLEY
- 2 TEASPOONS FINELY CHOPPED FRESH THYME
- 1 LARGE EGG
- 2 TABLESPOONS WHOLE MILK
- ½ CUP BREAD CRUMBS
- ¼ TEASPOON GROUND NUTMEG
- 1¼ LBS. GROUND PORK
- SALT AND PEPPER, TO TASTE
- 2 TEASPOONS CORNSTARCH
- 1 TABLESPOON WATER

1. Place the oil and butter in a large skillet and warm over medium heat. When the butter starts to foam, add the onions and toss to coat. Cover the pan and cook the onions, stirring occasionally, until they start to brown, about 10 minutes. Sprinkle salt, pepper, and the sugar over the onions and reduce the heat to medium-low. Cook the onions until they start to caramelize, about 25 minutes, while stirring occasionally.

2. Add the wine, raise the heat to high, and cook for 1 minute, while stirring constantly. Add the stock, parsley, and thyme and bring to a boil. Reduce the heat to low and simmer the sauce for 5 minutes.

3. While the onions are cooking, preheat the broiler to high, position a rack so that the tops of the meatballs will be approximately 6 inches below the broiler, and line a rimmed baking sheet with aluminum foil.

4. Place the egg, milk, bread crumbs, and nutmeg in a mixing bowl and stir until combined. Add the pork, season with salt and pepper, and stir until thoroughly combined. Working with wet hands, form the mixture into 2-inch meatballs, arrange them on the baking sheet, and spray the tops with cooking spray.

5. Place the meatballs in the oven and broil until browned all over, turning them as they cook. Remove the meatballs from the oven and add them to the sauce. Reduce the heat to low, cover the pan, and simmer, turning the meatballs occasionally, until they are cooked through, about 15 minutes.

6. Combine the cornstarch and water, stir the slurry into the sauce, and cook until it thickens slightly, about 2 minutes. Season with salt and pepper and serve immediately.

VARIATION

- Substitute ground turkey for the pork.

MEATBALLS IN APPLE & BRANDY CREAM

YIELD: 4 TO 6 SERVINGS / **ACTIVE TIME:** 20 MINUTES / **TOTAL TIME:** 55 MINUTES

The cuisine of France's Normandy region is characterized by the frequent use of apples, a special brandy called Calvados (made from apples or pears), and cream. This recipe is based on that trinity.

INGREDIENTS:

- 2 TABLESPOONS UNSALTED BUTTER
- 1 LARGE ONION, CHOPPED
- 2 GARLIC CLOVES, MINCED
- 1 LARGE EGG
- 2 TABLESPOONS WHOLE MILK
- ½ CUP BREAD CRUMBS
- 1¼ LBS. GROUND PORK
- SALT AND PEPPER, TO TASTE
- 2 GRANNY SMITH APPLES, PEELED, CORED, AND CHOPPED
- 1 CUP APPLE CIDER
- 1 CUP CHICKEN STOCK (SEE PAGE 660)
- ¼ CUP APPLEJACK OR CALVADOS
- 2 TABLESPOONS DIJON MUSTARD
- ½ CUP HEAVY CREAM
- 1 TABLESPOON CORNSTARCH

1. Preheat the broiler to high, position a rack so that the tops of the meatballs will be approximately 6 inches below the broiler, and line a rimmed baking sheet with aluminum foil.

2. Place the butter in a large skillet and melt over medium-high heat. Add the onion and garlic and sauté until the onion is translucent, about 3 minutes. Remove the pan from heat and set it aside.

3. Place the egg, milk, and bread crumbs in a mixing bowl and stir until combined. Add the pork and half of the onion mixture, season with salt and pepper, and stir until thoroughly combined. Working with wet hands, form the mixture into 2-inch meatballs, arrange them on the baking sheet, and spray the tops with cooking spray.

4. Place the meatballs in the oven and broil until browned all over, turning them as they cook. Remove the meatballs from the oven and set aside.

5. Add the apples, ¾ cup of the cider, the stock, brandy, and mustard to the onion mixture remaining in the skillet and bring to a boil over medium-high heat, stirring occasionally. Reduce the heat to medium and simmer the sauce for 10 minutes.

6. Add the meatballs and the cream to the sauce, reduce the heat to low, cover the pan, and simmer, turning the meatballs occasionally, until they are cooked through, about 15 minutes.

7. Combine the cornstarch and remaining cider, stir the slurry into the sauce, and cook until it has thickened slightly, about 2 minutes. Season with salt and pepper and serve.

VARIATIONS

- Add ⅔ cup chopped dried apples for a more assertive apple flavor.
- A mixture of ground veal and either ground chicken or ground turkey can be used in place of the pork.

MEATBALL CACCIATORE

YIELD: 4 TO 6 SERVINGS / **ACTIVE TIME:** 20 MINUTES / **TOTAL TIME:** 40 MINUTES

The saltiness of ham complements the robust tomato-and-vegetable sauce these meatballs are finished in.

INGREDIENTS:

- ¼ CUP OLIVE OIL
- 3 ONIONS, SLICED THIN
- 1 GREEN BELL PEPPER, STEMMED, SEEDS AND RIBS REMOVED, SLICED THIN
- 1 RED BELL PEPPER, STEMMED, SEEDS AND RIBS REMOVED, SLICED THIN
- 3 GARLIC CLOVES, MINCED
- 1 (14 OZ.) CAN CRUSHED TOMATOES, WITH THEIR LIQUID
- 1 CUP TOMATO SAUCE
- ½ CUP DRY WHITE WINE
- 2 TABLESPOONS FINELY CHOPPED FRESH PARSLEY
- 1 TABLESPOON ITALIAN SEASONING
- 1 BAY LEAF
- 1 LARGE EGG
- ½ CUP ITALIAN BREAD CRUMBS
- 1 LB. COOKED HAM, MINCED
- ½ LB. GROUND PORK
- SALT AND PEPPER, TO TASTE

1. Place the oil in a large skillet and warm over medium-high heat. When it starts to shimmer, add the onions, green pepper, red pepper, and garlic and sauté until the onions are translucent, about 3 minutes. Stir in the tomatoes, tomato sauce, ¼ cup of the wine, the parsley, Italian seasoning, and bay leaf and bring to a boil, stirring occasionally. Reduce the heat to low and simmer the sauce for 15 minutes.

2. While the sauce is simmering, preheat the broiler to high, position a rack so that the tops of the meatballs will be approximately 6 inches below the broiler, and line a rimmed baking sheet with aluminum foil.

3. Place the egg, remaining wine, and bread crumbs in a mixing bowl, stir to combine, and then add the ham and pork. Season with salt and pepper and stir until thoroughly combined. Working with wet hands, form the mixture into 1½-inch meatballs, arrange them on the baking sheet, and spray the tops with cooking spray.

4. Place the meatballs in the oven and broil until browned all over, turning them as they cook. Remove the meatballs from the oven and add them to the sauce. Reduce the heat to low, cover the pan, and simmer, turning the meatballs occasionally, until they are cooked through, about 15 minutes. Discard the bay leaf, season with salt and pepper, and serve.

VARIATIONS

- Use Italian sausage rather than ham and pork for a spicier meatball.
- Use ground turkey and ground turkey ham.

Italian seasoning, a mixture of basil, oregano, rosemary, and thyme, is used frequently in Mediterranean cuisines. Any one of those component herbs can be used by itself in the same quantity as the Italian seasoning in a recipe.

KROPPKAKOR

YIELD: 6 TO 8 SERVINGS / **ACTIVE TIME:** 25 MINUTES / **TOTAL TIME:** 50 MINUTES

Traditionally, the filling of these Swedish delicacies is seasoned only with allspice, but in the interest of balance, I've made a few additions.

INGREDIENTS:

- 1¾ LBS. YUKON GOLD POTATOES, PEELED AND CHOPPED
- 1½ TEASPOONS KOSHER SALT, PLUS MORE TO TASTE
- 2 LARGE EGGS, LIGHTLY BEATEN
- 1½ CUPS POTATO FLOUR
- ½ CUP ALL-PURPOSE FLOUR, PLUS MORE AS NEEDED
- 1 LB. BACON, CUT INTO SMALL CUBES
- 2 YELLOW ONIONS, DICED
- ½ TEASPOON ALLSPICE
- ½ TEASPOON GROUND CLOVES
- ½ TEASPOON CARDAMOM
- ½ TEASPOON GROUND NUTMEG
- BLACK PEPPER, TO TASTE
- LINGONBERRY JAM, FOR SERVING

1. Place the potatoes in a saucepan, cover with water, and bring to a boil. Cook until fork-tender, about 15 minutes. Drain, transfer to a mixing bowl, and let cool for 10 minutes. Mash until smooth, add the salt, eggs, and flours, and beat until the mixture forms a dough that is smooth and not sticky. If the dough is too sticky, incorporate more all-purpose flour a teaspoon at a time.

2. Pinch off a piece of dough large enough to roll into a ball the size of a golf ball. Place it on a flour-dusted work surface and roll into a ball. Flatten the balls into disks and cover with plastic wrap.

3. Place the bacon in a large skillet and cook over medium heat for 5 minutes in order to render the fat. Add the onions, reduce the heat to low, and cook until they start to soften, about 6 minutes. Add the allspice, cloves, cardamom, and nutmeg, season with salt and pepper, and cook until the bacon is crispy, about 5 minutes. Remove from heat and let cool.

4. Bring water to a boil in a large saucepan. Place 2 tablespoons of the bacon puree in the center of a disk and shape the dough around it to form a ball. Repeat until all of the puree has been used.

5. Carefully drop the balls into the boiling water and cook until they float to the top, about 10 minutes. Serve with the lingonberry jam.

VARIATION

- Serve with black currant jelly instead of the lingonberry jam.

PITEPALT

YIELD: 8 SERVINGS / **ACTIVE TIME:** 1 HOUR / **TOTAL TIME:** 2 HOURS

Kroppkakor's cousin from the north, this hearty Swedish dumpling will serve you well on a frigid day.

INGREDIENTS:

- ¾ LB. PORK BELLY, SKIN REMOVED AND CHOPPED
- 1 TABLESPOON OLIVE OIL, PLUS MORE AS NEEDED
- 1 TABLESPOON FINELY CHOPPED FRESH ROSEMARY
- 2 LBS. RUSSET POTATOES, PEELED AND GRATED
- 2 CUPS ALL-PURPOSE FLOUR, PLUS MORE AS NEEDED
- 1½ TABLESPOONS KOSHER SALT, PLUS MORE TO TASTE
- 6 TABLESPOONS UNSALTED BUTTER, MELTED, FOR SERVING
- LINGONBERRY JAM, FOR SERVING

1. Bring water to a boil in a small saucepan. Add the pork belly and cook for 5 minutes. Remove, transfer to a paper towel-lined plate, and pat the pork belly dry.

2. Place the olive oil in a large skillet and warm over medium-low heat. When the oil starts to shimmer, add half of the pork belly and sauté until browned all over, about 10 minutes. Place the sautéed pork belly in a bowl and repeat with the remaining pork belly. Add more oil to the pan if it starts to look dry. Add the rosemary to the bowl, stir to combine, and set the mixture aside.

3. Place the potatoes in a large bowl of cold water and soak for 5 minutes. Drain, return the potatoes to the bowl, and add the flour and salt. Stir the mixture until a thick dough forms. Shape the mixture into 1½-inch balls and make a deep indentation in each ball. Fill the depression with some of the pork belly mixture and smooth the dough over the filling. Repeat until all of the balls have been filled.

4. Bring a large saucepan of salted water to a boil. Use a slotted spoon to gently lower the dumplings into the water, gently stir to keep them from sticking, reduce the heat so that the water gently boils, and cook for 45 minutes. Place the cooked dumplings on a warmed platter, top with the melted butter and any remaining filling, and serve with the lingonberry jam.

LEMON & ROSEMARY MEATBALLS

YIELD: 4 TO 6 SERVINGS / **ACTIVE TIME:** 20 MINUTES / **TOTAL TIME:** 35 MINUTES

While traveling in Umbria a few years ago I fell in love with porchetta, a slow-roasted pork shoulder or loin stuffed with rosemary and garlic and drizzled with lemon. All those flavors appear in this quick and easy meatball version.

INGREDIENTS:

- 3 SLICES WHITE BREAD
- ¼ CUP WHOLE MILK
- 2 TABLESPOONS OLIVE OIL
- 2 SHALLOTS, CHOPPED
- 6 GARLIC CLOVES, MINCED
- 1 LARGE EGG
- ZEST AND JUICE OF 2 LEMONS
- ¼ CUP GRATED PARMESAN CHEESE
- 3 TABLESPOONS FINELY CHOPPED FRESH ROSEMARY
- 2 TABLESPOONS FINELY CHOPPED FRESH PARSLEY
- 1¼ LBS. GROUND PORK
- SALT AND PEPPER, TO TASTE

1. Preheat the oven to 450°F and line a rimmed baking sheet with aluminum foil. Tear the bread into small pieces, place them in a bowl with the milk, and stir to combine.

2. Place the oil in a small skillet and warm over medium-high heat. When it starts to shimmer, add the shallots and garlic and sauté until the shallots are translucent, about 3 minutes. Remove the pan from heat and set it aside.

3. Add the egg, lemon zest, Parmesan, rosemary, and parsley to the bread mixture and stir until combined. Add the pork and shallot mixture, season with salt and pepper, and stir until thoroughly combined. Working with wet hands, form the mixture into 1½-inch meatballs, arrange them on the baking sheet, and spray the tops with cooking spray.

4. Place the meatballs in the oven and bake for 12 to 15 minutes, until cooked through. Remove the pan from the oven, drizzle the lemon juice over the meatballs, and serve.

VARIATION

- Make the meatballs from ground veal or ground chicken.

MEATBALLS IN CHIPOTLE SAUCE

YIELD: 4 TO 6 SERVINGS / **ACTIVE TIME:** 25 MINUTES / **TOTAL TIME:** 40 MINUTES

Aromatic and spicy, this is not a dish for delicate palates.

INGREDIENTS:

¼ CUP OLIVE OIL

2 LARGE ONIONS, CHOPPED

4 GARLIC CLOVES, MINCED

1 LARGE EGG

2 TABLESPOONS WHOLE MILK

½ CUP BREAD CRUMBS

⅔ CUP FINELY CHOPPED FRESH CILANTRO

1 TABLESPOON CHILI POWDER

1 TABLESPOON DRIED OREGANO

1¼ LBS. GROUND PORK

SALT AND PEPPER, TO TASTE

CAYENNE PEPPER, TO TASTE

1¾ CUPS TOMATO SAUCE

2 TEASPOONS CUMIN

2 CHIPOTLE CHILI PEPPERS IN ADOBO, DRAINED AND MINCED

1. Preheat the broiler to high, position a rack so that the tops of the meatballs will be approximately 6 inches below the broiler, and line a rimmed baking sheet with aluminum foil.

2. Place the oil in a skillet and warm over medium-high heat. When it starts to shimmer, add the onions and garlic and sauté until the onions are translucent, about 3 minutes. Remove the pan from heat and set it aside.

3. Place the egg, milk, bread crumbs, ⅓ cup of the cilantro, the chili powder, and oregano in a mixing bowl and stir until combined. Add the pork and half of the onion mixture, season with salt and cayenne, and stir until thoroughly combined. Working with wet hands, form the mixture into 2-inch meatballs, arrange them on the baking sheet, and spray the tops with cooking spray.

4. Place the meatballs in the oven and broil until browned all over, turning them as they cook. Remove the meatballs from the oven and set aside.

5. Add the tomato sauce, cumin, and chipotles to the skillet containing the remaining onion mixture and bring to a boil over medium-high heat, stirring occasionally.

6. Add the meatballs to the sauce, reduce the heat to low, cover the pan, and simmer, turning the meatballs occasionally, until they are cooked through, about 15 minutes. Season with salt and black pepper, stir in the remaining cilantro, and serve.

VARIATION

• Make the meatballs from ground chicken or ground turkey.

MEXICAN MEATBALLS WITH ZUCCHINI

YIELD: 4 TO 6 SERVINGS / **ACTIVE TIME:** 20 MINUTES / **TOTAL TIME:** 45 MINUTES

Zucchini adds both subtle flavor and texture to this zesty dish. Serve it with some saffron-spiked rice, and top with Guacamole and Homemade Tomato Salsa (see pages 765 and 758, respectively), if you wish.

INGREDIENTS:

- 3 TABLESPOONS OLIVE OIL
- 1 ONION, CHOPPED
- 1 SMALL ZUCCHINI, MINCED
- 3 GARLIC CLOVES, MINCED
- 1 LARGE EGG
- 2 TABLESPOONS WHOLE MILK
- ½ CUP BREAD CRUMBS
- 1 TABLESPOON DRIED OREGANO
- 1 TEASPOON CUMIN
- 1¼ LBS. GROUND PORK
- SALT AND PEPPER, TO TASTE
- 1 (28 OZ.) CAN CRUSHED TOMATOES, DRAINED
- 2 CHIPOTLE CHILI PEPPERS IN ADOBO SAUCE, DRAINED
- ¼ CUP CHOPPED FRESH CILANTRO

1. Preheat the broiler to high, position a rack so that the tops of the meatballs will be approximately 6 inches below the broiler, and line a rimmed baking sheet with aluminum foil.

2. Place the oil in a skillet and warm over medium-high heat. When it starts to shimmer, add the onion, zucchini, and garlic and sauté until the onion is translucent, about 3 minutes. Remove the pan from heat and set it aside.

3. Place the egg, milk, bread crumbs, oregano, and cumin in a mixing bowl and stir until combined. Add the pork and the onion mixture, season with salt and pepper, and stir until thoroughly combined. Working with wet hands, form the mixture into 2-inch meatballs, arrange them on the baking sheet, and spray the tops with cooking spray.

4. Place the meatballs in the oven and broil until browned all over, turning them as they cook. Remove the meatballs from the oven and set aside.

5. Place the tomatoes and chipotles in a food processor and puree until smooth. Pour the mixture into a saucepan, stir in the cilantro, and bring the sauce to a boil over medium-high heat, stirring occasionally.

6. Add the meatballs to the sauce, reduce the heat to low, cover the pan, and simmer, turning the meatballs occasionally, until they are cooked through, about 15 minutes. Serve immediately.

VARIATION

- Make the meatballs from ground chicken or ground turkey.

CARIBBEAN MEATBALLS WITH MANGO

YIELD: 4 TO 6 SERVINGS / **ACTIVE TIME:** 25 MINUTES / **TOTAL TIME:** 1 HOUR

While curry powder is most often associated with Indian food, it's also very much at home in dishes hailing from the West Indies. These meatballs are spicy, but also sweet, thanks to the fresh fruit and the chutney.

INGREDIENTS:

- 3 TABLESPOONS OLIVE OIL
- 1 LARGE ONION, CHOPPED
- 3 GARLIC CLOVES, MINCED
- 1 LARGE EGG
- 2 TABLESPOONS WHOLE MILK
- 3 SLICES WHITE BREAD
- ½ TEASPOON GROUND GINGER
- ¼ TEASPOON GROUND NUTMEG
- 1¼ LBS. GROUND PORK
- SALT AND PEPPER, TO TASTE
- 1 TABLESPOON CURRY POWDER
- 1 CUP PINEAPPLE JUICE
- 1 CUP CHICKEN STOCK (SEE PAGE 660)
- ⅓ CUP MANGO CHUTNEY
- 2 CUPS CHOPPED FRESH MANGO
- 1 TABLESPOON CORNSTARCH
- 1 TABLESPOON WATER

1. Preheat the broiler to high, position a rack so that the tops of the meatballs will be approximately 6 inches below the broiler, and line a rimmed baking sheet with aluminum foil.

2. Place the oil in a large skillet and warm over medium-high heat. When it starts to shimmer, add the onion and garlic and sauté until the onion is translucent, about 3 minutes. Remove the pan from heat and set it aside.

3. Place the egg and milk in a mixing bowl and stir to combine. Tear the bread into tiny pieces and stir them into the mixture along with the ginger and nutmeg. Add the pork and half of the onion mixture, season with salt and pepper, and stir until thoroughly combined. Working with wet hands, form the mixture into 1½-inch meatballs, arrange them on the baking sheet, and spray the tops with cooking spray.

4. Place the meatballs in the oven and broil until browned all over, turning them as they cook. Remove the meatballs from the oven and set aside.

5. Add the curry powder to the onion mixture remaining in the skillet and cook over low heat for 1 minute, while stirring constantly. Stir in the pineapple juice, stock, and chutney, raise the heat to medium-high, and bring to a boil. Reduce the heat to medium and simmer the sauce for 10 minutes.

6. Add the meatballs and mango to the sauce, reduce the heat to low, cover the pan, and simmer, turning the meatballs occasionally, until they are cooked through, about 15 minutes.

7. Combine the cornstarch and water, stir the slurry into the sauce, and cook until it thickens slightly, about 2 minutes. Season with salt and pepper and serve.

VARIATIONS

- Instead of mango, use chopped papaya or pineapple.
- Substitute ground veal or ground turkey for the pork.

SWEET & SOUR MEATBALLS

YIELD: 4 TO 6 SERVINGS / **ACTIVE TIME:** 25 MINUTES / **TOTAL TIME:** 50 MINUTES

I remember making these meatballs for my sister and her college roommate in the 1960s. Guess what? They're still good. Plus, the rice to round out the meal is already in the meatballs.

INGREDIENTS:

- 1¼ LBS. GROUND PORK
- 1 CUP COOKED WHITE RICE
- 4 SCALLIONS, TRIMMED AND CHOPPED
- 4 GARLIC CLOVES, MINCED
- ¼ CUP SOY SAUCE
- 2 TABLESPOONS SESAME OIL
- BLACK PEPPER, TO TASTE
- ¾ CUP PINEAPPLE JUICE
- ½ CUP KETCHUP
- ⅓ CUP FIRMLY PACKED LIGHT BROWN SUGAR
- ¼ CUP APPLE CIDER VINEGAR
- ¼ CUP WATER
- 1 TABLESPOON CORNSTARCH
- 2 TABLESPOONS PEANUT OIL
- 2-INCH PIECE FRESH GINGER, PEELED AND GRATED
- ½ TEASPOON RED PEPPER FLAKES, OR TO TASTE
- 1 VIDALIA ONION, SLICED
- 1 RED BELL PEPPER, STEMMED, SEEDS AND RIBS REMOVED, AND SLICED
- 2 CUPS DICED FRESH PINEAPPLE

1. Preheat the oven to 450°F and line a rimmed baking sheet with aluminum foil. Place the pork, rice, scallions, two of the garlic cloves, 2 tablespoons of the soy sauce, the sesame oil, and pepper in a mixing bowl and stir until thoroughly combined. Working with wet hands, form the mixture into 1½-inch meatballs, arrange them on the baking sheet, and spray the tops with cooking spray.

2. Place the meatballs in the oven and bake for 12 to 15 minutes, until cooked through. Remove from the oven and set them aside.

3. While the meatballs are in the oven, place the pineapple juice, ketchup, brown sugar, vinegar, water, cornstarch, and remaining soy sauce in a bowl and stir until the sugar is dissolved. Set the mixture aside.

4. Place the peanut oil in a large skillet and warm over high heat. When the oil starts to shimmer, add the ginger, red pepper flakes, and remaining garlic and stir-fry until fragrant, about 15 seconds. Add the onion and bell pepper and stir-fry for 1 minute. Stir in the ketchup mixture and pineapple and cook, stirring frequently, until the sauce thickens slightly, about 2 minutes.

5. Add the meatballs to the sauce, cook until warmed through, and serve.

VARIATIONS

- Make the meatballs from beef, chicken, or veal.
- Instead of pineapple, try mango or papaya as the fruit.

STEAMED STICKY RICE MEATBALLS

YIELD: 4 TO 6 SERVINGS / **ACTIVE TIME:** 20 MINUTES / **TOTAL TIME:** 5 HOURS

Steamed, rice-coated meatballs are one of my favorite dim sum treats, so lovely that I never imagined they could be so easy to make at home.

INGREDIENTS:

- 2 CUPS GLUTINOUS RICE
- CABBAGE LEAVES, AS NEEDED
- ½ CUP DRIED SHIITAKE MUSHROOMS
- 1 LARGE EGG
- 2 TABLESPOONS SOY SAUCE
- 1½ TABLESPOONS CORNSTARCH
- 2 TEASPOONS SUGAR
- ½ CUP MINCED WATER CHESTNUTS
- ½ CUP PANKO
- 3 TABLESPOONS FINELY CHOPPED FRESH CILANTRO
- 2 GARLIC CLOVES, MINCED
- 2 SCALLIONS, TRIMMED AND CHOPPED
- 1-INCH PIECE FRESH GINGER, PEELED AND GRATED
- 1¼ LBS. GROUND PORK
- 1 CUP SWEET & SOUR DIPPING SAUCE (SEE PAGE 746), WARMED

1. Place the rice in a mixing bowl, cover with cold water, and let the rice soak for 4 hours. If time allows, let the rice soak overnight.

2. Line a steaming tray with cabbage leaves. Drain the rice and place it on a kitchen towel. Place the shiitake mushrooms in a bowl, cover with boiling water, and soak for 10 minutes. Drain the mushrooms and reserve 2 tablespoons of the soaking liquid. Remove the stems from the mushrooms and discard them. Chop the mushroom caps and set them aside.

3. Place the egg, reserved liquid, soy sauce, cornstarch, and sugar in a mixing bowl and stir to combine. Add the mushrooms, water chestnuts, panko, cilantro, garlic, scallions, ginger, and pork and stir until thoroughly combined.

4. Bring a few inches of water to a simmer in a large saucepan. Working with wet hands, form the mixture into 1½-inch balls and roll them in the rice, gently pressing down so that it adheres. Arrange the meatballs in the steaming tray and place it over the simmering water. Steam the meatballs until cooked through, about 30 to 35 minutes, adding more water to the saucepan as needed. Serve with the Sweet & Sour Dipping Sauce.

VARIATION

- Ground turkey or ground veal are equally good as the basis for these meatballs.

Fermented black bean paste contains tiny black soybeans preserved in salt, and it has a very pungent flavor. Due to the high amount of salt, the paste will last up to 2 years in the refrigerator once opened.

BEIJING MEATBALLS

YIELD: 4 TO 6 SERVINGS / **ACTIVE TIME:** 20 MINUTES / **TOTAL TIME:** 35 MINUTES

I made up this recipe in order to entice a friend's young child into eating more vegetables. The result was so pleasing that it became a featured part of my repertoire.

INGREDIENTS:

- 3 TABLESPOONS SESAME OIL
- 3 SCALLIONS, TRIMMED AND CHOPPED
- 3 GARLIC CLOVES, MINCED
- 1-INCH PIECE FRESH GINGER, PEELED AND GRATED
- 1 TABLESPOON FERMENTED BLACK BEAN PASTE
- 1 CARROT, PEELED AND MINCED
- 1 CELERY STALK, MINCED
- 1 LARGE EGG
- 3 TABLESPOONS HOISIN SAUCE
- 1 TABLESPOON SOY SAUCE
- 1 TABLESPOON CHILI GARLIC SAUCE
- ½ CUP COOKED WHITE RICE
- 1¼ LBS. GROUND PORK
- 1 CUP SESAME & HONEY MUSTARD SAUCE (SEE PAGE 738), FOR SERVING

1. Preheat the oven to 450°F and line a rimmed baking sheet with aluminum foil.

2. Place the oil in a skillet and warm over medium-high heat. When the oil starts to shimmer, add the scallions, garlic, ginger, and black bean paste and cook, stirring frequently, for 1 minute. Stir in the carrot and celery and sauté for 3 minutes, until the carrot just starts to soften. Remove the pan from heat and set it aside.

3. Place the egg, hoisin sauce, soy sauce, chili garlic sauce, and rice in a mixing bowl and stir until thoroughly combined. Add the pork and the vegetable mixture and stir until thoroughly combined. Working with wet hands, form the mixture into 1½-inch meatballs, arrange them on the baking sheet, and spray the tops with cooking spray.

4. Place the meatballs in the oven and bake for 12 to 15 minutes, until cooked through. Remove the pan from the oven and serve alongside a bowl of the Sesame & Honey Mustard Sauce.

VARIATION

- Substitute ground chicken or ground turkey for the pork.

SICHUAN MEATBALLS

YIELD: 6 TO 8 SERVINGS / **ACTIVE TIME:** 10 MINUTES / **TOTAL TIME:** 1 HOUR AND 15 MINUTES

This extremely fragrant recipe possesses equally heady flavors thanks to the unique buzz the Sichuan peppercorns supply.

1. Preheat the oven to 450°F and line a rimmed baking sheet with aluminum foil. Place the cumin seeds and Sichuan peppercorns in a dry skillet and toast over medium heat until they are fragrant, about 1 minute, taking care to not let them burn. Remove and grind to a fine powder with a mortar and pestle.

2. Place the olive oil in the skillet and warm over medium-high heat. When the oil starts to shimmer, add the onion and scallions and sauté until the onion is translucent, about 3 minutes. Remove the pan from heat and set it aside.

3. Place the pork, salt, dried chilies, red pepper flakes, toasted spice powder, and the onion mixture into a large bowl and stir to combine. Working with wet hands, form the mixture into 1½-inch balls, place them on the baking sheet, and spray the tops with cooking spray.

4. Place the meatballs in the oven and bake for 12 to 15 minutes, until cooked through. Remove from the oven, garnish with the cilantro, and serve with the Apple & Hoisin Dipping Sauce.

INGREDIENTS:

- 3 TABLESPOONS CUMIN SEEDS
- 1 TABLESPOON SICHUAN PEPPERCORNS
- 1 TABLESPOON OLIVE OIL
- 1 YELLOW ONION, SLICED
- 2 SCALLIONS, TRIMMED AND SLICED THIN, FOR GARNISH
- 1¼ LBS. GROUND PORK
- 1 TEASPOON KOSHER SALT
- 4 WHOLE DRIED RED CHILI PEPPERS
- 2 TEASPOONS RED PEPPER FLAKES
- ½ CUP CHOPPED FRESH CILANTRO, FOR GARNISH
- APPLE & HOISIN DIPPING SAUCE (SEE PAGE 742), FOR SERVING

GRILLED THAI MEATBALLS

YIELD: 4 TO 6 SERVINGS / **ACTIVE TIME:** 20 MINUTES / **TOTAL TIME:** 30 MINUTES

The potent flavors one associates with Thai food—fish sauce, garlic, and cilantro—are front and center in these meatballs.

INGREDIENTS:

- 2 TABLESPOONS SESAME OIL
- 4 SHALLOTS, DICED
- 4 GARLIC CLOVES, MINCED
- 3 TABLESPOONS FISH SAUCE
- 3 TABLESPOONS DRY SHERRY
- ½ CUP PANKO
- 2 TABLESPOONS FINELY CHOPPED FRESH CILANTRO
- 1 TABLESPOON SUGAR
- 2 TABLESPOONS CORNSTARCH
- 1¼ LBS. GROUND PORK
- SALT AND PEPPER, TO TASTE
- 1 CUP SWEET & SPICY DIPPING SAUCE (SEE PAGE 749), FOR SERVING

1. If using bamboo skewers, soak them in cold water. Preheat a charcoal or gas grill to medium-high heat (450°F). Place the oil in a small skillet and warm over medium-high heat. When the oil starts to shimmer, add the shallots and garlic and sauté until the shallots are translucent, about 3 minutes. Remove the pan from heat and set it aside.

2. Place the fish sauce, sherry, panko, cilantro, sugar, and cornstarch in a mixing bowl and stir until combined. Add the pork and the shallot mixture, season with salt and pepper, and stir until thoroughly combined again. Divide the mixture into 8 to 12 portions and form each portion into a sausage shape. Insert a skewer into each meatball so that the tip of the skewer just clears the top end.

3. Place the meatballs on the grill and cook, turning them as they brown, until cooked through, about 10 minutes. Serve immediately with the Sweet & Spicy Dipping Sauce.

VARIATION

- Ground turkey or ground veal are equally good as the basis for the meatballs.

POULTRY MEATBALLS

Famed 19th-century French gastronome Jean Anthelme Brillat-Savarin once wrote that "poultry is for the cook what canvas is for the painter." Its inherently mild flavor takes to many methods of seasoning, and it is relatively quick to cook.

Ground chicken and turkey are relatively new on the market and have become increasingly popular as people try to cut back on the amount of red meat in their diets. Keep in mind that they are interchangeable in this chapter's recipes; though I suggest one rather than the other in each recipe, that's based purely on personal preference.

APPLE & HERB TURKEY MEATBALLS

YIELD: 4 TO 6 SERVINGS / **ACTIVE TIME:** 15 MINUTES / **TOTAL TIME:** 30 MINUTES

Fresh apple adds moisture as well as a slight sweetness to these lean meatballs.

1. Preheat the oven to 450°F and line a rimmed baking sheet with aluminum foil. Place the egg, milk, bread crumbs, cheese, apple, sage, parsley, thyme, and allspice in a mixing bowl and stir until combined. Add the turkey, season with salt and pepper, and stir until thoroughly combined. Working with wet hands, form the mixture into 1½-inch meatballs, arrange them on the baking sheet, and spray the tops with cooking spray.

2. Place the meatballs in the oven and bake for 12 to 15 minutes, or until cooked through and no longer pink. Remove from the oven and serve with the Hot Honey Mustard.

VARIATION

- Make the meatballs with ground pork, ground veal, or some combination of the two.

INGREDIENTS:

- 1 LARGE EGG
- 2 TABLESPOONS WHOLE MILK
- ½ CUP BREAD CRUMBS
- ¼ CUP GRATED MONTEREY JACK CHEESE
- 1 GOLDEN DELICIOUS OR GRANNY SMITH APPLE, PEELED, CORED, AND GRATED
- 3 TABLESPOONS FINELY CHOPPED FRESH SAGE
- 2 TABLESPOONS FINELY CHOPPED FRESH PARSLEY
- 1 TABLESPOON FINELY CHOPPED FRESH THYME
- PINCH OF ALLSPICE
- 1¼ LBS. GROUND TURKEY
- SALT AND PEPPER, TO TASTE
- 1 CUP HOT HONEY MUSTARD (SEE PAGE 741), FOR SERVING

CHICKEN CROQUETTES

YIELD: 4 TO 6 SERVINGS / **ACTIVE TIME:** 20 MINUTES / **TOTAL TIME:** 1 HOUR AND 30 MINUTES

Croquettes of all types are satisfyingly delicious, easy to make, and a great way to utilize leftovers.

INGREDIENTS:

- 4 TABLESPOONS UNSALTED BUTTER
- 2 SHALLOTS, MINCED
- 1 CUP ALL-PURPOSE FLOUR
- ⅔ CUP MILK
- ⅔ CUP CHICKEN STOCK (SEE PAGE 660)
- 3 CUPS MINCED COOKED CHICKEN
- 2 TABLESPOONS FINELY CHOPPED FRESH PARSLEY
- 1 TABLESPOON CAJUN SEASONING
- 2 LARGE EGGS, LIGHTLY BEATEN
- 2 TABLESPOONS WATER
- 1 CUP BREAD CRUMBS
- VEGETABLE OIL, AS NEEDED
- 1 CUP MARINARA SAUCE (SEE PAGE 674), WARMED; OR CREAMY CHIPOTLE SAUCE (SEE PAGE 729)

1. Place the butter in a saucepan and melt it over medium heat. Add the shallots, sauté for 2 minutes, and stir in one-third of the flour. Reduce the heat to low and cook for 2 minutes, while stirring constantly. Add the milk and stock and bring to a boil, stirring to prevent lumps from forming. Reduce the heat to low, simmer the sauce for 2 minutes, and then remove the pan from the heat.

2. Stir the chicken, parsley, and Cajun seasoning into the sauce and transfer the mixture to a 9 x 13–inch baking pan. Cover with plastic wrap and refrigerate for 30 minutes.

3. Place the remaining flour on a sheet of plastic wrap. Place the eggs and water in a shallow bowl and stir to combine. Place the bread crumbs on another sheet of plastic wrap. Working with wet hands, form the chicken mixture into 2-inch balls. Roll the balls in the flour and then dip them into the egg mixture and bread crumbs until coated, gently pressing down to ensure the bread crumbs adhere to the croquettes. Place the croquettes on a parchment-lined baking sheet, cover with plastic wrap, and refrigerate for another 30 minutes.

4. Add oil to a Dutch oven until it is about 2 inches deep and warm it to 375°F over medium-high heat. Working in batches, place the croquettes in the oil and fry until they are golden brown, 3 to 5 minutes. Transfer the cooked croquettes to a paper towel–lined plate to drain. When all of the croquettes have been cooked, serve with Marinara Sauce or Creamy Chipotle Sauce.

VARIATIONS

- Use chopped ham, omitting the Cajun seasoning and adding 1 tablespoon chopped fresh sage, salt, and pepper.
- Use chopped fish or seafood—salmon, cod, halibut, shrimp, and crab all work well—omit the Cajun seasoning, and add 1 tablespoon Old Bay Seasoning.

SPICY GRILLED SOUTHWESTERN MEATBALLS

YIELD: 4 TO 6 SERVINGS / **ACTIVE TIME:** 15 MINUTES / **TOTAL TIME:** 30 MINUTES

Try these spicy morsels with Guacamole (see page 765) and slow-cooked beans. The crushed tortilla chips add both texture and flavor.

INGREDIENTS:

- 1 LARGE EGG
- 1 CUP MEXICAN TOMATO SAUCE (SEE PAGE 678)
- ½ CUP FINELY CRUSHED TORTILLA CHIPS
- 6 SCALLIONS, TRIMMED AND CHOPPED
- 4 GARLIC CLOVES, MINCED
- 3 TABLESPOONS FINELY CHOPPED FRESH CILANTRO
- 2 TEASPOONS FINELY CHOPPED CHIPOTLE CHILI PEPPERS IN ADOBO
- 2 TEASPOONS CUMIN
- 1 TEASPOON DRIED OREGANO
- 1¼ LBS. GROUND TURKEY
- SALT AND PEPPER, TO TASTE

1. If using bamboo skewers, soak them in cold water. Preheat your charcoal or gas grill to medium-high heat (450°F). Place the egg, 2 tablespoons of the tomato sauce, the crushed tortilla chips, scallions, garlic, cilantro, chipotles, cumin, and oregano in a mixing bowl and stir until thoroughly combined. Add the turkey, season with salt and pepper, and stir until thoroughly combined.

2. Divide the mixture into 8 to 12 portions and form each portion into a sausage shape. Insert a skewer into each meatball so that the tip of the skewer just clears the top end.

3. Place the meatballs on the grill and cook, turning them as they brown, until completely cooked through, 8 to 10 minutes. If using a charcoal grill, leave it uncovered while cooking the meatballs.

4. While the meatballs are on the grill, warm the remaining tomato sauce in a small saucepan and then serve it alongside the meatballs.

VARIATIONS

- Replace the turkey with ground pork or ground veal.
- Substitute uncooked chicken sausage for some of the ground turkey.

JERK CHICKEN MEATBALLS

YIELD: 6 TO 8 SERVINGS / **ACTIVE TIME:** 15 MINUTES / **TOTAL TIME:** 1 HOUR

Jamaica's famous spice blend lends its unique flavor to these meatballs. If you're interested in making a meal out of them, they are best served over a bowl of rice and beans.

INGREDIENTS:

- 1 TABLESPOON OLIVE OIL
- ½ YELLOW ONION, MINCED
- 1 SCALLION, TRIMMED AND MINCED
- 2 HABANERO PEPPERS, STEMMED, SEEDS AND RIBS REMOVED, AND MINCED
- 2-INCH PIECE FRESH GINGER, PEELED AND MINCED
- ¼ CUP PANKO
- 3 TABLESPOONS MILK
- 1 TABLESPOON FINELY CHOPPED FRESH THYME
- 2 TABLESPOONS BROWN SUGAR
- ½ TEASPOON CINNAMON
- ¼ TEASPOON GROUND NUTMEG
- 1½ TEASPOONS ALLSPICE
- 2 TABLESPOONS SOY SAUCE
- 1¼ LBS. GROUND CHICKEN
- SALT AND PEPPER, TO TASTE
- CARIBBEAN-STYLE PIGEON PEAS (SEE PAGE 608), FOR SERVING

1. Preheat the oven to 450°F and line a rimmed baking sheet with aluminum foil. Place the olive oil in a skillet and warm over medium-high heat. When the oil starts to shimmer, add the onion, scallion, and habanero pepper and sauté until the onion is translucent, about 3 minutes. Stir in the ginger and cook for 1 minute. Remove the pan from heat and set it aside.

2. Place the panko, milk, thyme, brown sugar, cinnamon, nutmeg, allspice, and soy sauce and stir to combine. Add the chicken and the onion mixture, season with salt and pepper, and stir until thoroughly combined. Working with wet hands, form the mixture into 1½-inch balls, arrange them on the baking sheet, and spray the tops with cooking spray.

3. Place the meatballs in the oven and bake for 12 to 15 minutes, until cooked through. Remove from the oven and serve alongside the Caribbean-Style Pigeon Peas.

SANTA FE CHICKEN MEATBALLS

YIELD: 4 TO 6 SERVINGS / **ACTIVE TIME:** 20 MINUTES / **TOTAL TIME:** 35 MINUTES

These meatballs contain some characteristically Southwestern flavors, such as cilantro, chili powder, and cumin. Since bell peppers contain a lot of water, place them in a colander and press down on them before adding them to the skillet. This way, they'll cook evenly with the onions and the other ingredients.

INGREDIENTS:

- 2 TABLESPOONS OLIVE OIL
- 1 SMALL ONION, CHOPPED
- ½ RED BELL PEPPER, CHOPPED
- 3 GARLIC CLOVES, MINCED
- 1 LARGE EGG
- 2 TABLESPOONS SOUR CREAM
- 2 TABLESPOONS HOT SAUCE
- ¾ CUP FINELY CRUSHED TORTILLA CHIPS
- ¼ CUP CHOPPED FRESH CILANTRO
- 1 TABLESPOON CHILI POWDER
- 1 TABLESPOON SMOKED PAPRIKA
- 1 TEASPOON CUMIN
- 1¼ LBS. GROUND CHICKEN
- SALT AND PEPPER, TO TASTE
- 1 CUP CREAMY CHIPOTLE SAUCE (SEE PAGE 729), FOR SERVING

1. Preheat the oven to 450°F and line a rimmed baking sheet with aluminum foil. Place the oil in a small skillet and warm over medium-high heat. When it starts to shimmer, add the onion, bell pepper, and garlic and sauté until the onion is translucent, about 3 minutes. Remove the pan from heat and set it aside.

2. Place the egg, sour cream, hot sauce, crushed tortilla chips, cilantro, chili powder, paprika, and cumin in a mixing bowl and stir until combined. Add the chicken and the onion mixture, season with salt and pepper, and stir until thoroughly combined. Working with wet hands, form the mixture into 1½-inch meatballs, arrange them on the baking sheet, and spray the tops with cooking spray.

3. Place the meatballs in the oven and bake for 12 to 15 minutes, until completely cooked through. Remove the pan from the oven and serve immediately with a bowl of the Creamy Chipotle Sauce.

VARIATIONS

- Replace the chicken with ground pork or ground veal.
- Substitute some uncooked chicken sausage for some of the chicken.
- For a less spicy preparation, substitute ketchup for the hot sauce.

GRILLED CRANBERRY & MAPLE TURKEY MEATBALLS

YIELD: 4 TO 6 SERVINGS / **ACTIVE TIME:** 15 MINUTES / **TOTAL TIME:** 30 MINUTES

Cranberries and maple syrup are treasured cornerstones of New England cuisine, and here they grace these delightful grilled meatballs with their charms.

INGREDIENTS:

- 1 LARGE EGG
- 2 TABLESPOONS WHOLE MILK
- ½ CUP CRUSHED CORNFLAKES
- 1 GOLDEN DELICIOUS APPLE, PEELED, CORED, AND GRATED
- ¼ CUP CHOPPED DRIED CRANBERRIES
- 2 TEASPOONS MUSTARD POWDER
- ½ TEASPOON DRIED THYME
- 1¼ LBS. GROUND TURKEY
- SALT AND PEPPER, TO TASTE
- ½ CUP SOUTHERN BARBECUE SAUCE (SEE PAGE 684)
- ½ CUP REAL MAPLE SYRUP
- ½ CUP APPLE CIDER VINEGAR
- ¼ CUP MINCED DRIED CRANBERRIES
- 1 TEASPOON LEMON ZEST
- ½ TEASPOON CINNAMON
- ½ TEASPOON GROUND GINGER

1. If using bamboo skewers, soak them in cold water. Preheat your charcoal or gas grill to medium-high heat (450°F). Place the egg, milk, cornflakes, apple, cranberries, 1 teaspoon of the mustard powder, and the thyme in a mixing bowl and stir until combined. Add the turkey, season with salt and pepper, and stir until thoroughly combined.

2. Place the barbecue sauce, maple syrup, vinegar, cranberries, lemon zest, cinnamon, ginger, and remaining mustard powder in a small saucepan and bring to a boil over medium-high heat, while stirring occasionally. Reduce the heat to low and simmer the sauce for 3 minutes, stirring occasionally. Divide the sauce between two small bowls and set them aside.

3. Divide the turkey mixture into 8 to 12 portions and form each portion into a sausage shape. Insert a skewer into each meatball so that the tip of the skewer just clears the top end.

4. Place the meatballs on the grill and cook, turning them as they brown and basting them with the sauce in one of the bowls, until completely cooked through, 8 to 10 minutes. If using a charcoal grill, leave it uncovered while cooking the meatballs. Discard the sauce used for basting and serve the meatballs with the remaining bowl of sauce.

VARIATIONS

- Replace the turkey with ground pork or ground veal.
- Substitute chopped dried apricots or dried currants for the cranberries.
- Add some hot sauce to the Southern Barbecue Sauce for a spicier dish.

CHICKEN TSUKUNE

YIELD: 4 TO 6 SERVINGS / **ACTIVE TIME:** 10 MINUTES / **TOTAL TIME:** 20 MINUTES

If you can find them, ground chicken thighs will give you the best results.

INGREDIENTS:

- 1¼ LBS. GROUND CHICKEN
- 1 LARGE EGG, LIGHTLY BEATEN
- 1 CUP PANKO
- 2 TEASPOONS MISO
- 2 TABLESPOONS SAKE
- 1½ TABLESPOONS MIRIN
- ½ TEASPOON BLACK PEPPER
- TARE SAUCE (SEE PAGE 750)

1. If using bamboo skewers, soak them in cold water and preheat a gas or charcoal grill to medium-high heat (450°F). Place the ground chicken meat, egg, panko, miso, sake, mirin, and the pepper in a bowl and stir to combine.

2. Working with wet hands, form the mixture into 1½-inch balls. Thread three meatballs on each skewer.

3. Divide the Tare Sauce between two bowls. Place the meatballs on the grill and cook, while turning, until browned all over and medium-rare, about 6 minutes. Baste the meatballs with the sauce in one of the bowls as they cook. Make sure to leave the grill uncovered if using a charcoal grill. Discard the sauce used to baste the meatballs and serve the meatballs with the remaining bowl of sauce.

CURRIED TURKEY MEATBALLS WITH DRIED CURRANTS & TOASTED ALMONDS

YIELD: 4 TO 6 SERVINGS / **ACTIVE TIME:** 20 MINUTES / **TOTAL TIME:** 50 MINUTES

This is a meatball version of Country Captain, a chicken dish that dates back to Colonial times. Serve it over rice to make the most of the rich gravy.

INGREDIENTS:

- 1 LARGE EGG
- 2 TABLESPOONS WHOLE MILK
- ½ CUP BREAD CRUMBS
- ½ CUP CHOPPED ALMONDS, TOASTED
- 2 TABLESPOONS FINELY CHOPPED FRESH PARSLEY
- 1¼ LBS. GROUND TURKEY
- SALT AND PEPPER, TO TASTE
- 3 TABLESPOONS OLIVE OIL
- 1 LARGE ONION, CHOPPED
- 1 RED BELL PEPPER, STEMMED, SEEDS AND RIBS REMOVED, AND DICED
- 2 GARLIC CLOVES, MINCED
- 2 TABLESPOONS CURRY POWDER
- ½ TEASPOON GROUND GINGER
- ½ TEASPOON DRIED THYME
- 1 (14 OZ.) CAN DICED TOMATOES, DRAINED
- ¼ CUP DRY SHERRY
- 1½ CUPS CHICKEN STOCK (SEE PAGE 660)
- ⅔ CUP DRIED CURRANTS
- 2 TEASPOONS CORNSTARCH
- 1 TABLESPOON WATER

1. Preheat the broiler to high, position a rack so that the tops of the meatballs will be approximately 6 inches below the broiler, and line a rimmed baking sheet with aluminum foil.

2. Place the egg, milk, bread crumbs, almonds, and parsley in a mixing bowl and stir until combined. Add the turkey, season with salt and pepper, and stir until thoroughly combined. Working with wet hands, form the mixture into 1½-inch meatballs, arrange them on the baking sheet, and spray the tops with cooking spray.

3. Place the oil in a large skillet and warm over medium-high heat. When it starts to shimmer, add the onion, bell pepper, and garlic and sauté until the onion is translucent, about 3 minutes. Stir in the curry powder, ginger, and thyme and cook for 1 minute. Add the tomatoes, sherry, stock, and currants and bring to a boil, while stirring occasionally. Reduce the heat to low and simmer the sauce for 10 minutes.

4. While the sauce is simmering, place the meatballs in the oven and broil until browned all over, turning them as they cook. Remove the meatballs from the oven and add them to the sauce. Reduce the heat to low, cover the pan, and simmer, turning the meatballs occasionally, until they are cooked through, about 15 minutes.

5. Combine the cornstarch and water, stir the slurry into the sauce, and cook until it thickens slightly, about 2 minutes. Season with salt and pepper and serve immediately.

VARIATIONS

- Replace the turkey with ground pork or ground veal.
- Substitute uncooked chicken sausage for some of the ground turkey.

CHICKEN MEATBALL PICCATA

YIELD: 4 TO 6 SERVINGS / **ACTIVE TIME:** 20 MINUTES / **TOTAL TIME:** 50 MINUTES

Have some pasta ready to go, as this luscious lemon-and-caper sauce cries out for its tender strands.

INGREDIENTS:

- 2 TABLESPOONS OLIVE OIL
- 1 SMALL ONION, CHOPPED
- 3 GARLIC CLOVES, MINCED
- 1 LARGE EGG
- 2 TABLESPOONS WHOLE MILK
- ½ CUP ITALIAN BREAD CRUMBS
- ½ CUP FINELY CHOPPED FRESH PARSLEY
- 1 TEASPOON ITALIAN SEASONING
- 1¼ LBS. GROUND CHICKEN
- SALT AND PEPPER, TO TASTE
- 2 TABLESPOONS UNSALTED BUTTER
- 3 TABLESPOONS ALL-PURPOSE FLOUR
- 1½ CUPS CHICKEN STOCK (SEE PAGE 660)
- ⅓ CUP FRESH LEMON JUICE
- ¼ CUP CAPERS, DRAINED AND RINSED

1. Preheat the broiler to high, position a rack so that the tops of the meatballs will be approximately 6 inches below the broiler, and line a rimmed baking sheet with aluminum foil.

2. Place the oil in a large skillet and warm over medium-high heat. When it starts to shimmer, add the onion and garlic and sauté until the onion is translucent, about 3 minutes. Remove the pan from heat and set it aside.

3. Place the egg, milk, bread crumbs, 2 tablespoons of the parsley, and the Italian seasoning in a mixing bowl and stir until combined. Add the chicken and half of the onion mixture, season with salt and pepper, and stir until thoroughly combined. Working with wet hands, form the mixture into 1½-inch meatballs, arrange them on the baking sheet, and spray the tops with cooking spray.

4. Place the meatballs in the oven and broil until browned all over, turning them as they cook. Remove the meatballs from the oven and set them aside.

5. Add the butter to the onion mixture remaining in the skillet and warm it over medium-high heat. Reduce the heat to low, add the flour and cook, while stirring constantly, for 2 minutes. Stir in the stock and lemon juice and bring to a boil over medium-high heat. Reduce the heat to medium-low, stir in the remaining parsley and the capers, and simmer the sauce for 3 minutes.

6. Add the meatballs to the sauce, reduce the heat to low, cover the pan, and simmer, turning the meatballs occasionally, until they are cooked through, about 15 minutes. Season with salt and pepper and serve.

VARIATION

- Replace the chicken with ground pork or ground veal.

CAPRESE CHICKEN

YIELD: 6 SERVINGS / **ACTIVE TIME:** 20 MINUTES / **TOTAL TIME:** 45 MINUTES

A twist on the classic salad that is sure to delight all with its color and flavor.

1. Preheat the oven to 450°F and line a rimmed baking sheet with aluminum foil.

2. Place the oil in a large skillet and warm over medium-high heat. When it starts to shimmer, add the onion, garlic, and red pepper flakes and sauté until the onion is translucent, about 3 minutes. Remove the pan from heat and set it aside.

3. Place the egg, milk, bread crumbs, Parmesan, mozzarella, parsley, and Italian seasoning in a mixing bowl and stir until combined. Add the chicken and the onion mixture, season with salt and pepper, and stir until thoroughly combined. Working with wet hands, form the mixture into 1½-inch meatballs, arrange them on the baking sheet, and spray the tops with cooking spray.

4. Place the meatballs in the oven and bake for about 10 minutes, until they are almost cooked through. Remove from the oven and place the meatballs in a baking dish or cast-iron skillet. Layer the tomatoes, mozzarella, and basil on top, place in the oven, and bake for 10 to 15 minutes, until the cheese is melted and starting to brown. Remove from the oven, drizzle the balsamic glaze over the top, and serve.

INGREDIENTS:

2 TABLESPOONS OLIVE OIL

1 SMALL ONION, MINCED

3 GARLIC CLOVES, MINCED

¼ TEASPOON RED PEPPER FLAKES

1 LARGE EGG

2 TABLESPOONS WHOLE MILK

½ CUP ITALIAN BREAD CRUMBS

¼ CUP GRATED PARMESAN CHEESE

¼ CUP GRATED FRESH MOZZARELLA CHEESE

2 TABLESPOONS FINELY CHOPPED FRESH PARSLEY

1 TEASPOON ITALIAN SEASONING

1¼ LBS. GROUND CHICKEN

SALT AND PEPPER, TO TASTE

1 LB. PLUM TOMATOES, SLICED

½ LB. FRESH MOZZARELLA CHEESE, DRAINED AND SLICED

LEAVES FROM 1 BUNCH FRESH BASIL

BALSAMIC GLAZE, FOR GARNISH

CHICKEN MEATBALL CACCIATORE

YIELD: 4 TO 6 SERVINGS / **ACTIVE TIME:** 25 MINUTES / **TOTAL TIME:** 55 MINUTES

Cacciatore is Italian for "hunter's style." No one's too sure how that relates to the vegetable-heavy sauce it has come to be associated with, but that may be because everyone is too busy enjoying it to bother to with questioning it.

INGREDIENTS:

- 1 CUP CHICKEN STOCK (SEE PAGE 660)
- ½ OZ. DRIED PORCINI MUSHROOMS
- 3 TABLESPOONS OLIVE OIL
- ¼ LB. PROSCIUTTO, MINCED
- 1 LARGE ONION, CHOPPED
- 4 GARLIC CLOVES, MINCED
- ½ LB. MUSHROOMS, SLICED
- 1 (28 OZ.) CAN DICED TOMATOES, DRAINED
- ¼ CUP CHOPPED FRESH PARSLEY
- 1 TEASPOON ITALIAN SEASONING
- 1 BAY LEAF
- 1 LARGE EGG
- 2 TABLESPOONS WHOLE MILK
- ½ CUP ITALIAN BREAD CRUMBS
- ¼ CUP GRATED PARMESAN CHEESE
- 1¼ LBS. GROUND CHICKEN
- SALT AND PEPPER, TO TASTE

1. Place the stock in a saucepan and bring it to a boil. Pour the stock over the porcini mushrooms and let them soak for 10 minutes. Drain the mushrooms and reserve the soaking liquid. Remove the stems from the mushrooms and discard. Chop the mushroom caps and set them aside. Strain the soaking liquid through cheesecloth and set aside.

2. While the mushrooms are soaking, place the oil in a large skillet and over medium-high heat. When it starts to shimmer, add the prosciutto, onion, and garlic and sauté until the onion is translucent, about 3 minutes. Add the button mushrooms, sauté for 2 minutes, and then stir in the porcini mushrooms, reserved liquid, tomatoes, 2 tablespoons of the parsley, the Italian seasoning, and the bay leaf. Bring to a boil, reduce the heat to low, and simmer the sauce for 10 minutes.

3. Preheat the broiler to high, position a rack so that the tops of the meatballs will be approximately 6 inches below the broiler, and line a rimmed baking sheet with aluminum foil.

4. Place the egg, milk, bread crumbs, Parmesan, and remaining parsley in a mixing bowl and stir until combined. Add the chicken, season with salt and pepper, and stir until thoroughly combined. Working with wet hands, form the mixture into 1½-inch meatballs, arrange them on the baking sheet, and spray the tops with cooking spray.

5. Place the meatballs in the oven and broil until browned all over, turning them as they cook.

6. Add the meatballs to the sauce, reduce the heat to low, cover the pan, and simmer, turning the meatballs occasionally, until they are cooked through, about 15 minutes. Season with salt and pepper and serve.

VARIATIONS

- Replace the chicken with ground chuck for a heartier dish.
- Substitute ground Italian sausage for some of the ground chicken.

BASIL AIOLI TURKEY MEATBALLS

YIELD: 4 TO 6 SERVINGS / **ACTIVE TIME:** 20 MINUTES / **TOTAL TIME:** 35 MINUTES

Adding the unique, almost-anise flavor of basil to a creamy aioli is a very simple path to a decadent dish.

INGREDIENTS:

- 2 TABLESPOONS OLIVE OIL
- 3 SHALLOTS, CHOPPED
- 4 GARLIC CLOVES, MINCED
- 1 CUP MAYONNAISE
- 1 CUP FIRMLY PACKED FRESH BASIL, CHOPPED
- ¼ CUP CHOPPED FRESH PARSLEY
- ¼ CUP CAPERS, DRAINED AND RINSED
- 2 TEASPOONS HERBES DE PROVENCE
- SALT AND PEPPER, TO TASTE
- 1 LARGE EGG
- ½ CUP BREAD CRUMBS
- 1¼ LBS. GROUND TURKEY

1. Preheat the oven to 450°F and line a rimmed baking sheet with aluminum foil. Place the oil in a small skillet and warm over medium-high heat. When it starts to shimmer, add two of the shallots and half of the garlic and sauté until the shallots are translucent, about 3 minutes.

2. Place the shallot mixture, mayonnaise, basil, parsley, capers, the remaining shallot and garlic, the Herbes de Provence, salt, and pepper in a mixing bowl and stir until thoroughly combined.

3. Place the egg, ½ cup of the aioli prepared in Step 2, and the bread crumbs in a separate mixing bowl and stir until combined. Add the turkey, season with salt and pepper, and stir until thoroughly combined. Working with wet hands, form the mixture into 1½-inch meatballs, arrange them on the baking sheet, and spray the tops with cooking spray.

4. Place the meatballs in the oven and bake for 12 to 15 minutes, or until completely cooked through. Remove from the oven and serve, accompanied by the remaining basil aioli.

VARIATIONS

- Replace the turkey with ground pork or ground veal.
- Substitute some chopped fresh oregano for a portion of the basil.

SUN-DRIED TOMATO & HERB CHICKEN MEATBALLS

YIELD: 4 TO 6 SERVINGS / **ACTIVE TIME:** 20 MINUTES / **TOTAL TIME:** 35 MINUTES

Sun-dried tomatoes are one of my favorite ingredients, as the fruit's natural sugars and succulent flavor become even more concentrated. These meatballs, which make for lovely hors d'oeuvres, also contain a variety of fresh herbs and creamy mozzarella.

1. Preheat the oven to 450°F and line a rimmed baking sheet with aluminum foil. Place the reserved oil in a skillet and warm over medium-high heat. When it starts to shimmer, add the onion, garlic, and celery and sauté until the onion is translucent, about 3 minutes. Remove the pan from heat and set it aside.

2. Place the egg, milk, bread crumbs, mozzarella, parsley, rosemary, and oregano in a mixing bowl and stir until combined. Add the chicken and the onion mixture, season with salt and pepper, and stir until thoroughly combined. Working with wet hands, form the mixture into 1½-inch meatballs, arrange them on the baking sheet, and spray the tops with cooking spray.

3. Place the meatballs in the oven and bake for 12 to 15 minutes, until completely cooked through. Remove the pan from the oven and serve with the Marinara Sauce.

VARIATIONS

- Replace the chicken with ground pork or ground veal.
- Substitute uncooked chicken sausage for some of the ground chicken.

INGREDIENTS:

- ⅔ CUP SUN-DRIED TOMATOES IN OLIVE OIL, DRAINED AND MINCED, OIL RESERVED
- 1 ONION, CHOPPED
- 2 GARLIC CLOVES, MINCED
- 1 CELERY STALK, CHOPPED
- 1 LARGE EGG
- 2 TABLESPOONS WHOLE MILK
- ½ CUP ITALIAN BREAD CRUMBS
- ½ CUP GRATED FRESH MOZZARELLA CHEESE
- 2 TABLESPOONS FINELY CHOPPED FRESH PARSLEY
- 2 TABLESPOONS FINELY CHOPPED FRESH ROSEMARY
- 1 TABLESPOON FINELY CHOPPED FRESH OREGANO
- 1¼ LBS. GROUND CHICKEN
- SALT AND PEPPER, TO TASTE
- 1 CUP MARINARA SAUCE (SEE PAGE 674), WARMED, FOR SERVING

TURKEY MEATBALL TETRAZZINI

YIELD: 4 TO 6 SERVINGS / **ACTIVE TIME:** 20 MINUTES / **TOTAL TIME:** 50 MINUTES

The combination of mushrooms and turkey in a cream sauce laced with sherry and Parmesan is irresistible.

INGREDIENTS:

- 4 TABLESPOONS UNSALTED BUTTER
- 2 TABLESPOONS OLIVE OIL
- 2 SHALLOTS, CHOPPED
- 2 GARLIC CLOVES, MINCED
- 1 CELERY STALK, CHOPPED
- 1 LARGE EGG
- 2 TABLESPOONS WHOLE MILK
- ½ CUP BREAD CRUMBS
- 1¼ LBS. GROUND TURKEY
- SALT AND PEPPER, TO TASTE
- ½ LB. MUSHROOMS, SLICED
- 3 TABLESPOONS ALL-PURPOSE FLOUR
- ½ CUP DRY SHERRY
- 1½ CUPS HALF-AND-HALF
- 1 CUP CHICKEN STOCK (SEE PAGE 660)
- ¾ CUP GRATED PARMESAN CHEESE

1. Preheat the broiler to high, position a rack so that the tops of the meatballs will be approximately 6 inches below the broiler, and line a rimmed baking sheet with aluminum foil.

2. Place 2 tablespoons of the butter and the oil in a large skillet and warm over medium-high heat. When the butter starts to foam, add the shallots, garlic, and celery and sauté until the shallots are translucent, about 3 minutes. Remove the pan from heat and set it aside.

3. Place the egg, milk, and bread crumbs in a mixing bowl and stir until combined. Add the turkey and the vegetable mixture, season with salt and pepper, and stir until thoroughly combined. Working with wet hands, form the mixture into 1½-inch meatballs, arrange them on the baking sheet, and spray the tops with cooking spray.

4. Place the meatballs in the oven and broil until browned all over, turning them as they cook. Remove the meatballs from the oven and set aside.

5. Place the remaining butter in a skillet and melt it over medium-high heat. Add the mushrooms, sauté for 3 minutes, and then reduce the heat to low. Stir in the flour and cook for 2 minutes. Add the sherry and bring the sauce to a boil, while stirring constantly to prevent lumps from forming. Reduce the heat to medium, simmer for 3 minutes, and then add the half-and-half, stock, and Parmesan. Simmer the sauce for another 2 minutes.

6. Add the meatballs to the sauce, reduce the heat to low, cover the pan, and simmer, turning the meatballs occasionally, until they are cooked through, about 15 minutes. Season with salt and pepper and serve.

VARIATIONS

- Replace the turkey with ground pork or ground veal.
- Soak ½ cup dried porcini mushrooms in ½ cup boiling water for 10 minutes. Drain the mushrooms and reserve the soaking liquid. Chop the mushrooms and strain the soaking liquid through cheesecloth. Add the reconstituted mushrooms to the sauce prior to adding the meatballs and use the soaking liquid in place of ½ cup of the stock.

TURKEY MEATBALL PROVENÇAL

YIELD: 4 TO 6 SERVINGS / **ACTIVE TIME:** 20 MINUTES / **TOTAL TIME:** 45 MINUTES

Olives and aromatic herbs are characteristic of the cuisine in sun-drenched Provence, and you'll find them—along with fennel and tomatoes—in these meatballs.

INGREDIENTS:

1 LARGE EGG

1¼ CUPS CHICKEN STOCK (SEE PAGE 660)

3 SLICES WHITE BREAD, TORN

½ CUP CHOPPED OIL-CURED BLACK OLIVES

¼ CUP CHOPPED FRESH PARSLEY

1 TABLESPOON HERBES DE PROVENCE

1¼ LBS. GROUND TURKEY

SALT AND PEPPER, TO TASTE

3 TABLESPOONS OLIVE OIL

2 LEEKS, WHITE PARTS ONLY, CHOPPED AND RINSED WELL

1 SMALL FENNEL BULB, TRIMMED AND DICED

2 GARLIC CLOVES, MINCED

1 (14 OZ.) CAN DICED TOMATOES, DRAINED

½ CUP DRY WHITE WINE

2 TEASPOONS ORANGE ZEST

2 TEASPOONS CORNSTARCH

1 TABLESPOON WATER

1. Preheat the broiler to high, position a rack so that the tops of the meatballs will be approximately 6 inches below the broiler, and line a rimmed baking sheet with aluminum foil.

2. Place the egg, 2 tablespoons of the stock, bread, olives, 2 tablespoons of the parsley, and the Herbes de Provence in a mixing bowl and stir until thoroughly combined. Add the turkey, stir until thoroughly combined, and season with salt and pepper. Working with wet hands, form the mixture into 1½-inch meatballs, arrange them on the baking sheet, and spray the tops with cooking spray.

3. Place the oil in a large skillet and warm over medium-high heat. When it starts to shimmer, add the leeks, fennel, and garlic and sauté until the leeks are translucent, about 3 minutes. Stir in the tomatoes, wine, orange zest, and the remaining stock and parsley and bring the sauce to a boil. Reduce the heat to medium-low, cover the pan, and simmer the sauce for 5 minutes.

4. Place the meatballs in the oven and broil until browned all over, turning them as they cook. Remove the meatballs from the oven and add them to the sauce. Reduce the heat to low, cover the pan, and simmer, turning the meatballs occasionally, until they are cooked through, about 15 minutes.

5. Combine the cornstarch and water, stir the slurry into the sauce, and cook until it thickens slightly, about 2 minutes. Season with salt and pepper and serve immediately.

VARIATIONS

- Replace the turkey with chopped fresh fish.
- Use celery instead of the fennel.

CHICKEN POT PIE

YIELD: 8 SERVINGS / **ACTIVE TIME:** 40 MINUTES / **TOTAL TIME:** 1 HOUR AND 15 MINUTES

Beloved meals don't get much easier than this. Even better, this pie freezes well, so if you make two you'll have another delicious dinner ready to go.

1. Preheat the oven to 350°F. Place the olive oil in a skillet and warm over medium-high heat. When the oil starts to shimmer, add the onion and garlic and sauté until the onion is translucent, about 3 minutes. Stir in the carrot, reduce the heat to medium-low, and cook until the carrot starts to soften and the onion starts to brown, about 8 minutes. Remove the pan from heat and set it aside.

2. Place the butter in a 12-inch cast-iron skillet and melt it over medium heat. Sprinkle the flour over the butter, reduce the heat to low, and stir until the mixture is a smooth paste. Gradually stir in the milk. When all of the milk has been incorporated, cook until the sauce starts to thicken, about 5 minutes.

3. Remove the pan from heat, add the meatballs, green beans, and sautéed vegetables, and season with salt and pepper. Place the puff pastry on a flour-dusted work surface and roll it out to about ¼ inch thick. Place the crust over the skillet and press down on the edge to seal.

4. Brush the crust with the half-and-half, place the pie in the oven, and bake for about 40 minutes, until the crust is golden brown and the filling is bubbling. Remove from the oven and let cool briefly before serving.

INGREDIENTS:

- 2 TABLESPOONS OLIVE OIL
- ½ YELLOW ONION, DICED
- 1 GARLIC CLOVE, CHOPPED
- 1 CARROT, PEELED AND CHOPPED
- 2 TABLESPOONS UNSALTED BUTTER
- 2 TABLESPOONS ALL-PURPOSE FLOUR, PLUS MORE AS NEEDED
- 1¼ CUPS MILK, AT ROOM TEMPERATURE
- CHICKEN & MUSHROOM MEATBALLS (SEE PAGE 303)
- ¾ CUP CHOPPED GREEN BEANS
- SALT AND PEPPER, TO TASTE
- 1 SHEET FROZEN PUFF PASTRY, THAWED
- 1 TABLESPOON HALF-AND-HALF

CHICKEN MEATBALL AU VIN

YIELD: 4 TO 6 SERVINGS / **ACTIVE TIME:** 25 MINUTES / **TOTAL TIME:** 1 HOUR AND 15 MINUTES

This is not quite the French classic coq au vin, but the flavor is so spot on that no one will mind the break from tradition.

INGREDIENTS:

- 1 LARGE EGG
- ¼ CUP WHOLE MILK
- ½ CUP BREAD CRUMBS
- ¼ CUP CHOPPED FRESH PARSLEY
- 2 TEASPOONS FINELY CHOPPED FRESH THYME
- 1¼ LBS. GROUND CHICKEN
- SALT AND PEPPER, TO TASTE
- ½ CUP ALL-PURPOSE FLOUR
- 4 OZ. BACON, CHOPPED
- 2 GARLIC CLOVES, MINCED
- ½ LB. SMALL MUSHROOMS, CHOPPED
- 2 CUPS DRY RED WINE
- 1 CUP CHICKEN STOCK (SEE PAGE 660)
- 1 BAY LEAF
- 1 LB. NEW POTATOES, SCRUBBED AND CHOPPED
- ½ LB. FROZEN PEARL ONIONS, THAWED

1. Preheat the oven to 375°F. Place the egg, milk, bread crumbs, 2 tablespoons of the parsley, and the thyme in a mixing bowl and stir until combined. Add the chicken, season with salt and pepper, and stir until thoroughly combined. Working with wet hands, form the mixture into 1½-inch balls, roll them in the flour, and place them on a parchment-lined baking sheet.

2. Place the bacon in a Dutch oven and cook over medium-high heat until it is crisp, about 6 minutes. Transfer the bacon to a paper towel–lined plate and add the meatballs to the rendered bacon fat. Cook, turning the meatballs occasionally, until they are browned all over. Remove the meatballs from the pan and discard all but 2 tablespoons of the bacon fat.

3. Place the Dutch oven back over medium-high heat and add the garlic and mushrooms. Sauté until the mushrooms just start to brown, about 5 minutes. Stir in the wine and bring to a boil. Cook for 2 minutes and then stir in the stock, remaining parsley, and the bay leaf. Return to a boil and then add the potatoes, bacon, and meatballs.

4. Cover the Dutch oven, place it in the oven, and bake for 45 minutes, until the potatoes are almost tender and the meatballs are cooked through. Add the onions to the stew, season with salt and pepper, and bake for another 10 minutes, until the potatoes are completely tender. Remove, discard the bay leaf, and serve.

CHICKEN & MUSHROOM MEATBALLS

YIELD: 4 TO 6 SERVINGS / **ACTIVE TIME:** 20 MINUTES / **TOTAL TIME:** 35 MINUTES

Meaty portobello mushrooms and delicate button mushrooms are the keys to these marvelous meatballs.

INGREDIENTS:

- 3 TABLESPOONS OLIVE OIL
- 2 TABLESPOONS UNSALTED BUTTER
- 2 SHALLOTS, CHOPPED
- 2 GARLIC CLOVES, MINCED
- ¼ LB. BUTTON MUSHROOMS, MINCED
- 2 PORTOBELLO MUSHROOM CAPS, STEMMED AND MINCED
- 3 TABLESPOONS FINELY CHOPPED FRESH PARSLEY
- 2 TEASPOONS HERBES DE PROVENCE
- 1 LARGE EGG
- 2 TABLESPOONS WHOLE MILK
- 3 SLICES WHITE BREAD, TORN INTO SMALL PIECES
- ¼ CUP GRATED FRESH MOZZARELLA CHEESE
- 1¼ LBS. GROUND CHICKEN
- SALT AND PEPPER, TO TASTE
- SWEET POTATO HASH (SEE PAGE 619), FOR SERVING

1. Preheat the oven to 450°F and line a rimmed baking sheet with aluminum foil. Place the oil and butter in a large skillet and warm over medium-high heat. When the butter starts to foam, add the shallots and garlic and sauté for 2 minutes. Add the mushrooms and sauté until the liquid they release has evaporated, 8 to 10 minutes. Stir in the parsley and Herbes de Provence, remove the pan from heat, and set it aside.

2. Place the egg, milk, bread, and cheese in a mixing bowl and stir until combined. Add the chicken and the mushroom mixture, season with salt and pepper, and stir until thoroughly combined. Working with wet hands, form the mixture into 1½-inch meatballs, arrange them on the baking sheet, and spray the tops with cooking spray.

3. Place the meatballs in the oven and bake for 12 to 15 minutes, until cooked through. Remove the pan from the oven and serve over the Sweet Potato Hash.

VARIATIONS

- Replace the ground chicken with ground turkey, ground pork, or ground veal.
- Substitute uncooked chicken sausage for a portion of the ground chicken.

BUFFALO CHICKEN MEATBALLS

YIELD: 6 TO 8 SERVINGS / **ACTIVE TIME:** 30 MINUTES / **TOTAL TIME:** 45 MINUTES

Purists will grieve the loss of the bones. The rest of us will happily take their share.

1. Place the chicken in a mixing bowl, season with salt and pepper, and stir to combine. Working with wet hands, form the mixture into 1½-inch meatballs, place them on a parchment-lined baking sheet, and let them firm up in the freezer for 15 minutes.

2. Place the butter in a saucepan and melt over medium heat. Stir in the vinegar, hot sauce, and cayenne, making sure not to breathe in the spicy steam, transfer the sauce to a mixing bowl, and cover it with aluminum foil.

3. Add vegetable oil to a Dutch oven until it is approximately 2 inches deep and warm it to 375°F over medium-high heat. While the oil is heating, place the cornstarch in a shallow dish and roll the meatballs in it until coated.

4. Working in batches, gently drop the meatballs into the hot oil and fry until golden brown and cooked through, about 8 minutes. Place the cooked meatballs on a paper towel–lined plate to drain. When all of the meatballs have been cooked, add them to the sauce and toss to coat. Serve with the Blue Cheese Sauce and celery sticks.

INGREDIENTS:

- 1¼ LBS. GROUND CHICKEN
- SALT AND PEPPER, TO TASTE
- 4 TABLESPOONS UNSALTED BUTTER
- 1 TABLESPOON WHITE VINEGAR
- ¾ CUP HOT SAUCE
- 1 TEASPOON CAYENNE PEPPER
- VEGETABLE OIL, AS NEEDED
- ½ CUP CORNSTARCH
- BLUE CHEESE SAUCE (SEE PAGE 717), FOR SERVING
- CELERY STICKS, FOR SERVING

MEATBALLS IN MOLE

YIELD: 4 TO 6 SERVINGS / **ACTIVE TIME:** 15 MINUTES / **TOTAL TIME:** 45 MINUTES

There's an intensity to this classic Mexican sauce that comes from a combination of spices, ground nuts, and cocoa powder.

1. Place the oil in a large skillet and warm over medium-high heat. When it starts to shimmer, add the onions and garlic and sauté until the onions are translucent, about 3 minutes. Remove one-third of the mixture and set it aside. Stir the chili powder and cumin into the skillet and cook for 1 minute.

2. Add 2¼ cups of the stock, the tomatoes, peanut butter, raisins, sugar, and cocoa powder to the skillet, raise the heat to high, and bring the sauce to a boil. Reduce the heat to low and simmer the sauce until it has thickened slightly, about 20 minutes. Season with salt and cayenne.

3. While the mole is simmering, preheat the broiler to high, position a rack so that the tops of the meatballs will be approximately 6 inches below the broiler, and line a rimmed baking sheet with aluminum foil.

4. Place the egg, tortilla chips, and remaining stock in a mixing bowl and stir until combined. Add the turkey and reserved vegetable mixture, season with salt and pepper, and stir until thoroughly combined. Working with wet hands, form the mixture into 1½-inch meatballs, arrange them on the baking sheet, and spray the tops with cooking spray.

5. Place the meatballs in the oven and broil until browned all over, turning them as they cook. Remove the meatballs from the oven and add them to sauce. Reduce the heat to low, cover the pan, and simmer, turning the meatballs occasionally, until they are cooked through, about 15 minutes. Season with salt, garnish with sesame seeds, and serve with the Spanish Rice.

VARIATIONS

- Replace the turkey with ground pork or ground veal.
- Substitute uncooked chicken sausage for some of the ground turkey.

INGREDIENTS:

3 TABLESPOONS OLIVE OIL

2 ONIONS, CHOPPED

6 GARLIC CLOVES, MINCED

3 TABLESPOONS CHILI POWDER

1 TABLESPOON CUMIN

2½ CUPS CHICKEN STOCK (SEE PAGE 660)

1 (14 OZ.) CAN DICED TOMATOES, DRAINED

¼ CUP PEANUT BUTTER

¼ CUP CHOPPED RAISINS

2 TABLESPOONS SUGAR

2 TABLESPOONS UNSWEETENED COCOA POWDER

SALT AND CAYENNE PEPPER, TO TASTE

1 LARGE EGG

¾ CUP CRUSHED TORTILLA CHIPS

1¼ LBS. GROUND TURKEY

SALT AND PEPPER, TO TASTE

SESAME SEEDS, FOR GARNISH

SPANISH RICE (SEE PAGE 552), FOR SERVING

CHICKEN MEATBALL KEBABS

YIELD: 4 TO 6 SERVINGS / **ACTIVE TIME:** 15 MINUTES / **TOTAL TIME:** 30 MINUTES

The sumptuous collection of herbs and spices in these grilled skewers is a celebration of the very best Middle Eastern cuisine has to offer.

INGREDIENTS:

- 1 LARGE EGG
- 2 TABLESPOONS WATER
- 2 TABLESPOONS TOMATO PASTE
- 2 SLICES WHOLE WHEAT BREAD, TORN
- ¼ CUP CHOPPED FRESH PARSLEY
- 2 SHALLOTS, CHOPPED
- 2 GARLIC CLOVES, MINCED
- 1 TABLESPOON CUMIN
- 2 TEASPOONS CORIANDER
- ½ TEASPOON CINNAMON
- 1¼ LBS. GROUND CHICKEN
- SALT AND CAYENNE PEPPER, TO TASTE

1. If using bamboo skewers, soak them in cold water. Preheat your gas or charcoal grill to medium-high (450°F). Place the egg, water, tomato paste, bread, parsley, shallots, garlic, cumin, coriander, and cinnamon in a mixing bowl and stir until thoroughly combined. Add the chicken, season with salt and cayenne, and stir until thoroughly combined.

2. Divide chicken mixture into 8 to 12 portions and form each portion into a sausage shape. Insert a skewer into each meatball so that the tip of the skewer just clears the top end. Place the meatballs on the grill and cook, turning them as they brown, until completely cooked through, 8 to 10 minutes. If using a charcoal grill, leave it uncovered while the meatballs are cooking. Serve immediately.

VARIATIONS

- Replace the chicken with ground pork or ground veal.
- Substitute some uncooked chicken sausage for some of the ground chicken.

BOMBAY TURKEY MEATBALLS

YIELD: 4 TO 6 SERVINGS / **ACTIVE TIME:** 20 MINUTES / **TOTAL TIME:** 1 HOUR

Chopped dried apricots add sweetness and nuts add crunch to these curry-flavored meatballs, which are topped with a yogurt-based sauce, and would be lovely beside some Naan (see page 540).

INGREDIENTS:

- ⅔ CUP PLAIN YOGURT
- ¼ CUP PINE NUTS
- 2 TABLESPOONS OLIVE OIL
- 1 ONION, MINCED
- 2 GARLIC CLOVES, MINCED
- 1 LARGE EGG
- 2 TABLESPOONS WHOLE MILK
- 2 SLICES WHITE BREAD, TORN
- ½ CUP CHOPPED DRIED APRICOTS
- ¼ CUP CHOPPED FRESH CILANTRO
- 1 TABLESPOON CURRY POWDER
- 1¼ LBS. GROUND TURKEY
- SALT AND PEPPER, TO TASTE
- 2 TEASPOONS CUMIN
- 1 TOMATO, CORED, SEEDED, AND MINCED
- SAAG ALOO (SEE PAGE 620), FOR SERVING

1. Preheat the oven to 450°F and line a rimmed baking sheet with aluminum foil. Place the yogurt in a fine sieve and set it over a mixing bowl. Shake the strainer gently a few times and allow yogurt to drain for at least 30 minutes at room temperature. Discard the whey and place yogurt in a small bowl. Set it aside.

2. While yogurt is draining, place the pine nuts in a small skillet and toast over medium heat, stirring frequently, until browned, 2 to 3 minutes. Remove from the skillet and set the pine nuts aside. Place the oil in the skillet and warm over medium-high heat. When it starts to shimmer, add the onion and garlic and sauté until the onion has started to soften, about 5 minutes. Remove the pan from heat and set it aside.

3. Place the egg, milk, bread, dried apricots, cilantro, and curry powder in a mixing bowl and stir until combined. Add the turkey and the onion mixture, season with salt and pepper, and stir until thoroughly combined. Working with wet hands, form the mixture into 1½-inch meatballs, arrange them on the baking sheet, and spray the tops with cooking spray.

4. Place the meatballs in the oven and bake for 12 to 15 minutes, until cooked through. Remove from the oven and set aside.

5. Add the cumin to the yogurt, stir to combine, and then fold in the tomato. Serve the yogurt sauce and Saag Aloo alongside the meatballs.

VARIATIONS

- Replace the turkey with ground pork or ground veal.
- Substitute dried currants or dried cranberries for the dried apricots.

CHICKEN VINDALOO

YIELD: 6 SERVINGS / **ACTIVE TIME:** 30 MINUTES / **TOTAL TIME:** 2 HOURS AND 30 MINUTES

A word of advice: add as much cayenne pepper as you and your family can handle, as this beloved preparation improves as it gets spicier.

INGREDIENTS:

- 1¼ LBS. GROUND CHICKEN
- 1 TABLESPOON GARAM MASALA
- 1 TEASPOON TURMERIC
- 2 TEASPOONS SWEET PAPRIKA
- 1 TEASPOON MUSTARD POWDER
- 2 TABLESPOONS SUGAR
- 1 TEASPOON CUMIN
- 1 TEASPOON CAYENNE PEPPER, OR TO TASTE
- ½ CUP RED WINE VINEGAR
- ¼ CUP TOMATO PASTE
- 5 TABLESPOONS OLIVE OIL
- SALT AND PEPPER, TO TASTE
- 1 LARGE YELLOW ONION, SLICED
- 6 GARLIC CLOVES, MINCED
- 1 TABLESPOON MINCED GINGER
- 1 (14 OZ.) CAN DICED TOMATOES, DRAINED
- FRESH CILANTRO, CHOPPED, FOR GARNISH
- 1 RED CHILI PEPPER, STEMMED, SEEDS AND RIBS REMOVED, AND SLICED, FOR GARNISH

1. Place the ground chicken, garam masala, turmeric, paprika, mustard powder, sugar, cumin, cayenne, vinegar, tomato paste, and 2 tablespoons of the olive oil in a mixing bowl, season the mixture with salt and pepper, and stir to combine.

2. Working with wet hands, form the mixture into 1½-inch meatballs and place them on a foil-lined baking sheet. Refrigerate for 30 minutes.

3. Preheat the broiler to high and position a rack so that the tops of the meatballs will be approximately 6 inches beneath the broiler. Remove the meatballs from the refrigerator and spray the tops with cooking spray. Place the meatballs in the oven and broil until they are browned all over, turning them as they cook. Remove from the oven and set aside.

4. Place the remaining olive oil in a Dutch oven and warm over medium-high heat and add the remaining oil. When the oil starts to shimmer, add the onion and cook until it is translucent, about 3 minutes. Reduce the heat to medium, add the garlic and ginger, and sauté for 1 minute.

5. Add the tomatoes and meatballs to the Dutch oven and bring to a boil. Reduce the heat to low, cover the pan, and simmer the meatballs, turning them occasionally, until they are cooked through, about 15 minutes. Garnish with the cilantro and chili pepper and serve.

GENERAL TSO'S MEATBALLS

YIELD: 6 TO 8 SERVINGS / **ACTIVE TIME:** 20 MINUTES / **TOTAL TIME:** 50 MINUTES

The takeout staple, ready to roll. Musaengchae is a Korean dish, but as it specializes in tempering spicy preparations, it's right at home next to these meatballs.

INGREDIENTS:

2 TABLESPOONS OLIVE OIL

1 SMALL ONION, CHOPPED

3 GARLIC CLOVES, MINCED

2-INCH PIECE FRESH GINGER, PEELED AND MINCED

1 LARGE EGG

2 TABLESPOONS WHOLE MILK

1¼ LBS. GROUND CHICKEN

SALT AND PEPPER, TO TASTE

1½ TEASPOONS TOASTED SESAME OIL

3 TABLESPOONS SOY SAUCE

1 CUP CHICKEN STOCK (SEE PAGE 660)

2 TABLESPOONS SRIRACHA, OR TO TASTE

3 TABLESPOONS SUGAR

2 TABLESPOONS CORNSTARCH

MUSAENGCHAE (SEE PAGE 583), FOR SERVING

1. Preheat the broiler to high, position a rack so that the tops of the meatballs will be approximately 6 inches below the broiler, and line a rimmed baking sheet with aluminum foil.

2. Place the olive oil in a large skillet and warm over medium-high heat. When it starts to shimmer, add the onion, garlic, and ginger and sauté until the onion is translucent, about 3 minutes. Remove the pan from heat and set it aside.

3. Place the egg, milk, chicken, and onion mixture in a mixing bowl, season with salt and pepper, and stir until thoroughly combined. Working with wet hands, form the mixture into 1½-inch meatballs, arrange them on the baking sheet, and spray the tops with cooking spray.

4. Place the meatballs in the oven and broil until browned all over, turning them as they cook. Remove the meatballs from the oven and set aside.

5. Place the sesame oil, soy sauce, stock, sriracha, and sugar in a skillet and bring to a boil over medium-high heat. Add the meatballs to the sauce, reduce the heat to low, cover the pan, and simmer, turning the meatballs occasionally, until they are cooked through, about 15 minutes.

6. Stir in the cornstarch and cook the sauce until it thickens slightly, about 2 minutes. Serve with Musaengchae.

CRUNCHY TURKEY MEATBALLS

YIELD: 4 TO 6 SERVINGS / **ACTIVE TIME:** 20 MINUTES / **TOTAL TIME:** 35 MINUTES

Extremely aromatic thanks to the toasted sesame oil, scallions, and ginger, these crispy balls are a great addition to a cocktail party menu. Any sauce along the lines of the Sweet & Spicy Dipping Sauce on page 749 will pair well with these meatballs.

INGREDIENTS:

2 TABLESPOONS SESAME OIL

4 SCALLIONS, TRIMMED AND CHOPPED

2-INCH PIECE FRESH GINGER, PEELED AND GRATED

3 GARLIC CLOVES, MINCED

1 LARGE EGG

3 TABLESPOONS FISH SAUCE

1 CUP PANKO

½ CUP MINCED WATER CHESTNUTS

¼ CUP CHOPPED FRESH CILANTRO

1¼ LBS. GROUND TURKEY

SALT, TO TASTE

RED PEPPER FLAKES, TO TASTE

1. Preheat the oven to 450°F and line a rimmed baking sheet with aluminum foil. Place the sesame oil in a small skillet and warm over medium-high heat. When it starts to shimmer, add the scallions, ginger, and garlic and sauté until the scallions are translucent, about 3 minutes. Remove the pan from heat and set it aside.

2. Place the egg, fish sauce, ½ cup of the panko, the water chestnuts, and cilantro in a mixing bowl and stir until combined. Add the turkey and scallion mixture, season with salt and red pepper flakes, and stir until thoroughly combined. Working with wet hands, form the mixture into 1½-inch meatballs, roll the meatballs in the remaining panko, arrange them on the baking sheet, and spray the tops with cooking spray.

3. Place the meatballs in the oven and bake for 12 to 15 minutes, until completely cooked through. Remove from the oven and serve.

VARIATIONS

- Replace the turkey with ground pork or ground veal.
- Substitute cooked white rice for the panko.

Lemongrass, an herb that is used frequently in Thai and Vietnamese cooking, is characterized by a strong citrus flavor and a spicy finish similar to that of ginger. Fresh lemongrass is sold by the stalk, and looks like a pale, fibrous, woody scallion. To trim it, cut the lower bulb 5 inches from the stalk and discard the fibrous upper part. Trim away the outer layers, as you would peel an onion; then bruise the stem to release the flavor. If you can't find lemongrass, substitute 1 teaspoon lemon zest plus 2 tablespoons fresh lemon juice for each stalk of lemongrass specified in a recipe, along with a pinch of ground ginger.

AROMATIC THAI CHICKEN MEATBALLS

YIELD: 4 TO 6 SERVINGS / **ACTIVE TIME:** 20 MINUTES / **TOTAL TIME:** 35 MINUTES

Lemongrass is the primary flavoring agent in these succulent bites, which have just a hint of spice from the red pepper flakes.

1. Preheat the oven to 450°F and line a rimmed baking sheet with aluminum foil. Place the lemongrass, scallions, garlic, fish sauce, water, and red pepper flakes in a blender and puree until smooth.

2. Place the egg and milk in a mixing bowl, add the lemongrass puree and the rice, and stir until combined. Add the chicken, season with salt and pepper, and stir until thoroughly combined. Working with wet hands, form the mixture into 1½-inch meatballs, roll the meatballs in the panko, arrange them on the baking sheet, and spray the tops with cooking spray.

3. Place the meatballs in the oven and bake for 12 to 15 minutes, until cooked through. Remove the pan from the oven and serve, accompanied by a bowl of the Sweet & Sour Sauce.

VARIATION

• Replace the chicken with ground pork or ground veal.

INGREDIENTS:

- 2 LEMONGRASS STALKS, TRIMMED AND MINCED
- 4 SCALLION WHITES, SLICED
- 2 GARLIC CLOVES
- 1 TABLESPOON FISH SAUCE
- 1 TABLESPOON WATER
- ½ TEASPOON RED PEPPER FLAKES, OR TO TASTE
- 1 LARGE EGG
- 2 TABLESPOONS WHOLE MILK
- ¾ CUP COOKED WHITE RICE
- 1¼ LBS. GROUND CHICKEN
- SALT AND PEPPER, TO TASTE
- ¾ CUP PANKO
- 1 CUP SWEET & SOUR DIPPING SAUCE (SEE PAGE 746), FOR SERVING

BASQUE MEATBALLS

YIELD: 4 TO 6 SERVINGS / **ACTIVE TIME:** 20 MINUTES / **TOTAL TIME:** 1 HOUR

The Basque region lies in the Pyrenees between France and Spain and its cuisine is marked by rustic, hearty fare. These chicken meatballs are delicate, but the seasonings in the sauce provide the dish some punch.

1. Place the oil in a large skillet and warm over medium-high heat. When the oil starts to shimmer, add the onions and garlic and sauté until the onions are translucent, about 3 minutes. Remove one-third of the mixture from the pan and set it aside. Stir the ham and bell pepper into the skillet and cook for 3 minutes, while stirring frequently. Stir in the paprika and thyme and cook for 1 minute.

2. Add 1¼ cups of the stock, the sherry, tomatoes, and red pepper flakes and bring the sauce to a boil. Reduce the heat to medium-low and simmer the sauce for 15 minutes, stirring occasionally.

3. While the sauce is simmering, preheat the broiler to high, position a rack so that the tops of the meatballs will be approximately 6 inches below the broiler, and line a rimmed baking sheet with aluminum foil.

4. Place the egg, remaining stock, and bread crumbs in a mixing bowl and stir until combined. Add the chicken and the reserved vegetable mixture, season with salt and pepper, and stir until thoroughly combined. Working with wet hands, form the mixture into 1½-inch meatballs, arrange them on the baking sheet, and spray the tops with cooking spray.

5. Place the meatballs in the oven and broil until browned all over, turning them as they cook. Remove the meatballs from the oven and add them to the sauce. Reduce the heat to low, cover the pan, and simmer, turning the meatballs occasionally, until they are cooked through, about 15 minutes. Season with salt and pepper and serve over the Shakshuka.

VARIATIONS

- Replace the chicken with ground pork, ground veal, or ground chuck.
- Substitute uncooked chicken sausage for some of the ground chicken.

INGREDIENTS:

¼ CUP OLIVE OIL

2 LARGE ONIONS, CHOPPED

6 GARLIC CLOVES, MINCED

4 OZ. BAKED HAM, MINCED

1 RED BELL PEPPER, STEMMED, SEEDS AND RIBS REMOVED, AND CHOPPED

2 TABLESPOONS SMOKED PAPRIKA

2 TEASPOONS FINELY CHOPPED FRESH THYME

1½ CUPS CHICKEN STOCK (SEE PAGE 660)

¾ CUP DRY SHERRY

1 (14 OZ.) CAN DICED TOMATOES, DRAINED

RED PEPPER FLAKES, TO TASTE

1 LARGE EGG

½ CUP BREAD CRUMBS

1¼ LBS. GROUND CHICKEN

SALT AND PEPPER, TO TASTE

SHAKSHUKA (SEE PAGE 644), FOR SERVING

MEATBALLS MADE WITH MULTIPLE MEATS

In most of this book, the centerpiece of the recipe is a single type of meat. It can be a red meat, pork, poultry, or even fish, but you know to expect a singular flavor.

That's not the case with the following recipes, which are all made from a combination of meats. This adds a degree of complexity to the preparation, and a depth of flavor to the resulting dishes. Most of these recipes are drawn from European cuisines, but you'll also find some that fall under a Latin American or American influence.

CLASSIC ITALIAN AMERICAN MEATBALLS

YIELD: 4 TO 6 SERVINGS / **ACTIVE TIME:** 20 MINUTES / **TOTAL TIME:** 50 MINUTES

After years of experimentation to get the recipe just right, these have become my favorite meatballs. The herbs and spices give them a complex flavor, and the cheeses add the ideal amount of moisture.

INGREDIENTS:

- 2 TABLESPOONS OLIVE OIL
- 1 SMALL ONION, MINCED
- 3 GARLIC CLOVES, MINCED
- ¼ TEASPOON RED PEPPER FLAKES
- 1 LARGE EGG
- 2 TABLESPOONS WHOLE MILK
- ½ CUP ITALIAN BREAD CRUMBS
- ¼ CUP GRATED PARMESAN CHEESE
- ¼ CUP GRATED FRESH MOZZARELLA CHEESE
- 2 TABLESPOONS FINELY CHOPPED FRESH PARSLEY
- 1 TEASPOON ITALIAN SEASONING
- ½ LB. GROUND PORK
- ½ LB. GROUND CHUCK
- ¼ LB. GROUND VEAL
- SALT AND PEPPER, TO TASTE
- 2 CUPS MARINARA SAUCE (SEE PAGE 674)

1. Preheat the broiler to high, position a rack so that the tops of the meatballs will be approximately 6 inches below the broiler, and line a rimmed baking sheet with aluminum foil.

2. Place the oil in a large skillet and warm over medium-high heat. When it starts to shimmer, add the onion, garlic, and red pepper flakes and sauté until the onion is translucent, about 3 minutes. Remove the pan from heat and set it aside.

3. Place the egg, milk, bread crumbs, Parmesan, mozzarella, parsley, and Italian seasoning in a mixing bowl and stir until combined. Add the pork, beef, veal, and the onion mixture, season with salt and pepper, and stir until thoroughly combined. Working with wet hands, form the mixture into 1½-inch meatballs, arrange them on the baking sheet, and spray the tops with cooking spray.

4. Place the meatballs in the oven and broil until browned all over, turning them as they cook. Remove the meatballs from the oven and set aside.

5. Place the sauce in the skillet and warm over medium heat. Add the meatballs to the sauce, reduce the heat to low, cover the pan, and simmer, turning the meatballs occasionally, until they are cooked through, about 15 minutes. Season with salt and pepper and serve.

VARIATIONS

- For traditional spaghetti and meatballs, cook ½ to 1 lb. pasta and serve with some grated Parmesan cheese on the side.
- Cut the cooked meatballs into small pieces and then use as a pizza topping.
- For a meatball sandwich, make an indentation in the center of a roll or section of bread to accommodate the size of the meatballs. Then top the meatballs with grated or sliced fresh mozzarella cheese and bake the sandwich in a 375°F oven for 10 to 12 minutes, or until the meatballs are warmed through and the cheese has melted.

SPINACH & PARMESAN MEATBALLS

YIELD: 4 TO 6 SERVINGS / **ACTIVE TIME:** 20 MINUTES / **TOTAL TIME:** 35 MINUTES

While you can serve these on top of spaghetti with more sauce, I make them for hors d'oeuvre and use the sauce for dipping.

1. Preheat the oven to 450°F and line a rimmed baking sheet with aluminum foil. Place the oil in a small skillet and warm over medium-high heat. When it starts to shimmer, add the shallots, garlic, and celery and sauté until the shallots are translucent, about 3 minutes. Add the spinach to the skillet and sauté until it has wilted, about 2 minutes. Remove the pan from heat and set it aside.

2. Place the egg, milk, bread crumbs, Parmesan, parsley, and oregano in a mixing bowl and stir until combined. Add the meat and the vegetable mixture, season with salt and red pepper flakes, and stir until thoroughly combined. Working with wet hands, form the mixture into 1½-inch meatballs, arrange them on the baking sheet, and spray the tops with cooking spray.

3. Place the meatballs in the oven and bake for 12 to 15 minutes, until cooked through. Remove the pan from the oven and serve with the Marinara Sauce.

INGREDIENTS:

- 2 TABLESPOONS OLIVE OIL
- 2 SHALLOTS, CHOPPED
- 2 GARLIC CLOVES, MINCED
- 1 CELERY STALK, MINCED
- ½ LB. FROZEN CHOPPED SPINACH, THAWED AND SQUEEZED DRY
- 1 LARGE EGG
- 2 TABLESPOONS WHOLE MILK
- ½ CUP ITALIAN BREAD CRUMBS
- ⅓ CUP GRATED PARMESAN CHEESE
- 2 TABLESPOONS FINELY CHOPPED FRESH PARSLEY
- 2 TABLESPOONS FINELY CHOPPED FRESH OREGANO
- 1¼ LBS. GROUND PORK, VEAL, AND BEEF MIXTURE
- SALT, TO TASTE
- RED PEPPER FLAKES, TO TASTE
- 1 CUP MARINARA SAUCE (SEE PAGE 674), FOR SERVING

BEEF & SAUSAGE MEATBALLS

YIELD: 4 TO 6 SERVINGS / **ACTIVE TIME:** 20 MINUTES / **TOTAL TIME:** 35 MINUTES

Sun-dried tomatoes, wine, herbs, and cheese give these meatballs a robust flavor that can stand up to the sausage.

INGREDIENTS:

- ½ CUP SUN-DRIED TOMATOES IN OLIVE OIL, DRAINED AND MINCED, OIL RESERVED
- 2 SHALLOTS, CHOPPED
- 3 GARLIC CLOVES, MINCED
- 1 LARGE EGG
- 3 TABLESPOONS DRY RED WINE
- ½ CUP ITALIAN BREAD CRUMBS
- ⅓ CUP GRATED FRESH MOZZARELLA CHEESE
- 2 TABLESPOONS FINELY CHOPPED FRESH PARSLEY
- 1 TABLESPOON FINELY CHOPPED FRESH OREGANO
- ¾ LB. GROUND CHUCK
- ½ LB. SWEET OR HOT GROUND ITALIAN SAUSAGE
- SALT AND PEPPER, TO TASTE
- 1 CUP MARINARA SAUCE (SEE PAGE 674), FOR SERVING

1. Preheat the oven to 450°F and line a rimmed baking sheet with aluminum foil. Place the reserved oil in a small skillet and warm over medium-high heat. When it starts to shimmer, add the shallots and garlic and sauté until the shallots are translucent, about 3 minutes. Remove the pan from heat and set it aside.

2. Place the egg, wine, bread crumbs, cheese, parsley, and oregano in a mixing bowl and stir until thoroughly combined. Add the beef, sausage, sun-dried tomatoes, and vegetable mixture, season with salt and pepper, and stir until thoroughly combined. Working with wet hands, form the mixture into 1½-inch meatballs, arrange them on the baking sheet, and spray the tops with cooking spray.

3. Place the meatballs in the oven and bake for 12 to 15 minutes, until cooked through. Remove from the oven and serve with the Marinara Sauce.

VARIATION

- Substitute ground chicken or ground turkey for both or either of the meats.

SICILIAN MEATBALLS

YIELD: 4 TO 6 SERVINGS / **ACTIVE TIME:** 20 MINUTES / **TOTAL TIME:** 45 MINUTES

The North African influence upon Sicily resulted in pine nuts and dried currants becoming characteristic ingredients of the region's cuisine.

INGREDIENTS:

- 2 TABLESPOONS OLIVE OIL
- ½ SMALL RED ONION, CHOPPED
- 2 GARLIC CLOVES, MINCED
- 1 LARGE EGG
- 2 TABLESPOONS WHOLE MILK
- ½ CUP ITALIAN BREAD CRUMBS
- ¼ CUP GRATED PARMESAN CHEESE
- ¼ CUP PINE NUTS, TOASTED
- 3 TABLESPOONS MINCED DRIED CURRANTS
- 2 TABLESPOONS FINELY CHOPPED FRESH OREGANO
- 2 TABLESPOONS FINELY CHOPPED FRESH PARSLEY
- ¾ LB. GROUND PORK
- ½ LB. SWEET OR HOT GROUND ITALIAN SAUSAGE
- SALT AND PEPPER, TO TASTE
- 2 CUPS ROMESCO SAUCE (SEE PAGE 680)

1. Preheat the broiler to high, position a rack so that the tops of the meatballs will be approximately 6 inches below the broiler, and line a rimmed baking sheet with aluminum foil.

2. Place the oil in a large skillet and warm over medium-high heat. When it starts to shimmer, add the onion and garlic and sauté until the onion is translucent, about 3 minutes. Remove the pan from heat and set it aside.

3. Place the egg, milk, bread crumbs, Parmesan, pine nuts, currants, oregano, and parsley in a mixing bowl and stir until combined. Add the pork, sausage, and onion mixture, season with salt and pepper, and stir until thoroughly combined. Working with wet hands, form the mixture into 1½-inch meatballs, arrange them on the baking sheet, and spray the tops with cooking spray.

4. Place the meatballs in the oven and broil until browned all over, turning them as they cook. Remove the meatballs from the oven and set them aside.

5. Place the sauce in the skillet and warm over medium heat. Add the meatballs to the sauce, reduce the heat to low, cover the pan, and simmer, turning the meatballs occasionally, until they are cooked through, about 15 minutes. Season with salt and pepper and serve.

VARIATION

- Substitute ground chicken or ground turkey for both or either of the meats; do not make them with all sausage, however, because the texture will become too lumpy.

MEDITERRANEAN MEATBALLS

YIELD: 4 TO 6 SERVINGS / **ACTIVE TIME:** 25 MINUTES / **TOTAL TIME:** 1 HOUR AND 45 MINUTES

These meatballs, made with bulgur to add texture as well as the wholesome goodness of grains, hail from the Greek islands.

INGREDIENTS:

- 1 LARGE EGG
- ⅔ CUP DRY RED WINE
- ½ CUP BULGUR WHEAT
- ⅔ CUP CHOPPED FRESH PARSLEY
- 3 SCALLIONS, TRIMMED AND CHOPPED
- 4 GARLIC CLOVES, MINCED
- 2 TEASPOONS CUMIN
- 2 TEASPOONS CORIANDER
- ¾ LB. GROUND LAMB
- ½ LB. GROUND BEEF
- SALT AND PEPPER, TO TASTE
- ¼ CUP OLIVE OIL
- 1 ONION, CHOPPED
- 1 (28 OZ.) CAN CRUSHED TOMATOES, DRAINED
- 1 CINNAMON STICK
- 1 BAY LEAF

1. Place the egg and 2 tablespoons of the wine in a mixing bowl and stir to combine. Add the bulgur, ½ cup of the parsley, the scallions, two of the garlic cloves, the cumin, and coriander and stir until combined. Stir in the lamb and beef, season with salt and pepper, and knead the mixture for 2 minutes. Refrigerate for 1 hour.

2. Place the olive oil in a large skillet and warm over medium-high heat. When it starts to shimmer, add the onion and remaining garlic and sauté until the onion is translucent, about 3 minutes. Stir in the remaining wine, tomatoes, cinnamon stick, and bay leaf and bring to a boil over medium-high heat, stirring occasionally. Reduce heat to low and simmer the sauce for 10 minutes.

3. Preheat the broiler to high, position a rack so that the tops of the meatballs will be approximately 6 inches below the broiler, and line a rimmed baking sheet with aluminum foil.

4. Working with wet hands, form the meat mixture into 1½-inch meatballs, arrange them on the baking sheet, and spray the tops with cooking spray. Place the meatballs in the oven and broil until browned all over, turning them as they cook. Remove the meatballs from the oven and add them to the sauce.

5. Reduce the heat to low, cover the pan, and simmer, turning the meatballs occasionally, until they are cooked through, about 15 minutes. Remove the cinnamon stick and bay leaf and discard them. Season the sauce with salt and pepper and serve.

VARIATION

- Substitute buckwheat groats or couscous for the bulgur.

LEMONY GREEK MEATBALLS

YIELD: 4 TO 6 SERVINGS / **ACTIVE TIME:** 20 MINUTES / **TOTAL TIME:** 35 MINUTES

Garlic, oregano, and lemon form an almost holy trinity in Greek cuisine. Here, they partner with some red wine to produce a simple and lovely sauce.

INGREDIENTS:

- 2 TABLESPOONS OLIVE OIL
- ½ SMALL RED ONION, MINCED
- 3 GARLIC CLOVES, MINCED
- 1 LARGE EGG
- 2 TABLESPOONS WHOLE MILK
- ½ CUP ITALIAN BREAD CRUMBS
- ¼ CUP CHOPPED FRESH PARSLEY
- 2 TABLESPOONS FINELY CHOPPED FRESH OREGANO
- ¾ LB. GROUND LAMB
- ½ LB. GROUND CHUCK
- SALT AND PEPPER, TO TASTE
- 1 CUP DRY RED WINE
- 2 TABLESPOONS FRESH LEMON JUICE

1. Preheat the oven to 450°F and line a rimmed baking sheet with aluminum foil. Place the oil in a small skillet and warm over medium-high heat. When it starts to shimmer, add the onion and garlic and sauté until the onion is translucent, about 3 minutes. Remove the pan from heat and set it aside.

2. Place the egg, milk, bread crumbs, half of the parsley, and the oregano in a mixing bowl and stir until combined. Add the lamb, beef, and half of the vegetable mixture, season with salt and pepper, and stir until thoroughly combined. Working with wet hands, form the mixture into 1½-inch meatballs, arrange them on the baking sheet, and spray the tops with cooking spray.

3. Place the meatballs in the oven and bake for 12 to 15 minutes, until cooked through. Remove from the oven and place them in a shallow bowl.

4. While the meatballs are in the oven, add the wine to the onion mixture remaining in the skillet and bring to a boil over high heat, stirring occasionally. Cook until liquid has reduced by half and then stir in the remaining parsley and the lemon juice. Cook for another 2 minutes, season with salt and pepper, and then pour the sauce over the meatballs. Stir until they are evenly coated and serve.

VARIATION

- Substitute ground chicken or ground turkey for either or both of the meats. If using poultry, opt for white wine rather than red.

GRILLED GREEK MEATBALLS

YIELD: 4 TO 6 SERVINGS / **ACTIVE TIME:** 20 MINUTES / **TOTAL TIME:** 35 MINUTES

In Greek, meatballs have a different name depending on how they're cooked: *keftedes* are fried or grilled; meatballs in a sauce are referred to as *yuvarlakia*.

INGREDIENTS:

- 3 TABLESPOONS OLIVE OIL
- 2 SHALLOTS, CHOPPED
- 3 GARLIC CLOVES, CHOPPED
- 1 LARGE EGG
- 2 TABLESPOONS FRESH LEMON JUICE
- 1 TABLESPOON TOMATO PASTE
- ½ CUP ITALIAN BREAD CRUMBS
- 2 TABLESPOONS FINELY CHOPPED FRESH PARSLEY
- 2 TABLESPOONS FINELY CHOPPED FRESH MINT
- 1 TABLESPOON FINELY CHOPPED FRESH THYME
- 1 TABLESPOON FINELY CHOPPED FRESH OREGANO
- 1 TEASPOON LEMON ZEST
- ¾ LB. GROUND CHUCK
- ¾ LB. GROUND LAMB
- SALT AND PEPPER, TO TASTE
- 1 CUP GREEK FETA SAUCE (SEE PAGE 730), FOR SERVING

1. If using bamboo skewers, soak them in cold water. Preheat your gas or charcoal grill to medium-high heat (450°F). Place the oil in a small skillet and warm over medium-high heat. When it starts to shimmer, add the shallots and garlic and sauté until the shallots are translucent, about 3 minutes. Remove the pan from heat and set it aside.

2. Place the egg, lemon juice, tomato paste, bread crumbs, parsley, mint, thyme, oregano, and lemon zest in a mixing bowl and stir until combined. Add the beef, lamb, and onion mixture, season with salt and pepper, and stir until thoroughly combined. Divide the mixture into 8 to 12 portions and form each portion into a sausage shape. Insert a skewer into each meatball so that the tip of the skewer just clears the top end.

3. Place the skewers on the grill and cook, turning them as they brown, until cooked through, 6 to 8 minutes. If using a charcoal grill, leave it uncovered while cooking the meatballs. Serve alongside the Greek Feta Sauce.

SWEDISH MEATBALLS

YIELD: 4 TO 6 SERVINGS / **ACTIVE TIME:** 20 MINUTES / **TOTAL TIME:** 45 MINUTES

Allspice and nutmeg, in addition to a combination of meats and a creamy sauce, define the quintessential Swedish meatball, known as *köttbullar*. Variations on this recipe have been served at American cocktail parties for generations.

INGREDIENTS:

- 4 TABLESPOONS UNSALTED BUTTER
- 1 SMALL ONION, CHOPPED
- ¼ CUP MILK
- 1 LARGE EGG
- 1 LARGE EGG YOLK
- 3 SLICES WHITE BREAD
- ¼ TEASPOON ALLSPICE
- ¼ TEASPOON GRATED FRESH NUTMEG
- PINCH OF GROUND GINGER
- ¾ LB. GROUND PORK
- ½ LB. GROUND CHUCK
- SALT AND PEPPER, TO TASTE
- ¼ CUP ALL-PURPOSE FLOUR
- 2½ CUPS BEEF STOCK (SEE PAGE 663)
- ½ CUP HEAVY CREAM

1. Preheat the broiler to high, position a rack so that the tops of the meatballs will be approximately 6 inches below the broiler, and line a rimmed baking sheet with aluminum foil.

2. Place 2 tablespoons of the butter in a large skillet and melt it over medium-high heat. Add the onion and sauté until it is translucent, about 3 minutes. Remove the pan from heat and set it aside.

3. Place the milk, egg, and egg yolk in a mixing bowl and stir to combine. Tear the bread into small pieces and add them to the mixing bowl along with the allspice, nutmeg, and ginger. Stir in the pork, beef, and the onion mixture, season with salt and pepper, and stir until thoroughly combined. Working with wet hands, form the mixture into 1½-inch meatballs, arrange them on the baking sheet, and spray the tops with cooking spray.

4. Place the meatballs in the oven and broil until browned all over, turning them as they cook. Remove the meatballs from the oven and set them aside.

5. Place the remaining butter in the skillet and melt it over low heat. Stir in the flour, cook for 2 minutes while stirring constantly, and then raise the heat to medium-high. Stir in the stock and cream and bring to a boil.

6. Add the meatballs to the sauce, reduce the heat to low, cover the pan, and simmer, turning the meatballs occasionally, until they are cooked through, about 15 minutes. Season with salt and pepper and serve.

VARIATIONS

- Substitute ground chicken or ground turkey for both or either of the meats.
- Add ¼ cup chopped fresh dill to the sauce.

MUSTARD & DILL MEATBALLS

YIELD: 4 TO 6 SERVINGS / **ACTIVE TIME:** 15 MINUTES / **TOTAL TIME:** 30 MINUTES

Here's another Scandinavian-inspired preparation, this one featuring fresh dill as well as the sharp taste of Dijon mustard.

INGREDIENTS:

- 1 LARGE EGG
- ¾ CUP SOUR CREAM
- 1 TABLESPOON MAYONNAISE
- 3 SLICES CARAWAY RYE BREAD, TORN
- ⅓ CUP CHOPPED FRESH DILL
- 3 TABLESPOONS DIJON MUSTARD
- 2 SCALLIONS, TRIMMED AND CHOPPED
- PINCH OF ALLSPICE
- PINCH OF GROUND NUTMEG
- ¾ LB. GROUND PORK
- ½ LB. GROUND VEAL
- SALT AND PEPPER, TO TASTE

1. Preheat the oven to 450°F and line a rimmed baking sheet with aluminum foil. Place the egg, ¼ cup of the sour cream, mayonnaise, bread, 2 tablespoons of the dill, 1 tablespoon of the mustard, the scallions, allspice, and nutmeg in a mixing bowl and stir until combined.

2. Add the pork and veal, season with salt and pepper, and stir until thoroughly combined. Working with wet hands, form the mixture into 1½-inch meatballs, arrange them on the baking sheet, and spray the tops with cooking spray.

3. Place the meatballs in the oven and bake for 12 to 15 minutes, until cooked through.

4. While the meatballs are in the oven, place the remaining sour cream, dill, and mustard in a small bowl and stir to combine. Remove the meatballs from the oven and serve alongside the sour cream-and-dill dipping sauce.

VARIATION

- Substitute ground chicken or ground turkey for either or both of the meats.

SPANISH MEATBALLS IN TOMATO & GARLIC SAUCE

YIELD: 4 TO 6 SERVINGS / **ACTIVE TIME:** 20 MINUTES / **TOTAL TIME:** 50 MINUTES

Small meatballs in tomato sauce are one of the traditional bites served in Spanish tapas bars. You can serve these as an hors d'oeuvre, or over some Patatas Bravas (see page 623).

INGREDIENTS:

- ¼ CUP OLIVE OIL
- 1 LARGE ONION, MINCED
- 1 LARGE RED BELL PEPPER, STEMMED, SEEDS AND RIBS REMOVED, AND MINCED
- 6 GARLIC CLOVES, MINCED
- 1 LARGE EGG
- ½ CUP DRY RED WINE
- ½ CUP BREAD CRUMBS
- ⅓ CUP CHOPPED FRESH PARSLEY
- 2 TABLESPOONS SMOKED PAPRIKA
- ¾ LB. GROUND CHUCK
- ¾ LB. GROUND PORK
- SALT AND PEPPER, TO TASTE
- 1 (28 OZ.) CAN CRUSHED TOMATOES, DRAINED
- 1 TABLESPOON DRIED OREGANO

1. Preheat the broiler to high, position a rack so that the tops of the meatballs will be approximately 6 inches below the broiler, and line a rimmed baking sheet with aluminum foil.

2. Place the oil in a large skillet and warm over medium-high heat. When it starts to shimmer, add the onion, bell pepper, and garlic and sauté until the onion is translucent, about 3 minutes. Remove the pan from heat and set it aside.

3. Place the egg, 3 tablespoons of the wine, the bread crumbs, ¼ cup of the parsley, and the paprika in a mixing bowl and stir until combined. Add the beef, pork, and half of the onion mixture, season with salt and pepper, and stir until thoroughly combined. Working with wet hands, form the mixture into 1½-inch meatballs, arrange them on the baking sheet, and spray the tops with cooking spray.

4. Place the meatballs in the oven and broil until browned all over, turning them as they cook. Remove the meatballs from the oven and set aside.

5. Add the remaining wine, tomatoes, and oregano to the onion mixture remaining in the skillet and bring to a boil over medium-high heat, stirring occasionally. Reduce the heat to medium and simmer the sauce for 10 minutes.

6. Add the meatballs to the sauce, reduce the heat to low, cover the pan, and simmer, turning the meatballs occasionally, until they are cooked through, about 15 minutes. Season with salt and pepper and serve.

VARIATION

- Substitute ground chicken or ground turkey for either or both of the meats. If using poultry, substitute white wine for the red wine.

CAROLINA BBQ MEATBALLS

YIELD: 4 TO 6 SERVINGS / **ACTIVE TIME:** 15 MINUTES / **TOTAL TIME:** 30 MINUTES

The barbecue tradition in the Carolinas features mustard in the sauce, which gives it a sharp bite and allows the flavor to keep from getting suffocated by the smoke from the grill.

INGREDIENTS:

- 1 LARGE EGG
- 2 TABLESPOONS WHOLE MILK
- 3 SLICES CARAWAY RYE BREAD, TORN
- 3 SCALLIONS, TRIMMED AND CHOPPED
- 2 TABLESPOONS FINELY CHOPPED FRESH PARSLEY
- 2 TEASPOONS FINELY CHOPPED FRESH THYME
- ¼ TEASPOON ALLSPICE
- PINCH OF GROUND NUTMEG
- ¾ LB. GROUND CHUCK
- ½ LB. GROUND PORK
- SALT AND PEPPER, TO TASTE
- 1 CUP SOUTHERN BARBECUE SAUCE (SEE PAGE 684)
- ¼ CUP DIJON MUSTARD

1. If using bamboo skewers, soak them in cold water. Preheat your gas or charcoal grill to medium-high heat (450°F). Place the egg, milk, bread, scallions, parsley, thyme, allspice, and nutmeg in a mixing bowl and stir until combined. Add the beef and pork, season with salt and pepper, and stir until thoroughly combined.

2. Divide the mixture into 8 to 12 portions and form each one into a sausage shape. Insert a skewer into each meatball so that the tip of the skewer just clears the top end.

3. Combine the barbecue sauce and mustard and divide it between two bowls.

4. Place the meatballs on the grill and cook, turning them as they brown and basting the meatballs with the sauce in one of the bowls, until cooked through, 8 to 10 minutes. If using a charcoal grill, leave it uncovered while cooking the meatballs. Discard the sauce used to baste the meatballs, and serve them with the remaining bowl of sauce.

VARIATION

- Substitute ground chicken or ground turkey for either one or both of the meats.

GRILLED CAJUN MEATBALLS

YIELD: 4 TO 6 SERVINGS / **ACTIVE TIME:** 20 MINUTES / **TOTAL TIME:** 35 MINUTES

Andouille sausage is a spicy, smoked pork sausage used primarily in Cajun cooking. If andouille is unavailable, use another smoked pork sausage such as kielbasa, and add a bit more cayenne.

INGREDIENTS:

- ½ LB. SMOKED ANDOUILLE SAUSAGE, CHOPPED AND CASING REMOVED
- 2 TABLESPOONS OLIVE OIL
- 1 LARGE ONION, CHOPPED
- 2 GARLIC CLOVES, MINCED
- 1 LARGE EGG
- 2 TABLESPOONS WHOLE MILK
- 1 TABLESPOON WORCESTERSHIRE SAUCE
- ½ CUP BREAD CRUMBS
- ½ CUP GRATED SHARP CHEDDAR CHEESE
- ¾ LB. GROUND CHUCK
- SALT AND PEPPER, TO TASTE
- 1 CUP DILL & SCALLION SAUCE (SEE PAGE 718), FOR SERVING

1. If using bamboo skewers, soak them in cold water. Preheat your gas or charcoal grill to medium-high (450°F). Place the sausage in a food processor and pulse until it is minced. Set it aside.

2. Place the oil in a small skillet and warm over medium-high heat. When it starts to shimmer, add the onion and garlic and sauté until the onion is translucent, about 3 minutes. Remove the pan from heat and set it aside.

3. Place the egg, milk, Worcestershire sauce, bread crumbs, and cheese in a mixing bowl and stir until combined. Add the beef, sausage, and onion mixture, season with salt and pepper, and stir until thoroughly combined. Divide the mixture into 8 to 12 portions and form each one into a sausage shape. Insert a skewer into each meatball so that the tip just clears the top end.

4. Place the meatballs on the grill and cook, turning them as they brown, until cooked through, 6 to 8 minutes. If using a charcoal grill, leave it uncovered while the meatballs are cooking. Serve the meatballs with the Dill & Scallion Sauce.

VARIATION

- For milder meatballs, omit the andouille and use ground pork sausage, or omit the sausage entirely and substitute plain ground pork.

MUFFULETTA MEATBALLS

YIELD: 4 TO 6 SERVINGS / **ACTIVE TIME:** 15 MINUTES / **TOTAL TIME:** 30 MINUTES

The muffuletta sandwich, which these meatballs are based upon, is a submarine sandwich with layers of cold cuts topped with cheese and an olive salad. The Central Grocery in New Orleans' French Quarter has been making them since 1906, but they're available throughout the city. These meatballs have so much going on that no sauce is necessary.

INGREDIENTS:

- 1 LARGE EGG
- 2 TABLESPOONS WHOLE MILK
- 2 SLICES WHITE BREAD, TORN
- 4 OZ. HAM, MINCED
- 4 OZ. GENOA OR HARD SALAMI, MINCED
- ½ CUP CHOPPED PIMENTO-STUFFED GREEN OLIVES
- ½ CUP GRATED FONTINA CHEESE
- 2 GARLIC CLOVES, MINCED
- 2 TABLESPOONS FINELY CHOPPED FRESH PARSLEY
- 1 TABLESPOON WHITE WINE VINEGAR
- 2 TEASPOONS FINELY CHOPPED FRESH OREGANO
- ¾ LB. GROUND PORK
- SALT AND CAYENNE PEPPER, TO TASTE

1. Preheat the oven to 450°F and line a rimmed baking sheet with aluminum foil. Place the egg, milk, bread, ham, salami, olives, cheese, garlic, parsley, vinegar, and oregano in a mixing bowl and stir to combine.

2. Add the pork, season with salt and cayenne, and stir until thoroughly combined. Working with wet hands, form the mixture into 1½-inch meatballs, arrange them on the baking sheet, and spray the tops with cooking spray.

3. Place the meatballs in the oven and bake for 12 to 15 minutes, until cooked through. Remove from the oven and serve immediately.

VARIATION

• Substitute ground chicken or ground turkey for the ground pork.

BBQ PUMPERNICKEL MEATBALLS

YIELD: 4 TO 6 SERVINGS / **ACTIVE TIME:** 20 MINUTES / **TOTAL TIME:** 45 MINUTES

This classic hors d'oeuvre was commonly served at cocktail parties in the 1950s. It gets a bit of an update here, with water chestnuts and lots of herbs entering the fray.

1. Preheat the broiler to high, position a rack so that the tops of the meatballs will be approximately 6 inches below the broiler, and line a rimmed baking sheet with aluminum foil.

2. Place the oil in a large skillet and warm over medium-high heat. When it starts to shimmer, add the onion, bell pepper, and garlic and sauté until the onion is translucent, about 3 minutes. Remove the pan from heat and set it aside.

3. Place the egg, Worcestershire sauce, hot sauce, bread, water chestnuts, sage, and paprika and stir until combined. Add the beef, lamb, and onion mixture, season with salt and pepper, and stir until thoroughly combined. Working with wet hands, form the mixture into 1½-inch meatballs, arrange them on the baking sheet, and spray the tops with cooking spray.

4. Place the meatballs in the oven and broil until browned all over, turning them as they cook. Remove the meatballs from the oven and set them aside.

5. Add the wine to the skillet, bring to a boil over high heat, and cook until reduced by half. Turn off the heat and stir in the barbecue sauce.

6. Add the meatballs to the sauce, set the heat to low, cover the pan, and simmer, turning the meatballs occasionally, until they are cooked through, about 15 minutes. Season with salt and pepper and serve.

VARIATION

- Substitute ground chicken or ground turkey for either or both of the meats.

INGREDIENTS:

- 2 TABLESPOONS OLIVE OIL
- ½ SMALL RED ONION, MINCED
- ½ GREEN BELL PEPPER, MINCED
- 2 GARLIC CLOVES, MINCED
- 1 LARGE EGG
- 2 TABLESPOONS WORCESTERSHIRE SAUCE
- ¼ TEASPOON HOT SAUCE, OR TO TASTE
- 3 SLICES PUMPERNICKEL BREAD, TORN
- ½ CUP CHOPPED WATER CHESTNUTS
- 2 TABLESPOONS FINELY CHOPPED FRESH SAGE
- 1 TABLESPOON SMOKED PAPRIKA
- ¾ LB. GROUND BEEF
- ½ LB. GROUND LAMB
- SALT AND PEPPER, TO TASTE
- 1 CUP DRY RED WINE
- 1 CUP COFFEE & BOURBON BARBECUE SAUCE (SEE PAGE 687)

SWEET & SOUR TEX-MEX MEATBALLS

YIELD: 4 TO 6 SERVINGS / **ACTIVE TIME:** 20 MINUTES / **TOTAL TIME:** 45 MINUTES

These meatballs are cooked in a blend of jalapeño pepper jelly and chili sauce, both of which have sweet, sour, and spicy aspects.

INGREDIENTS:

- 2 TABLESPOONS OLIVE OIL
- 1 SMALL ONION, MINCED
- ½ RED BELL PEPPER, MINCED
- 4 GARLIC CLOVES, MINCED
- 1 LARGE EGG
- 1 CUP TOMATO SAUCE
- ¾ CUP CRUSHED TORTILLA CHIPS
- 3 TABLESPOONS FINELY CHOPPED FRESH CILANTRO
- 3 TABLESPOONS DICED MILD GREEN CHILIES
- 1 TABLESPOON DRIED OREGANO
- 2 TEASPOONS CUMIN
- ¾ LB. GROUND CHUCK
- ½ LB. GROUND PORK
- SALT AND PEPPER, TO TASTE
- ½ CUP CHILI SAUCE
- ½ CUP JALAPEÑO PEPPER JELLY

1. Preheat the broiler to high, position a rack so that the tops of the meatballs will be approximately 6 inches below the broiler, and line a rimmed baking sheet with aluminum foil.

2. Place the oil in a large skillet and warm over medium-high heat. When it starts to shimmer, add the onion, bell pepper, and garlic and sauté until the onion is translucent, about 3 minutes. Remove the pan from heat and set it aside.

3. Place the egg, 2 tablespoons of the tomato sauce, the crushed tortilla chips, cilantro, chilies, oregano, and cumin in a mixing bowl and stir until thoroughly combined. Add the beef, pork, and half of the onion mixture, season with salt and pepper, and stir until thoroughly combined. Working with wet hands, form the mixture into 1½-inch meatballs, arrange them on the baking sheet, and spray the tops with cooking spray.

4. Place the meatballs in the oven and broil until browned all over, turning them as they cook. Remove the meatballs from the oven and set aside.

5. Add the chili sauce, jelly, and remaining tomato sauce to the onion mixture left in the skillet and bring the sauce to a boil over medium-high heat, stirring occasionally.

6. Add the meatballs to the sauce, reduce the heat to low, cover the pan, and simmer, turning the meatballs occasionally, until they are cooked through, about 15 minutes. Serve immediately.

VARIATION

- Substitute ground chicken or ground turkey for either or both of the meats.

MEATLOAF MEATBALLS

YIELD: 4 TO 6 SERVINGS / **ACTIVE TIME:** 25 MINUTES / **TOTAL TIME:** 40 MINUTES

Homey and inviting, these meatballs are the round iteration of old-fashioned American meatloaf, right down to the ketchup glaze. Serve with mashed potatoes and Creamed Spinach (see page 635).

INGREDIENTS:

- 2 TABLESPOONS UNSALTED BUTTER
- 2 TABLESPOONS OLIVE OIL
- 1 SMALL ONION, CHOPPED
- 2 GARLIC CLOVES, MINCED
- ½ LB. MUSHROOMS, CHOPPED
- 1 LARGE EGG
- ¾ CUP KETCHUP
- 2 TABLESPOONS WHOLE MILK
- ½ CUP ROLLED OATS
- 2 TABLESPOONS FINELY CHOPPED FRESH PARSLEY
- 2 TABLESPOONS WORCESTERSHIRE SAUCE
- 2 TEASPOONS FINELY CHOPPED FRESH THYME
- ¾ LB. GROUND PORK
- ½ LB. GROUND VEAL

1. Preheat the oven to 450°F and line a rimmed baking sheet with aluminum foil. Place the butter and oil in a large skillet and warm over medium-high heat. When the butter starts to foam, add the onion and garlic and sauté for 2 minutes. Add the mushrooms and cook until they start to soften, about 5 minutes. Remove the pan from heat and set it aside.

2. Place the egg, ¼ cup of the ketchup, milk, oats, parsley, Worcestershire sauce, and thyme in a mixing bowl and stir until thoroughly combined. Add the pork, veal, and vegetable mixture, season with salt and pepper, and stir until thoroughly combined. Working with wet hands, form the mixture into 1½-inch meatballs, arrange them on the baking sheet, and spray the tops with cooking spray.

3. Place the meatballs in the oven and bake for 12 to 15 minutes, until cooked through.

4. When the meatballs are close to being done, place the remaining ketchup in the skillet and warm over medium heat. Remove from heat, add the meatballs, stir until they are coated, and serve.

VARIATIONS

- Substitute ground chicken or ground turkey for either or both of the meats.
- For more flavor, incorporate some bottled chili sauce.

BEEF & CHORIZO MEATBALLS

YIELD: 4 TO 6 SERVINGS / **ACTIVE TIME:** 20 MINUTES / **TOTAL TIME:** 35 MINUTES

Chorizo in Spain is cured; the Mexican version needs to be cooked, and it packs more of a punch.

INGREDIENTS:

- 3 TABLESPOONS OLIVE OIL
- ¼ SMALL RED ONION, CHOPPED
- 3 GARLIC CLOVES, MINCED
- 1 LARGE EGG
- 2 TABLESPOONS WHOLE MILK
- ¼ CUP BREAD CRUMBS
- ¾ CUP GRATED JALAPEÑO JACK CHEESE
- 3 TABLESPOONS FINELY CHOPPED FRESH CILANTRO
- 1 TABLESPOON CHILI POWDER
- 2 TEASPOONS CUMIN
- 1 TEASPOON DRIED OREGANO
- 1 LB. GROUND CHUCK
- ½ LB. CHORIZO, CHOPPED AND CASING REMOVED
- SALT AND CAYENNE PEPPER, TO TASTE
- 1 CUP GREEN CHILI CHOW CHOW (SEE PAGE 692), FOR SERVING

1. Preheat the oven to 450°F and line a rimmed baking sheet with aluminum foil. Place the oil in a small skillet and warm over medium-high heat. When it starts to shimmer, add the onion and garlic and sauté until the onion is translucent, about 3 minutes. Remove the pan from heat and set it aside.

2. Place the egg, milk, bread crumbs, cheese, cilantro, chili powder, cumin, and oregano in a mixing bowl and stir until combined. Add the beef, chorizo, and the onion mixture to the mixing bowl, season with salt and cayenne, and stir until thoroughly combined. Working with wet hands, form the mixture into 1½-inch meatballs, arrange them on the baking sheet, and spray the tops with cooking spray.

3. Place the meatballs in the oven and bake for 12 to 15 minutes, until cooked through. Remove from the oven and serve with the Green Chili Chow Chow.

VARIATION

- Substitute the Portuguese linguiça for the chorizo, and use ground pork in place of the beef.

BEEF BOURGUIGNON MEATBALLS

YIELD: 4 TO 6 SERVINGS / **ACTIVE TIME:** 20 MINUTES / **TOTAL TIME:** 45 MINUTES

A hearty entree for a cold fall evening, especially if served over some buttered egg noodles.

INGREDIENTS:

- 6 STRIPS OF BACON, CHOPPED
- 1 ONION, CHOPPED
- 2 GARLIC CLOVES, MINCED
- 1 LARGE EGG
- 2 TABLESPOONS WHOLE MILK
- ½ CUP BREAD CRUMBS
- ½ CUP GRATED SWISS CHEESE
- ¼ CUP GRATED PARMESAN CHEESE
- 2 TABLESPOONS FINELY CHOPPED FRESH PARSLEY
- 1 TABLESPOON FINELY CHOPPED FRESH THYME
- ¾ LB. GROUND BEEF
- ½ LB. GROUND PORK
- SALT AND PEPPER, TO TASTE
- 1 CUP BEEF STOCK (SEE PAGE 663)
- 1 CUP DRY RED WINE
- 2 TEASPOONS CORNSTARCH
- 1 TABLESPOON WATER

1. Preheat the broiler to high, position a rack so that the tops of the meatballs will be approximately 6 inches below the broiler, and line a rimmed baking sheet with aluminum foil.

2. Place the bacon in a large skillet and cook over medium-high heat until it is crispy, about 6 minutes. Transfer the bacon to a paper towel–lined plate, remove all but 2 tablespoons of the rendered bacon fat from the skillet, and add the onion and garlic. Sauté until the onion is translucent, about 3 minutes. Remove the pan from heat and set it aside.

3. Place the egg, milk, bread crumbs, Swiss cheese, ¼ cup of the Parmesan, the parsley, and thyme and stir until combined. Add the beef, pork, bacon, and the onion mixture, season with salt and pepper, and stir until thoroughly combined. Working with wet hands, form the mixture into 1½-inch meatballs, arrange them on the baking sheet, and spray the tops with cooking spray.

4. Place the meatballs in the oven and broil until browned all over, turning them as they cook. Remove the meatballs from the oven and set them aside.

5. Add the stock and wine to the skillet and bring to a boil over high heat. Reduce the heat to medium-high and cook until the sauce has reduced by one-third.

6. Add the meatballs to the sauce, reduce the heat to low, cover the pan, and simmer, turning the meatballs occasionally, until they are cooked through, about 15 minutes.

7. Combine the cornstarch and water, stir the slurry into the sauce, and cook until it thickens slightly, about 2 minutes. Season with salt and pepper and serve immediately.

VARIATION

- Substitute ground chicken or ground turkey for both or either of the meats. If using poultry, substitute Chicken Stock (see page 660) and white wine for the Beef Stock and red wine.

SEAFOOD MEATBALLS

People are eating more fish and seafood every year, both at home and out at restaurants. Although these recipes were developed with a specific variety of fish in mind, it is more important to use the freshest fish in the market rather than focus on a particular species.

Some of these recipes are fried, others are baked or poached gently in a flavorful sauce. It may take a little more time to create the mixtures from which these meatballs are made, but as they do not require any browning before being cooked, the total amount of time required of you to get them to the table is commonly shorter.

CAJUN SHRIMP BALLS

YIELD: 4 TO 6 SERVINGS / **ACTIVE TIME:** 20 MINUTES / **TOTAL TIME:** 1 HOUR AND 15 MINUTES

Shrimp are a favorite food in Louisiana, and these vibrantly flavored offerings provide an easy way to enjoy them.

INGREDIENTS:

- 2 TABLESPOONS OLIVE OIL
- 1 SMALL ONION, CHOPPED
- 2 GARLIC CLOVES, MINCED
- 1 CELERY STALK, CHOPPED
- ½ RED BELL PEPPER, MINCED
- 1½ LBS. LARGE SHRIMP, PEELED AND DEVEINED
- 2 LARGE EGG WHITES
- ¼ CUP BREAD CRUMBS
- 3 TABLESPOONS FINELY CHOPPED FRESH CHIVES
- 3 TABLESPOONS FINELY CHOPPED FRESH PARSLEY
- ½ TEASPOON HOT SAUCE, OR TO TASTE
- CAJUN SEASONING, TO TASTE
- CAJUN OKRA & TOMATOES (SEE PAGE 636), FOR SERVING

1. Place the oil in a skillet and warm over medium heat. When it starts to shimmer, add the onion, garlic, celery, and red bell pepper and sauté until the vegetables are soft, about 8 minutes. Scrape the vegetables into a mixing bowl and set them aside.

2. Mince ½ pound of the shrimp and add it to the sautéed vegetables. Place the egg whites and the remaining shrimp in a food processor and puree until smooth. Add the puree to the mixing bowl along with the bread crumbs, chives, parsley, hot sauce, and Cajun seasoning. Stir until thoroughly combined and refrigerate the mixture for 30 minutes. Preheat the oven to 400°F and line a rimmed baking sheet with aluminum foil.

3. Working with wet hands, form the mixture into 1-inch balls, arrange them on the baking sheet, and spray the tops with cooking spray. Place in the oven and bake for 12 to 15 minutes, until cooked through. Remove from the oven and serve with the Cajun Okra & Tomatoes.

VARIATION

- Substitute scallops or any firm-fleshed whitefish like cod or tilapia for the shrimp.

To “devein” shrimp means to remove the black column that runs along the back, which is actually the intestinal tract. To do this, hold the shrimp in one hand with the backside facing up. Slice down the middle of the back with a paring knife and pull out the “vein” in one piece.

FRIED SHRIMP BALLS

YIELD: 4 TO 6 SERVINGS / **ACTIVE TIME:** 20 MINUTES / **TOTAL TIME:** 50 MINUTES

Light, fluffy, and crunchy, these balls are similar to the topping for shrimp toast that can be found on the menus at many Chinese restaurants in the United States.

INGREDIENTS:

- 1½ LBS. LARGE SHRIMP, PEELED AND DEVEINED
- 2 LARGE EGG WHITES
- 2 TABLESPOONS CORNSTARCH
- ½ CUP CHOPPED WATER CHESTNUTS
- 3 SCALLIONS, TRIMMED AND CHOPPED
- 2-INCH PIECE FRESH GINGER, PEELED AND GRATED
- 2 TABLESPOONS DRY SHERRY
- 1 TABLESPOON SOY SAUCE
- 1 TABLESPOON SESAME OIL
- SALT AND PEPPER, TO TASTE
- 1½ CUPS PANKO
- VEGETABLE OIL, AS NEEDED
- 1 CUP SWEET & SOUR DIPPING SAUCE (SEE PAGE 746), FOR SERVING

1. Mince ½ pound of the shrimp and place it in a mixing bowl. Place the egg whites, cornstarch, and remaining shrimp in a food processor and puree until smooth. Add the puree to the mixing bowl with the water chestnuts, scallions, ginger, sherry, soy sauce, sesame oil, salt, and pepper. Stir until thoroughly combined and refrigerate the mixture for 30 minutes.

2. Place the panko in a shallow bowl. Working with wet hands, form the shrimp mixture into 1-inch balls and roll them in the panko, gently pressing down so that the panko adheres.

3. Add oil to a Dutch oven until it is approximately 2 inches deep and warm to 375°F over medium-high heat. Working in batches, add the shrimp balls and fry until golden brown, 2 to 3 minutes. Transfer the cooked shrimp balls to a paper towel–lined plate to drain. When all of the shrimp balls have been cooked, serve them with the Sweet & Sour Dipping Sauce.

VARIATION

- Substitute scallops or any firm-fleshed whitefish like cod or tilapia for the shrimp.

SHRIMP BALLS IN CREOLE SAUCE

YIELD: 4 TO 6 SERVINGS / **ACTIVE TIME:** 25 MINUTES / **TOTAL TIME:** 1 HOUR AND 15 MINUTES

Another shrimp-based preparation that mines the culinary genius of Louisiana.

INGREDIENTS:

- 1½ LBS. LARGE SHRIMP, PEELED AND DEVEINED
- 2 LARGE EGG WHITES
- ¼ CUP BREAD CRUMBS
- 2 TABLESPOONS FINELY CHOPPED FRESH PARSLEY
- HOT SAUCE, TO TASTE
- CAJUN SEASONING, TO TASTE
- 2 TABLESPOONS OLIVE OIL
- 1 LARGE ONION, CHOPPED
- 3 GARLIC CLOVES, MINCED
- 1 CELERY STALK, CHOPPED
- ½ RED BELL PEPPER, CHOPPED
- 1 (28 OZ.) CAN DICED TOMATOES, WITH THEIR LIQUID
- 1 TABLESPOON FINELY CHOPPED FRESH THYME
- 1 TABLESPOON FINELY CHOPPED FRESH OREGANO
- 1 BAY LEAF
- SALT AND PEPPER, TO TASTE

1. Mince ½ pound of the shrimp and place them in a mixing bowl. Place the egg whites and remaining shrimp in a food processor and puree until smooth. Add the puree to the mixing bowl along with the bread crumbs, parsley, hot sauce, and Cajun seasoning. Stir until thoroughly combined and refrigerate the mixture for 30 minutes.

2. Place the oil in a large skillet and warm over medium-high heat. When it starts to shimmer, add the onion, garlic, celery, and bell pepper and sauté until the onion is translucent, about 3 minutes. Stir in the tomatoes, thyme, oregano, and bay leaf and bring to a boil over medium-high heat, stirring occasionally. Reduce the heat to medium and simmer the sauce for 10 minutes.

3. Working with wet hands, form the shrimp mixture into 1-inch balls and gently lower them into the simmering sauce. Raise the heat and bring the sauce to a boil. Reduce the heat to low, cover the pan, and simmer until they are cooked through, about 15 minutes, turning the meatballs over after about 10 minutes. Remove the bay leaf and discard it. Season with salt and pepper and serve.

VARIATIONS

- Substitute scallops or any firm-fleshed whitefish like cod or tilapia for the shrimp.
- This sauce is also delicious with ground chicken or turkey meatballs.

SOUTHWESTERN CRAB BALLS

YIELD: 4 TO 6 SERVINGS / **ACTIVE TIME:** 20 MINUTES / **TOTAL TIME:** 35 MINUTES

This recipe is a riff on traditional crab cakes. You can also make them into larger patties and serve them on hamburger buns.

1. Preheat the oven to 425°F and line a rimmed baking sheet with aluminum foil. Place the crab on a dark work surface and carefully pick it over to remove any and all shell fragments. Set the crab aside.

2. Place the butter in a small skillet and melt it over medium-high heat. Add the scallions, bell pepper, and garlic and sauté until the vegetables start to soften, about 5 minutes. Remove the pan from heat and set it aside.

3. Place the mayonnaise, egg, cilantro, paprika, chili powder, Worcestershire sauce, thyme, salt, and cayenne in a mixing bowl and stir to combine. Stir in the bread crumbs and then fold in the crab.

4. Working with wet hands, form the mixture into 1½-inch balls, arrange them on the baking sheet, and spray the tops with cooking spray. Place the crab balls in the oven and bake them for 12 to 15 minutes, until cooked through. Remove from the oven and serve, accompanied by a bowl of Creamy Chipotle Sauce.

VARIATIONS

- In addition to cooked fish or seafood of any kind, try cooked and minced chicken or pork.
- Substitute canned tuna that has been drained and flaked for the crab.

INGREDIENTS:

1 LB. LUMP CRABMEAT

3 TABLESPOONS UNSALTED BUTTER

4 SCALLIONS, TRIMMED AND CHOPPED

½ RED BELL PEPPER, CHOPPED

2 GARLIC CLOVES, MINCED

⅓ CUP MAYONNAISE

1 LARGE EGG

3 TABLESPOONS FINELY CHOPPED FRESH CILANTRO

1 TABLESPOON PAPRIKA

1 TABLESPOON CHILI POWDER

2 TEASPOONS WORCESTERSHIRE SAUCE

½ TEASPOON DRIED THYME

SALT AND CAYENNE PEPPER, TO TASTE

½ CUP BREAD CRUMBS

1 CUP CREAMY CHIPOTLE SAUCE (SEE PAGE 729), FOR SERVING

SCALLOP BALLS IN TARRAGON SAUCE

YIELD: 4 TO 6 SERVINGS / **ACTIVE TIME:** 25 MINUTES / **TOTAL TIME:** 1 HOUR AND 30 MINUTES

Seafood in an herb-enriched cream sauce is found in many European cuisines, and this delicate dish is drawn from classic French cooking. Serve it over rice or place it in an ovenproof casserole topped with a puff pastry crust and bake it as a pot pie.

1. Rinse the scallops and pat them dry with paper towels; if using sea scallops, cut each one into eight pieces. Wrap the scallops in plastic wrap and freeze for 20 minutes, until they have firmed up slightly.

2. Place 2 tablespoons of the butter in a large skillet and melt over medium-high heat. Add the leeks, carrot, and celery and sauté until the leeks are translucent, about 3 minutes. Stir in the wine, clam juice, and bay leaf and bring to a boil. Reduce the heat to low, cover the pan, and cook the sauce for 10 minutes. Strain and reserve both the solids and the liquid.

3. Place the egg whites, 2 tablespoons of the half-and-half, and the bread crumbs in a mixing bowl and stir until combined. Place the scallops in a food processor and pulse until minced. Add the scallops to the mixing bowl, season with salt and pepper, and stir until thoroughly combined. Refrigerate the mixture for 30 minutes.

4. Place the remaining butter in the skillet and melt it over low heat. Add the flour and cook for 2 minutes, while stirring constantly. Stir in the parsley, tarragon, reserved cooking liquid and solids, and the remaining half-and-half, raise the heat to medium heat, and bring to a boil. Reduce the heat to low and simmer the sauce for 2 minutes.

5. Form the scallop mixture into 1-inch balls and gently lower them into the simmering sauce. Raise the heat and bring the sauce to a boil. Reduce the heat to low, cover the pan, and simmer until they are cooked through, about 25 minutes, turning the scallop balls over after 15 minutes. Remove the bay leaf and discard it. Season with salt and pepper and serve.

VARIATION

- Substitute shrimp or any firm-fleshed whitefish like cod or tilapia for the scallops.

INGREDIENTS:

- 1½ LBS. BAY OR SEA SCALLOPS
- 4 TABLESPOONS UNSALTED BUTTER
- 2 LEEKS, WHITE PARTS ONLY, CHOPPED AND RINSED WELL
- 1 CARROT, PEELED AND CHOPPED
- 1 CELERY STALK, CHOPPED
- 1 CUP DRY WHITE WINE
- 1 CUP CLAM JUICE
- 1 BAY LEAF
- 2 LARGE EGG WHITES
- 1 CUP HALF-AND-HALF
- ½ CUP BREAD CRUMBS
- SALT AND PEPPER, TO TASTE
- 3 TABLESPOONS ALL-PURPOSE FLOUR
- 2 TABLESPOONS FINELY CHOPPED FRESH PARSLEY
- 2 TABLESPOONS FINELY CHOPPED FRESH TARRAGON

FRIED SCALLOP BALLS

YIELD: 4 TO 6 SERVINGS / **ACTIVE TIME:** 25 MINUTES / **TOTAL TIME:** 55 MINUTES

Easy to make and loaded with the bright and clean flavors Mexican cuisine is known for, these fried puffs are surprisingly delicate.

1. Rinse the scallops and pat them dry. Mince ½ pound of the scallops and place them in a mixing bowl. Place the egg whites, cream, cornstarch, and remaining scallops in a food processor and puree until smooth. Add the puree to the mixing bowl along with the onion, bell pepper, cilantro, garlic, chili powder, cumin, salt, and pepper. Stir until thoroughly combined and refrigerate the mixture for 30 minutes.

2. Place the bread crumbs in a shallow bowl. Working with wet hands, form the scallop mixture into 1-inch balls and roll them in the bread crumbs, gently pressing down so that they adhere.

3. Add oil to a Dutch oven until it is approximately 2 inches deep and warm to 375°F over medium-high heat. Working in batches, add the scallop balls and fry until golden brown and cooked through, about 3 minutes. Transfer the cooked scallop balls to a paper towel–lined plate to drain. When all of the scallop balls have been cooked, serve alongside the Creamy Chipotle Sauce.

VARIATIONS

- Substitute shrimp or any firm-fleshed whitefish like cod or tilapia for the scallops.
- To put an Asian-inspired twist on these scallop balls, omit the chili powder and cumin, substitute chopped scallions for the red onion, and add 2 tablespoons grated fresh ginger to the mixture.

INGREDIENTS:

1½ LBS. BAY SCALLOPS OR SEA SCALLOPS

2 LARGE EGG WHITES

3 TABLESPOONS HEAVY CREAM

2 TABLESPOONS CORNSTARCH

¼ CUP MINCED RED ONION

½ RED BELL PEPPER, MINCED

3 TABLESPOONS FINELY CHOPPED FRESH CILANTRO

2 GARLIC CLOVES, MINCED

1 TABLESPOON CHILI POWDER

2 TEASPOONS CUMIN

SALT AND PEPPER, TO TASTE

¾ CUP BREAD CRUMBS

VEGETABLE OIL, AS NEEDED

1 CUP CREAMY CHIPOTLE SAUCE (SEE PAGE 729), FOR SERVING

SOUTHWESTERN CLAM & CORN FRITTERS

YIELD: 4 TO 6 SERVINGS / **ACTIVE TIME:** 25 MINUTES / **TOTAL TIME:** 25 MINUTES

Both clams and corn have an inherently sweet flavor, and they are delicious when cooked together—which is why many clam chowders also include corn.

1. Place the clams in a fine sieve and drain them over a bowl to reserve the liquid. Press down on the clams with a spoon to extract as much liquid as possible.

2. Place the egg, cream, and ¼ cup of the extracted clam juice in a mixing bowl and stir to combine. Add the flour, cumin, oregano, baking powder, corn, scallions, garlic, cilantro, chilies, and clams, season with salt and cayenne, and stir until thoroughly combined.

3. Preheat the oven to 150°F, line a baking sheet with paper towels, and place it in the oven. Add oil to a Dutch oven until it is approximately 2 inches deep and warm to 375°F over medium-high heat. Drop tablespoons of the batter into the oil and fry until the fritters are golden-brown and cooked through, about 3 minutes. Transfer the cooked fritters to the baking sheet to keep warm. When all of the fritters have been cooked, serve them with the Southwestern Barbecue Sauce.

VARIATION

- Substitute scallops, shrimp, or any firm-fleshed whitefish like cod or tilapia for the clams.

INGREDIENTS:

1 LB. MINCED CLAMS

1 LARGE EGG

½ CUP HEAVY CREAM

1½ CUPS ALL-PURPOSE FLOUR

1 TABLESPOON CUMIN

2 TEASPOONS DRIED OREGANO

1½ TEASPOONS BAKING POWDER

½ CUP COOKED CORN KERNELS

2 SCALLIONS, TRIMMED AND MINCED

2 GARLIC CLOVES, MINCED

2 TABLESPOONS FINELY CHOPPED FRESH CILANTRO

2 TABLESPOONS DICED GREEN CHILIES

SALT AND CAYENNE PEPPER, TO TASTE

VEGETABLE OIL, AS NEEDED

1 CUP SOUTHWESTERN BARBECUE SAUCE (SEE PAGE 684), FOR SERVING

GEFILTE FISH BALLS

YIELD: 4 TO 6 SERVINGS / **ACTIVE TIME:** 45 MINUTES / **TOTAL TIME:** 4 HOURS AND 30 MINUTES

Gefilte fish, which is always made with freshwater fish, dates from the Middle Ages in Germany, where it was conceived as a way to stretch fresh fish in order to feed a crowd.

INGREDIENTS:

- 1½ LBS. FISH FILLETS (COMBINATION OF WHITEFISH, CARP, AND PIKE)
- 3 LARGE EGGS
- 2 LARGE ONIONS
- 2 CELERY STALKS
- 3 CARROTS
- ½ CUP MATZO MEAL
- SALT AND PEPPER, TO TASTE
- 8 CUPS FISH STOCK (SEE PAGE 672), PLUS MORE AS NEEDED
- ½ CUP PREPARED HORSERADISH

1. Rinse the fish, pat it dry with paper towels, and cut it into 1-inch pieces. Wrap the fish in plastic wrap and freeze for 20 minutes, or until it has firmed up.

2. Place the fish in a food processor and pulse until it is minced. Place it in a bowl, stir in the eggs, and then grate half of 1 onion into the bowl. Grate 1 celery stalk and 1 carrot and add them to the bowl with the matzo meal, salt, and pepper. Stir until thoroughly combined and then refrigerate the mixture for 2 hours.

3. Place the stock in a saucepan, season with salt and pepper, and bring to a boil over medium-high heat. Slice the remaining onion, celery, and carrots and add them to the stock. Form the fish mixture into 1½-inch balls and gently lower them into the stock. Reduce the heat to low, cover the pot, and simmer the fish balls until cooked through and very tender, about 1½ hours. Add more stock as needed to keep the fish balls submerged.

4. Remove the fish balls and carrots from the pot and let them cool to room temperature. Wrap them tightly with plastic wrap and refrigerate until completely cooled. Serve chilled, topping the fish balls with the carrot slices and horseradish.

VARIATIONS

- Add ¼ cup chopped dill to the fish mixture.
- Add 2 minced garlic cloves to the fish mixture.

ITALIAN COD BALLS

YIELD: 4 TO 6 SERVINGS / **ACTIVE TIME:** 20 MINUTES / **TOTAL TIME:** 50 MINUTES

This recipe is actually more Italian American than authentically Italian; but the addition of spinach and cheeses gives it plenty of flavor.

INGREDIENTS:

- 1¼ LBS. COD FILLETS
- 1 LARGE EGG
- 2 TABLESPOONS WHOLE MILK
- 1 CUP ITALIAN BREAD CRUMBS
- ¼ CUP GRATED FRESH MOZZARELLA CHEESE
- 3 TABLESPOONS GRATED PARMESAN CHEESE
- 3 TABLESPOONS FINELY CHOPPED FRESH PARSLEY
- 1 TABLESPOON FINELY CHOPPED FRESH OREGANO
- 4 OZ. FROZEN SPINACH, THAWED AND SQUEEZED DRY
- MARINARA SAUCE (SEE PAGE 674), FOR SERVING

1. Rinse the cod, pat it dry with paper towels, and cut it into 1-inch pieces. Wrap the fish in plastic wrap and freeze for 20 minutes, or until it has firmed up.

2. Preheat the oven to 425°F and line a rimmed baking sheet with aluminum foil. Place the egg, milk, ½ cup of the bread crumbs, the mozzarella, Parmesan, parsley, and oregano in a mixing bowl and stir until thoroughly combined.

3. Place the cod in a food processor and pulse until it is minced. Add the spinach and the cod to the mixing bowl, season with salt and pepper, and stir until thoroughly combined. Working with wet hands, form the mixture into 1½-inch balls and roll them in the remaining bread crumbs, gently pressing down to ensure that they adhere. Arrange the cod balls on the baking sheet and spray the tops with cooking spray.

4. Place the cod balls in the oven and bake for 12 to 15 minutes, until cooked through. Remove from the oven and serve with a bowl of Marinara Sauce for dipping.

VARIATION

- Substitute salmon or any firm-fleshed whitefish like halibut for the cod.

NEW ENGLAND COD BALLS

YIELD: 4 TO 6 SERVINGS / **ACTIVE TIME:** 20 MINUTES / **TOTAL TIME:** 35 MINUTES

While living on Nantucket I devised myriad recipes to make use of the famed local cod, and this is one of the best results of that particular endeavor.

INGREDIENTS:

- 2 TABLESPOONS UNSALTED BUTTER
- 1 SMALL ONION, MINCED
- ½ GREEN BELL PEPPER, MINCED
- 1 LARGE EGG
- 1 CUP TARTAR SAUCE (SEE PAGE 722)
- ¾ CUP FINELY CRUSHED POTATO CHIPS
- 2 TABLESPOONS FINELY CHOPPED FRESH PARSLEY
- 2 TEASPOONS FINELY CHOPPED FRESH THYME
- SALT AND PEPPER, TO TASTE
- 1¼ LBS. COOKED COD FILLETS, FLAKED

1. Preheat the oven to 425°F and line a rimmed baking sheet with aluminum foil. Place the butter in a small skillet and melt it over medium-high heat. When it starts to shimmer, add the onion and bell pepper and sauté until the onion is translucent, about 3 minutes. Remove the pan from heat and set it aside.

2. Place the egg, 2 tablespoons of the Tartar Sauce, the potato chips, parsley, thyme, salt, and pepper and stir to combine. Fold in the cod and the onion mixture. Working with wet hands, form the mixture into 1½-inch balls, arrange them on the baking sheet, and spray the tops with cooking spray.

3. Place the cod balls in the oven and bake for 12 to 15 minutes, until cooked through. Remove from the oven and serve with the remaining Tartar Sauce.

VARIATIONS

- In addition to cooked fish or seafood of any kind, try cooked and finely chopped chicken or pork.
- Substitute canned tuna, drained and flaked, for the cod.

TILAPIA BALLS IN COCONUT & MACADAMIA SAUCE

YIELD: 4 TO 6 SERVINGS / **ACTIVE TIME:** 25 MINUTES / **TOTAL TIME:** 1 HOUR AND 30 MINUTES

The buttery richness of macadamia nuts and coconut milk make this dish a decadent treat.

1. Rinse the tilapia, pat dry with paper towels, and cut it into 1-inch pieces. Wrap the fish in plastic wrap and freeze for 20 minutes, or until it has firmed up.

2. Place the sesame oil in a large skillet and warm over medium-high heat. When it starts to shimmer, add the scallions, garlic, and ginger and sauté until the scallions are translucent, about 3 minutes. Scrape the mixture into a mixing bowl and set it aside.

3. Place the egg, 2 tablespoons of the coconut milk, and the panko in a separate mixing bowl and stir until combined. Place the tilapia in a food processor, pulse until minced, and then add it to the mixture. Stir in one-third of the scallion mixture, season with salt and pepper, and stir until thoroughly combined. Refrigerate the mixture for 30 minutes.

4. Place the olive oil in the skillet and warm over medium-high heat. When it starts to shimmer, add the mushrooms and sauté until they start to soften, about 3 minutes. Stir in the macadamia nuts, cook for 1 minute, and then add the fish sauce and the remaining scallion mixture and coconut milk. Reduce the heat to medium and bring the sauce to a boil.

5. Form the fish mixture into 1-inch balls and gently lower them into the sauce. Reduce the heat to low, cover the pan, and simmer the fish balls until they are cooked through, about 25 minutes, turning them over after 15 minutes.

6. Combine the cornstarch and water, stir the slurry into the sauce, and cook until it thickens slightly, about 2 minutes. Season with salt and pepper, garnish with the cilantro, and serve immediately.

VARIATION

- Substitute salmon or any firm-fleshed whitefish for the tilapia.

INGREDIENTS:

1¼ LBS. TILAPIA FILLETS

2 TABLESPOONS SESAME OIL

5 SCALLIONS, TRIMMED AND CHOPPED

3 GARLIC CLOVES, MINCED

3-INCH PIECE FRESH GINGER, PEELED AND GRATED

1 LARGE EGG

1 (14 OZ.) CAN COCONUT MILK

½ CUP PANKO

SALT AND PEPPER, TO TASTE

2 TABLESPOONS OLIVE OIL

⅓ LB. SHIITAKE MUSHROOMS, STEMMED AND SLICED

1 CUP CHOPPED SALTED MACADAMIA NUTS

2 TABLESPOONS FISH SAUCE

2 TEASPOONS CORNSTARCH

1 TABLESPOON WATER

¼ CUP FINELY CHOPPED FRESH CILANTRO, FOR GARNISH

HALIBUT BALLS IN GUMBO

YIELD: 4 TO 6 SERVINGS / **ACTIVE TIME:** 45 MINUTES / **TOTAL TIME:** 1 HOUR AND 30 MINUTES

Gumbo, from the Ethiopian word *gombo* (meaning "okra"), is a classic preparation in Louisiana. In this case, however, the gumbo is not thickened with okra, but with filé powder, which is made from the ground roots of a sassafras tree.

INGREDIENTS:

- ⅓ CUP OLIVE OIL
- ½ CUP ALL-PURPOSE FLOUR
- 1½ LBS. HALIBUT FILLETS
- 2 TABLESPOONS UNSALTED BUTTER
- 1 ONION, CHOPPED
- ½ GREEN BELL PEPPER, CHOPPED
- 1 CELERY STALK, CHOPPED
- 3 GARLIC CLOVES, MINCED
- 1 LARGE EGG
- 2 CUPS FISH STOCK (SEE PAGE 672)
- ½ CUP BREAD CRUMBS
- SALT AND PEPPER, TO TASTE
- 1 TABLESPOON FINELY CHOPPED FRESH THYME
- 2 BAY LEAVES
- 1 (14 OZ.) CAN DICED TOMATOES, DRAINED
- ½ TEASPOON HOT SAUCE, OR TO TASTE
- 1 TABLESPOON FILÉ POWDER

1. Preheat the oven to 450°F. Place the oil and flour in a Dutch oven. Place the pot in the oven and bake the roux for 20 to 30 minutes, stirring occasionally, until it has browned.

2. Rinse the halibut, pat dry with paper towels, and cut it into 1-inch pieces. Wrap the fish in plastic wrap and freeze for 20 minutes, or until it has firmed up.

3. Place the butter in a large skillet and melt it over medium-high heat. Add the onion, bell pepper, celery, and garlic and sauté until the onion is translucent, about 3 minutes. Remove the pan from heat and set it aside.

4. Place the egg, 2 tablespoons of the fish stock, and the bread crumbs in a mixing bowl and stir until combined. Place the halibut in a food processor and pulse until it is minced. Add the halibut to the mixing bowl, season with salt and pepper, and stir until thoroughly combined. Refrigerate the mixture for at least 30 minutes.

5. Place the roux over medium heat, add the remaining fish stock, and stir constantly until the mixture comes to a boil and starts to thicken. Add the thyme, bay leaves, tomatoes, hot sauce, and the vegetable mixture and season with salt and pepper. Bring to a boil, reduce the heat to medium-low, and simmer the gumbo for 20 minutes, stirring occasionally.

6. Form fish mixture into 1-inch balls and gently lower them into the simmering sauce. Raise the heat and bring the sauce back to a boil. Reduce the heat to low, cover the pot, and simmer the fish balls until they are cooked through, about 25 minutes, turning them over after 15 minutes. Remove the bay leaves and discard them. Remove the pan from the heat and stir in the filé powder. Season with salt and pepper and serve.

VARIATIONS

- Substitute salmon or any firm-fleshed whitefish for the halibut.
- Use clam juice instead of the stock.
- Add a cup of sliced okra when the remaining Fish Stock is used in Step 5.

A roux is a mixture of fat and flour used to thicken soups and sauces. The first step when making any roux is to cook the flour in the fat, so that the dish doesn't end up tasting like paste. For white sauces, this is done over low heat and the fat used is butter. Many Creole and Cajun dishes, such as gumbo, use a fuller-flavored brown roux that is made with oil or drippings and cooked to a deep brown. This darker roux gives dishes an almost nutty flavor.

TILAPIA BALL CURRY

YIELD: 4 TO 6 SERVINGS / **ACTIVE TIME:** 20 MINUTES / **TOTAL TIME:** 1 HOUR

The coconut milk tempers the spice just enough to ensure that your experience is pure pleasure.

INGREDIENTS:

2 TABLESPOONS OLIVE OIL

2 YELLOW ONIONS, PEELED AND SLICED

2 RED BELL PEPPERS, STEMMED, SEEDS AND RIBS REMOVED, AND SLICED

3 TABLESPOONS MASHED GINGER

1 GARLIC CLOVE, MASHED

3 TABLESPOONS GREEN CURRY PASTE

3 TABLESPOONS FISH SAUCE

1 TABLESPOON MADRAS CURRY POWDER

1 (14 OZ.) CAN COCONUT MILK

2 TABLESPOONS CHOPPED THAI BASIL, PLUS MORE FOR GARNISH

TILAPIA BALLS (SEE PAGE 385)

FRESH CILANTRO, FINELY CHOPPED, FOR GARNISH

LIME WEDGES, FOR SERVING

1. Place the olive oil in a skillet and warm over medium-high heat. When the oil starts to shimmer, add the onions, peppers, ginger, and garlic and sauté until the vegetables start to soften, 5 to 7 minutes.

2. Stir in the curry paste and cook until fragrant, about 2 minutes. Add the fish sauce, Madras curry powder, coconut milk, and Thai basil and stir until incorporated. Place the fish balls in the curry and cook until warmed through, about 5 minutes. Garnish with cilantro and serve with lime wedges.

MUSTARD & DILL SALMON BALLS

YIELD: 4 TO 6 SERVINGS / **ACTIVE TIME:** 25 MINUTES / **TOTAL TIME:** 1 HOUR AND 15 MINUTES

The use of aromatic fresh dill can be found in Greek cuisine, as well as in Scandinavian countries. This dish has northern European inspiration because it blends the fresh herb with piquant mustard.

INGREDIENTS:

- 1¼ LBS. SALMON FILLETS, SKIN REMOVED
- 1 LARGE EGG
- ½ CUP MAYONNAISE
- ⅓ CUP DIJON MUSTARD
- ½ CUP BREAD CRUMBS
- ⅓ CUP CHOPPED FRESH DILL
- SALT AND PEPPER, TO TASTE
- ¼ CUP SOUR CREAM
- 2 TEASPOONS FRESH LEMON JUICE

1. Rinse the salmon, pat it dry with paper towels, and cut into 1-inch pieces. Wrap the fish in plastic wrap and freeze for 20 minutes, or until it has firmed up.

2. Preheat the oven to 425°F and line a rimmed baking sheet with aluminum foil. Place the egg, 2 tablespoons of the mayonnaise, 2 tablespoons of the mustard, the bread crumbs, and 3 tablespoons of the dill in a mixing bowl and stir until combined. Place the salmon in a food processor and pulse until it is minced. Add the salmon to the mixture, season with salt and pepper, and stir until thoroughly combined.

3. Working with wet hands, form the mixture into 1½-inch balls, arrange them on the baking sheet, and spray the tops with cooking spray. Place the salmon balls in the oven and bake for 12 to 15 minutes, until cooked through.

4. While the salmon balls are in the oven, combine the sour cream, lemon juice, and the remaining mayonnaise, mustard, and dill. Serve alongside the baked salmon balls.

VARIATIONS

- Substitute tuna or any firm-fleshed whitefish like halibut or cod for the salmon.
- Serve with Hollandaise Sauce (see page 726) instead of the mustard & dill mayo.

SALMON BALLS NIÇOISE

YIELD: 4 TO 6 SERVINGS / **ACTIVE TIME:** 30 MINUTES / **TOTAL TIME:** 1 HOUR AND 15 MINUTES

These baked salmon balls, dotted with olives, are greatly improved from the salmon cakes I ate as a child, which suffered from canned, instead of fresh, salmon.

INGREDIENTS:

- 1¼ LBS. SALMON FILLETS, SKIN REMOVED
- 1 LARGE EGG
- 2 TABLESPOONS MAYONNAISE
- 1 TABLESPOON DIJON MUSTARD
- ½ CUP MASHED POTATOES
- ¼ CUP CHOPPED OIL-CURED BLACK OLIVES
- 1 SHALLOT, MINCED
- 2 TABLESPOONS FINELY CHOPPED FRESH PARSLEY
- 2 TABLESPOONS SMALL CAPERS, DRAINED AND RINSED
- 1 TABLESPOON HERBES DE PROVENCE
- SALT AND PEPPER, TO TASTE
- 1 CUP SUN-DRIED TOMATO SAUCE (SEE PAGE 679), FOR SERVING

1. Rinse the salmon, pat dry with paper towels, and cut it into 1-inch pieces. Wrap the fish in plastic wrap and freeze for 20 minutes, or until it has firmed up.

2. Preheat the oven to 425°F and line a rimmed baking sheet with aluminum foil. Place the egg, mayonnaise, mustard, potatoes, olives, shallot, parsley, capers, and Herbes de Provence in a mixing bowl and stir until combined. Place the salmon in a food processor and pulse until minced. Add the salmon to the mixture, season with salt and pepper, and stir until thoroughly combined.

3. Working with wet hands, form the mixture into 1½-inch balls, arrange them on the baking sheet, and spray the tops with cooking spray. Place the salmon balls in the oven and bake for 12 to 15 minutes, until cooked through. Remove from the oven and serve with the Sun-Dried Tomato Sauce.

VARIATION

- Substitute tuna or any firm-fleshed whitefish like halibut or cod for the salmon.

CREAMY SNAPPER BALLS

YIELD: 4 TO 6 SERVINGS / **ACTIVE TIME:** 30 MINUTES / **TOTAL TIME:** 1 HOUR AND 30 MINUTES

These lean and luscious balls made from red snapper are poached in a brightly colored cream sauce that is laced with the pleasant bite of tequila.

INGREDIENTS:

- 1½ LBS. RED SNAPPER FILLETS, SKIN REMOVED
- 4 LARGE DRIED ANCHO CHILI PEPPERS, STEMMED, SEEDED, AND TORN
- 2 TABLESPOONS OLIVE OIL
- 1 ONION, CHOPPED
- 1 LARGE EGG
- 1 CUP HALF-AND-HALF
- ½ CUP PANKO
- SALT AND PEPPER, TO TASTE
- 2 TABLESPOONS BALSAMIC VINEGAR
- 4 GARLIC CLOVES, PEELED
- 2 TEASPOONS DRIED OREGANO
- ⅓ CUP TEQUILA
- 2 TEASPOONS CORNSTARCH
- 1 TABLESPOON WATER
- ¼ CUP CHOPPED FRESH CILANTRO

1. Rinse the snapper, pat dry with paper towels, and cut it into 1-inch pieces. Wrap the fish in plastic wrap and freeze for 20 minutes, or until it has firmed up. Place the dried chilies in a bowl, cover them with boiling water, and let them soak for 15 minutes.

2. Place the oil in a large skillet and warm over medium-high heat. When it starts to shimmer, add the onion and sauté until it is translucent, about 3 minutes. Remove the pan from heat and set it aside.

3. Place the egg, 2 tablespoons of the half-and-half, and the panko in a mixing bowl and stir until combined. Place the snapper in a food processor and pulse until it is minced. Add half of the onion and all of the snapper to the mixing bowl, season with salt and pepper, and stir until thoroughly combined. Refrigerate the mixture for 30 minutes.

4. Place the vinegar, garlic, oregano, chilies, and the soaking liquid in a food processor and puree until smooth. Add the puree to the onion left in the skillet along with the tequila and remaining half-and-half. Bring to a boil over medium-high heat, stirring occasionally. Reduce the heat to low and simmer the sauce for 10 minutes.

5. Form the fish mixture into 1-inch balls and gently lower them into the simmering sauce. Raise the heat and bring the sauce to a boil. Reduce the heat to low, cover the pan, and simmer the fish balls until cooked through, about 25 minutes, turning them over after 15 minutes.

6. Combine the cornstarch and water, stir the slurry into the sauce, and cook until it thickens slightly, about 2 minutes. Season with salt and pepper, stir in the cilantro, and serve immediately.

VARIATION

- Substitute salmon or any firm-fleshed whitefish like halibut, grouper, or cod for the snapper.

SWEET & SAVORY SALMON BALLS

YIELD: 4 TO 6 SERVINGS / **ACTIVE TIME:** 20 MINUTES / **TOTAL TIME:** 50 MINUTES

The Omega-3 fatty acids in salmon make this fish a popular choice, and the sweet-and-savory fusion that is so indicative of Asian cooking makes this preparation a favorite at parties everywhere.

INGREDIENTS:

- 1¼ LBS. SALMON FILLETS, SKIN REMOVED
- 1 LARGE EGG
- 2 TABLESPOONS HOISIN SAUCE
- 2 TABLESPOONS MAYONNAISE
- 1 TABLESPOON SESAME OIL
- 1 TABLESPOON SOY SAUCE
- 1 CUP PANKO
- ¼ CUP CHOPPED FRESH CILANTRO
- 3 SCALLIONS, TRIMMED AND CHOPPED
- 1-INCH PIECE FRESH GINGER, PEELED AND GRATED
- 2 GARLIC CLOVES, MINCED
- SALT AND PEPPER, TO TASTE
- 1 CUP PONZU SAUCE (SEE PAGE 749), FOR SERVING

1. Rinse the salmon, pat dry with paper towels, and cut it into 1-inch pieces. Wrap the fish in plastic wrap and freeze for 20 minutes, or until it has firmed up.

2. Preheat the oven to 425°F and line a rimmed baking sheet with aluminum foil. Place the egg, hoisin sauce, mayonnaise, sesame oil, soy sauce, ½ cup of the panko, the cilantro, scallions, ginger, and garlic in a mixing bowl and stir until combined. Place the salmon in a food processor and pulse until it is minced. Add the salmon to the mixture, season with salt and pepper, and stir until thoroughly combined.

3. Working with wet hands, form the mixture into 1½-inch balls and roll them in the remaining bread crumbs, gently pressing down to make sure they adhere. Arrange the salmon balls on the baking sheet and spray the tops with cooking spray.

4. Place the salmon balls in the oven and bake for 12 to 15 minutes, until cooked through. Remove the pan from the oven and serve, accompanied by a bowl of Ponzu Sauce.

VARIATION

- Substitute tuna or any firm-fleshed whitefish like halibut or cod for the salmon.

GREEK TUNA BALLS

YIELD: 4 TO 6 SERVINGS / **ACTIVE TIME:** 25 MINUTES / **TOTAL TIME:** 50 MINUTES

While I prefer the imported Italian tuna packed in olive oil because it has more flavor and moisture, there's so much going on in this sauce that any type of canned tuna will be just fine.

INGREDIENTS:

2 TABLESPOONS MAYONNAISE

1 LARGE EGG

½ CUP ITALIAN BREAD CRUMBS

¼ CUP GRATED PARMESAN CHEESE

3 (6 OZ.) CANS TUNA, DRAINED AND FLAKED

SALT AND PEPPER, TO TASTE

2 TABLESPOONS OLIVE OIL

1 SMALL ONION, CHOPPED

3 GARLIC CLOVES, MINCED

1 CELERY STALK, CHOPPED

1 (28 OZ.) CAN CRUSHED TOMATOES, WITH THEIR LIQUID

½ CUP DRY WHITE WINE

¾ CUP PITTED AND CHOPPED KALAMATA OLIVES

¼ CUP CAPERS, DRAINED AND RINSED

¼ CUP CHOPPED FRESH PARSLEY

3 TABLESPOONS FINELY CHOPPED FRESH OREGANO

1 BAY LEAF

1. Preheat the oven to 425°F and line a rimmed baking sheet with aluminum foil. Place the mayonnaise, egg, bread crumbs, and cheese in a mixing bowl and stir to combine. Fold in the tuna and season with salt and pepper.

2. Working with wet hands, form the mixture into 1½-inch balls, arrange them on the baking sheet, and spray the tops with cooking spray.

3. Place in the oven and bake for 8 to 10 minutes, until lightly browned. Remove from the oven and set aside.

4. While the tuna balls are in the oven, place the oil in a skillet and warm over medium-high heat. When it starts to shimmer, add the onion, garlic, and celery and sauté until the onion is translucent, about 3 minutes. Stir in the tomatoes, wine, olives, capers, parsley, oregano, and bay leaf and bring the sauce to a boil. Reduce the heat to medium and simmer the sauce for 15 minutes.

5. Add the tuna balls to the sauce and simmer for 10 minutes. Remove the bay leaf and discard it, season with salt and pepper, and serve immediately.

VARIATIONS

- In addition to cooked fish or seafood of any kind, try cooked and minced chicken or pork.
- Substitute 3 (6 oz.) cans of salmon, drained, skin and bones removed and discarded, and flaked for the tuna.

GRILLED TUNA BALLS WITH WASABI MAYONNAISE

YIELD: 4 TO 6 SERVINGS / **ACTIVE TIME:** 20 MINUTES / **TOTAL TIME:** 1 HOUR AND 15 MINUTES

Tuna steaks grilled rare are very popular, even with people who prefer other foods well done. There are so many luscious flavors in this recipe, which is a seared take on the Hawaiian poke bowl.

INGREDIENTS:

- 1¼ LBS. TUNA STEAKS
- 3 SCALLION WHITES, CHOPPED
- 2 GARLIC CLOVES, MINCED
- 2-INCH PIECE FRESH GINGER, PEELED AND GRATED
- 2 TABLESPOONS FISH SAUCE
- 1 TABLESPOON MIRIN
- SALT AND PEPPER, TO TASTE
- 1 TABLESPOON WASABI POWDER
- 2 TABLESPOONS COLD WATER
- ⅔ CUP MAYONNAISE
- 3 TABLESPOONS MINCED PICKLED GINGER
- 2 TEASPOONS SESAME OIL

1. If using bamboo skewers, soak them in cold water. Rinse the tuna, pat dry with paper towels, and cut it into 1-inch pieces, discarding any sinew. Wrap the fish in plastic wrap and freeze for 20 minutes, or until it has firmed up.

2. Place the tuna in a food processor and pulse until minced. Place the tuna in a mixing bowl, add the scallions, garlic, grated ginger, fish sauce, mirin, salt, and pepper, and stir until thoroughly combined. Divide the mixture into 8 to 12 portions and form each one into a sausage shape. Insert a skewer into each meatball so that the tip of the skewer just clears the top end. Cover the skewers with plastic wrap and refrigerate for 30 minutes.

3. While the meatballs are in the refrigerator, preheat your gas or charcoal grill to medium-high heat (450°F). Place the wasabi and water in a mixing bowl and stir until the mixture is a paste. Stir in the mayonnaise, pickled ginger, and sesame oil and store in the refrigerator.

4. Place the meatballs on the grill and cook, turning them as they brown, until just cooked through, 4 to 6 minutes. If using a charcoal grill, leave it uncovered while cooking the meatballs. Serve with the wasabi sauce.

VARIATION

- Substitute salmon or any firm-fleshed whitefish like halibut or cod for the tuna.

GRILLED TUNA BALLS WITH AIOLI

YIELD: 4 TO 6 SERVINGS / **ACTIVE TIME:** 25 MINUTES / **TOTAL TIME:** 1 HOUR AND 15 MINUTES

This recipe is the next generation of the old-school tuna tartare. The flavorful contrast of the seared exterior and almost raw interior of these skewers is what makes them special.

1. If using bamboo skewers, soak them in cold water. Rinse the tuna, pat dry with paper towels, and cut it into 1-inch pieces, discarding any sinew. Wrap the fish in a sheet of plastic wrap and freeze for 20 minutes, or until it has firmed up.

2. Place the tuna in a food processor and pulse until minced. Place the tuna in a mixing bowl, add the parsley, shallots, capers, horseradish, lemon juice, mustard, salt, and pepper and stir until thoroughly combined. Divide the mixture into 8 to 12 portions and form each one into a sausage shape. Insert a skewer into each meatball so that the tip of the skewer just clears the top end. Cover the skewers with plastic wrap and refrigerate for 30 minutes.

3. While the meatballs are in the refrigerator, preheat your gas or charcoal grill to medium-high heat (450°F). Place the meatballs on the grill and cook, turning them as they brown, until just cooked through, 4 to 6 minutes. If using a charcoal grill, leave it uncovered while cooking the meatballs. Serve alongside the Easy Aioli.

VARIATION

- Substitute salmon or any firm-fleshed whitefish like halibut or cod for the tuna.

INGREDIENTS:

1¼ LBS. TUNA STEAKS

½ CUP CHOPPED FRESH PARSLEY

2 SHALLOTS, CHOPPED

3 TABLESPOONS CAPERS, DRAINED AND RINSED

2 TABLESPOONS PREPARED HORSERADISH

2 TABLESPOONS FRESH LEMON JUICE

2 TABLESPOONS DIJON MUSTARD

SALT AND PEPPER, TO TASTE

1 CUP EASY AIOLI (SEE PAGE 725), FOR SERVING

TAKOYAKI

YIELD: 4 SERVINGS / **ACTIVE TIME:** 20 MINUTES / **TOTAL TIME:** 20 MINUTES

These octopus balls are the perfect party food: unusual and delicious enough to impress and simple enough to partner with a nice, cold beer.

INGREDIENTS:

2 TEASPOONS SAKE

2 TEASPOONS MIRIN

2 TEASPOONS SOY SAUCE

2 TEASPOONS OYSTER SAUCE

2 TEASPOONS WORCESTERSHIRE SAUCE

1 TABLESPOON SUGAR

1 TABLESPOON KETCHUP

SALT AND WHITE PEPPER, TO TASTE

2 TABLESPOONS WATER, PLUS MORE AS NEEDED

1 LARGE EGG

1½ CUPS CHICKEN STOCK (SEE PAGE 660)

¾ CUP ALL-PURPOSE FLOUR

1 CUP MINCED COOKED OCTOPUS

2 SCALLION GREENS, SLICED THIN

¼ CUP MINCED PICKLED GINGER

TAKOYAKI SAUCE (SEE PAGE 753), FOR SERVING

1. Place the sake, mirin, soy sauce, oyster sauce, Worcestershire sauce, sugar, ketchup, salt, and white pepper in a mixing bowl and stir to combine. Set the mixture aside.

2. Place the water, egg, and stock in a bowl and stir until combined. Sprinkle the flour over the mixture and stir until all of the flour has been incorporated and the mixture is a thick batter. Add the sake-and-mirin mixture and stir to incorporate. Pour the batter into a measuring cup with a spout.

3. Grease the wells of an aebleskiver pan with cooking spray and place it over medium heat. When the pan is hot, fill the wells of the pan halfway and add a pinch of octopus, scallion, and pickled ginger to each. Fill the wells the rest of the way with the batter, until they are almost overflowing. Cook for approximately 2 minutes and carefully flip each ball over. Turn as needed until they are golden brown on both sides and piping hot. Serve immediately alongside the Takoyaki Sauce.

TIP: You can also use a cast-iron skillet to prepare the takoyaki, though they will not have the traditional round shape. To prepare them in a skillet, simply add the batter in ¼ cup portions, sprinkle the octopus, scallion, and pickled ginger on top, and use a thin spatula to flip them over.

VEGETARIAN MEATBALLS

The following recipes are for "meatballs" that contain no meat. Instead, you'll find a wide range of ingredients bound together before being baked or fried. Many of the ingredients used—dried beans, for instance—are an excellent source of protein and other nutrients, too, so don't fret.

In my omnivore household, most of the recipes here are served as an hors d'oeuvre or a side dish to lend a simple entree a touch of intrigue. But many are satisfying enough to be served over a tossed salad for a light lunch. Please note: serving sizes are in terms of main-dish portions to remain consistent with recipes in the rest of the book. If serving them as a side or snack, they can easily feed twice that number.

FALAFEL

YIELD: 6 TO 8 SERVINGS / **ACTIVE TIME:** 30 MINUTES / **TOTAL TIME:** 24 HOURS

While falafel can be made with fava beans, it is usually prepared with garbanzo beans. What differentiates falafel from other bean balls is that the beans are soaked—but not cooked—before they are ground. That is why dried beans are specified; canned beans would add too much moisture.

INGREDIENTS:

- 1 LB. DRIED GARBANZO BEANS
- 1 SMALL ONION, DICED
- 3 GARLIC CLOVES
- ¼ CUP ALL-PURPOSE FLOUR
- 2 TABLESPOONS FINELY CHOPPED FRESH PARSLEY
- 1 TABLESPOON FRESH LEMON JUICE
- 1 TABLESPOON CORIANDER
- 2 TEASPOONS CUMIN
- 1 TEASPOON BAKING SODA
- SALT AND CAYENNE PEPPER, TO TASTE
- VEGETABLE OIL, AS NEEDED
- 1 CUP TAHINI OR TRADITIONAL HUMMUS (SEE PAGES 733 OR 710, RESPECTIVELY), FOR SERVING

1. Cover the garbanzo beans with cold water and soak overnight.

2. Drain the beans and place them in a food processor. Add the onion, garlic, flour, parsley, lemon juice, coriander, cumin, baking soda, salt, and cayenne and blitz until the mixture is a smooth paste, scraping the work bowl as necessary.

3. Form the mixture into 1-inch balls, place them on a parchment-lined baking sheet, cover tightly with plastic wrap, and refrigerate for 20 minutes.

4. Add oil to a Dutch oven until it is approximately 2 inches deep and warm to 375°F over medium-high heat. Working in batches, add the falafel and fry until browned all over, about 3 minutes. Transfer the cooked falafel to a paper towel–lined plate to drain. When all of the falafel have been cooked, serve them with Tahini or Traditional Hummus.

VARIATION

- Omit the coriander and cumin, and add 2 tablespoons chili powder; substitute cilantro for the parsley. This will make these more American than Middle Eastern.

BLACK-EYED PEA BALLS

YIELD: 4 TO 6 SERVINGS / **ACTIVE TIME:** 30 MINUTES / **TOTAL TIME:** 24 HOURS

Called *akla* in Ghana and *akara* in other parts of the African continent, these spicy morsels are similar to falafel. And, like falafel, the beans are soaked but not cooked before frying. They are traditionally eaten with a spicy relish, but I prefer a sauce for dipping.

INGREDIENTS:

- ½ LB. DRIED BLACK-EYED PEAS
- 1 ONION, CHOPPED
- 3 GARLIC CLOVES
- 1 SMALL JALAPEÑO OR SERRANO PEPPER, STEMMED, SEEDS AND RIBS REMOVED, AND CHOPPED
- 1 LARGE EGG
- 3 TABLESPOONS WATER
- SALT AND PEPPER, TO TASTE
- VEGETABLE OIL, AS NEEDED
- 1 CUP SOFRITO (SEE PAGE 677), WARMED, FOR SERVING

1. Cover the black-eyed peas with cold water and soak overnight.

2. Drain the beans and place them in a food processor. Add the onion, garlic, chili pepper, egg, water, salt, and pepper and blitz until the mixture is a smooth paste, scraping the work bowl as necessary.

3. Form the mixture into 1-inch balls, place them on a parchment-lined baking sheet, cover tightly with plastic wrap, and refrigerate for 20 minutes.

4. Add oil to a Dutch oven until it is approximately 2 inches deep and warm it to 375°F over medium-high heat. Working in batches, add the balls and fry until they are golden brown, about 3 minutes. Transfer the cooked balls to a paper towel–lined plate to drain. When all of the balls have been cooked, serve alongside a bowl of Sofrito.

VARIATION

- Replace the black-eyed peas with kidney beans or small navy beans.

LENTIL BALLS

YIELD: 4 TO 6 SERVINGS / **ACTIVE TIME:** 20 MINUTES / **TOTAL TIME:** 1 HOUR AND 15 MINUTES

Lentils are the "meatiest" of the legumes, and you will find that even devout carnivores adore these flavorful treats, which benefit from a touch of Middle Eastern flair.

INGREDIENTS:

- 2 CUPS LENTILS, PICKED OVER, RINSED, AND DRAINED
- 1 TEASPOON KOSHER SALT, PLUS MORE TO TASTE
- ¾ CUP PINE NUTS
- 1 LARGE EGG
- 2 TABLESPOONS TOMATO JUICE
- 1 TABLESPOON TOMATO PASTE
- 1 CUP BREAD CRUMBS
- 2 TABLESPOONS OLIVE OIL
- 1 ONION, CHOPPED
- 2 GARLIC CLOVES, MINCED
- 2 TEASPOONS CORIANDER
- 1 TEASPOON CUMIN
- BLACK PEPPER, TO TASTE
- 1 CUP GREEK FETA SAUCE (SEE PAGE 730), FOR SERVING

1. Place the lentils in a large saucepan, cover with water, and add the salt. Bring to a boil over medium-high heat, reduce the heat to low, cover the pan, and simmer the lentils until they are tender, about 20 minutes. Drain the lentils and set them aside.

2. While the lentils are simmering, place the pine nuts in a small dry skillet and toast over medium-high heat, shaking the pan frequently, until the pine nuts are browned, about 2 minutes. Remove the nuts from the pan and set them aside.

3. Place the egg, tomato juice, tomato paste, and ½ cup of the bread crumbs in a mixing bowl and stir until combined. Add the lentils and stir until the mixture is thoroughly combined.

4. Place the oil in a skillet and warm over medium-high heat. When it starts to shimmer, add the onion and garlic and sauté until the onion is translucent, about 3 minutes. Stir in the coriander and cumin and cook for 1 minute. Stir the onion mixture into the lentil mixture.

5. Place ½ cup of the pine nuts and 1 cup of the lentil mixture in a food processor and blitz until smooth. Return the mixture to the mixing bowl and stir in the remaining pine nuts. Season with salt and pepper and refrigerate for 30 minutes. Preheat the oven to 450°F and line a rimmed baking sheet with aluminum foil.

6. Place the remaining bread crumbs in a shallow bowl. Working with wet hands, form the mixture into 1½-inch balls and roll them in the bread crumbs, gently pressing down to make sure that they adhere. Arrange the lentil balls on the baking sheet and spray the tops with cooking spray.

7. Place the lentil balls in the oven and bake for 12 to 15 minutes, until cooked through. Remove from the oven and serve with the Greek Feta Sauce.

VEGETARIAN SHEPHERD'S PIE

YIELD: 4 TO 6 SERVINGS / **ACTIVE TIME:** 45 MINUTES / **TOTAL TIME:** 1 HOUR AND 30 MINUTES

The chard, mushrooms, and Lentil Balls make this humble pie feel richer on the palate than the stomach.

INGREDIENTS:

- 6 RUSSET POTATOES, PEELED AND CHOPPED
- ½ TEASPOON KOSHER SALT, PLUS MORE TO TASTE
- 11 TABLESPOONS UNSALTED BUTTER, DIVIDED INTO INDIVIDUAL TABLESPOONS
- ½ CUP MILK
- ¼ CUP PLAIN YOGURT
- BLACK PEPPER, TO TASTE
- 1 SMALL ONION, MINCED
- 3 CUPS CHOPPED MUSHROOMS
- 1 BUNCH SWISS CHARD, WASHED AND CHOPPED
- 1 TABLESPOON WORCESTERSHIRE SAUCE
- LENTIL BALLS (SEE PAGE 412)

1. Preheat the oven to 350°F. Place the potatoes in a large saucepan and cover with cold water. Add the salt. Bring the water to a boil, reduce to a simmer, and cook the potatoes until fork-tender, about 20 minutes.

2. Drain the potatoes and place them in a large bowl. Add 6 tablespoons of the butter, the milk, and the yogurt and mash the potatoes until they are smooth and creamy. Season with salt and pepper and set aside.

3. In a 12-inch cast-iron skillet, melt 3 tablespoons of the butter over medium heat. Add the onion and sauté until it is translucent, about 3 minutes. Add the mushrooms, the chopped stems of the chard (not the leaves), and the Worcestershire sauce. Cook for about 3 minutes, stirring frequently, then reduce the heat to low and continue to cook until the chard stems are tender, another 5 minutes.

4. Increase the heat to medium and add the chard leaves. Cook, while stirring constantly, until the leaves wilt, about 3 minutes. Remove the skillet from heat and season with salt and pepper.

5. Place the Lentil Balls on top of the vegetable mixture, then spread the mashed potatoes over the top, smoothing the surface with a rubber spatula. Cut the remaining 2 tablespoons of butter into slivers and dot the potatoes with them.

6. Cover with foil and bake for 25 minutes. Remove the foil and bake for another 10 minutes, until the potatoes are just browned and the filling is bubbly. Remove and briefly let cool before serving.

BLACK BEAN BALLS

YIELD: 4 TO 6 SERVINGS / **ACTIVE TIME:** 25 MINUTES / **TOTAL TIME:** 1 HOUR

These flavorful treats feature a host of traditional Southwestern ingredients—including chili powder, chilies, and cilantro.

1. Place the olive oil in a large skillet and warm over medium-high heat. When it starts to shimmer, add the onion, garlic, and chili peppers and sauté until the onion is translucent, about 3 minutes. Stir in the chili powder and cumin, cook for 1 minute, and then add the black beans, cilantro, and water. Bring the mixture to a boil, reduce heat to medium-low, and simmer, stirring frequently, for 3 minutes.

2. Transfer the mixture to a food processor and puree until smooth. Scrape the mixture into a mixing bowl and season with salt and pepper. Form the mixture into 1-inch balls, place them on a parchment-lined baking sheet, cover tightly with plastic wrap, and refrigerate for 30 minutes.

3. Add vegetable oil to a Dutch oven until it is approximately 2 inches deep and warm to 375°F over medium-high heat. Working in batches, add the black bean balls to the oil and fry until crispy, about 3 minutes. Transfer the cooked balls to a paper towel–lined plate to drain. When all of the black bean balls have been cooked, serve alongside a bowl of Creamy Chipotle Sauce or Tomatillo Salsa.

VARIATION

- Substitute kidney beans, garbanzo beans, or small navy beans for the black beans.

INGREDIENTS:

- 2 TABLESPOONS OLIVE OIL
- 1 ONION, CHOPPED
- 3 GARLIC CLOVES, MINCED
- 2 JALAPEÑO OR SERRANO PEPPERS, STEMMED, SEEDS AND RIBS REMOVED, AND CHOPPED
- 2 TABLESPOONS CHILI POWDER
- 1½ TABLESPOONS CUMIN
- 2 (14 OZ.) CANS BLACK BEANS, DRAINED AND RINSED
- ½ CUP CHOPPED FRESH CILANTRO
- ½ CUP WATER
- SALT AND PEPPER, TO TASTE
- VEGETABLE OIL, AS NEEDED
- 1 CUP CREAMY CHIPOTLE SAUCE OR TOMATILLO SALSA (SEE PAGES 729 OR 761, RESPECTIVELY), FOR SERVING

Chili powder is a spice blend that you can make at home. To do so, combine 2 tablespoons ground red chili pepper, 2 tablespoons paprika, 1 tablespoon coriander, 1 tablespoon garlic powder, 1 tablespoon onion powder, 2 teaspoons cumin, 2 teaspoons cayenne pepper, 1 teaspoon black pepper, and 1 teaspoon dried oregano.

BOLLITOS DE YUCA

YIELD: 4 SERVINGS / **ACTIVE TIME:** 20 MINUTES / **TOTAL TIME:** 4 HOURS

A classic recipe from the Dominican Republic. As yuca is very mild, the Tropical Salsa makes for an ideal match.

1. Place the yuca and salt in a large saucepan and cover with water. Bring to a boil and cook until the yuca is tender, about 20 minutes. Drain, place the yuca in a food processor, and blitz until smooth.

2. Stir the butter, parsley, and milk into the yuca puree, season with salt, and let the mixture cool to room temperature.

3. Place 1 tablespoon of the mixture in the palm of one hand. Flatten it, put a cheese cube in the center and form a ball around the cheese. Place the balls on a baking sheet and repeat with the remaining puree and cheese. Place the balls on a parchment-lined baking sheet and refrigerate for 2 hours.

4. Add vegetable oil to a Dutch oven until it is approximately 2 inches deep and warm to 350°F over medium heat. Place the egg in a small bowl and whisk until scrambled. Place the flour in another bowl. Dip a ball into the egg, then into the flour until it is completely coated. Shake to remove any excess and gently drop the balls into the oil. Fry, turning them as they cook, until they are golden brown all over, 3 to 5 minutes. Transfer the cooked balls to a paper towel-lined plate to drain. When all of the balls have been cooked, serve with the Tropical Salsa.

INGREDIENTS:

- 1 LB. YUCA, PEELED
- 1 TABLESPOON KOSHER SALT, PLUS MORE TO TASTE
- 2 TABLESPOONS UNSALTED BUTTER
- 1 TEASPOON FINELY CHOPPED FRESH PARSLEY
- ¼ CUP MILK
- ½ LB. CHEDDAR CHEESE, CUT INTO 1-INCH CUBES
- 1 EGG
- ¼ CUP ALL-PURPOSE FLOUR
- VEGETABLE OIL, AS NEEDED
- TROPICAL SALSA (SEE PAGE 762), FOR SERVING

KIDNEY BEAN & SWEET POTATO BALLS

YIELD: 4 TO 6 SERVINGS / **ACTIVE TIME:** 30 MINUTES / **TOTAL TIME:** 1 HOUR AND 15 MINUTES

These colorful balls are mildly seasoned to let the sweet potatoes shine, and make a great side for any grilled meat.

INGREDIENTS:

- ½ LB. SWEET POTATOES, PEELED AND CHOPPED
- SALT AND PEPPER, TO TASTE
- 3 SCALLIONS, TRIMMED AND CHOPPED
- 2 TABLESPOONS FINELY CHOPPED FRESH PARSLEY
- 1 TABLESPOON FINELY CHOPPED FRESH SAGE
- 1 (14 OZ.) CAN KIDNEY BEANS, DRAINED AND RINSED
- 2 GARLIC CLOVES
- ½ TEASPOON BAKING POWDER
- VEGETABLE OIL, AS NEEDED
- 1 CUP SOUTHERN BARBECUE SAUCE (SEE PAGE 684), FOR SERVING

1. Place the sweet potatoes in a saucepan, cover with water, season with salt, and bring to a boil over high heat. Reduce the heat to medium and cook the sweet potatoes until fork-tender, about 20 minutes. Drain the sweet potatoes and place them in a mixing bowl. Mash until smooth and then stir in the scallions, parsley, and sage.

2. Place the beans, garlic, baking powder, salt, and pepper in a food processor and blitz until the mixture is a smooth paste, scraping the work bowl as necessary. Add the mixture to the mashed sweet potatoes and stir until thoroughly combined. Form the mixture into 1-inch balls, place them on a parchment-lined baking sheet, cover with plastic wrap, and refrigerate for 30 minutes.

3. Add oil to a Dutch oven until it is approximately 2 inches deep and warm to 375°F over medium-high heat. Working in batches, add the balls to the oil and fry until crispy and golden brown. Transfer the cooked balls to a paper towel–lined plate to drain. When all of the balls have been cooked, serve them with the Southern Barbecue Sauce.

VARIATION

- Substitute black-eyed peas, garbanzo beans, or small navy beans in place of the kidney beans.

ARANCINI

YIELD: 4 TO 6 SERVINGS / **ACTIVE TIME:** 45 MINUTES / **TOTAL TIME:** 3 HOURS

In Italian, *arancini* means "little oranges," and these cheese-stuffed rice balls are a staple of Sicilian cooking. If you happen to have some leftover risotto, they can come together much quicker than the time indicated above.

INGREDIENTS:

- 5 CUPS CHICKEN STOCK (SEE PAGE 660)
- 3 TABLESPOONS UNSALTED BUTTER
- 1 ONION, CHOPPED
- 2 GARLIC CLOVES, MINCED
- 2 CUPS ARBORIO RICE
- ¾ CUP WHITE WINE
- 1¼ CUPS GRATED PARMESAN CHEESE
- SALT AND PEPPER, TO TASTE
- 2 LARGE EGGS
- 1½ CUPS ITALIAN BREAD CRUMBS
- 2 OZ. FRESH MOZZARELLA CHEESE, CUT INTO ½-INCH CUBES
- VEGETABLE OIL, AS NEEDED

1. Place the stock in a saucepan and warm over medium heat until it just comes to a simmer. Remove from heat and set the stock aside.

2. Place the butter in a heavy saucepan and melt it over medium-high heat. Add the onion and garlic and sauté until the onion is translucent, about 3 minutes. Add the rice, stir to coat with butter, and raise the heat to high. Add the wine and cook, stirring constantly, until it has been absorbed, 2 to 3 minutes. Reduce the heat to medium and incorporate the warmed stock 1 cup at a time. Stir constantly and wait for the rice to absorb the stock before adding the next portion. Stir ¾ cup of the Parmesan into the risotto, season with salt and pepper, and place it in a 9 x 13–inch baking pan. Refrigerate for 2 hours.

3. Place the eggs, remaining Parmesan, ½ cup of the bread crumbs, and 2 cups of the risotto in a mixing bowl and stir until combined. Place the remaining bread crumbs in a shallow bowl. Measure out a tablespoon of the mixture, press a piece of mozzarella into it, and form a ball around the cheese. Roll the arancini in the bread crumbs and place it on a parchment-lined baking sheet. Repeat until all of the rice mixture has been used.

4. Preheat the oven to 150°F. Add oil to a Dutch oven until it is approximately 2 inches deep and warm to 375°F over medium-high heat. Line a baking sheet with paper towels and place it in the oven. Working in batches, add the arancini to the oil and fry until crispy and golden brown about 3 minutes. Transfer the cooked arancini to the baking sheet to drain and keep warm. Serve once all of the arancini have been cooked.

VARIATIONS

- Add ½ teaspoon crushed saffron to the stock and the interiors of the rice balls will take on a bright yellow color.
- Sauté ⅓ lb. chopped wild mushrooms in 2 tablespoons unsalted butter and add them to the risotto with the Parmesan.
- Add 2 cups chopped fresh spinach or half of a 10 oz. package of frozen chopped spinach to the risotto as it cooks.
- Stir 1 cup cooked and pureed asparagus into the stock as it warms.
- Add ¼ cup chopped fresh herbs (some combination of parsley, basil, oregano, thyme, and rosemary) to the risotto as it cooks.

DILL PICKLE ARANCINI

YIELD: 8 SERVINGS / **ACTIVE TIME:** 30 MINUTES / **TOTAL TIME:** 1 HOUR AND 30 MINUTES

It seems impossible when you have the original, but the addition of dill pickles does lift arancini to even greater heights.

1. Place the stock in a large saucepan, bring it to a simmer, remove it from heat, and set it aside. Place the butter in a skillet and melt it over medium-high heat. Add the rice and onion and cook until the onion is translucent, about 3 minutes. Deglaze the skillet with the white wine and cook until the wine has been almost completely absorbed, about 2 minutes. Reduce the heat to medium and incorporate the warmed stock 1 cup at a time, stirring constantly and waiting until the stock has been absorbed before adding the next portion. Stir the cheese and pickles into the risotto, season with salt and pepper, and place it in a 9 x 13–inch baking pan. Refrigerate for 2 hours.

2. Preheat the oven to 150°F. Add oil to a Dutch oven until it is approximately 2 inches deep and warm over medium-high heat until it reaches 375°F. Line a baking sheet with paper towels and place it in the oven. Place the eggs in a bowl and the panko in a shallow bowl. Form the risotto into 1½-inch balls, dip them in the eggs, and then roll them in the panko, gently pressing down to make sure it adheres.

3. Working in batches, add the arancini to the oil and fry until crispy and golden brown, about 3 minutes. Transfer the cooked arancini to the baking sheet to drain and keep warm. Serve once all of the arancini have been cooked.

INGREDIENTS:

- 8 CUPS CHICKEN STOCK (SEE PAGE 660)
- 1 STICK OF UNSALTED BUTTER
- 2 CUPS ARBORIO RICE
- 1 SMALL WHITE ONION, MINCED
- 1 CUP WHITE WINE
- 1½ CUPS GRATED HAVARTI CHEESE WITH DILL
- 1½ CUPS CHOPPED DILL PICKLES
- SALT AND PEPPER, TO TASTE
- VEGETABLE OIL, AS NEEDED
- 6 LARGE EGGS, BEATEN
- 5 CUPS PANKO

RICE & CHEDDAR BALLS

YIELD: 4 TO 6 SERVINGS / **ACTIVE TIME:** 30 MINUTES / **TOTAL TIME:** 3 HOURS AND 30 MINUTES

These fried morsels are an Americanized version of arancini, with much of the flavor coming from the liquid in which the rice is cooked.

INGREDIENTS:

- 1 CUP WATER
- 1 CUP WHOLE MILK
- 1 CUP LONG-GRAIN WHITE RICE
- 2 TABLESPOONS PAPRIKA
- 1 TEASPOON MUSTARD POWDER
- 2 TABLESPOONS UNSALTED BUTTER
- 4 SCALLIONS, TRIMMED AND CHOPPED
- ½ RED BELL PEPPER, MINCED
- 2 LARGE EGGS
- 2 TEASPOONS FINELY CHOPPED FRESH THYME
- 2 CUPS GRATED CHEDDAR CHEESE
- SALT AND PEPPER, TO TASTE
- 1 CUP BREAD CRUMBS
- VEGETABLE OIL, AS NEEDED
- 1 CUP MARINARA SAUCE (SEE PAGE 674), WARMED, FOR SERVING

1. Place the water, milk, rice, paprika, and mustard powder in a saucepan and stir to combine. Bring to a boil over medium-high heat, stirring occasionally. Cover the pan, reduce the heat to low, and cook until the liquid has been absorbed and the rice is tender, 15 to 18 minutes. Remove the pan from the heat and set it aside.

2. While the rice is cooking, place the butter in a small skillet and melt it over medium-high heat. Add the scallions and red pepper and sauté until the vegetables have started to soften, about 5 minutes. Remove the pan from heat and set it aside.

3. Place the eggs, thyme, cheddar, rice, and vegetable mixture in a mixing bowl, season with salt and pepper, and stir until thoroughly combined. Place the mixture in a 9 x 13–inch baking pan and refrigerate for 1 hour.

4. Place the bread crumbs in a shallow bowl. Working with wet hands, form the rice mixture into 1½-inch balls and roll them in the bread crumbs, gently pressing down to make sure they adhere.

5. Preheat the oven to 150°F. Add oil to a Dutch oven until it is approximately 2 inches deep and warm over medium-high heat until it reaches 375°F. Line a baking sheet with paper towels and place it in the oven. Working in batches, add the rice balls to the oil and fry until crispy and golden brown. Transfer the cooked rice balls to the baking sheet to drain and keep warm. When all of the rice balls have been cooked, serve with the Marinara Sauce.

CORN FRITTERS

YIELD: 4 TO 6 SERVINGS / **ACTIVE TIME:** 25 MINUTES / **TOTAL TIME:** 25 MINUTES

Crispy corn fritters make for a wonderful hors d'oeuvre or side dish, and they are as at home on the breakfast table as the dinner table.

INGREDIENTS:

- 1 LB. CORN KERNELS
- SALT AND PEPPER, TO TASTE
- 2 LARGE EGGS
- 3 SCALLION WHITES, CHOPPED
- 1 GARLIC CLOVE, MINCED
- 3 TABLESPOONS FINELY CHOPPED FRESH CILANTRO
- 1 CUP ALL-PURPOSE FLOUR
- ¼ CUP CORNMEAL
- 1 TABLESPOON SUGAR
- 1 TABLESPOON BAKING POWDER
- 2 TEASPOONS CORIANDER
- VEGETABLE OIL, AS NEEDED
- 1 CUP SOUTHERN BARBECUE SAUCE (SEE PAGE 684), WARMED, FOR SERVING

1. Place the corn in a saucepan, cover with water, and season the water with salt. Bring to a boil over high heat and then cook the corn until tender, about 2 minutes. Drain and transfer to a food processor, reserving 2 tablespoons of kernels if desired. Add the eggs, puree until smooth, and scrape the mixture into a mixing bowl.

2. Stir the scallions, garlic, and cilantro into the corn mixture, as well as the reserved kernels, if using. Place the flour, cornmeal, sugar, baking powder, coriander, salt, and pepper in another mixing bowl and stir until combined. Add the dry mixture to the corn mixture and stir until just combined.

3. Preheat the oven to 150°F. Add oil to a Dutch oven until it is approximately 2 inches deep and warm over medium-high heat until it reaches 375°F. Line a baking sheet with paper towels and place it in the oven. Working in batches, drop tablespoons of the batter into the oil and fry until crispy and golden brown, 2 to 3 minutes. Transfer the cooked fritters to the baking sheet in the oven to drain and keep warm. Serve with the Southern Barbecue Sauce once all of the batter has been used.

VARIATIONS

- Omit the scallions, garlic, cilantro, and coriander, add an additional 1 tablespoon of sugar, and serve the fritters for breakfast with some warmed maple syrup.
- Omit the cilantro and coriander and add ¼ cup chopped pimentos and 1 teaspoon dried sage.

EGGPLANT BALLS

YIELD: 4 TO 6 SERVINGS / **ACTIVE TIME:** 30 MINUTES / **TOTAL TIME:** 1 HOUR AND 30 MINUTES

For generations of Italians in the southern part of the country, meat was quite scarce, so cooks utilized eggplant and other hearty vegetables. These balls, known as *pitticelle di murignani* in Calabria, are just one glorious result of that tradition.

INGREDIENTS:

- 3 (1 LB.) EGGPLANTS
- 2 LARGE EGGS
- ½ CUP GRATED PARMESAN CHEESE
- 1½ CUPS ITALIAN BREAD CRUMBS, PLUS MORE AS NEEDED
- 3 TABLESPOONS FINELY CHOPPED FRESH PARSLEY
- 2 TABLESPOONS FINELY CHOPPED FRESH OREGANO
- SALT AND PEPPER, TO TASTE
- VEGETABLE OIL, AS NEEDED
- 1 CUP MARINARA SAUCE (SEE PAGE 674), WARMED, FOR SERVING

1. Preheat the oven to 450°F and line a rimmed baking sheet with aluminum foil. Poke holes in the eggplants, place them on a baking sheet, and roast until completely tender, about 40 minutes, turning the eggplants over halfway through. Remove from the oven, cut the eggplants in half, and let them cool.

2. When the eggplants are cool enough to handle, scrape the flesh into a food processor, discard the skins, and add any juices that accumulated in the pan. Puree the eggplant until smooth and then place it in a mixing bowl.

3. Add the eggs, cheese, ½ cup of the bread crumbs, parsley, oregano, salt, and pepper to the eggplant and stir until the mixture holds together. If necessary, incorporate additional bread crumbs to make the mixture cohesive.

4. Place the remaining bread crumbs in a shallow bowl. Working with wet hands, form the mixture into 1½-inch balls and roll them in the bread crumbs, gently pressing down to make sure that they adhere.

5. Preheat the oven to 150°F. Add oil to a Dutch oven until it is approximately 2 inches deep and warm over medium-high heat until it reaches 375°F. Line a baking sheet with paper towels and place it in the oven. Working in batches, place the eggplant balls in the oil and fry until crispy and golden brown, 3 to 4 minutes. Transfer the cooked balls to the baking sheet in the oven to drain and keep warm. Serve alongside the Marinara Sauce once all of the eggplant balls have been cooked.

VARIATIONS

- For the Sicilian version of these eggplant balls, add ½ cup toasted pine nuts and ½ cup dried currants (soak the currants in hot water for 10 minutes and then drain) to the eggplant mixture.
- For the Neapolitan spin, add ½ cup pitted and chopped olives (green or black will work) to the eggplant mixture.

TOFU & MUSHROOM BALLS

YIELD: 4 TO 6 SERVINGS / **ACTIVE TIME:** 25 MINUTES / **TOTAL TIME:** 40 MINUTES

These are surprisingly meaty thanks to the sautéed mushrooms.

1. Preheat the oven to 425°F and line a rimmed baking sheet with aluminum foil. Place the oil in a skillet and warm over medium-high heat. When it starts to shimmer, add the onion and garlic and sauté until the onion is translucent, about 3 minutes. Stir in the mushrooms, season with salt and pepper, and sauté, stirring frequently, until the liquid the mushrooms release has evaporated, about 7 minutes. Place the mixture in a mixing bowl and set it aside.

2. Place the tofu, egg, bread crumbs, parsley, and rosemary in a food processor and puree until smooth. Add the puree to the mixing bowl, season with salt and pepper, and stir until thoroughly combined. Working with wet hands, form the mixture into 1½-inch balls, arrange them on the baking sheet, and spray the tops with cooking spray.

3. Place the balls in the oven and bake for 12 to 15 minutes, until cooked through. Remove from the oven and serve, accompanied by a bowl of Marinara Sauce for dipping.

VARIATION

- Use portobello mushrooms for an even earthier flavor.

INGREDIENTS:

- 3 TABLESPOONS OLIVE OIL
- 1 ONION, CHOPPED
- 3 GARLIC CLOVES, MINCED
- 2 CUPS CHOPPED BUTTON MUSHROOMS
- SALT AND PEPPER, TO TASTE
- 1 (14 OZ.) PACKAGE EXTRA-FIRM TOFU, DRAINED AND CHOPPED
- 1 LARGE EGG
- ¼ CUP ITALIAN BREAD CRUMBS
- 3 TABLESPOONS FINELY CHOPPED FRESH PARSLEY
- 2 TABLESPOONS FINELY CHOPPED FRESH ROSEMARY
- 1 CUP MARINARA SAUCE (SEE PAGE 674), WARMED, FOR SERVING

SAUERKRAUT BALLS

YIELD: 4 TO 6 SERVINGS / **ACTIVE TIME:** 30 MINUTES / **TOTAL TIME:** 30 MINUTES

Anyone who grew up in the American Midwest knows about sauerkraut balls held together by mashed potatoes; they are an integral part of many parties, springing from a tradition brought by German immigrants.

INGREDIENTS:

- 1 LB. POTATOES, PEELED AND CHOPPED
- SALT AND PEPPER, TO TASTE
- 1 LB. SAUERKRAUT
- 2 LARGE EGGS
- ¾ CUP WHOLE-GRAIN DIJON MUSTARD
- 3 SCALLIONS, TRIMMED AND CHOPPED
- 2 TABLESPOONS FINELY CHOPPED FRESH PARSLEY
- 1 TABLESPOON CARAWAY SEEDS, CRUSHED
- 1 CUP BREAD CRUMBS
- VEGETABLE OIL, AS NEEDED
- ½ CUP MAYONNAISE
- ½ CUP SOUR CREAM

1. Place the potatoes in a saucepan, cover with water, season the water with salt, bring to a boil, and cook until the potatoes are fork-tender, about 20 minutes. Drain the potatoes, place them in a mixing bowl, and mash until smooth. Set the potatoes aside.

2. While the potatoes are cooking, place the sauerkraut in a bowl, cover with cold water, and soak for 12 minutes, changing the water every 3 minutes. Drain the sauerkraut, press down on it to remove as much water as possible, and then chop it.

3. Add the eggs and ¼ cup of the mustard to the potatoes and stir to combine. Add the scallions, parsley, caraway seeds, and sauerkraut, season with salt and pepper, and stir until thoroughly combined.

4. Place the bread crumbs in a shallow bowl. Working with wet hands, form the mixture into 1½-inch balls and roll them in the bread crumbs, gently pressing down to make sure that they adhere.

5. Preheat the oven to 150°F. Add oil to a Dutch oven until it is approximately 2 inches deep and warm over medium-high heat until it reaches 375°F. Line a baking sheet with paper towels and place it in the oven.

6. While the oil is warming, place the mayonnaise, sour cream, and remaining mustard in a small bowl, stir to combine, and set the sauce aside.

7. Working in batches, place the sauerkraut balls in the oil and fry until crispy and golden brown, 3 to 4 minutes. Transfer the cooked balls to the baking sheet in the oven to drain and keep warm. When all of the sauerkraut balls have been cooked, serve with the mustard-and-sour cream sauce.

VARIATION

• Add ½ cup grated cheese, such as cheddar, to the mashed potatoes.

GOLDEN POTATO & ONION BALLS

YIELD: 4 TO 6 SERVINGS / **ACTIVE TIME:** 30 MINUTES / **TOTAL TIME:** 45 MINUTES

My take on *gougères*, a French hors d'oeuvre made with puff pastry. The combination of sweet caramelized onion and potato is one of my favorites, and I confidently serve these alongside any grilled or broiled entrée.

INGREDIENTS:

2 TABLESPOONS OLIVE OIL

1 STICK OF UNSALTED BUTTER, PLUS 2 TABLESPOONS

2 LARGE ONIONS, CHOPPED

SALT AND PEPPER, TO TASTE

2 TEASPOONS SUGAR

2 LBS. RED POTATOES, PEELED AND CHOPPED

1 CUP ALL-PURPOSE FLOUR

2 EGGS

1. Place the oil and the 2 tablespoons of butter in a large skillet and warm over medium heat. When the butter starts to foam, add the onions, stir to coat, and cover the pan. Cook the onions until browned, about 10 minutes. Sprinkle salt, pepper, and the sugar over the onions, reduce the heat to medium-low, and cook until they are caramelized, about 25 minutes.

2. While the onions are cooking, place the potatoes in a saucepan, cover with water, season the water with salt, bring to a boil, and cook until the potatoes are fork-tender, about 20 minutes. Drain the potatoes, place them in a mixing bowl, and mash until smooth. Set the potatoes aside.

3. Place 1 cup of water in a saucepan and bring to a boil over high heat. Add the remaining butter and stir until it has melted. Add the flour and stir until the dough comes together and stops sticking to the sides of the pan. Remove the pan from the stove and incorporate the eggs one at a time. Place the dough in a mixing bowl and stir in the onions and mashed potatoes. Season with salt and pepper and form the mixture into 1-inch balls.

4. Preheat the oven to 150°F. Add oil to a Dutch oven until it is approximately 2 inches deep and warm over medium-high heat until it reaches 375°F. Line a baking sheet with paper towels and place it in the oven. Working in batches, place the balls in the oil and fry until crispy and golden brown, 2 to 3 minutes. Transfer the cooked balls to the baking sheet in the oven to drain and keep warm. Serve once all of the balls have been cooked.

VARIATION

- Omit the onions and add ¾ cup grated cheddar cheese, Gruyère cheese, or a smoked cheese to the mixture.

CHEESE & SPINACH BALLS

YIELD: 4 TO 6 SERVINGS / **ACTIVE TIME:** 25 MINUTES / **TOTAL TIME:** 40 MINUTES

These baked spheres are a classic hors d'oeuvre, particularly when you double up on the cheese and serve them with some Blue Cheese Sauce.

INGREDIENTS:

1 (10 OZ.) PACKAGE FROZEN CHOPPED SPINACH, THAWED

6 TABLESPOONS UNSALTED BUTTER

1 ONION, CHOPPED

2 GARLIC CLOVES, MINCED

3 LARGE EGGS

¾ CUP GRATED PARMESAN CHEESE

2 TABLESPOONS FINELY CHOPPED FRESH PARSLEY

1 TABLESPOON FINELY CHOPPED FRESH THYME

1 CUP ITALIAN BREAD CRUMBS

SALT AND PEPPER, TO TASTE

1 CUP BLUE CHEESE SAUCE (SEE PAGE 717), FOR SERVING

1. Preheat the oven to 425°F and line a rimmed baking sheet with aluminum foil. Place the spinach in a colander and press down to remove as much liquid from it as possible. Set the spinach aside.

2. Place the butter in a small skillet and melt it over medium-high heat. Add the onion and garlic and sauté until the onion is translucent, about 3 minutes. Remove the pan from heat and set it aside.

3. Place the eggs, cheese, parsley, thyme, ½ cup of bread crumbs, spinach, and the onion mixture in a bowl, season with salt and pepper, and stir until thoroughly combined.

4. Place remaining bread crumbs in a shallow bowl. Working with wet hands, form the mixture into 1½-inch balls and roll them in the bread crumbs, gently pressing down to make sure that they adhere. Arrange the balls on the baking sheet and spray the tops with cooking spray.

5. Place the spinach balls in the oven and bake for 12 to 15 minutes, until cooked through. Remove from the oven and serve with the Blue Cheese Sauce.

VARIATIONS

- Replace the spinach with cooked and minced broccoli or asparagus.
- Use cheddar cheese instead of Parmesan.

CREAM CHEESE BALLS

YIELD: 4 TO 6 SERVINGS / **ACTIVE TIME:** 20 MINUTES / **TOTAL TIME:** 50 MINUTES

A "master recipe" from which endless variations can be made. I serve these little balls with either crackers or thin pretzel sticks or carrots that the guests can use like toothpicks.

INGREDIENTS:

- 1 LB. CREAM CHEESE, AT ROOM TEMPERATURE
- 4 TABLESPOONS UNSALTED BUTTER, AT ROOM TEMPERATURE
- ½ CUP CHOPPED PIMENTO-STUFFED GREEN OLIVES
- 3 SCALLIONS, TRIMMED AND CHOPPED
- 2 GARLIC CLOVES, MINCED
- 2 TABLESPOONS WORCESTERSHIRE SAUCE
- 2 TEASPOONS HERBES DE PROVENCE
- SALT, TO TASTE
- RED PEPPER FLAKES, TO TASTE
- ½ CUP CHOPPED FRESH PARSLEY

1. Place the cream cheese and butter in a mixing bowl and beat with a handheld mixer at medium speed until light and fluffy. Stir in the olives, scallions, garlic, Worcestershire sauce, and Herbes de Provence, season with salt and red pepper flakes, and stir until thoroughly combined.

2. Form the mixture into 1-inch balls and roll them in the parsley, gently pressing down to make sure it adheres. Place the balls on a parchment-lined baking sheet, cover with plastic wrap, and refrigerate for 30 minutes before serving.

VARIATIONS

- Roll the balls in toasted sesame seeds rather than parsley.
- Substitute soy sauce for the Worcestershire sauce and chopped shiitake mushrooms for the olives.
- Use ½ cup chopped pimentos in place of the olives.

ROASTED PINE NUT & PESTO BALLS

YIELD: 6 TO 8 SERVINGS / **ACTIVE TIME:** 25 MINUTES / **TOTAL TIME:** 55 MINUTES

These balls can be made in a matter of minutes with store-bought pesto. But making pesto at home is easy, and much tastier.

INGREDIENTS:

- 1 CUP PINE NUTS
- 2 GARLIC CLOVES
- 1 CUP FIRMLY PACKED FRESH BASIL LEAVES
- ¼ CUP OLIVE OIL
- ½ LB. CREAM CHEESE, AT ROOM TEMPERATURE
- SALT AND PEPPER, TO TASTE

1. Preheat the oven to 350°F. Place ¾ cup of the pine nuts on a baking sheet, place them in the oven, and roast for 5 to 7 minutes, until lightly browned. Remove from the oven and set them aside.

2. Place the garlic, basil, olive oil, and remaining pine nuts in a food processor and puree until smooth. Place the mixture in a mixing bowl and add the cream cheese. Stir until thoroughly combined and season with salt and pepper.

3. Place the toasted pine nuts in a shallow bowl. Form the mixture into ¾-inch balls and roll them in the toasted pine nuts, gently pressing down to make sure that they adhere. Place the balls on a parchment-lined baking sheet, cover with plastic wrap, and refrigerate for 30 minutes before serving.

VARIATION

- Replace the pesto with ½ cup sun-dried tomatoes packed in olive oil. Drain and puree the tomatoes before adding them to the mixture.

DUDHI KOFTA

YIELD: 6 SERVINGS / **ACTIVE TIME:** 30 MINUTES / **TOTAL TIME:** 1 HOUR AND 30 MINUTES

An ideal recipe for the surplus of zucchini that every summer seems to bring.

INGREDIENTS:

- 2 LBS. ZUCCHINI, TRIMMED AND GRATED
- 2 TEASPOONS KOSHER SALT
- 1 SMALL RED ONION, CHOPPED
- ¼ CUP RAW CASHEWS
- 2 GARLIC CLOVES, MINCED
- 1-INCH PIECE FRESH GINGER, PEELED AND MINCED
- 4 BIRD'S EYE CHILI PEPPERS, STEMMED, SEEDS AND RIBS REMOVED, AND MINCED
- ½ CUP CHICKPEA FLOUR
- 2 TABLESPOONS FINELY CHOPPED FRESH CILANTRO
- VEGETABLE OIL, AS NEEDED

1. Place the grated zucchini in a bowl, add the salt, and stir to combine. Let stand for 20 minutes.

2. Place the onion, cashews, garlic, ginger, and chilies in a food processor and blitz until the mixture is a chunky paste.

3. Place the zucchini in a kitchen towel and wring it to remove as much liquid as possible. Place the zucchini in a mixing bowl and add the onion-and-cashew paste. Stir to combine, add the chickpea flour and cilantro, and fold to incorporate. The dough should be slightly wet.

4. Add vegetable oil to a Dutch oven until it is about 2 inches deep and heat it to 300°F. As the oil warms, form the dough into 1½-inch balls. Working in batches, place the balls in the oil and fry until crispy and golden brown, about 5 minutes. Transfer the cooked kofta to a paper towel–lined plate to drain. Serve once all of the kofta have been cooked.

MUTHIA

YIELD: 6 TO 8 SERVINGS / **ACTIVE TIME:** 20 MINUTES / **TOTAL TIME:** 30 MINUTES

These Indian cabbage balls are packed with flavor and nutrients. However, if cabbage isn't your thing, feel free to substitute any leafy green in its place.

INGREDIENTS:

- 1½ TEASPOONS KOSHER SALT, PLUS MORE TO TASTE
- 1 GREEN CABBAGE, OUTER LEAVES RESERVED, REMAINDER CHOPPED
- 1½ CUPS CHICKPEA FLOUR, PLUS MORE AS NEEDED
- 2 TABLESPOONS COCONUT OIL, MELTED
- 2-INCH PIECE FRESH GINGER, PEELED AND MINCED
- 2 TABLESPOONS MINCED FRESNO CHILI PEPPER
- 1 TABLESPOON CORIANDER
- 1½ TEASPOONS CUMIN
- ½ TEASPOON TURMERIC
- CILANTRO & LIME YOGURT (SEE PAGE 737), FOR SERVING

1. Bring salted water to a boil in a large saucepan and prepare an ice bath. Add the chopped cabbage to the boiling water and cook for 1 minute. Drain and add the cabbage to the ice bath. Drain again and squeeze the cabbage to remove as much liquid as possible. Place on a kitchen towel to dry.

2. Place the chickpea flour and coconut oil in a bowl and stir to combine. Add the remaining ingredients, except for the yogurt, and the cabbage and stir until the dough starts to hold together. Place the dough on a flour-dusted work surface and knead until it is smooth and stiff. Form the mixture into 1½-inch balls.

3. Bring a few inches of water to a simmer in a saucepan and line a steaming tray with the reserved cabbage leaves. Place the muthia in the tray and steam until they are shiny and firm, about 20 minutes. Serve with the Cilantro & Lime Yogurt.

ITALIAN SEITAN MEATBALLS

YIELD: 6 TO 8 SERVINGS / **ACTIVE TIME:** 30 MINUTES / **TOTAL TIME:** 1 HOUR

Crispy on the outside and pleasantly chewy inside thanks to the seitan, these meatballs are as fun as they are tasty.

1. Bring a few inches of water to a simmer in a saucepan. Place the sun-dried tomatoes and walnuts in a food processor and pulse until they are a smooth paste. Add the remaining ingredients to the food processor and pulse until the mixture is a crumbly dough, scraping the work sides as needed until combined into a crumbly dough.

2. Form the mixture into 1-inch balls and place them in a steaming tray. Set the steaming tray over the simmering water and steam the meatballs until they are cooked through, about 25 minutes, turning the meatballs over halfway through.

3. Place the olive oil in a skillet and warm over medium-high heat. When it starts to shimmer, add the meatballs in batches and cook, turning occasionally, until they are browned all over. Serve with the Marinara Sauce once all of the meatballs have been cooked.

INGREDIENTS:

- ⅓ CUP SUN-DRIED TOMATOES IN OLIVE OIL, DRAINED
- ½ CUP WALNUTS
- 1¼ CUPS SEITAN (SEE PAGE 450 FOR HOMEMADE)
- 1 CUP COOKED LENTILS
- 2 TABLESPOONS FINELY CHOPPED FRESH BASIL
- 1½ TEASPOONS ONION POWDER
- 1 TEASPOON GARLIC POWDER
- ½ TEASPOON BLACK PEPPER
- 1 TABLESPOON OLIVE OIL
- 1 CUP MARINARA SAUCE (SEE PAGE 674), FOR SERVING

HOMEMADE SEITAN

YIELD: APPROXIMATELY ½ LB. / **ACTIVE TIME:** 15 MINUTES / **TOTAL TIME:** 45 MINUTES

If you can't find premade seitan or don't care for the options in your local market, it is easy to make at home with the purchase of some unusual ingredients. You will need to find vital wheat gluten, which is wheat flour that has been stripped of any starch and dried. Health food stores or stores that specialize in baking will likely carry it, but you can also order online from King Arthur Flour or Bob's Red Mill. Nutritional yeast is the same species of yeast used for making bread and beer but has been deactivated. In other words, it is not "alive" and cannot be used for leavening or fermenting; rather, it is meant to be used as a seasoning. It has a cheesy, nutty taste that is terrific on popcorn and other savory dishes. You can look for it in the bulk spice section at your local supermarket or order it online. Once you have made a batch of seitan, you can cut it to suit your recipe and cook as you would meat or tofu.

INGREDIENTS:

- 1 CUP VITAL WHEAT GLUTEN
- ¼ CUP NUTRITIONAL YEAST
- 1 TEASPOON GARLIC POWDER
- ½ CUP VEGETABLE STOCK (SEE PAGE 664 FOR HOMEMADE) OR WATER, PLUS MORE FOR POACHING
- 1 TEASPOON SOY SAUCE

1. In a mixing bowl, mix the gluten, yeast, and garlic powder until blended.

2. Incorporate the stock or water and soy sauce a little at a time until a dough forms. If it is too dry, add extra stock or water. Knead the dough for a few minutes until it feels elastic and all of the ingredients are thoroughly incorporated. Divide into two pieces and shape each one into a disk.

3. Bring a pot of stock, water, or a combination of the two, deep enough to cover the dough, to a boil. Put the disks in the pot and reduce heat to a simmer. Poach for 30 minutes. Turn off the heat and let cool in the pot.

BUDDHA SEITAN

YIELD: 4 TO 6 SERVINGS / **ACTIVE TIME:** 35 MINUTES / **TOTAL TIME:** 45 MINUTES

If you're not a fan of seitan, substitute your eggplant or your favorite vegetables—the sauce is so good that a delightful dinner is guaranteed.

INGREDIENTS:

- ½ CUP WATER
- ⅓ CUP SUGAR
- ¼ CUP MUSHROOM SOY SAUCE
- ½ CUP SOY SAUCE, PLUS 2 TABLESPOONS
- ¼ CUP WHITE WINE VINEGAR
- 1 LB. SEITAN (SEE PAGE 450 FOR HOMEMADE)
- 2 GARLIC CLOVES, MINCED
- 1-INCH PIECE FRESH GINGER, PEELED AND MINCED
- 1 TEASPOON RED PEPPER FLAKES, OR TO TASTE
- ⅓ CUP OLIVE OIL
- 2 TABLESPOONS CORNSTARCH
- AVOCADO OIL, AS NEEDED
- JASMINE RICE, COOKED, FOR SERVING

1. Place the water, sugar, mushroom soy sauce, the ½ cup of soy sauce, and white wine vinegar in a bowl and stir to combine. Set the sauce aside.

2. Place the seitan, garlic, ginger, red pepper flakes, olive oil, and remaining soy sauce in a food processor and pulse until combined. Form the mixture into 1-inch balls.

3. Place the cornstarch in a shallow dish and dredge the seitan balls in it until they are coated. Reserve the remaining cornstarch.

4. Add avocado oil to a Dutch oven until it is about 2 inches deep and warm to 350°F. Working in batches, gently drop the seitan balls in the oil and fry until golden brown, turning them as they cook, 3 to 5 minutes. Transfer the cooked seitan to a paper towel–lined plate to drain.

5. Pour the sauce into a skillet and bring to a boil over medium-high heat. Stir in the cornstarch and cook until the sauce has thickened slightly. Add the seitan balls, stir until coated, and serve over the jasmine rice.

VEGETARIAN SPAGHETTI & MEATBALLS

YIELD: 6 TO 8 SERVINGS / **ACTIVE TIME:** 10 MINUTES / **TOTAL TIME:** 20 MINUTES

The increased availability of zucchini noodles has made things much easier for both vegetarians and those looking to avoid carbs.

1. Place the olive oil in a skillet and warm over medium-high heat. When it starts to shimmer, add the zucchini noodles and cook until tender, about 5 minutes.

2. Stir in the Parmesan, sauce, and meatballs and cook until warmed through. Remove the pan from heat, garnish with additional Parmesan, and serve.

INGREDIENTS:

- 2 TABLESPOONS OLIVE OIL
- 1 LB. ZUCCHINI NOODLES
- ¼ CUP GRATED PARMESAN CHEESE, PLUS MORE FOR GARNISH
- 2 CUPS MARINARA SAUCE (SEE PAGE 674)
- ITALIAN SEITAN MEATBALLS (SEE PAGE 449)

DESSERT BALLS

This chapter stretches the definition of "meatball," but there are so many wonderful "ground and round" sweets that it makes sense to include some confections in this book. So make some of these quick and easy recipes, like homemade chocolate truffles, cream puffs filled with ice cream, cookies, and crispy fritters.

BASIC CHOCOLATE TRUFFLES

YIELD: 36 TRUFFLES / **ACTIVE TIME:** 30 MINUTES / **TOTAL TIME:** 4 HOURS AND 30 MINUTES

Once you learn how easy it is to make these truffles, you'll never have to pony up for those expensive ones again. See the variations to make them in your favorite flavors—from coconut to orange.

INGREDIENTS:

- 1 LB. QUALITY BITTERSWEET CHOCOLATE
- 1¼ CUPS HEAVY CREAM
- PINCH OF KOSHER SALT
- ½ CUP UNSWEETENED COCOA POWDER

1. Place the chocolate in a food processor and pulse until chopped. Set it aside.

2. Place the cream in a saucepan and bring to a simmer over medium heat, stirring frequently. Stir in the salt and chocolate, remove the pan from the heat, cover it, and let the mixture sit for 5 minutes. Stir the mixture until smooth and transfer to a square 9-inch baking pan. Refrigerate for 4 hours.

3. Place the cocoa powder in a shallow bowl. Form 2-teaspoon portions of the mixture into balls, roll them in the cocoa, and place on a parchment-lined baking sheet. Cover with plastic wrap and refrigerate for 30 minutes before serving.

VARIATIONS

- Instead of cocoa powder, coat the truffles in toasted coconut, finely chopped nuts, or colored candy sprinkles.
- Add 2 to 4 tablespoons of your favorite liqueur to the truffle mixture.
- Add 1 tablespoon orange zest to the mixture.
- Form the truffles around a small nut, such as a hazelnut or a peanut.

Cold hands make shaping truffles easy. Keep a bowl of ice water and a roll of paper towels nearby while rolling them. Submerge your hands in the water until they are very cold. Then dry them and roll some truffles, repeating as necessary.

CHOCOLATE & GOAT CHEESE TRUFFLES

YIELD: 48 TRUFFLES / **ACTIVE TIME:** 30 MINUTES / **TOTAL TIME:** 2 HOURS

The sharpness of the goat cheese balances the sweetness of the chocolate in these unusual, but delightful, truffles.

INGREDIENTS:

- ½ LB. QUALITY BITTERSWEET CHOCOLATE
- ½ LB. GOAT CHEESE, AT ROOM TEMPERATURE
- ¼ CUP CONFECTIONERS' SUGAR
- ½ TEASPOON PURE VANILLA EXTRACT
- ½ CUP UNSWEETENED COCOA POWDER

1. Place the chocolate in a food processor and pulse until chopped. Place the chocolate in a heatproof bowl and bring 2 inches of water to a simmer in a saucepan. Place the chocolate over the water and let it melt, stirring occasionally.

2. Place the goat cheese, confectioners' sugar, and vanilla in a mixing bowl and beat with a handheld mixer at medium speed until light and fluffy. With the mixer running, gradually add the chocolate and beat until thoroughly incorporated. Place the mixture in a square 9-inch baking pan and refrigerate for 1 hour, until it is firm.

3. Place the cocoa powder in a shallow bowl. Form 2-teaspoon portions of the mixture into balls, roll them in the cocoa, and place on a parchment-lined baking sheet. Cover with plastic wrap and refrigerate for 30 minutes before serving.

VARIATIONS

- Incorporate 2 tablespoons of your favorite liqueur.
- Roll the balls in grated white chocolate instead of cocoa powder.

EXTRA-CHOCOLATY TRUFFLES

YIELD: 30 TRUFFLES / **ACTIVE TIME:** 30 MINUTES / **TOTAL TIME:** 4 HOURS AND 30 MINUTES

Due to the unsweetened cocoa powder that is added to the mix, these truffles are for those who love chocolate, but don't want too much sugar in their confections.

INGREDIENTS:

½ LB. QUALITY BITTERSWEET CHOCOLATE

½ CUP HEAVY CREAM

4 TABLESPOONS UNSALTED BUTTER, CUT INTO SMALL PIECES

PINCH OF KOSHER SALT

⅔ CUP UNSWEETENED COCOA POWDER

1. Place the chocolate in a food processor and pulse until chopped. Set it aside.

2. Place the cream and butter in a saucepan and bring to a simmer over medium heat, stirring frequently. Stir in the salt, ¼ cup of the cocoa powder, and the chocolate, remove the pan from the heat, cover it, and let the mixture sit for 5 minutes. Stir the mixture until smooth and transfer to a square 9-inch baking pan. Refrigerate for 4 hours.

3. Place the remaining cocoa powder in a shallow bowl. Form 2-teaspoon portions of the mixture into balls, roll them in the cocoa, and place on a parchment-lined baking sheet. Cover with plastic wrap and refrigerate for 30 minutes before serving.

VARIATIONS

- Use milk chocolate instead of bittersweet chocolate.
- Add ½ cup chopped toasted nuts to the mixture.

HONEY & NUT TRUFFLES

YIELD: 16 TRUFFLES / **ACTIVE TIME:** 10 MINUTES / **TOTAL TIME:** 2 HOURS

Peanut butter and chocolate get all of the attention, but it is the honey that steals the show here.

1. Place the peanut butter, honey, and salt in a bowl and stir until well combined. Form teaspoons of the mixture into balls, place them on a parchment-lined baking sheet, and refrigerate for 1 hour.

2. Remove the baking sheet from the refrigerator. Place the chocolate chips in microwave-safe bowl and microwave until melted, removing to stir every 15 seconds.

3. Dip the balls into the melted chocolate until completely coated. Place them back on the baking sheet. When all of the truffles have been coated, place them in the refrigerator and chill until the chocolate is set.

INGREDIENTS:

½ CUP PEANUT BUTTER

¼ CUP HONEY

¼ TEASPOON KOSHER SALT

1 CUP SEMISWEET CHOCOLATE CHIPS

WHITE CHOCOLATE & ALMOND TRUFFLES

YIELD: 30 TRUFFLES / **ACTIVE TIME:** 30 MINUTES / **TOTAL TIME:** 4 HOURS AND 30 MINUTES

Almonds and creamy white chocolate are a winning combination in these easy-to-make truffles.

INGREDIENTS:

- 1 LB. QUALITY WHITE CHOCOLATE
- 1 CUP WHIPPING CREAM
- 1 CUP NATURAL ALMOND BUTTER
- ½ CUP SUGAR
- PINCH OF KOSHER SALT
- 1 CUP BLANCHED ALMONDS

1. Place the chocolate in a food processor and pulse until chopped. Set it aside.

2. Place the cream, almond butter, sugar, and salt in a saucepan and bring to a simmer over medium heat, stirring frequently. Stir in the chocolate, remove the pan from the heat, cover it, and let the mixture sit for 5 minutes. Stir the mixture until smooth and transfer to a square 9-inch baking pan. Refrigerate for 4 hours.

3. While the mixture is in the refrigerator, preheat the oven to 350°F. Place the almonds on a baking sheet, place them in the oven, and roast for 5 to 7 minutes, until lightly browned. Remove from the oven, place the almonds in a food processor, and pulse until finely ground.

4. Place the almonds in a shallow bowl. Form 2-teaspoon portions of the mixture into balls, roll them in the almonds, and place on a parchment-lined baking sheet. Cover with plastic wrap and refrigerate for 30 minutes before serving.

VARIATIONS

- Use dark chocolate or milk chocolate instead of white chocolate.
- Coat the truffles in melted milk chocolate instead of nuts.
- For peanut truffles, use natural peanut butter and chopped peanuts or commercial peanut butter and then omit the sugar from the recipe.
- Form the truffles around a small nut.

AVOCADO & CHOCOLATE TRUFFLES

YIELD: 36 TRUFFLES / **ACTIVE TIME:** 10 MINUTES / **TOTAL TIME:** 45 MINUTES

Unorthodox, yes. But avocado's rich, fresh flavor allows these truffles to stick the landing.

1. Place the chocolate chips in a microwave-safe bowl and microwave on medium until melted, removing to stir every 10 seconds.

2. Place the avocados, vanilla, and salt in a bowl and stir to combine. Fold in the melted chocolate, cover the bowl, and refrigerate for 30 minutes.

3. Place the cocoa powder in a shallow bowl. Form approximately ¾-tablespoon portions of the mixture into balls, roll them in the cocoa powder, and serve.

INGREDIENTS:

- 3 CUPS SEMISWEET CHOCOLATE CHIPS
- FLESH OF 2 AVOCADOS
- 2 TEASPOONS PURE VANILLA EXTRACT
- ½ TEASPOON KOSHER SALT
- ½ CUP UNSWEETENED COCOA POWDER

CHOCOLATE & PEANUT BUTTER TRUFFLES

YIELD: 36 TRUFFLES / **ACTIVE TIME:** 15 MINUTES / **TOTAL TIME:** 4 HOURS AND 15 MINUTES

As everyone knows, peanut butter and chocolate were made for each other.

INGREDIENTS:

- 3 CUPS MILK CHOCOLATE CHIPS
- 1½ STICKS OF UNSALTED BUTTER
- ½ LB. CRUNCHY PEANUT BUTTER
- ⅓ CUP HEAVY CREAM

1. Place the 1 cup of the chocolate chips, the butter, peanut butter, and cream in a heatproof bowl and stir to combine. Place the bowl over a half-full saucepan of simmering water and stir until the mixture is smooth and combined. Remove from heat, cover with plastic wrap, and refrigerate for 2 hours.

2. Line a large baking sheet with parchment paper. Form generous teaspoons of the mixture into balls, place them on the baking sheet, and freeze for 1 hour.

3. Place the remaining chocolate in a microwave-safe bowl and microwave on medium until melted, removing to stir every 10 seconds. Using a fork or skewer, dip the truffles in the melted chocolate, shaking off any excess. Return to the baking sheet and let sit at room temperature until the chocolate has set, about 1 hour.

CASHEW & COCONUT TRUFFLES

YIELD: 24 TRUFFLES / **ACTIVE TIME:** 15 MINUTES / **TOTAL TIME:** 1 HOUR AND 15 MINUTES

The nutty crunch provided by the cashews is balanced nicely by the creamy coconut.

INGREDIENTS:

- ½ LB. RAW CASHEWS
- 1 CUP ALL-PURPOSE FLOUR
- ⅓ CUP UNSWEETENED COCOA POWDER
- ½ TEASPOON TURMERIC
- ⅛ TEASPOON CINNAMON
- 1½ STICKS OF UNSALTED BUTTER
- ¾ CUP ALMOND BUTTER
- 1 CUP SUGAR
- ⅔ CUP UNSWEETENED SHREDDED COCONUT

1. Place the cashews in a food processor and pulse until minced. Transfer the cashews to a mixing bowl and stir in the flour, cocoa powder, turmeric, and cinnamon. Set the mixture aside.

2. Place the butter, almond butter, and sugar in a saucepan and melt over medium heat, while stirring occasionally. Add the mixture to the cashew mixture and stir until thoroughly combined. Cover the bowl with plastic wrap and refrigerate for 30 minutes.

3. Place the coconut in a shallow bowl. Form tablespoons of the mixture into balls, roll them in the shredded coconut, and place the truffles on a parchment-lined baking sheet. Cover with plastic wrap and refrigerate for 30 minutes before serving.

BOURBON BALLS

YIELD: 60 BALLS / **ACTIVE TIME:** 30 MINUTES / **TOTAL TIME:** 4 HOURS AND 45 MINUTES

These are a holiday season staple, and as most of the preparation is done by refrigeration, they will come in handy during the inevitable time crunch that occurs as Christmas approaches.

INGREDIENTS:

- 1 CUP PECAN HALVES
- 1½ CUPS CONFECTIONERS' SUGAR
- ¼ CUP UNSWEETENED COCOA POWDER
- ½ CUP BOURBON
- 2 TABLESPOONS LIGHT CORN SYRUP
- 2½ CUPS FINELY CRUSHED VANILLA WAFERS

1. Preheat the oven to 350°F. Place the pecans on a baking sheet, place them in the oven, and roast for 5 to 7 minutes, until lightly browned. Remove the pan from the oven, place the pecans in a food processor, and pulse until finely ground. Set the pecans aside.

2. Sift 1 cup of the sugar and the cocoa powder into a mixing bowl and then stir in the bourbon, corn syrup, vanilla wafers, and pecans. Refrigerate the mixture for 30 minutes.

3. Sift the remaining sugar into a shallow bowl. Form the mixture into 1-inch balls and roll them in the sugar. Place the balls on a platter or a parchment-lined baking sheet and refrigerate for 4 hours before serving.

VARIATIONS

- Use rum instead of bourbon.
- Use Frangelico instead of bourbon and hazelnuts rather than pecans.
- Make them without the cocoa powder.
- Use Grand Marnier instead of bourbon, omit the cocoa powder, and add 1 tablespoon orange zest.
- Add 1 cup minced bittersweet chocolate or miniature chocolate chips.
- Roll balls in finely ground nuts instead of confectioners' sugar.
- Use ginger snaps or crushed chocolate cookies instead of vanilla wafers.
- Omit the cocoa powder, use rum, and add ¾ cup toasted coconut.
- Add ½ teaspoon cinnamon or apple pie spice to the mixture.
- Add ¾ cup minced raisins or other dried fruit.

CHOCOLATE & KAHLÚA BALLS

YIELD: 48 BALLS / **ACTIVE TIME:** 30 MINUTES / **TOTAL TIME:** 5 HOURS

I sampled delicate confections similar to these in Hawaii a few years ago and couldn't wait to try and replicate them at home. The combination of chocolate with coconut and liqueur is a grown-up delight.

INGREDIENTS:

- 1 CUP MACADAMIA NUTS
- 1½ CUPS SWEETENED SHREDDED COCONUT
- 6 OZ. QUALITY BITTERSWEET CHOCOLATE
- ½ CUP EVAPORATED MILK
- PINCH OF KOSHER SALT
- 2½ CUPS CHOCOLATE COOKIE CRUMBS
- ½ CUP CONFECTIONERS' SUGAR
- ½ CUP KAHLÚA
- ½ TEASPOON PURE VANILLA EXTRACT

1. Preheat the oven to 350°F. Place the macadamia nuts on a baking sheet, place them in the oven, and roast for 5 to 7 minutes, until lightly browned. Remove the pan from the oven, place the nuts in a food processor, and pulse until finely ground. Set them aside. Place the coconut on another baking sheet and roast for 10 to 12 minutes, until browned. Remove from the oven and set the coconut aside.

2. Place the chocolate in a food processor and pulse until chopped. Set it aside.

3. Place the evaporated milk in a saucepan and bring to a simmer over medium heat, stirring frequently. Stir in the salt and chocolate, remove the pan from the heat, cover it, and let the mixture sit for 5 minutes. Stir the mixture until smooth and then transfer it to a mixing bowl. Stir in the nuts, cookie crumbs, confectioners' sugar, Kahlúa, and vanilla and refrigerate for 30 minutes.

4. Place the coconut in a shallow bowl. Form the mixture into 1-inch balls and roll them in the coconut. Place the balls on a platter or parchment-lined baking sheet and refrigerate for 4 hours before serving.

VARIATIONS

- Use crushed ginger snaps or crushed vanilla wafers instead of chocolate cookie crumbs.
- Use Grand Marnier rather than Kahlúa and add ½ cup finely chopped dried apricots to the mixture.
- Use almonds, pecans, or hazelnuts in place of the macadamia nuts.

CRISPY PEANUT BUTTER BALLS

YIELD: 24 BALLS / **ACTIVE TIME:** 10 MINUTES / **TOTAL TIME:** 40 MINUTES

The taste of these treats will shift with the type of granola you use. My favorite combination contains nuts, as well as dried cranberries.

1. Place the peanut butter and honey in a mixing bowl and stir until combined. Stir in the granola, orange juice, and orange zest.

2. Spray your hands with cooking spray. Form the mixture into 1½-inch balls and arrange them on a parchment-lined baking sheet. Refrigerate for 30 minutes before serving.

VARIATIONS

- Use milk instead of orange juice, omit the orange zest, and add ½ teaspoon cinnamon to the peanut butter-and-honey mixture before adding the granola.
- Substitute almond butter for the peanut butter. If using natural almond butter, add ½ cup confectioners' sugar.
- Add ¾ cup chopped dried fruit.
- Add ¾ cup miniature chocolate or butterscotch chips.

INGREDIENTS:

½ CUP PEANUT BUTTER

3 TABLESPOONS HONEY

2 CUPS GRANOLA

2 TABLESPOONS FRESH ORANGE JUICE

1 TABLESPOON ORANGE ZEST

CARAMEL POPCORN BALLS

YIELD: 36 BALLS / **ACTIVE TIME:** 15 MINUTES / **TOTAL TIME:** 45 MINUTES

Children of all ages adore these. I've made them very large, wrapped them in cellophane, and hung them on my Christmas tree as edible ornaments that were given as favors to guests as they left my holiday party.

INGREDIENTS:

- 1 CUP FIRMLY PACKED LIGHT BROWN SUGAR
- ½ CUP WATER
- ½ CUP LIGHT CORN SYRUP
- 2 TABLESPOONS UNSALTED BUTTER
- 4 CUPS MINIATURE MARSHMALLOWS
- ½ TEASPOON CINNAMON
- 10 CUPS SALTED POPCORN, WARM

1. Place the sugar, water, and corn syrup in a saucepan and bring to a boil over medium-high heat. Swirl the pan frequently, but do not stir the mixture. Cook until the mixture acquires a nut-brown color, about 5 minutes.

2. Remove the pan from heat and stir in the butter, marshmallows, and cinnamon. Place the pan over low heat and stir until smooth.

3. Place the popcorn in a large mixing bowl, making sure to remove and discard any kernels that did not pop. Pour the caramel over the popcorn and stir to coat the kernels evenly.

4. Spray your hands with cooking spray and form the mixture into 3-inch balls. Arrange them on a parchment-lined baking sheet and refrigerate for 30 minutes before serving.

VARIATIONS

- Substitute 1 cup chopped toasted nuts for 1 cup of popcorn.
- Add ½ cup chopped dried fruit to the mixture.
- Substitute ground ginger for the cinnamon.

DRIED FRUIT & COCONUT BALLS

YIELD: 30 BALLS / **ACTIVE TIME:** 25 MINUTES / **TOTAL TIME:** 55 MINUTES

Simple, but the combination of fruits along with the sweet honey is really satisfying.

INGREDIENTS:

- 1 CUP CASHEWS
- 1½ CUPS SWEETENED SHREDDED COCONUT
- ½ CUP MINCED DRIED APRICOTS
- ½ CUP DRIED CURRANTS
- ½ CUP MINCED DRIED DATES
- ½ CUP GRAHAM CRACKER CRUMBS
- ⅓ CUP HONEY, PLUS MORE AS NEEDED
- ⅓ CUP OATS

1. Preheat the oven to 350°F. Place cashews on a baking sheet, place them in the oven, and roast for 5 to 7 minutes, until lightly browned. Remove from the oven, place the cashews in a food processor, and pulse until minced. Place the coconut on another baking sheet, place it in the oven, and roast for 10 to 12 minutes, until browned. Remove from the oven and set it aside.

2. Place the dried fruits, graham cracker crumbs, honey, oats, cashews, and ½ cup of the coconut in a mixing bowl and stir until thoroughly combined. Incorporate additional honey if the mixture is having trouble holding together.

3. Place the remaining coconut in a shallow bowl. Spray your hands with cooking spray, form the mixture into 2-inch balls, and roll them in the coconut. Place the balls on a platter or a parchment-lined baking sheet and refrigerate for 30 minutes before serving.

VARIATIONS

- Use any combination of dried fruits.
- Substitute any variety of nut for the cashews.
- Substitute crushed ginger snaps for the graham cracker crumbs.

HAZELNUT BALLS

YIELD: 48 BALLS / **ACTIVE TIME:** 20 MINUTES / **TOTAL TIME:** 45 MINUTES

Buttery, aromatic hazelnuts are my favorite. Here, they manage to perfume as well as flavor these delicious treats.

INGREDIENTS:

2 STICKS OF UNSALTED BUTTER, AT ROOM TEMPERATURE, PLUS MORE AS NEEDED

1½ CUPS HAZELNUTS, SKINS REMOVED

1 TEASPOON PURE VANILLA EXTRACT

2 CUPS CONFECTIONERS' SUGAR

2¼ CUPS ALL-PURPOSE FLOUR

PINCH OF KOSHER SALT

1. Preheat the oven to 350°F and grease two baking sheets with butter. Place the hazelnuts on another baking sheet, place them in the oven, and roast for 5 to 7 minutes, until lightly browned. Remove from the oven, place the nuts in a food processor, and pulse until minced. Set the hazelnuts aside.

2. Place the butter, vanilla, and ⅔ cup of the sugar in a mixing bowl and beat with a handheld mixer at medium speed until light and fluffy. Reduce the speed to low, add the flour and salt, and beat until just combined. Stir in the minced nuts, form the dough into ¾-inch balls, and place them on the prepared baking sheets. Place in the oven and bake for 15 to 18 minutes, until firm. Remove from the oven and let cool slightly.

3. Sift the remaining sugar into a shallow bowl and roll the balls in the sugar until coated. Place on wire racks to cool completely before serving.

VARIATIONS

- Omit the vanilla and add 1 tablespoon lemon zest.
- Add minced white chocolate to the mixture.
- Rather than hazelnuts use chopped almonds, peanuts, or cashews.
- Instead of nuts, use 1 cup chopped apricots, candied cherries, or some combination of dried and candied fruits.

The skins of hazelnuts are bitter and must be removed before using them in a preparation. Look for hazelnuts that have already had their skins removed. If you can't find them, arrange the hazelnuts in a single layer on a baking sheet and bake at 350°F for 25 minutes, keeping a close eye on them to ensure that they don't burn. Pour the hot nuts onto a kitchen towel and rub them back and forth until the skins come off.

MOCHA BALLS

YIELD: 36 BALLS / **ACTIVE TIME:** 20 MINUTES / **TOTAL TIME:** 45 MINUTES

Whoever came up with the glorious combination of chocolate and coffee, aka mocha, must have a special place in culinary heaven reserved for them.

INGREDIENTS:

- 1 STICK OF UNSALTED BUTTER, AT ROOM TEMPERATURE AND CHOPPED, PLUS MORE AS NEEDED
- 1 TABLESPOON INSTANT ESPRESSO POWDER
- 2 TABLESPOONS BOILING WATER
- ⅓ CUP GRANULATED SUGAR
- 1 LARGE EGG
- ½ TEASPOON PURE VANILLA EXTRACT
- 3 TABLESPOONS UNSWEETENED COCOA POWDER
- 1⅓ CUPS ALL-PURPOSE FLOUR
- PINCH OF KOSHER SALT
- 1 CUP CONFECTIONERS' SUGAR

1. Preheat the oven to 350°F and grease two baking sheets with butter. Place the espresso powder and water in a small bowl and stir until the espresso powder has dissolved. Set the mixture aside.

2. Place the butter and granulated sugar in a mixing bowl and beat with a handheld mixer at medium speed until light and fluffy. Incorporate the egg and vanilla, add the cocoa powder and espresso, and beat until combined, scraping the bowl as necessary. Reduce the speed to low, add the flour and salt, and beat until the mixture just holds together.

3. Form the dough into 1-inch balls and place them on the baking sheets. Bake for 15 to 18 minutes, until firm. Remove from the oven and let the balls cool slightly.

4. Sift the confectioners' sugar into a shallow bowl and roll the balls in it until they are coated. Place the balls on wire racks and let them cool completely before serving.

VARIATIONS

- For straight coffee balls, increase the instant espresso powder to 2 tablespoons and omit the cocoa powder.
- To ramp up the flavor, increase the amount of instant espresso powder to 1½ tablespoons and increase the cocoa powder to ¼ cup.

MEXICAN WEDDING COOKIES

YIELD: 36 COOKIES / **ACTIVE TIME:** 20 MINUTES / **TOTAL TIME:** 45 MINUTES

Also known as *polvorones*, these rich and buttery cookies are similar to shortbread. In Mexico they are made with lard, but I prefer unsalted butter.

INGREDIENTS:

- 1 LB. UNSALTED BUTTER, AT ROOM TEMPERATURE, PLUS MORE AS NEEDED
- 1¾ CUPS CONFECTIONERS' SUGAR
- 1 CUP CAKE FLOUR
- 1 CUP SELF-RISING FLOUR
- 1 CUP FINELY CHOPPED BLANCHED ALMONDS
- ½ TEASPOON PURE VANILLA EXTRACT

1. Preheat the oven to 350°F and grease two baking sheets with butter.

2. Place the butter in a mixing bowl with 1¼ cups of the sugar and beat with a handheld mixer at medium speed until light and fluffy. Add the cake flour, self-rising flour, almonds, and vanilla to the bowl and mix until just combined. The dough will be very stiff; add a few drops of hot water, if necessary, to make it pliable.

3. Form the dough into ¾-inch balls and place them 1 inch apart on the prepared baking sheets. Bake for 15 to 18 minutes, or until firm. Remove the pans from the oven.

4. Sift the remaining sugar into a shallow bowl and add a few cookies at a time, rolling them around in the sugar to coat them well. Transfer cookies to a rack to cool completely.

VARIATION

- Use pecans or walnuts in place of the almonds. Toast them in a 350°F oven for 5 to 7 minutes before chopping them.

BANANA FRITTERS

YIELD: 24 FRITTERS / **ACTIVE TIME:** 20 MINUTES / **TOTAL TIME:** 20 MINUTES

Serve these with ice cream, whipped cream, or all by themselves—there's no way to go wrong with these crispy treats.

1. Place the egg, milk, and bananas in a mixing bowl and stir to combine. Place the flour, granulated sugar, baking powder, cinnamon, ginger, and salt in a separate mixing bowl and stir to combine. Add the dry mixture to the wet mixture and stir until just combined.

2. Add oil to a Dutch oven until it is approximately 2 inches deep and warm to 375°F over medium-high heat. Preheat the oven to 150°F, line a baking sheet with paper towels, and place it in the oven.

3. Drop tablespoons of the batter into the oil and fry, turning them as they brown, until golden brown and crispy. Transfer the cooked fritters to the baking sheet in the oven. When all of the fritters have been cooked, dust them with the confectioners' sugar and serve.

VARIATIONS

- Use any juicy fruit; I've used a combination of banana and mango, and another featuring pineapple, peaches, and raspberries.
- Replace 2 tablespoons of the milk with rum or a liqueur.

INGREDIENTS:

1 LARGE EGG

½ CUP WHOLE MILK

1½ CUPS CHOPPED BANANAS

1⅓ CUPS ALL-PURPOSE FLOUR

3 TABLESPOONS GRANULATED SUGAR

1½ TEASPOONS BAKING POWDER

½ TEASPOON CINNAMON

½ TEASPOON GROUND GINGER

PINCH OF KOSHER SALT

VEGETABLE OIL, AS NEEDED

½ CUP CONFECTIONERS' SUGAR

FRIED ICE CREAM BALLS

YIELD: 4 TO 6 SERVINGS / **ACTIVE TIME:** 30 MINUTES / **TOTAL TIME:** 8 HOURS AND 30 MINUTES

This is hardly a spur-of-the-moment dessert; the ice cream balls spend many hours freezing between steps, so it's not a bad idea to start this preparation the day before you plan to fry and serve them. They are always a hit, however, and easy to make. The contrast between the crispy coating and chilly, soft ice cream is glorious.

INGREDIENTS:

1 QUART ICE CREAM, SLIGHTLY THAWED

3 LARGE EGGS

2 TABLESPOONS SUGAR

1 TEASPOON PURE VANILLA EXTRACT

6 CUPS CORNFLAKES

VEGETABLE OIL, AS NEEDED

1½ CUPS CHOCOLATE SAUCE (SEE PAGE 770), WARMED, FOR SERVING

1. Line a baking sheet with plastic wrap and place it in the freezer for 10 minutes. Remove the sheet from the freezer and scoop a dozen 1 oz. portions of the ice cream onto it. Cover with plastic wrap and freeze for 3 hours, until the ice cream is very hard.

2. Place the eggs, sugar, and vanilla in a mixing bowl and stir to combine. Place the cornflakes in a food processor and pulse until finely ground.

3. Place the cornflakes in a shallow bowl. Dip the scoops of ice cream into the egg, let the excess drip off, and then roll them in the cornflakes. Return the coated balls to the freezer and freeze for at least 1 hour. Reserve the remaining cornflakes and refrigerate the remaining egg mixture.

4. After 1 hour, repeat the coating process. Freeze the ice cream balls for another 4 hours.

5. Add oil to a Dutch oven until it is approximately 2 inches deep and warm to 375°F over medium heat. Working in batches of two or three, add the balls to the oil and fry for about 30 seconds. Transfer the fried balls to a paper towel–lined plate to drain. When all of the ice cream balls have been cooked, serve alongside the Chocolate Sauce.

VARIATION

- Roll the balls in crushed puffed rice cereal, graham cracker crumbs, or cookie crumbs instead of cornflakes.

EGGNOG FRITTERS WITH MAPLE SAUCE

YIELD: 24 FRITTERS / **ACTIVE TIME:** 20 MINUTES / **TOTAL TIME:** 20 MINUTES

Eggnog, flavored with spices and brandy, is not only a holiday treat, as its unique flavor makes these fritters welcome any time of year.

INGREDIENTS:

- 2 LARGE EGGS
- 1 CUP WHOLE MILK
- ¼ CUP BRANDY
- 1¼ TEASPOONS PURE VANILLA EXTRACT
- 2½ CUPS ALL-PURPOSE FLOUR
- ½ CUP SUGAR
- 2 TEASPOONS BAKING POWDER
- 1 TEASPOON BAKING SODA
- 1 TEASPOON APPLE PIE SPICE
- PINCH OF KOSHER SALT
- 1 CUP REAL MAPLE SYRUP
- ½ TEASPOON CINNAMON
- VEGETABLE OIL, AS NEEDED

1. Place the eggs, milk, 2 tablespoons of the brandy, and ¾ teaspoon of the vanilla in a mixing bowl and stir to combine. Place the flour, sugar, baking powder, baking soda, apple pie spice, and salt in another mixing bowl and stir to combine. Add the dry mixture to the wet mixture and stir until just combined.

2. Place the maple syrup, cinnamon, and remaining brandy and vanilla in a small saucepan and bring to a simmer over medium heat, stirring frequently. Remove the pan from heat and set it aside.

3. Add oil to a Dutch oven until it is approximately 2 inches deep and warm to 375°F over medium-high heat. Preheat the oven to 150°F, line a baking sheet with paper towels, and place it in the oven. Drop tablespoons of the batter into the oil and fry, turning them as they brown, until golden brown and crispy. Transfer the cooked fritters to the baking sheet in the oven. When all of the fritters have been cooked, serve them with the maple sauce.

VARIATION

- Use Grand Marnier and 2 teaspoons orange zest in place of the brandy and apples.

SWEET RICOTTA FRITTERS

YIELD: 24 FRITTERS / **ACTIVE TIME:** 20 MINUTES / **TOTAL TIME:** 20 MINUTES

Ricotta cheese has a creamy flavor and texture that make these fritters light and delicious. In addition, it allows the hint of orange to really pop.

INGREDIENTS:

- 4 LARGE EGGS
- ⅓ CUP GRANULATED SUGAR
- 1 LB. RICOTTA CHEESE
- 2 TEASPOONS ORANGE ZEST
- ½ TEASPOON PURE VANILLA EXTRACT
- 1 TABLESPOON BAKING POWDER
- PINCH OF KOSHER SALT
- 1 CUP ALL-PURPOSE FLOUR
- VEGETABLE OIL, AS NEEDED
- ⅓ CUP CONFECTIONERS' SUGAR

1. Place the eggs, granulated sugar, ricotta, orange zest, and vanilla in a mixing bowl and beat with a handheld mixer at medium speed until smooth. Incorporate the baking powder and salt, reduce the speed to low, add the flour, and beat until just combined.

2. Add oil to a Dutch oven until it is approximately 2 inches deep and warm to 375°F over medium-high heat. Preheat the oven to 150°F, line a baking sheet with paper towels, and place it in the oven. Drop tablespoons of the batter into the oil and fry, turning them as they brown, until golden brown and crispy. Transfer the cooked fritters to the baking sheet in the oven. When all of the fritters have been cooked, dust them with the confectioners' sugar and serve.

VARIATIONS

- Omit the orange zest and add ½ teaspoon cinnamon and a pinch of ground nutmeg.
- Add ½ cup minced dried fruit to the batter.
- Drizzle warm honey over the fritters instead of dusting them with confectioners' sugar.

PROFITEROLES WITH ICE CREAM & CARAMEL

YIELD: 36 CREAM PUFFS / **ACTIVE TIME:** 30 MINUTES / **TOTAL TIME:** 1 HOUR

Profiteroles are baby cream puffs filled with ice cream and traditionally topped with a chocolate sauce or glaze. The dough is called *pâte a choux* in classic French cooking; it's a useful one to have in your repertoire.

INGREDIENTS:

- 1 CUP WATER
- 6 TABLESPOONS UNSALTED BUTTER
- 2 TEASPOONS SUGAR
- ½ TEASPOON KOSHER SALT
- ¼ TEASPOON PURE VANILLA EXTRACT
- ¾ CUP ALL-PURPOSE FLOUR
- 5 LARGE EGGS
- 3 CUPS ICE CREAM
- 1½ CUPS CARAMEL (SEE PAGE 769)

1. Preheat the oven to 425°F and line two baking sheets with parchment paper. Place the water, butter, sugar, salt, and vanilla in a saucepan and bring to a boil over medium-high heat, stirring occasionally. Remove the pan from the heat, add the flour, and stir until the mixture is smooth.

2. Place the saucepan over high heat and cook, while stirring it constantly, until the dough begins to leave the side of the pan and film the bottom of it.

3. Transfer the dough to a mixing bowl and incorporate four of the eggs, working them in one at a time and scraping down the bowl as needed. Place the dough in a piping bag fitted with a round nozzle and pipe mounds that are approximately 1 inch in diameter and ½ inch high on the baking sheets, leaving 2 inches between the mounds.

4. Place the remaining egg in a bowl and beat until scrambled. Brush the tops of the mounds with the egg. Place in the oven and bake for about 20 minutes, until the pastries are golden brown and dry to the touch. Remove from the oven and use a paring knife to cut a slit in the side of each pastry to allow the steam to escape. Turn off the oven, place the pastries back in the oven, leave the door ajar, and let the pastries sit for 5 minutes before transferring them to a wire rack to cool completely.

5. To serve, split the puffs in half, fill them with ice cream, and place the halves back together. Top with the Caramel and serve.

VARIATIONS

- Fill the pastries with any flavor of mousse or pudding.
- Top them with Chocolate Sauce (see page 770).
- For a savory version, omit the sugar, add a pinch of freshly ground black pepper, and fill them with egg salad, smoked salmon, or cream cheese with chives.

COOKIE DOUGH POPS

YIELD: 15 TO 20 POPS / **ACTIVE TIME:** 15 MINUTES / **TOTAL TIME:** 3 HOURS AND 15 MINUTES

The simple addition of lollipop sticks makes these balls a whole lotta fun.

INGREDIENTS:

- 1 STICK OF UNSALTED BUTTER, AT ROOM TEMPERATURE
- ⅓ CUP GRANULATED SUGAR
- ⅓ CUP PACKED DARK BROWN SUGAR
- ½ TEASPOON KOSHER SALT
- ½ TEASPOON PURE VANILLA EXTRACT
- 1 CUP ALL-PURPOSE FLOUR
- 1 CUP SEMISWEET CHOCOLATE CHIPS
- ½ LB. WHITE, MILK, OR DARK CHOCOLATE, MELTED
- CHOPPED NUTS (OPTIONAL)
- RAINBOW OR CHOCOLATE SPRINKLES (OPTIONAL)

1. Place the butter, granulated sugar, and brown sugar in the bowl of a stand mixer and beat until it is light and fluffy. Add the salt and vanilla and beat until combined.

2. Add the flour in two batches and beat until almost all of it has been incorporated. Before the flour is completely blended in, add the chocolate chips and mix until well combined. Cover the dough with plastic wrap and place in the refrigerator for 1 hour.

3. Line a baking sheet with parchment paper. Remove the mixture from the refrigerator and scoop out teaspoon-sized balls of dough. Roll them into spheres and place on the baking sheet. Insert lollipop sticks into each sphere.

4. Dip each pop into the melted chocolate until completely coated. Decorate them with nuts or sprinkles, if desired, and place them back on the baking sheet. Place in the refrigerator and chill until the chocolate is set, about 2 hours.

CARAMEL & COCONUT MACAROONS

YIELD: 16 MACAROONS / **ACTIVE TIME:** 20 MINUTES / **TOTAL TIME:** 2 HOURS

The chocolate is optional here because these macaroons already have plenty going on.

1. Place the butter, milk, Caramel, and salt in a small saucepan and cook over medium heat. Once the butter has melted, add the coconut and stir until it is completely coated.

2. Line a baking sheet with parchment paper and spray your hands with cooking spray. Form tablespoons of the caramel-and-coconut mixture into balls, place them on the sheet, and refrigerate for 1 hour.

3. If using the chocolate chips, place them in a microwave-safe bowl and microwave on medium until melted, removing to stir every 20 seconds. Dip half of the cooled macaroons into the melted chocolate and place them back on the baking sheet. Once all the macaroons have been dipped, drizzle the remaining chocolate over the top. Place in the refrigerator and chill until the chocolate has hardened, about 30 minutes.

INGREDIENTS:

- 6 TABLESPOONS UNSALTED BUTTER, MELTED
- 3 TABLESPOONS WHOLE MILK
- 2 CUPS CARAMEL (SEE PAGE 769)
- 1 TEASPOON KOSHER SALT
- 4 CUPS SWEETENED SHREDDED COCONUT
- 4 OZ. DARK CHOCOLATE CHIPS (OPTIONAL)

CHRISTMAS IN THE CARIBBEAN

YIELD: 36 COOKIES / **ACTIVE TIME:** 20 MINUTES / **TOTAL TIME:** 1 HOUR

The sweet lime glaze and the coconut make these treats the next best thing to an actual tropical island vacation.

INGREDIENTS:

3 TABLESPOONS CREAM CHEESE, AT ROOM TEMPERATURE

ZEST AND JUICE OF 1 LIME

1½ CUPS CONFECTIONERS' SUGAR

2½ CUPS ALL-PURPOSE FLOUR

¾ CUP CASTER SUGAR

¼ TEASPOON KOSHER SALT

2 STICKS OF UNSALTED BUTTER, DIVIDED INTO TABLESPOONS AND AT ROOM TEMPERATURE

2 TEASPOONS PURE VANILLA EXTRACT

1½ CUPS SWEETENED SHREDDED COCONUT

1. Preheat the oven to 350°F and line two baking sheets with parchment paper. Place 1 tablespoon of the cream cheese and 1 tablespoon of the lime juice in a mixing bowl and stir until the mixture is smooth. Add the confectioners' sugar, and whisk until the mixture is smooth and thin, adding the remaining lime juice in 1-teaspoon increments until the glaze reaches the desired consistency. Set the glaze aside.

2. Place the flour, caster sugar, salt, and lime zest in a separate mixing bowl and whisk to combine. Add the butter one piece at a time and use a pastry blender to work the mixture until it is a coarse meal. Add the vanilla and remaining cream cheese and work the mixture until it is a smooth dough.

3. Form the mixture into balls and place them on the baking sheets. Bake for about 15 minutes, until light brown. Remove from the oven and let cool slightly.

4. Place the coconut in a shallow bowl. Brush the glaze over the balls and roll them in the coconut. Refrigerate for 30 minutes before serving.

TANG YUAN DANGO

YIELD: 6 SERVINGS / **ACTIVE TIME:** 30 MINUTES / **TOTAL TIME:** 2 HOURS

Topping these sweet rice balls with freeze-dried berries adds a burst of color and flavor.

1. Place the strawberries and sugar in a heatproof mixing bowl and stir to combine. Place 1 inch of water in a small saucepan and bring it to a boil. Cover the bowl with plastic wrap, place it over the saucepan, and let cook for 1 hour. Check the water level every 15 minutes and add more if it has evaporated. After 1 hour, turn off the heat and let the syrup cool. When cool, strain and discard the solids.

2. Bring water to a boil in a large pot. Place the flour, water, and ¾ cup of the syrup in a large mixing bowl and use a fork to work the mixture until combined and very dry. Remove 2 tablespoons of the mixture and roll each tablespoon into a ball. Place the balls in the boiling water and cook until they float to the surface and double in size, about 5 minutes. Return the balls to the mixture, add the canola oil, and use the fork to incorporate.

3. Bring the water back to a boil and prepare an ice bath. Place the mixture on a flour-dusted work surface and knead until it is a smooth and slightly tacky dough. If the dough is too dry or too sticky, incorporate water or flour as needed.

4. Divide the dough into 18 pieces, roll them into balls, and use a slotted spoon to gently lower them into the pot. Gently stir to keep them from sticking to the bottom and then cook until they float to the surface and double in size, about 8 minutes. Remove with a slotted spoon, refresh in the ice bath, drain, and skewer the balls in sets of three. Garnish with the freeze-dried strawberries, drizzle some of the remaining syrup over the top, and serve.

INGREDIENTS:

- 4 CUPS FRESH STRAWBERRIES, HULLED AND CHOPPED
- 1¼ CUPS SUGAR
- 1½ CUPS SWEET RICE FLOUR (GLUTINOUS RICE FLOUR), PLUS MORE AS NEEDED
- ⅓ CUP WATER, PLUS MORE AS NEEDED
- 2 TABLESPOONS CANOLA OIL
- FREEZE-DRIED STRAWBERRIES, FOR GARNISH

JIAN DUI

YIELD: 4 SERVINGS / **ACTIVE TIME:** 1 HOUR / **TOTAL TIME:** 1 HOUR

One of the most beloved Asian sweet dumplings, red bean paste is another popular filling for these crispy and chewy balls.

INGREDIENTS:

- ¼ CUP ROASTED PEANUTS, CHOPPED
- 2½ TABLESPOONS GRANULATED SUGAR
- ⅛ TEASPOON KOSHER SALT
- 2 CUPS SWEET RICE FLOUR (GLUTINOUS RICE FLOUR), PLUS MORE FOR DUSTING
- ¾ CUP WATER
- ⅔ CUP FIRMLY PACKED LIGHT BROWN SUGAR
- PEANUT OIL, AS NEEDED
- ⅓ CUP SESAME SEEDS

1. Place the peanuts, granulated sugar, and salt in a food processor and pulse until ground. Be careful not to process the mixture too much and make peanut butter. Place the mixture in a small bowl and set aside. Place the sweet rice flour in a separate bowl and make a well in the center. Place the water in a small pot and bring it to a boil. Add the brown sugar, stir until dissolved, and then pour the syrup into the well. Stir the mixture until a ball of dough forms.

2. Transfer the dough to a flour-dusted work surface and knead until smooth. The dough needs to be hot, so be careful. Cut the dough into 2 pieces and roll each one into a log. The dough tends to dry quickly, so keep a bowl of water near the work surface and dip your hands into it as necessary. Cut each log into eight pieces and roll each piece into a ball. Cover the pieces with plastic wrap to keep them from drying out.

3. Place a ball in the palm of one hand and use the thumb of your free hand to make a hole in the center of the ball. Fill with 1 teaspoon of the peanut mixture and smooth the dough over the filling. Pinch the seam and twist to remove any excess dough. Roll into a smooth ball, place on a parchment-lined baking sheet, and cover with plastic wrap. Repeat with the remaining balls and filling.

4. Add peanut oil to a Dutch oven until it is 2 inches deep and bring to 350°F over medium heat. Place the sesame seeds in a shallow bowl. Dip each ball into the bowl of water, shake to remove any excess, and roll them in the sesame seeds until coated.

5. Working in batches of four, drop the balls into the hot oil and cook, gently stirring initially, until they float to the surface, about 3 minutes. Push the balls to the edge of the Dutch oven and baste them with the hot oil as they cook. Cook for another 3 to 4 minutes and transfer to a paper towel–lined plate. Serving the balls warm is preferred, but they are also delicious at room temperature.

LUQAIMAT

YIELD: 4 SERVINGS / **ACTIVE TIME:** 30 MINUTES / **TOTAL TIME:** 1 HOUR AND 30 MINUTES

This sweet and simple dumpling is typically the reward at the end of a fast during Ramadan.

INGREDIENTS:

- 1 CUP ALL-PURPOSE FLOUR
- ½ TEASPOON INSTANT YEAST
- ½ CUP NONFAT MILK POWDER
- 2 TABLESPOONS SUGAR
- ½ TEASPOON CARDAMOM
- PINCH OF SAFFRON
- ⅓ CUP LUKEWARM WATER (90°F), PLUS MORE AS NEEDED
- VEGETABLE OIL, AS NEEDED
- ½ CUP DATE SYRUP OR HONEY
- 1 TABLESPOON SESAME SEEDS, TOASTED

1. Place the flour, yeast, milk powder, sugar, cardamom, and saffron in a mixing bowl and stir until combined. While working the mixture with your hands, gradually incorporate the water until a dough forms. Cover with a dry kitchen towel and rest for 1 hour.

2. Add vegetable oil to a Dutch oven until it is 2 inches deep and bring it to 350°F over medium heat. Wet your hands and roll tablespoons of the dough into balls. Drop them into the hot oil and fry, while stirring, until they are dark brown, about 3 to 5 minutes. Transfer to a paper towel–lined plate to drain and cool.

3. When all of the dumplings have been cooked, place them in a serving bowl, add the date syrup or honey and the toasted sesame seeds. Toss to coat and serve immediately.

GALUSTE CU PRUNE

YIELD: 4 SERVINGS / **ACTIVE TIME:** 30 MINUTES / **TOTAL TIME:** 1 HOUR

As beautiful as they are delicious, these are the pride of Romania.

INGREDIENTS:

- 3 PLUMS, PITTED AND QUARTERED
- 3 TABLESPOONS CONFECTIONERS' SUGAR
- 1½ LBS. YUKON GOLD POTATOES, PEELED AND CHOPPED
- 2 EGGS
- 1 CUP ALL-PURPOSE FLOUR
- 3 TABLESPOONS SEMOLINA FLOUR
- ¼ TEASPOON KOSHER SALT
- 1 TABLESPOON OLIVE OIL
- 3 TABLESPOONS UNSALTED BUTTER
- 2 CUPS BREAD CRUMBS
- 6 TABLESPOONS GRANULATED SUGAR

1. Place the plums in a small bowl, sprinkle the confectioners' sugar on top, and toss to combine. Set aside.

2. Place the potatoes in a saucepan, cover with water, and bring to a boil. Cook until they are fork-tender, about 20 minutes. Drain the potatoes, place them in a large mixing bowl, and mash until smooth. Add the eggs, flours, and salt and stir until the dough just holds together.

3. Bring water to a boil in a large saucepan and add the olive oil. Place the butter in a skillet and melt over medium heat. Add the bread crumbs, reduce the heat to low, and cook, while stirring frequently, until the bread crumbs are golden brown. Remove from heat, add the granulated sugar, and stir to combine. Let the mixture cool completely.

4. Divide the dough into 12 pieces and flatten them to ¼ inch thick. Place one of the sugar-coated plums in the center of each piece, shape the dough around the plum, and gently roll into a ball.

5. Place the balls in the boiling water and cook until they rise to the surface, about 4 minutes. Remove them with a strainer and roll them in the bread crumb mixture until completely coated. Place the balls on a platter and let cool completely before serving.

LEMON & COCONUT SNOWBALLS

YIELD: 24 BALLS / **ACTIVE TIME:** 5 MINUTES / **TOTAL TIME:** 35 MINUTES

These tropical-leaning treats are no-bake, making them perfect for those days when it is far too hot to even think about turning on the oven.

1. Place the flour, two-thirds of the coconut, and the sugar in a large mixing bowl and stir to combine. Place the remaining coconut in a shallow bowl and set aside.

2. Add the remaining ingredients and stir until the mixture is a rough dough. Form tablespoons of the dough into balls and then roll them in the coconut. Place the balls on a parchment-lined baking sheet, cover with plastic wrap, and refrigerate for 30 minutes before serving.

INGREDIENTS:

- 1 CUP ALL-PURPOSE FLOUR
- ¾ CUP UNSWEETENED SHREDDED COCONUT
- 2 CUPS SUGAR
- ZEST AND JUICE OF ½ LEMON
- ½ CUP CREAM CHEESE, AT ROOM TEMPERATURE
- 1 TEASPOON PURE VANILLA EXTRACT

CHIA & SESAME BLISS BALLS

YIELD: 12 BALLS / **ACTIVE TIME:** 10 MINUTES / **TOTAL TIME:** 30 MINUTES

One bite and you'll recognize that the bliss in the name is far from hyperbole.

INGREDIENTS:

- 2 STICKS OF UNSALTED BUTTER
- ¼ CUP UNSWEETENED COCOA POWDER
- 1 TEASPOON PURE ALMOND EXTRACT
- ½ TEASPOON PURE VANILLA EXTRACT
- 1 CUP SUGAR
- ½ CUP WHITE CHIA SEEDS
- 2 TABLESPOONS SESAME SEEDS

1. Place the butter, cocoa powder, extracts, and sugar in a bowl and beat with a handheld mixer on medium speed until the mixture is fluffy. Cover the bowl and freeze until the mixture is set, about 20 minutes.

2. Combine the chia seeds and sesame seeds in a shallow bowl. Form 2-tablespoon portions of the mixture into balls and roll them in the seed mixture. Serve immediately or store in the refrigerator.

PISTACHIO BALLS

YIELD: 12 BALLS / **ACTIVE TIME:** 10 MINUTES / **TOTAL TIME:** 30 MINUTES

If you're a fan of pistachio ice cream, try adding a teaspoon of almond extract to the mixture.

INGREDIENTS:

- 1 STICK OF UNSALTED BUTTER
- ½ CUP PEANUT BUTTER
- ¼ CUP UNSWEETENED COCOA POWDER
- ½ CUP SUGAR
- PINCH OF KOSHER SALT
- 1 TABLESPOON DRIED CRANBERRIES, MINCED
- ¾ CUP CHOPPED PISTACHIOS

1. Place the butter and peanut butter in a microwave-safe bowl and microwave on medium until melted, removing to stir every 15 seconds. Stir in all of the remaining ingredients, except for the pistachios, cover the bowl, and freeze until set, about 20 minutes.

2. Place the chopped pistachios in a shallow bowl. Form 2-tablespoon portions of the mixture into balls and roll them in the nuts. Serve immediately or store in the refrigerator.

CHOCOLATE & HAZELNUT BALLS

YIELD: 18 BALLS / **ACTIVE TIME:** 10 MINUTES / **TOTAL TIME:** 1 HOUR

The delicious and decadent spread known as Nutella serves as the inspiration for these treats.

1. Preheat the oven to 350°F and line a springform pan with parchment paper. Place the semisweet chocolate chips in a microwave-safe bowl and microwave on medium until melted, removing to stir every 15 seconds.

2. Place the egg yolks and sugar in a mixing bowl and beat with a handheld mixer until pale and very thick. Stir in the melted chocolate and then fold in the ground hazelnuts.

3. Place the egg whites and salt in a separate mixing bowl and beat until the mixture holds stiff peaks. Working in three increments, fold the mixture into the hazelnut mixture.

4. Scrape the batter into the pan, place it in the oven, and bake for about 25 minutes, until the cake is dry to the touch. Remove and let cool completely on a wire rack.

5. Cut the cake into pieces and add them to a food processor in batches. Pulse until they are crumbs and then place the crumbs in a mixing bowl. Stir in the frosting until you are able to form the mixture into balls; you may not need to use all of the frosting. Form the mixture into golf ball–sized spheres, place them on a parchment-lined baking sheet, and store them in the freezer.

6. Place the bittersweet chocolate chips in a heatproof bowl. Warm the cream in a saucepan until it is just about to come to a boil. Pour the cream over the chocolate, let stand for 1 minute, and then stir until smooth.

7. Let the mixture cool for 5 minutes and remove the balls from the freezer. Dip them into the chocolate until completely coated, place them back on the baking sheet, and freeze until the chocolate has set, about 15 minutes.

INGREDIENTS:

- ½ CUP SEMISWEET CHOCOLATE CHIPS
- 5 LARGE EGGS, YOLKS AND WHITES SEPARATED
- 1 CUP SUGAR
- 5 OZ. HAZELNUTS, SKINS REMOVED AND FINELY GROUND
- PINCH OF KOSHER SALT
- 2 CUPS BITTERSWEET CHOCOLATE CHIPS
- ½ CUP HEAVY CREAM

SIDES AND ACCOMPANIMENTS

It's true that if you eat enough of any of these meatballs, they will make a meal. But it's nice to balance out all that protein with vegetables, and soak up all the delicious sauces with various starches. Here are some recipes that allow you to do just that, so you can mix and match with the meatballs any way you deem fit.

RUSTIC WHOLE WHEAT BREAD

YIELD: 1 LOAF / **ACTIVE TIME:** 30 MINUTES / **TOTAL TIME:** 21 HOURS

Bread making is a delicate art, as the wrong measurements can lead to a flat loaf and a disappointed baker. That being said, this whole wheat masterpiece will leave no one disappointed, especially when it's served while still warm alongside sauced meatballs.

INGREDIENTS:

3¼ CUPS ALL-PURPOSE FLOUR, PLUS MORE AS NEEDED

1¼ CUPS WHOLE WHEAT FLOUR

1½ CUPS WATER (90°F)

JUST UNDER ¼ TEASPOON ACTIVE DRY YEAST

2¼ TEASPOONS KOSHER SALT

1. Place the flours and water in a large mixing bowl and use your hands to combine the mixture into a dough. Cover the bowl with a kitchen towel and let the mixture sit for 45 minutes to 1 hour.

2. Sprinkle the yeast and salt over the dough and fold until they have been incorporated. Cover the bowl with the kitchen towel and let stand for 30 minutes. Remove the towel, fold a corner of the dough into the center, and cover. Repeat every 30 minutes until all of the corners have been folded in.

3. After the last fold, cover the dough with the kitchen towel and let it sit for 12 to 14 hours.

4. Dust a work surface lightly with flour and place the dough on it. Fold each corner of the dough into the center, flip the dough over, and roll it into a smooth ball. Dust your hands with flour as needed. Be careful not to roll or press the dough too hard, as this will prevent the dough from expanding properly. Dust a bowl with flour and place the dough, seam side down, in the bowl. Let stand until it has roughly doubled in size, about 1 hour and 15 minutes.

5. Cut a round piece of parchment paper that is 1 inch larger than the circumference of your cast-iron Dutch oven. When the dough has approximately 1 hour left in its rise (this is also known as "proofing"), preheat the oven to 475°F and place the covered Dutch oven in the oven as it warms.

6. When the dough has roughly doubled in size, invert it onto a lightly floured work surface. Use a very sharp knife to score one side of the loaf. Using oven mitts, remove the Dutch oven from the oven. Use a bench scraper to transfer the dough onto the piece of parchment, scored side up. Hold the sides of the parchment and carefully lower the dough into the Dutch oven. Cover the Dutch oven and place it in the oven for 20 minutes.

7. Remove the lid and bake the loaf for an additional 20 minutes. Remove from the oven and let cool on a wire rack for at least 2 hours before slicing.

RUSTIC WHITE BREAD

YIELD: 1 LOAF / **ACTIVE TIME:** 30 MINUTES / **TOTAL TIME:** 21 HOURS

Don't be thrown by the "white" in the name. Letting the dough rest overnight allows an incredible amount of flavor to develop, resulting in a loaf that is anything but bland.

INGREDIENTS:

4½ CUPS ALL-PURPOSE FLOUR, PLUS MORE AS NEEDED

1½ CUPS WATER (90°F)

JUST UNDER ¼ TEASPOON ACTIVE DRY YEAST

2¼ TEASPOONS KOSHER SALT

1. Place the flour and water in a large mixing bowl and use your hands to combine the mixture into a dough. Cover the bowl with a kitchen towel and let the mixture sit for 45 minutes to 1 hour.

2. Sprinkle the yeast and salt over the dough and fold until they have been incorporated. Cover the bowl with the kitchen towel and let stand for 30 minutes. Remove the towel, fold a corner of the dough into the center, and cover. Repeat every 30 minutes until all of the corners have been folded in.

3. After the last fold, cover the dough with the kitchen towel and let it sit for 12 to 14 hours.

4. Dust a work surface lightly with flour and place the dough on it. Fold each corner of the dough to the center, flip the dough over, and roll it into a smooth ball. Dust your hands with flour as needed. Be careful not to roll or press the dough too hard, as this will prevent the dough from expanding properly. Dust a bowl with flour and place the dough, seam side down, in the bowl. Let stand until it has roughly doubled in size, about 1 hour and 15 minutes.

5. Cut a round piece of parchment paper that is 1 inch larger than the circumference of your cast-iron Dutch oven. When the dough has approximately 1 hour left in its rise (this is also known as "proofing"), preheat the oven to 475°F and place the covered Dutch oven in the oven as it warms.

6. When the dough has roughly doubled in size, invert it onto a lightly floured work surface. Use a very sharp knife to score one side of the loaf. Using oven mitts, remove the Dutch oven from the oven. Use a bench scraper to transfer the dough onto the piece of parchment, scored side up. Hold the sides of the parchment and carefully lower the dough into the Dutch oven. Cover the Dutch oven and place it in the oven for 20 minutes.

7. Remove the lid and bake the loaf for an additional 20 minutes. Remove from the oven and let cool on a wire rack for at least 2 hours before slicing.

CORN BREAD

YIELD: 16 SERVINGS / **ACTIVE TIME:** 40 MINUTES / **TOTAL TIME:** 2 HOURS AND 15 MINUTES

Incorporating a creamy corn puree into the batter makes all the difference here.

INGREDIENTS:

- 5 EARS OF CORN, SILK REMOVED
- 10 TABLESPOONS UNSALTED BUTTER
- 1 CUP DICED ONION
- 3 GARLIC CLOVES, MINCED
- 2 TEASPOONS KOSHER SALT, PLUS MORE TO TASTE
- 2¾ CUPS HEAVY CREAM
- 2 CUPS ALL-PURPOSE FLOUR
- 2 CUPS CORNMEAL
- ¼ CUP BROWN SUGAR
- 1½ TABLESPOONS BAKING POWDER
- ½ TEASPOON CAYENNE PEPPER
- ½ TEASPOON PAPRIKA
- 1½ CUPS HONEY
- 6 EGGS
- ¼ CUP SOUR CREAM

1. Preheat the oven to 400°F.

2. Place the ears of corn on a baking sheet, place it in the oven, and bake for 25 minutes, until the kernels have a slight give to them. Remove from the oven and let cool. When the ears of corn are cool enough to handle, remove the husks and cut the kernels from the cob. Lower the oven temperature to 300°F.

3. Place 2 tablespoons of the butter in a large saucepan and melt over medium heat. Add the onion and garlic, season with salt, and cook until the onion is translucent. Set ¾ cup of the corn kernels aside and add the rest to the pan. Add 2 cups of the cream and a pinch of salt and cook until the corn is very tender, about 15 to 20 minutes.

4. Strain, reserve the cream, and transfer the solids to the blender. Puree until smooth, adding the cream as needed if the mixture is too thick. Season to taste and allow the puree to cool completely.

5. Place the flour, cornmeal, salt, brown sugar, baking powder, cayenne pepper, and paprika in a large mixing bowl and stir until combined. Place 2 cups of the corn puree, the honey, eggs, remaining cream, and sour cream in a separate large mixing bowl and stir until combined. Gradually add the dry mixture to the wet mixture and stir to combine. When all of the wet mixture has been incorporated, add the reserved corn kernels and fold the mixture until they are evenly distributed.

6. Grease an 11 x 7–inch baking pan and pour the batter into it. Place the pan in the oven and bake until a toothpick inserted into the center comes out clean, about 35 minutes. Remove from the oven and briefly cool before cutting.

DINNER ROLLS

YIELD: 12 ROLLS / **ACTIVE TIME:** 1 HOUR / **TOTAL TIME:** 3 HOURS

These classic dinner rolls are light, flaky, buttery perfection. Use them to make meatball sliders, or serve them beside your favorites.

INGREDIENTS:

- 1¼ CUPS WHOLE MILK, HEATED TO 110°F
- 3 TABLESPOONS SUGAR
- 1 TABLESPOON ACTIVE DRY YEAST
- 1 STICK OF UNSALTED BUTTER
- ¾ TEASPOON KOSHER SALT
- 2 EGGS, AT ROOM TEMPERATURE AND LIGHTLY BEATEN
- 3½ CUPS CAKE OR BREAD FLOUR, PLUS MORE AS NEEDED

1. In a small bowl, combine ½ cup warm milk and the sugar. Sprinkle the yeast over it, stir, and set aside so the yeast can proof (about 10 minutes).

2. While the yeast is proofing, melt the butter in a 12-inch cast-iron skillet over medium-low heat, and remove from heat when melted.

3. When the yeast mix is frothy, stir in 3 tablespoons of the melted butter, the remaining milk, the salt, and the eggs. Then stir in the flour, mixing until all ingredients are incorporated. Transfer to a lightly floured surface and knead the dough for 5 to 10 minutes, until it is soft, springy, and elastic.

4. Coat the bottom and sides of a large mixing bowl (ceramic is best) with butter. Place the ball of dough in the bowl, cover loosely with plastic wrap, put it in a naturally warm, draft-free location, and let it rise until doubled in size, about 45 minutes to 1 hour.

5. Prepare a lightly floured surface to work on. Punch down the dough in the bowl and transfer it to the floured surface. Warm the skillet containing the butter so that it is melted again.

6. Break off pieces of the dough and shape them into 2-inch balls with your hands. Roll the balls in the butter in the skillet, and leave them in the skillet.

7. Cover the skillet loosely with a clean kitchen towel, put it in the warm, draft-free spot, and let the rolls rise until doubled in size, about 30 minutes. While they're rising, preheat the oven to 350°F.

8. When the rolls have risen and the oven is ready, cover the skillet with aluminum foil and bake in the oven for 20 minutes. Remove the foil and finish cooking, another 15 minutes or so, until the rolls are golden on top and light and springy. Serve warm.

GARLIC KNOTS

YIELD: ABOUT 36 KNOTS / **ACTIVE TIME:** 45 MINUTES / **TOTAL TIME:** 1 HOUR AND 30 MINUTES

These knots will get a great crust on them if you bake them in a cast-iron skillet, and then they can be bathed in garlic-parsley butter and put on a plate. Don't expect them to hang around for long, which is why this is a double batch of dough.

INGREDIENTS:

FOR THE SAUCE

- 1 STICK OF UNSALTED BUTTER
- 8 GARLIC CLOVES, MINCED
- ⅓ CUP MINCED PARSLEY LEAVES
- 2 TEASPOONS KOSHER SALT

FOR THE KNOTS

- 1½ CUPS WATER (105°F)
- 2 TEASPOONS ACTIVE DRY YEAST
- 4 CUPS ALL-PURPOSE FLOUR, PLUS MORE AS NEEDED
- 2 TEASPOONS KOSHER SALT
- 1 TABLESPOON OLIVE OIL
- PARMESAN CHEESE, GRATED, FOR GARNISH (OPTIONAL)

1. To prepare the sauce, melt the butter in a saucepan over medium heat. Add the garlic and reduce heat to medium-low. Allow to cook, stirring occasionally, for about 3 minutes. This takes some of the pungency out of the garlic and also infuses the butter with the flavor. Stir in the parsley and salt.

2. To prepare the knots, place the warm water and yeast in a large bowl and gently stir. When the mixture starts to foam, stir in the flour and salt and mix until the dough is just combined. It will be sticky.

3. Turn the dough out on a flour-dusted surface and start kneading until the flour is incorporated, adding more if necessary to make the dough malleable and smooth but not overdone.

4. Lightly grease a bowl and put the dough in it. Allow to rise until doubled in size, about an hour. Preheat the oven to 450°F.

5. Transfer to a lightly floured surface and push and stretch the dough into a large rectangle. If it resists, let it rest before stretching it further. Cut the rectangle into strips, and tie the strips into knots. Spread the olive oil over the bottom of a 12-inch cast-iron skillet. Tuck the knots into the skillet so they are slightly separated. Bake for about 15 minutes, until golden brown.

6. When the garlic knots come out of the oven, place a kitchen towel over your hand to pull them off the skillet into a large mixing bowl. Scoop a large spoonful of the garlic-parsley sauce over the knots and toss to coat, adding a bit more if necessary. Use another spoon to transfer the coated knots to a plate.

7. Continue to work in batches in the skillet until the dough is used up, or save the remaining dough in the refrigerator for up to 3 days. The sauce can also be refrigerated for several days and reheated. If desired, sprinkle grated Parmesan on top before serving.

FOCACCIA

YIELD: 4 TO 6 SERVINGS / **ACTIVE TIME:** 1 HOUR AND 30 MINUTES / **TOTAL TIME:** 3 HOURS

This is essentially a raised flatbread—like a crustier pizza—to which all kinds of yummy things can be added.

INGREDIENTS:

- 1 PACKET ACTIVE DRY YEAST (2¼ TEASPOONS)
- 2 CUPS WATER (105°F)
- 4-4½ CUPS ALL-PURPOSE FLOUR, PLUS MORE AS NEEDED
- 2 TEASPOONS KOSHER SALT
- 2 TABLESPOONS OLIVE OIL, PLUS MORE TO TASTE
- SALT AND PEPPER PEPPER, TO TASTE
- PARMESAN CHEESE, GRATED, FOR TOPPING

1. Proof the yeast by mixing it with the warm water. Let sit for 10 minutes until foamy.

2. In a bowl, combine the flour, salt, and yeast mix. Stir to combine. Transfer to a lightly floured surface and knead the dough until it loses its stickiness, adding more flour as needed, about 10 minutes.

3. Coat the bottom and sides of a large mixing bowl (ceramic is best) with a tablespoon of the olive oil. Place the ball of dough in the bowl, cover loosely with plastic wrap, put it in a naturally warm, draft-free location, and let it rise until doubled in size, about 45 minutes to 1 hour.

4. Preheat the oven to 450°F.

5. When doubled in size, turn the dough out onto a lightly floured surface and divide it in two. Put a tablespoon of the olive oil in a 12-inch cast-iron skillet and press one of the pieces of dough into it. Drizzle some olive oil over it and sprinkle with salt and pepper, then with Parmesan. Cover loosely with plastic wrap and let rise for about 20 minutes. With the other piece, press it out onto a piece of parchment paper, follow the same procedure to top it, and let it rise.

6. Put the skillet on the middle rack of the oven and bake for 25 to 30 minutes, until golden brown. Remove from oven and let rest for 5 minutes before removing from the pan to cool further. Wipe any crumbs off the skillet, coat with more olive oil, and transfer the other round to the skillet. Bake for about 25 minutes, remove from skillet, and let cool.

TIP: If desired, you can put the extra dough in a plastic bag and store it in the refrigerator for up to 3 days to use later.

PIZZA DOUGH

YIELD: 2 BALLS OF DOUGH / **ACTIVE TIME:** 30 MINUTES / **TOTAL TIME:** 1 HOUR

With this super-easy recipe, you can create amazing pizzas that can be personalized with almost anything you have in the refrigerator or pantry, from traditional cheese to "gourmet." And while the flavor will become more complex and the crust crispier if you allow the dough to rise for a couple of hours (or up to 3 days in the refrigerator), you can also roll it out and bake it within 15 minutes of making it.

INGREDIENTS:

¾ CUP WATER (105°F)

1 TEASPOON ACTIVE DRY YEAST

2 CUPS ALL-PURPOSE FLOUR, PLUS MORE AS NEEDED

1½ TEASPOONS KOSHER SALT

1 TABLESPOON OLIVE OIL

1. If you'll be making pizza within the hour, preheat the oven to 450°F.

2. In a large bowl, add the warm water and yeast, stirring to dissolve the yeast. When the mixture starts to foam, stir in the flour and salt and work the mixture until the dough is just combined. It will be sticky.

3. Turn the dough out on a flour-dusted surface and start kneading until the flour is incorporated, adding more if necessary to make the dough elastic and smooth, but not overdone.

4. If cooking immediately, allow the dough to rest for 15 minutes. While it's doing so, put a 10-inch cast-iron skillet in the oven. Prepare the toppings for the pizza. If preparing ahead of time, place dough in the refrigerator for up to 3 days.

5. When the dough is ready, put a piece of parchment paper under it. Start rolling and pushing it out to form a 9-inch round that will fit in the skillet. If it bounces back, let it rest before pushing or rolling it out again.

6. When the round is shaped, remove the skillet from the oven. Add the olive oil and brush to distribute over the bottom. Transfer the dough to the skillet and add the toppings.

7. Bake for 12 to 15 minutes, until the crust starts to brown and the toppings are hot and bubbling. Remove and allow to cool for 5 minutes before lifting or sliding the pizza out and serving.

CORN TORTILLAS

YIELD: 20 TORTILLAS / **ACTIVE TIME:** 50 MINUTES / **TOTAL TIME:** 50 MINUTES

You really should be making your own corn tortillas, as a warm tortilla lifted straight from a griddle or skillet is a thing of beauty. The main ingredient, masa harina, is a corn flour that is available in most grocery stores.

INGREDIENTS:

- 2 CUPS MASA HARINA, PLUS MORE AS NEEDED
- ½ TEASPOON KOSHER SALT
- 1 CUP WATER (110°F), PLUS MORE AS NEEDED
- 2 TABLESPOONS VEGETABLE OIL OR MELTED LARD

1. Place the masa harina and salt in a bowl and stir to combine. Slowly add the warm water and oil (or lard) and stir until they are incorporated and a soft dough forms. The dough should be quite soft and not at all sticky. If it is too dry, add more water. If the dough is too wet, add more masa harina.

2. Wrap the dough in plastic (or place it in a resealable bag) and let it rest at room temperature for 30 minutes. It can be stored in the refrigerator for up to 24 hours; just be careful not to let it dry out.

3. Cut a 16-inch piece of plastic wrap and lay half of it across the bottom plate of a tortilla press.

4. Place a large griddle across two burners and warm over high heat.

5. Pinch off a small piece of the dough and roll it into a ball. Place in the center of the lined tortilla press, fold the plastic over the top of the dough, and press down the top plate to flatten the dough. Do not use too much force. If the tortilla is too thin, you will have a hard time getting it off of the plastic. Open the press and carefully peel off the tortilla. Reset the plastic.

6. Place the tortilla on the hot, dry griddle and toast for 30 to 45 seconds. Flip over and cook for another minute. Remove from the griddle and set aside. Repeat the process with the remaining dough.

PARATHA

YIELD: 8 SERVINGS / **ACTIVE TIME:** 25 MINUTES / **TOTAL TIME:** 30 MINUTES

This buttery, unleavened South Asian flatbread comes together quickly and is great for dipping in spicy sauces.

INGREDIENTS:

- 2 CUPS PASTRY FLOUR, PLUS MORE AS NEEDED
- 1 CUP WHOLE WHEAT FLOUR
- ¼ TEASPOON KOSHER SALT
- 1 CUP WATER (110°F)
- 5 TABLESPOONS VEGETABLE OIL, PLUS MORE AS NEEDED
- 5 TABLESPOONS GHEE OR MELTED UNSALTED BUTTER

1. Place the flours and salt in the bowl of a stand mixer. Turn on low and slowly add the warm water. Beat until incorporated and then slowly add the vegetable oil. When the oil has been incorporated, place the dough on a lightly floured work surface and knead until it is quite smooth, about 8 minutes.

2. Divide the dough into eight small balls and dust them with flour.

3. Use your hands to roll out each ball into a long rope. Spiral each rope into a large disk.

4. Use a rolling pin to flatten the spiraled disks until they are no more than ¼-inch thick. Lightly brush each disk with a small amount of vegetable oil.

5. Place a skillet or griddle over very high heat for about 4 minutes. Brush the surface with some of the ghee or melted butter and place a disk of the dough on the surface. Cook until it is blistered and brown, about 1 minute. Turn over and cook the other side. Transfer the cooked paratha to a plate and repeat with the remaining disks. Serve warm or at room temperature.

TIP: If you want to freeze any extras, make sure to place parchment paper between them to prevent them from melding together.

PITA BREAD

YIELD: 16 PITAS / **ACTIVE TIME:** 1 HOUR / **TOTAL TIME:** 2 HOURS

Pitas are delicious, somewhat chewy bread pockets that originated in the Mediterranean region. They can be filled with just about anything and are popular around the world, but are especially prevalent in Middle Eastern cuisine.

INGREDIENTS:

- 1 PACKET OF ACTIVE DRY YEAST (2¼ TEASPOONS)
- 2½ CUPS WARM WATER (105°F)
- 3 CUPS ALL-PURPOSE FLOUR, PLUS MORE AS NEEDED
- 1 TABLESPOON OLIVE OIL, PLUS MORE AS NEEDED
- 1 TABLESPOON KOSHER SALT
- 3 CUPS WHOLE WHEAT FLOUR
- UNSALTED BUTTER, AS NEEDED

1. Proof the yeast by mixing it with the warm water. Let sit for about 10 minutes until foamy.

2. In a large bowl, add the yeast mixture into the all-purpose flour and stir until it forms a stiff dough. Cover and let the dough rise for about 1 hour.

3. Add the oil and salt to the dough and stir in the whole wheat flour in ½-cup increments. When finished, the dough should be soft. Turn onto a lightly floured surface and knead it until it is smooth and elastic, about 10 minutes.

4. Coat the bottom and sides of a large mixing bowl (ceramic is best) with butter. Place the ball of dough in the bowl, cover loosely with plastic wrap, put it in a naturally warm, draft-free location, and let it rise until doubled in size, about 45 minutes to 1 hour.

5. On a lightly floured surface, punch down the dough and cut into 16 pieces. Put the pieces on a baking sheet and cover with a kitchen towel while working with individual pieces.

6. Roll out the pieces with a rolling pin until they are approximately 7 inches in diameter. Stack them between sheets of plastic wrap.

7. Warm a 10-inch cast-iron skillet over high heat and lightly oil the bottom. Cook the individual pitas for about 20 seconds on one side, then flip and cook for about a minute on the other side, until bubbles form. Turn again and continue to cook until the pita puffs up, another minute or so. Keep the skillet lightly oiled while cooking, and store the pitas on a plate under a clean kitchen towel until ready to serve.

NAAN

YIELD: 8 PIECES / **ACTIVE TIME:** 1 HOUR / **TOTAL TIME:** 3 TO 4 HOURS

This is the bread that is traditionally served with Indian cuisine. It's usually cooked in a tandoor (clay oven) in India, but a cast-iron skillet works just fine.

INGREDIENTS:

- 1½ TEASPOONS ACTIVE DRY YEAST
- ½ TABLESPOON SUGAR
- 1 CUP WATER (105°F)
- 3 CUPS ALL-PURPOSE FLOUR OR 1½ CUPS ALL-PURPOSE AND 1½ CUPS WHOLE WHEAT PASTRY FLOUR, PLUS MORE AS NEEDED
- ¼ TEASPOON KOSHER SALT
- 1 TEASPOON BAKING POWDER
- ½ CUP PLAIN YOGURT
- 4 TABLESPOONS UNSALTED BUTTER, MELTED, PLUS MORE AS NEEDED
- ¼ CUP OLIVE OIL

1. Proof the yeast by mixing it with the sugar and ½ cup of the warm water. Let sit for 10 minutes until foamy.

2. In a bowl, add the remaining water, flour, salt, baking powder, and yeast mixture. Stir to combine. Add the yogurt and 2 tablespoons of the butter and stir to form a soft dough.

3. Transfer to a lightly floured surface and knead the dough until it is springy and elastic, about 10 minutes.

4. Coat the bottom and sides of a large mixing bowl (ceramic is best) with butter. Place the ball of dough in the bowl, cover loosely with plastic wrap, put it in a naturally warm, draft-free location, and let it rise until doubled in size, about 1 to 2 hours.

5. Punch down the dough. Lightly flour a work surface again, take out the dough, and roll it into a large circle. Cut it into 8 slices (like a pie).

6. Place the skillet over high heat and warm until it is very hot, about 5 minutes. Working with individual pieces of dough, roll them out to soften the sharp edges and make the pieces look more like teardrops. Brush both sides with olive oil and, working with one at a time, place the bread in the skillet.

7. Cook for 1 minute, turn the dough with tongs, cover the skillet, and cook the other side for about a minute (no longer). Transfer the cooked naan to a plate and cover with foil to keep warm while cooking the remaining pieces. Serve warm.

TIP: You can add herbs or spices to the dough or the pan to make naan with different flavors, like adding ¼ cup chopped fresh parsley to the dough, or sprinkling the skillet lightly with cumin, coriander, or turmeric (or a combination) before cooking the pieces of naan. You can also use a seasoned olive oil to brush the pieces before cooking—one that has been infused with hot pepper flakes or roasted garlic will be lovely.

POTATO & PARSNIP LATKES

YIELD: 4 SERVINGS / **ACTIVE TIME:** 40 MINUTES / **TOTAL TIME:** 1 HOUR

The parsnips improve the traditional latke tremendously, as they add sweetness as well as a nice, crispy texture.

INGREDIENTS:

- 2 RUSSET POTATOES, PEELED AND GRATED
- 3 PARSNIPS, PEELED, TRIMMED, CORED, AND GRATED
- 1 TABLESPOON ALL-PURPOSE FLOUR
- 1 EGG
- SALT AND PEPPER, TO TASTE
- 1 TABLESPOON OLIVE OIL

1. Preheat the oven to 350°F. Place the grated potatoes in a colander and squeeze one handful at a time until no more liquid can be removed from them. Transfer to a bowl, add the parsnips, flour, and egg, and stir to combine. Season the mixture with salt and pepper.

2. Place the oil in a large skillet and warm over medium-high heat. When it starts to shimmer, add ¼-cup portions of the latke mixture to the pan and gently press down to flatten them into patties. Reduce heat to medium-low and cook until brown on both sides, about 8 to 10 minutes per side.

3. When both sides are perfectly brown, test the latkes to see if the interior is fully cooked. If not, place them on a baking sheet and bake in the oven for an additional 10 minutes. Let the cooked latkes cool briefly and serve.

INJERA

YIELD: 12 INJERA / **ACTIVE TIME:** 30 MINUTES / **TOTAL TIME:** 2 TO 3 DAYS

To make authentic injera, all you need is time. Letting the dough ferment for a few days improves the flavor along with the nutritional properties of this traditional Ethiopian bread.

INGREDIENTS:

3 CUPS TEFF FLOUR

5⅓ CUPS WATER, PLUS MORE AS NEEDED

1 TEASPOON KOSHER SALT

OLIVE OIL, AS NEEDED

1. Place the flour and 4 cups of the water in a large mixing bowl and stir until combined. Cover with plastic wrap and let the mixture rest at room temperature for 2 to 3 days. The batter is ready when bubbles have formed on the surface and the mixture has a sour smell.

2. Do not stir the mixture. Pour out as much of the water as possible, being careful not to pour out the wet flour on the bottom. Bring the remaining water to boil in a small saucepan.

3. Take 1½ cups of the fermented batter and place it in the boiling water, stirring vigorously, until the mixture has thickened.

4. Add the mixture in the saucepan to the original batter and stir until thoroughly combined. Add the salt and cook until the mixture reaches the consistency of a pancake batter. Add more water if necessary to achieve the desired consistency.

5. Coat the bottom of a cast-iron skillet with olive oil and warm over medium heat. When the oil starts to shimmer, tilt the pan and pour in enough batter to cover the whole surface of the skillet. After 2 minutes, cover with a lid and cook until bubbles have formed on the surface and the bottom side of the injera is not sticking to the pan. Transfer to a parchment-lined baking sheet and repeat until all of the batter has been used. Place parchment paper between the cooked injera so that they do not stick together.

PICKLED BEETS

YIELD: 4 PINTS / **ACTIVE TIME:** 30 MINUTES / **TOTAL TIME:** 2 HOURS

This recipe works with any type of beet, but candy-striped beets look fantastic pickled in the jar. And keep in mind that red will stain a serving board and your guests' fingers.

1. Scrub and trim the beets. Bring water to a boil in a large saucepan, add the beets, and reduce the heat to a simmer. Cook for 30 minutes, or until beets are tender. Remove and let the beets cool. When the beets are cool enough to handle, rinse them under cold water, quarter the beets, and set them aside.

2. Place the vinegar, water, sugar, and salt in a Dutch oven, bring to a boil, and then add the beets and onions. Reduce the heat and simmer for 5 to 10 minutes.

3. Pour the mixture into mason jars, packing tightly. Pour additional liquid over the beets and onions, leaving about ½ inch of space free at the top. Let cool before using or storing in the refrigerator, where they will keep for up to 2 weeks.

INGREDIENTS:

- 4 LBS. BEETS
- 2½ CUPS WHITE VINEGAR
- 1¼ CUPS WATER
- 1¼ CUPS SUGAR
- 1 TEASPOON PICKLING SALT
- 2 SMALL ONIONS, SLICED THIN

HOT & SPICY CARROTS

YIELD: 1 PINT / **ACTIVE TIME:** 15 MINUTES / **TOTAL TIME:** 1 HOUR AND 30 MINUTES

Rich meatballs taste even more decadent when countered by tangy pickled vegetables.

1. Wash the carrots and cut them into matchsticks or rounds. The rounds should be about the size of a quarter. Pat dry.

2. Place the vinegar, salt, sugar, and water in a mixing bowl and stir until the sugar dissolves. Add the carrots to the mixture and let marinate for at least 1 hour before serving.

3. For best flavor, store the carrots in the refrigerator for up to 5 days.

INGREDIENTS:

- ½ LB. LARGE CARROTS, PEELED
- 1 CUP UNSEASONED RICE VINEGAR
- 1 TEASPOON KOSHER SALT
- 2 TABLESPOONS SUGAR, PLUS 2 TEASPOONS
- 1 CUP WATER

RETRO BREAD & BUTTER PICKLES

YIELD: ½ CUP / **ACTIVE TIME:** 5 MINUTES / **TOTAL TIME:** 12 HOURS

These are classics, and great a addition to a meatball sandwich.

INGREDIENTS:

- ½ ENGLISH HOTHOUSE CUCUMBER OR 2 PERSIAN CUCUMBERS, SLICED THIN
- 1 SMALL ONION, SLICED THIN
- 2 JALAPEÑO PEPPERS, STEMMED, SEEDS AND RIBS REMOVED, AND SLICED THIN
- 4 SPRIGS FRESH DILL
- 2 TABLESPOONS CORIANDER SEEDS
- 2 TABLESPOONS MUSTARD SEEDS
- 2 TEASPOONS CELERY SALT
- 2 CUPS DISTILLED WHITE VINEGAR
- 1 CUP SUGAR
- 2 TABLESPOONS KOSHER SALT

1. Pack the cucumber slices, onion, jalapeños, dill sprigs, coriander seeds, mustard seeds, and celery salt into a 1-quart jar.

2. Bring the vinegar, sugar, and salt to a boil in a medium saucepan, stirring to dissolve sugar and salt. Carefully pour the brine into the jars and let the pickles cool before using or storing in the refrigerator, where they will keep for up to 1 week.

SPANISH RICE

YIELD: 6 SERVINGS / **ACTIVE TIME:** 10 MINUTES / **TOTAL TIME:** 45 MINUTES

Flank this with the Beef & Chorizo Meatballs (see page 358) and drizzle some of the Chimichurri Redux (see page 766) over the dish for a flavor-packed meal.

INGREDIENTS:

- 2 CUPS LONG-GRAIN RICE
- 2 TABLESPOONS OLIVE OIL
- 1 CUP TOMATO SAUCE
- 1 TEASPOON KOSHER SALT
- 1 GARLIC CLOVE, MINCED
- 3 CUPS WATER
- 1 CUP CHICKEN STOCK (SEE PAGE 660)
- 1 TEASPOON CUMIN
- PINCH OF GARLIC POWDER

1. Place the oil in a large skillet and warm over medium-high heat. Add the rice and cook until it turns golden brown, about 5 minutes.

2. Stir in the remaining ingredients and bring to a boil. Reduce the heat to low, cover the pan, and cook until the rice is tender and all of the liquid has been absorbed, about 35 minutes. Remove from heat and let the rice sit for 5 minutes before fluffing it with a fork and serving.

WHOLE WHEAT PASTA DOUGH

YIELD: 1¾ LBS. / **ACTIVE TIME:** 1 HOUR / **TOTAL TIME:** 2 TO 3 HOURS

Whether you're looking for healthier pasta alternatives or are a fan of chewier pastas like linguine, whole wheat pasta is an excellent conduit for thick, creamy sauces.

INGREDIENTS:

4 CUPS FINE WHOLE WHEAT FLOUR, PLUS MORE AS NEEDED

1½ TEASPOONS KOSHER SALT

4 LARGE EGG YOLKS

1 TABLESPOON OLIVE OIL

2 TABLESPOONS WATER, PLUS MORE AS NEEDED

1. On a flat work surface, combine the flour and salt and form it into a tall mound. Create a well in the center, then add the egg yolks, oil, and the 2 tablespoons of water. Using a fork or your fingertips, gradually start pulling the flour into the pool of egg, beginning with the flour at the inner rim of the well. Continue to gradually add flour until the dough starts holding together in a single floury mass, adding more water—1 tablespoon at a time—if the mixture is too dry to stick together. Once the dough feels firm and dry and can form a craggy-looking ball, it is time to start kneading.

2. Begin by working the remaining flour on the work surface into the ball of dough. Using the heel of your hand, push the ball of dough away from you in a downward motion. Turn the dough 45 degrees each time you repeat this motion, as doing so incorporates the flour more evenly. The dough should have a smooth, elastic texture. If the dough still feels wet, tacky, or sticky, dust it with flour and continue kneading. If it feels too dry and is not completely sticking together, wet your hands with water and continue kneading. Wet your hands as many times as you need in order to help the dough shape into a ball. Knead for 8 to 10 minutes to create a dough that is smooth and springy and to eliminate any air bubbles and bits of unincorporated flour in the dough. The dough has been sufficiently kneaded when it is very smooth and gently pulls back into place when stretched.

3. Wrap the ball of dough tightly in plastic wrap and let rest for at least 1 hour and up to 2 hours. If using within a few hours, leave it out on the kitchen counter; otherwise, refrigerate it (it will keep for up to 3 days). If refrigerated, the dough may experience some discoloration, but it won't affect the flavor.

4. Cut the dough into four even pieces. Set one piece on a smooth work surface and wrap up the rest in plastic wrap to prevent drying. Shape the dough into a ball, place it on the work surface, and, with the palm of your hand, push down on it so that it looks like a thick pita. Using a rolling pin, roll the dough to ½ inch thick. Try as much as possible to keep the thickness and width of the dough "patty" even, as it will help the dough fit through the pasta maker more easily.

ALL-YOLK PASTA DOUGH

YIELD: ¾ LB. / **ACTIVE TIME:** 1 HOUR / **TOTAL TIME:** 2 TO 3 HOURS

The use of only egg yolks produces a rich, golden dough that creates tender pasta. It is perfect for thin, fragile, or small, filled pastas.

INGREDIENTS:

- 1½ CUPS ALL-PURPOSE FLOUR
- ⅓ CUP "00" FLOUR, PLUS MORE AS NEEDED
- 8 LARGE EGG YOLKS
- 2 TABLESPOONS WATER (90°F), PLUS MORE AS NEEDED

1. On a flat work surface, form the flours into a mound. Create a well in the center, then add the egg yolks and the 2 tablespoons of water. Using a fork or your fingertips, gradually start pulling the flour into the pool of egg, beginning with the flour at the inner rim of the well. Continue to gradually add flour until the dough starts holding together in a single floury mass, adding more water—1 tablespoon at a time—if the mixture is too dry to stick together. Once the dough feels firm and dry and can form a craggy-looking ball, it is time to start kneading.

2. Begin by incorporating the remaining flour on the work surface into the ball of dough. Using the heel of your hand, push the ball of dough away from you in a downward motion. Turn the dough 45 degrees each time you repeat this motion, as doing so incorporates the flour more evenly. The dough should have a smooth, elastic texture. If the dough still feels wet, tacky, or sticky, dust it with flour and continue kneading. If it feels too dry and is not completely sticking together, wet your hands with water and continue kneading. Wet your hands as many times as you need in order to help the dough shape into a ball. Knead for 8 to 10 minutes to create a dough that is smooth and springy and to eliminate any air bubbles and bits of unincorporated flour in the dough. The dough has been sufficiently kneaded when it is very smooth and gently pulls back into place when stretched.

3. Wrap the ball of dough tightly in plastic wrap and let rest for at least 1 hour and up to 2 hours. If using within a few hours, leave it out on the kitchen counter; otherwise, refrigerate it (it will keep for up to 3 days). If refrigerated, the dough may experience some discoloration, but it won't affect the flavor).

4. Cut the dough into four even pieces. Set one piece on a smooth work surface and wrap up the rest in plastic wrap to prevent drying. Shape the dough into a ball, place it on the work surface, and, with the palm of your hand, push down on it so that it looks like a thick pita. Using a rolling pin, roll the dough to ½ inch thick. Try as much as possible to keep the thickness and width of the dough "patty" even, as it will help the dough fit through the pasta maker more easily.

TIP: This dough is suitable for popular noodles such as linguine and spaghetti.

THREE-EGG BASIC PASTA DOUGH

YIELD: ABOUT 1 LB. / **ACTIVE TIME:** 1 HOUR / **TOTAL TIME:** 2 TO 3 HOURS

This simple, delicious pasta recipe is sure to become your go-to.

INGREDIENTS:

2¾ CUPS ALL-PURPOSE FLOUR, PLUS MORE AS NEEDED

3 LARGE EGGS

1 EGG YOLK

2 TABLESPOONS WATER (90°F), PLUS MORE AS NEEDED

1. On a flat work surface, form the flour into a mound. Create a well in the center, then add the eggs, egg yolk, and the 2 tablespoons of water. Using a fork or your fingertips, gradually start pulling the flour into the pool of egg, beginning with the flour at the inner rim of the well. Continue to gradually add flour until the dough starts holding together in a single floury mass, adding more water—1 tablespoon at a time—if the mixture is too dry to stick together. Once the dough feels firm and dry and can form a craggy-looking ball, it is time to start kneading.

2. Begin by incorporating the remaining flour on the work surface into the ball of dough. Using the heel of your hand, push the ball of dough away from you in a downward motion. Turn the dough 45 degrees each time you repeat this motion, as doing so incorporates the flour more evenly. The dough should have a smooth, elastic texture. If the dough still feels wet, tacky, or sticky, dust it with flour and continue kneading. If it feels too dry and is not completely sticking together, wet your hands with water and continue kneading. Wet your hands as many times as you need in order to help the dough shape into a ball. Knead for 8 to 10 minutes to create a dough that is smooth and springy, and to eliminate any air bubbles and bits of unincorporated flour in the dough. The dough has been sufficiently kneaded when it is very smooth and gently pulls back into place when stretched.

3. Wrap the ball of dough tightly in plastic wrap and let rest for at least 1 hour and up to 2 hours. If using within a few hours, leave it out on the kitchen counter, otherwise refrigerate it (it will keep for up to 3 days). If refrigerated, the dough may experience some discoloration (but it won't affect the flavor at all).

4. Cut the dough into four even pieces. Set one piece on a smooth work surface and wrap up the rest in plastic wrap to prevent drying. Shape the dough into a ball, place it on the work surface, and, with the palm of your hand, push down on it so that it looks like a thick pita. Using a rolling pin, roll the dough to ½ inch thick. Try as much as possible to keep the thickness and width of the dough "patty" even, as it will help the dough fit through the pasta maker more easily.

TIP: This dough is suitable for popular noodles such as fettuccine, pappardelle, and tagliatelle.

FARFALLE

YIELD: ¾ LB. / **ACTIVE TIME:** 45 MINUTES / **TOTAL TIME:** 1 TO 3 HOURS

Farfalle means "butterfly" in Italian, and these lighter-than-air pasta shapes are well worth their elegant name. They work well with tomato- or cream-based sauces, but feel free to experiment with your favorites.

INGREDIENTS:

- ALL-YOLK PASTA DOUGH (SEE PAGE 556)
- SEMOLINA FLOUR, AS NEEDED
- SALT, TO TASTE

1. Prepare the dough as directed, rolling the dough to the second-thinnest setting (generally notch 4) for pasta sheets that are about ⅛ inch thick. Lay the pasta sheets on lightly floured parchment-lined baking sheets and cover loosely with plastic wrap. Work quickly to keep the pasta sheets from drying out, which makes it harder for the pasta to stick together.

2. Working with one pasta sheet at a time, place it on a lightly floured work surface and trim both ends to create a rectangle. Using a pastry cutter, cut the pasta sheet lengthwise into 1- to 1¼-inch-wide ribbons. Carefully separate the ribbons from each other, then, using a ridged pastry cutter, cut the ribbons into 2-inch pieces. To form the butterfly shape, place the index finger of your nondominant hand on the center of the piece of pasta. Then place the thumb and index finger of your dominant hand on the sides of the rectangle—right in the middle—and pinch the dough together to create a butterfly shape. Firmly pinch the center again to help it hold its shape. Leave the ruffled ends of the farfalle untouched. Repeat with all the pasta sheets.

3. Set the farfalle on lightly floured parchment-lined baking sheets so they are not touching. Allow them to air-dry for at least 30 minutes and up to 3 hours, and then cook. Alternatively, you can place them, once air-dried, in a bowl, cover with a kitchen towel, and refrigerate for up to 3 days. Or freeze on the baking sheets, transfer to freezer bags, and store in the freezer for up to 2 months. Do not thaw them prior to cooking (they will become mushy) and add an extra minute or so to their cooking time.

4. To cook the farfalle, bring a large pot of salted water to a boil. Add the farfalle and cook until the pasta is tender but still chewy, 2 to 3 minutes.

FAZZOLETTI

YIELD: ABOUT 1 LB. / **ACTIVE TIME:** 30 MINUTES / **TOTAL TIME:** 1 HOUR AND 30 MINUTES

These thin, square, or rectangular pasta shapes resemble handkerchiefs, which is where they get their name. Don't worry about making perfect squares; they taste just as good when uneven.

INGREDIENTS:

- THREE-EGG BASIC PASTA DOUGH (SEE PAGE 557)
- SEMOLINA FLOUR, AS NEEDED
- SALT, TO TASTE

1. Prepare the dough as directed, rolling the dough to the thinnest setting (generally notch 5) for pasta sheets that are about 1⁄16 inch thick. Lay the pasta sheets on lightly floured parchment-lined baking sheets and let them air-dry for 15 minutes.

2. Cut each pasta sheet into as many 2½-inch squares or 1½ × 2½–inch rectangles as possible. Set them on lightly floured parchment-covered baking sheets so they are not touching. Gather any scraps together into a ball, put it through the pasta maker to create additional pasta sheets, and cut those as well. Allow them to air-dry for 1 hour, turning them over once halfway through, and then cook. Alternatively, you can place them, once air-dried, in a bowl, cover with a kitchen towel, and refrigerate for up to 3 days.

3. To cook the fazzoletti, cook for about 1 minute in a pot of boiling, salted water, until they are tender but still chewy.

GARGANELLI

YIELD: 1½ LBS. / **ACTIVE TIME:** 1 HOUR AND 30 MINUTES / **TOTAL TIME:** 4 HOURS AND 30 MINUTES

This Bolognese pasta requires a delicate touch and a bit of patience, but once you get the hang of rolling the squares around the chopstick, you're sure to want it for every meal.

1. Combine all of the ingredients and prepare the dough as directed in the Whole Wheat Pasta Dough on page 555. Then use a pasta maker to roll the dough to the second-thinnest setting (generally notch 4) for pasta sheets that are about ⅛ inch thick. Lay the pasta sheets on flour-dusted, parchment-lined baking sheets and cover them loosely with plastic wrap.

2. Working with one pasta sheet at a time, lightly dust it with flour. Cut it into 1½-inch-wide strips and then cut the strips into 1½-inch squares. Repeat with the remaining pasta sheets. Cover the squares loosely with plastic wrap. Gather any scraps together into a ball, put it through the pasta maker to create additional pasta sheets, and cut those as well.

3. To make each garganello, place one square of pasta dough on a lightly floured work surface with one of the corners pointing toward you. Using a chopstick, gently roll the square of pasta around the chopstick, starting from the corner closest to you, until a tube forms. Once completely rolled, press down slightly as you seal the ends together, then carefully slide the pasta tube off the chopstick and lightly dust with flour. Set them on flour-dusted, parchment-lined baking sheets and allow them to air-dry for 1 hour, turning them over halfway through.

4. To cook the garganelli, cook for 2 to 3 minutes in a pot of boiling, salted water, until they are tender but still chewy.

INGREDIENTS:

- 2¼ CUPS SEMOLINA FLOUR, PLUS MORE AS NEEDED
- 1½ TEASPOONS KOSHER SALT, PLUS MORE TO TASTE
- 3 LARGE EGGS
- 2 TABLESPOONS OLIVE OIL
- 2 TABLESPOONS WATER

NODI

YIELD: ABOUT 1 LB. / **ACTIVE TIME:** 1 HOUR AND 30 MINUTES / **TOTAL TIME:** 3 TO 4 HOURS

This gondola-inspired pasta is formed by creating a knot in the center of a thin noodle.

INGREDIENTS:

1¾ CUPS SEMOLINA FLOUR, PLUS MORE AS NEEDED

1 TEASPOON KOSHER SALT, PLUS MORE TO TASTE

½ TEASPOON FENNEL SEEDS, FINELY GROUND

⅔ CUP WATER (105°F)

1. Put the flour, salt, and fennel seeds in a large bowl and add the water. Begin mixing with a fork until the mixture starts to roughly stick together and look coarse. Gather it together with your hands and transfer it to a lightly floured work surface.

2. Using the heel of your hand, push the ball of dough away from you in a downward motion. Turn the dough 45 degrees each time you repeat this motion, as doing so incorporates the flour more evenly. If the dough feels too dry, wet your hands as many times as you need in order to help shape the dough into a ball. Knead for 10 minutes.

3. Cover the dough tightly with plastic wrap to keep it from drying out and let rest for at least 1 hour, but 2 hours is even better. If using within a few hours, leave out on the kitchen counter. Otherwise, put it in the refrigerator, where it will keep for up to 3 days.

4. Between the palms of your hands or on a lightly floured work surface, roll the dough into a 2-inch-thick log and cut it across into 18 rounds of even thickness (the easiest way to do this is to cut the roll in half and continue cutting each piece in half until you have 18 pieces). Cover all the pieces but the one you are working with to keep them from drying out.

5. With the palms of your hands, roll the piece of dough left out into a long rope ⅛ inch thick. Now make the knots. Starting on one end of the rope, tie a simple knot, gently pull on both ends to slightly tighten the knot, then cut the knot off the rope, leaving a tail on each side of about ⅜ inch long. Keep making and cutting off knots in this manner until you use up all of the rope. Repeat with the remaining pieces of dough. Set the finished knots on lightly floured, parchment-lined baking sheets so they are not touching. Allow them to air-dry for 2 hours, turning them over once halfway through, and then cook. Alternatively, you can place them, once air-dried, in a bowl, cover with a kitchen towel, and refrigerate for up to 3 days.

6. To cook the nodi, place in a large pot of boiling, salted water for 2 to 3 minutes, until they are tender but still firm.

ORECCHIETTE

YIELD: ABOUT 1 LB. / **ACTIVE TIME:** 1 HOUR AND 30 MINUTES / **TOTAL TIME:** 4 HOURS

Orecchiette means "little ears" and refers to this pasta's flattened shape. Orecchiette provide an interesting texture contrast when cooked, as the center is soft while the outer edge is just the slightest bit chewy.

INGREDIENTS:

- 2 CUPS SEMOLINA FLOUR, PLUS MORE AS NEEDED
- 1 TEASPOON KOSHER SALT, PLUS MORE TO TASTE
- ¾ CUP WATER, PLUS MORE AS NEEDED

1. Combine the flour and salt in a large bowl. Add the water a little at a time while mixing with a fork. Continue mixing the dough until it starts holding together in a single floury mass. If it is still too dry to stick together, add more water, 1 teaspoon at a time, until it does. Work the dough with your hands until it feels firm and dry and can be formed into a craggy-looking ball.

2. Transfer the dough to a lightly floured work surface and knead it for 10 minutes. Because it is made with semolina flour, the dough can be quite stiff and hard. You can also mix and knead this in a stand mixer; don't try it with a handheld mixer—the dough is too stiff and could burn the motor out. Using the heel of your hand, push the ball of dough away from you in a downward motion. Turn the dough 45 degrees each time you repeat this motion, as doing so incorporates the flour more evenly. Wet your hands as needed if the dough is too sticky. After 10 minutes of kneading, the dough will only be slightly softer (most of the softening is going to occur when the dough rests, which is when the gluten network within the dough will relax). Shape into a ball, cover tightly with plastic wrap, and let rest in the refrigerator for at least 2 hours, and up to 2 days.

3. Cut the dough into four equal sections. Take one dough section and shape it into an oval with your hands. Cover the remaining sections with plastic wrap to prevent it from drying out. Place on a lightly floured work surface and, with the palms of your hands, roll it against the surface until it becomes a long ½-inch-thick rope. Using a sharp paring knife, cut the rope into ¼-inch discs, lightly dusting with semolina flour so they don't stick together.

4. To form the orecchiette, place a disc on the work surface. Stick your thumb in flour, place it on top of the disc, and, applying a little pressure, drag your thumb, and the accompanying dough, across to create an ear-like shape. Flour your thumb before making each orecchiette for best results. Lightly dust the orecchiette with flour and set them on lightly floured parchment-covered baking sheets so they are not touching. Allow them to air-dry for 1 hour, turning them over once halfway through, and then cook. Alternatively, you can place them, once air-dried, in a bowl, cover with a kitchen towel, and refrigerate for up to 3 days.

5. To cook the orecchiette, place in a large pot of boiling, salted water until they are tender but still chewy, 3 to 4 minutes.

RIBBON PASTA

YIELD: ABOUT 1 LB. / **ACTIVE TIME:** 20 MINUTES / **TOTAL TIME:** 1 HOUR

Ribbon pasta includes things like pappardelle, tagliatelle, and the classic fettuccine, and it is one of the easiest pasta types to make on your own. With a little practice, you can have these churned out in as little as a half hour—so long as you don't mind using a little elbow grease.

INGREDIENTS:

THREE-EGG BASIC PASTA DOUGH (SEE PAGE 557)

SEMOLINA FLOUR, AS NEEDED

SALT, TO TASTE

1. Prepare the dough as directed, rolling the dough to the second thinnest setting (generally notch 4) or thinnest setting (generally notch 5 or 6) to form pasta sheets that are, respectively, ⅛ or 1⁄16 inch thick. Lay the pasta sheets on lightly floured parchment-lined baking sheets. Let the sheets air-dry for 15 minutes, turning them over halfway through (doing this will make them easier to cut).

2. Lightly flour the surface of a pasta sheet and gently roll it up, starting from a short end, to create a pasta roll. Use a very sharp knife to gently slice the roll across to your preferred width. Cut into 1- to 1½-inch-wide strips for pappardelle; ¾-inch-wide strips for tagliatelle; and ½- to ¼-inch-wide strips for fettuccine.

3. Lightly dust the cut roll with flour, then begin to gently unfold the strips, one by one, as you shake off any excess flour. Arrange them straight and spread out or lay them down by shaping them in a coil (referred to as a bird's nest). Repeat with all the pasta sheets. Let air-dry for 30 minutes and then cook. Alternatively, cover them with a kitchen towel and refrigerate for up to 3 days.

4. To cook the pasta, bring a large pot of water to a boil. Once it is boiling, add salt (1 tablespoon for every 4 cups water) and stir. Add the pasta and stir for the first minute to prevent any sticking and to untangle the strands of pasta. Tagliolini will not require additional cooking, so drain them as soon as they hit the water and you stir to disentangle them. Cook the remaining pasta ribbons until tender but still chewy, anywhere from 1 to 3 minutes.

TAJARIN

YIELD: ½ LB. / **ACTIVE TIME:** 20 MINUTES / **TOTAL TIME:** 1 HOUR

These delicate, flat noodles are best broken up in a soup or served alongside roasted proteins and vegetables.

INGREDIENTS:

ALL-YOLK PASTA DOUGH (SEE PAGE 556)

SEMOLINA FLOUR, AS NEEDED

SALT, TO TASTE

1. Prepare the dough as directed, rolling the dough to the thinnest setting (generally notch 5) for pasta sheets that are about 1⁄16 inch thick. Cut into 8-inch-long sheets. Lay the pasta sheets on lightly floured parchment-lined baking sheets and air-dry for 15 minutes.

2. Working with one pasta sheet at a time, lightly dust it with semolina flour, then gently roll it up, starting from a short end. Using a very sharp knife, gently slice the roll across into 1⁄12-inch-wide strips. Lightly dust the cut roll with flour, then gently begin unfolding the strips, one by one, as you shake off any excess flour. Arrange them either straight and spread out or curled in a coil. Repeat with all the pasta sheets. Allow them to air-dry for 30 minutes and then cook. Alternatively, you can place them, once air-dried, on a baking sheet, cover with a kitchen towel, and refrigerate for up to 3 days.

3. To cook the tajarin, bring a large pot of salted water to a boil. Cook until the pasta is tender but still chewy, typically no more than 2 minutes. Drain and serve with the sauce of your choice.

TROFIE

YIELD: ABOUT 1 LB. / **ACTIVE TIME:** 40 MINUTES / **TOTAL TIME:** 4 TO 5 HOURS

Trofie are thin, spiraled noodles that work best with strong sauces, including pesto and ragùs.

INGREDIENTS:

2¾ CUPS ALL-PURPOSE FLOUR

1 TEASPOON KOSHER SALT, PLUS MORE TO TASTE

1 CUP WATER

SEMOLINA FLOUR, AS NEEDED

1. Place the flour and salt in a large bowl, mix well with a fork, and add the water. Mix with the fork until all the water has been absorbed, then start working the dough with your hands. In a few minutes the crumbly mixture will begin to come together as a coarse dough.

2. Transfer the dough, along with any bits stuck to the bowl, to a lightly floured work surface. Begin to knead the dough. Using the heel of your hand, push the ball of dough away from you in a downward motion. Turn the dough 45 degrees each time you repeat this motion, as doing so incorporates the flour more evenly. Knead the dough for about 10 minutes. Cover the dough with plastic wrap to keep it from drying out and let rest at room temperature for 1 hour, but 2 hours is even better.

3. Between the palms of your hands or on a lightly floured work surface, roll the dough into a 2-inch-thick log and cut it across into eight pieces (the easiest way to do this is to cut the roll in half and continue cutting each piece in half until you have eight pieces). Cover all the dough pieces but the one you are working with to keep them from drying out. Shape each piece of dough into a ball, and then roll it until it is a long, ½ inch-thick rope. Cut into ½-inch pieces and dust them with flour.

4. Working with one piece at a time, press down on the dough with your fingertips and roll the dough down the palm of your other hand. This action will cause the piece of dough to turn into a narrow spiral with tapered ends. Repeat with the remaining pieces of dough. Dust the spirals with flour, set them on flour-dusted, parchment-lined baking sheets, and allow them to air-dry for 2 hours, turning them over halfway through.

5. To cook the trofie, cook for 3 to 4 minutes in a pot of boiling, salted water, until they are tender but still chewy.

CHINESE EGG NOODLES

YIELD: ABOUT 1 LB. / **ACTIVE TIME:** 45 MINUTES / **TOTAL TIME:** 2 HOURS

This noodle is a staple of recipes like lo mein and chow mein, as well as many Asian soups. It is incredibly easy to make and, of course, delicious.

INGREDIENTS:

- 2 CUPS ALL-PURPOSE FLOUR, PLUS MORE AS NEEDED
- 1 TEASPOON KOSHER SALT, PLUS MORE TO TASTE
- 2 LARGE EGGS, LIGHTLY BEATEN
- 3 TABLESPOONS WATER, PLUS MORE AS NEEDED

1. Stir the flour and salt together in a large bowl. Add the eggs and stir until a floury dough forms. Add the 3 tablespoons of water and continue to work the mixture until you almost cannot see any remaining traces of flour. If you find, even after adding the water, that your dough is still very floury, add more water, 1 tablespoon at a time, and continue mixing it with your hands until the dough starts coming together more easily. Start kneading the dough in the bowl with your dominant hand. Continue kneading in the bowl until a smooth ball forms; this should take about 10 minutes. Wrap the dough tightly in plastic wrap and let rest at room temperature for 40 to 50 minutes to allow the gluten in the dough to relax.

2. Unwrap the dough and place it on a lightly floured work surface. Using a rolling pin, begin "beating" the dough, turning it over after every 10 whacks or so. Continue doing this for 6 minutes. Then, shape the dough into a ball, cover with plastic wrap, and let rest at room temperature for another 30 minutes.

3. Return the dough to the work surface (no need to flour again). Cut it in half and wrap one half in plastic wrap to prevent drying. Roll the other half into a large, thin sheet about twice the length and breadth of the length of your rolling pin (you should be able to almost see your hand through it). Lightly flour both sides of the sheet of dough and then fold the sheet of dough twice over itself to create a three-layered fold (like a letter).

4. Using a very sharp knife, slice across the roll into evenly spaced strands. You can make them as thin or thick as you'd like. As you cut the dough, be sure to hold the knife perpendicular to the surface and lightly push the newly cut strip away from the roll with the knife to completely separate it. Continue until you have cut the entire roll, then lightly dust the slivered noodles with flour to prevent any sticking. Transfer the noodles to a parchment-lined baking sheet, shaking off any excess flour if necessary. You can leave them nested or unspool them according to your preference, as they will unravel and straighten once boiled. Repeat with the remaining dough. Cook in a pot of boiling, salted water for 3 to 4 minutes, or cover and refrigerate for up to 1 day.

UDON NOODLES

YIELD: 1 LB. / **ACTIVE TIME:** 1 HOUR / **TOTAL TIME:** 2 TO 3 HOURS

Japanese udon noodles are best when homemade, as the packaged versions lack some of the chewiness and bulk of the fresh variety.

INGREDIENTS:

- ¼ CUP WATER (105°F), PLUS MORE AS NEEDED
- 1 TEASPOON FINE SEA SALT
- 2¼ CUPS CAKE FLOUR OR "00" FLOUR
- POTATO STARCH OR CORNSTARCH, FOR DUSTING

1. Stir the water and salt together in a small bowl until the salt dissolves. Put the flour in a large bowl and make a well in the center. Add the salted water in a stream while stirring the flour. Once all the water has been added, begin working the dough with your hands to incorporate all the flour. If the dough is too dry, add water in 1-teaspoon increments until the dough sticks together.

2. Transfer the dough to a work surface that you have dusted very lightly with the potato starch or cornstarch. Knead the dough with the palm of your dominant hand, turning it 45 degrees with each pressing, until the dough becomes uniformly smooth and slowly springs back when pressed by a finger, about 10 minutes. Cover the dough tightly with plastic wrap and let rest for 1 to 2 hours to relax the gluten.

3. Cut the dough into two pieces. Set one on a lightly dusted work surface and wrap the other in plastic wrap to prevent drying. Pat the piece of dough into a rectangular shape and, using a lightly dusted rolling pin, roll the dough into a ⅛-inch-thick rectangle. Lightly dust the dough and then fold it twice over itself to create a three-layered fold, as you would a letter.

4. Using a very sharp knife, slice the roll into ⅛-inch-wide strands. As you cut the dough, be sure to hold the knife perpendicular to the surface and lightly push the newly cut strip away from the roll with the knife to completely separate it. Continue until you have cut the entire roll, then lightly dust the slivered pasta to prevent any sticking. Transfer the noodles to a parchment-lined baking sheet, shaking off any excess starch if necessary. Repeat with the remaining dough. Udon noodles quickly turn brittle and break when handled, so cook as soon as you finish making them.

5. To cook the udon, cook for about 1 minute in a pot of boiling, salted water, until they are tender but still chewy.

SIMPLE STIR-FRIED BOK CHOY

YIELD: 2 SERVINGS / **ACTIVE TIME:** 10 MINUTES / **TOTAL TIME:** 10 MINUTES

Bok choy is sweet and delicate; the perfect accompaniment to any main dish. This is a perfect simple side, and adding a splash of mirin at the end of cooking brings out the sweetness of the vegetable without overwhelming it.

INGREDIENTS:

- 1 TABLESPOON OLIVE OIL
- ½ LB. BOK CHOY, SLICED
- 2 GARLIC CLOVES, MINCED
- 1 TABLESPOON MIRIN
- 1 TEASPOON SOY SAUCE
- SALT, TO TASTE

1. Place the oil in a small pan and warm over medium-high heat. When it starts to shimmer, add the bok choy and sauté until the green part of the cabbage has wilted, about 5 minutes.

2. Add garlic and cook for 2 minutes, then add the mirin and soy sauce, stir to combine, and cook for 1 more minute.

3. Season with salt and serve.

KIMCHI

YIELD: 4 CUPS / **ACTIVE TIME:** 30 MINUTES / **TOTAL TIME:** 3 TO 7 DAYS

Simple and versatile, kimchi is the perfect introduction to all that fermentation has to offer.

INGREDIENTS:

- 1 HEAD NAPA CABBAGE, CUT INTO STRIPS
- ½ CUP KOSHER SALT
- 2-INCH PIECE FRESH GINGER, PEELED AND MINCED
- 2 GARLIC CLOVES, MINCED
- 1 TEASPOON SUGAR
- 5 TABLESPOONS RED PEPPER FLAKES
- 3 BUNCHES SCALLIONS, TRIMMED AND SLICED
- FILTERED WATER, AS NEEDED

1. Place the cabbage and salt in a large bowl and stir to combine. Work the mixture with your hands, squeezing to remove as much liquid as possible. Let the mixture rest for 2 hours.

2. Add the remaining ingredients, except for the water. Stir the mixture until well combined and squeeze to remove as much liquid as possible.

3. Transfer the mixture to a container and press down so it is tightly packed. The liquid should be covering the mixture. If it is not, add water until the mixture is covered.

4. Cover the jar and let the mixture sit at room temperature for 3 to 7 days, removing the lid daily to release the gas that has built up. When the taste is to your liking, store in an airtight container in the refrigerator.

MUSAENGCHAE

YIELD: 6 SERVINGS / **ACTIVE TIME:** 10 MINUTES / **TOTAL TIME:** 10 MINUTES

A traditional Korean side dish that is capable of freshening up any table it appears on.

1. Place all of the ingredients in a mixing bowl and stir to combine. Let marinate for 1 hour at room temperature before serving.

INGREDIENTS:

- 2 CUPS SHREDDED DAIKON RADISH
- 2 CUCUMBERS, SLICED THIN
- 1 TEASPOON GOCHUJANG POWDER
- 2 TABLESPOONS RICE VINEGAR
- 1 TABLESPOON KOSHER SALT
- 1 TABLESPOON SUGAR

GRILLED CABBAGE

YIELD: 4 SERVINGS / **ACTIVE TIME:** 15 MINUTES / **TOTAL TIME:** 45 MINUTES

This deceptively simple preparation of grilled cabbage results in a mellow, tasty side.

1. Preheat your grill to medium heat and cut the head of cabbage into 8 wedges.

2. Remove the core and place the wedges on a large piece of aluminum foil. Season with the garlic powder, salt, and pepper. Create a packet by folding the foil over and crimping the edges.

3. When the grill is about 400°F, place the packet on the grill, cover the grill, and cook until tender, 30 to 40 minutes. Remove the cabbage from the packet, place it on the grill, and cook until it is charred on both sides. Serve immediately.

INGREDIENTS:

1 LARGE HEAD CABBAGE

1½ TEASPOONS GARLIC POWDER

SALT AND PEPPER, TO TASTE

ENSALADA CHILEANA

YIELD: 6 SERVINGS / **ACTIVE TIME:** 10 MINUTES / **TOTAL TIME:** 45 MINUTES

A simple salad that is positively divine when tomatoes are at their peak.

INGREDIENTS:

2 RED ONIONS, SLICED

SALT, TO TASTE

4 TOMATOES, CUT INTO WEDGES

1 TABLESPOON OLIVE OIL

FRESH CHIVES, FINELY CHOPPED, FOR GARNISH

1. Place the onions in a bowl of salted ice water and soak for 30 minutes.

2. Drain the onions, squeeze to remove any excess liquid, and place in a bowl. Add the tomatoes and toss to combine. Season with salt, stir in the olive oil, and toss to coat. Garnish with the chives and serve.

BASIC RED CABBAGE SLAW

YIELD: 2 TO 4 SERVINGS / **ACTIVE TIME:** 10 MINUTES / **TOTAL TIME:** 2 TO 3 HOURS

This is a topper that should be made a few hours ahead of time to give the cabbage time to soften.

INGREDIENTS:

1 SMALL HEAD RED CABBAGE, CORED AND SLICED AS THIN AS POSSIBLE

1 TEASPOON KOSHER SALT, PLUS MORE TO TASTE

JUICE OF 1 LIME

1 BUNCH FRESH CILANTRO, CHOPPED

1. Place the cabbage in a large bowl, sprinkle the salt on top, and toss to distribute. Use your hands to work the salt into the cabbage, then let it sit for 2 to 3 hours.

2. Once it has rested, taste to gauge the saltiness: if too salty, rinse under cold water and let drain; if just right, add the lime juice and cilantro, stir to combine, and serve.

SAVORY HALWA

YIELD: 4 TO 6 SERVINGS / **ACTIVE TIME:** 10 MINUTES / **TOTAL TIME:** 30 MINUTES

Halwa is an Indian dish that is usually prepared as a dessert. By removing the sugar, it becomes an ideal partner for the Bombay Turkey Meatballs (see page 311).

INGREDIENTS:

- 2 TABLESPOONS UNSALTED BUTTER
- 1 LB. CARROTS, PEELED AND GRATED
- ½ TEASPOON CARDAMOM
- 2 CUPS MILK
- SALT, TO TASTE

1. Place the butter in a saucepan and melt over medium heat. Add the carrots and cardamom and cook until the carrots start to soften, about 5 minutes.

2. Add the milk, bring to a simmer, and cook until the milk has reduced and the carrots are very tender, about 10 minutes. Season with salt and serve.

STIR-FRIED CARROT NOODLES

YIELD: 4 SERVINGS / **ACTIVE TIME:** 30 MINUTES / **TOTAL TIME:** 30 MINUTES

Showing the versatility of carrots, this recipe sends them through the spiralizer to make "noodles" and then tops them with a rich peanut-sesame sauce.

INGREDIENTS:

- 2 TEASPOONS SESAME SEEDS
- 2 TABLESPOONS SMOOTH PEANUT BUTTER
- 2 TABLESPOONS WATER
- 2 TABLESPOONS SEASONED RICE VINEGAR
- 1 TABLESPOON SOY SAUCE
- 1 TABLESPOON LIGHT BROWN SUGAR
- 2 TEASPOONS TOASTED SESAME OIL
- 1 TEASPOON CHILI SAUCE, PLUS MORE TO TASTE
- 1-INCH PIECE FRESH GINGER, PEELED AND GRATED
- 2 TABLESPOONS PEANUT OIL, PLUS MORE AS NEEDED
- 4-6 LARGE CARROTS, PEELED AND SPIRALIZED OR GRATED
- SALT, TO TASTE
- 6 SCALLIONS, TRIMMED AND CHOPPED, FOR GARNISH

1. Place the sesame seeds in a small skillet and toast over medium heat until golden brown and aromatic, about 2 minutes. Transfer the sesame seeds to a small bowl and set aside.

2. Place the peanut butter, water, vinegar, soy sauce, brown sugar, sesame oil, chili sauce, and ginger in a small saucepan, whisk to combine, and bring to a gentle boil over medium-low heat. Cook, stirring frequently, until the sauce thickens, 4 to 5 minutes. Remove the sauce from heat and set aside.

3. Warm a wok or a large skillet over medium heat for 2 to 3 minutes. Raise heat to medium-high and add the peanut oil. When the oil begins to shimmer, add half of the carrots and a pinch of salt and stir-fry until the carrots have softened, about 2 minutes. Transfer the carrots to a bowl and set aside. Repeat the process with the remaining carrots, adding peanut oil if necessary.

4. Add the sauce to the bowl and toss until the carrots are evenly coated. Garnish with the toasted sesame seeds and scallions and serve.

BLUE CHEESE POLENTA

YIELD: 6 SERVINGS / **ACTIVE TIME:** 25 MINUTES / **TOTAL TIME:** 1 HOUR

The blue cheese amplifies the creaminess, and turns polenta's mild flavor into something memorable.

1. Place the cornmeal, the stock, and the water in a large pot. Bring to a boil over medium-high heat, reduce heat so that the mixture simmers, and cook, stirring occasionally, until the mixture is thick and creamy, about 40 minutes to 1 hour.

2. Stir in the butter and half of the blue cheese. Season the polenta with salt and pepper and remove the pan from heat. Sprinkle the remaining blue cheese on top and serve.

INGREDIENTS:

2 CUPS MEDIUM-GRAIN CORNMEAL

3 CUPS CHICKEN STOCK (SEE PAGE 660)

2 CUPS WATER

1 STICK OF UNSALTED BUTTER

4 OZ. BLUE CHEESE, CRUMBLED

SALT AND PEPPER, TO TASTE

POLENTA FRIES

YIELD: 4 SERVINGS / **ACTIVE TIME:** 30 MINUTES / **TOTAL TIME:** 2 HOURS AND 30 MINUTES

The creamy texture and beautiful golden hue of these would be great alongside the Sweet & Sour Tex-Mex Meatballs on page 354.

INGREDIENTS:

- 2½ CUPS MILK
- 2½ CUPS VEGETABLE STOCK (SEE PAGE 664)
- 2 CUPS MEDIUM-GRAIN CORNMEAL
- 2 TABLESPOONS UNSALTED BUTTER
- 1 TEASPOON KOSHER SALT, PLUS MORE TO TASTE
- ½ TEASPOON BLACK PEPPER
- ½ TEASPOON DRIED OREGANO
- ½ TEASPOON DRIED THYME
- ½ TEASPOON DRIED ROSEMARY
- VEGETABLE OIL, AS NEEDED
- ¼ CUP GRATED PARMESAN CHEESE, FOR GARNISH
- 2 TABLESPOONS FINELY CHOPPED FRESH ROSEMARY, FOR GARNISH

1. Grease a large, rimmed baking sheet with cooking spray. Place the milk and stock in a saucepan and bring to a boil. Whisk in the polenta, reduce the heat to low and cook, stirring constantly, until all of the liquid has been absorbed and the polenta is creamy, about 5 minutes.

2. Stir in the butter, salt, pepper, oregano, thyme, and rosemary. When they have been incorporated, transfer the polenta to the greased baking sheet and even out the surface with a rubber spatula. Refrigerate for 2 hours.

3. Carefully invert the baking sheet over a cutting board so that the polenta falls onto it. Slice in half lengthwise and cut each piece into 4-inch-long and 1-inch-wide strips.

4. Add oil to a Dutch oven until it is approximately 2 inches deep and bring it to 375°F. Working in batches of two, place the strips in the oil and fry, turning as they cook, until golden brown, 2 to 4 minutes. Transfer the cooked fries to a paper towel–lined plate to drain. When all of the fries have been cooked, sprinkle the Parmesan and rosemary over them and serve.

CAULIFLOWER RICE

YIELD: 2 SERVINGS / **ACTIVE TIME:** 10 MINUTES / **TOTAL TIME:** 10 MINUTES

This simple dish provides the texture of rice with the nutritional benefits of cauliflower. It can be used in stir-fries or to accompany curries and is excellent on its own with a little butter.

INGREDIENTS:

1 LARGE HEAD CAULIFLOWER, TRIMMED AND CHOPPED

¼ CUP OLIVE OIL

SALT AND PEPPER, TO TASTE

1. Place the cauliflower in a food processor and pulse until it becomes granular.

2. Place the oil in a large skillet and warm over medium heat. When the oil starts to shimmer, add the cauliflower, cover the pan, and cook until tender, 3 to 5 minutes.

3. Season with salt and pepper and serve.

SPINACH & MUSHROOM QUINOA

YIELD: 6 SERVINGS / **ACTIVE TIME:** 20 MINUTES / **TOTAL TIME:** 5 HOURS

Folding in the herbs at the end of your preparation packs this side dish with tons of fresh flavor.

1. Place all of the ingredients, except for the spinach and fresh herbs, in a slow cooker and cook on high until the quinoa is slightly fluffy, about 4 hours.

2. Add the spinach and turn off the heat. Keep the slow cooker covered and let sit for 1 hour.

3. Fluff the quinoa with a fork, add the basil, dill, and thyme, and fold to incorporate. Season with salt and pepper and serve.

INGREDIENTS:

- 1½ CUPS QUINOA, RINSED
- 2½ CUPS VEGETABLE STOCK (SEE PAGE 664)
- 1 YELLOW ONION, CHOPPED
- ½ RED BELL PEPPER, CHOPPED
- ¾ LB. PORTOBELLO MUSHROOMS, CHOPPED
- 2 GARLIC CLOVES, MINCED
- 1 TABLESPOON KOSHER SALT, PLUS MORE TO TASTE
- 1 TABLESPOON BLACK PEPPER, PLUS MORE TO TASTE
- 3 CUPS BABY SPINACH
- 1½ CUPS FRESH BASIL LEAVES, FINELY CHOPPED
- ¼ CUP FINELY CHOPPED FRESH DILL
- 2 TABLESPOONS FINELY CHOPPED FRESH THYME

SWEET & SPICY ROASTED BARLEY

YIELD: 4 SERVINGS / **ACTIVE TIME:** 20 MINUTES / **TOTAL TIME:** 1 HOUR AND 30 MINUTES

Partner this hearty dish with one of the lighter meatball preparations, such as the Cajun Shrimp Balls on page 366.

1. Preheat the oven to 375°F. Place the carrots in a 9 x 13–inch baking pan, drizzle the olive oil over them, and season with salt and pepper. Place in the oven and roast until the carrots are slightly soft to the touch, about 45 minutes.

2. While the carrots are cooking, open the Pasilla peppers and discard the seeds and stems. Place the peppers in a bowl, add the boiling water, and cover the bowl with aluminum foil.

3. When the carrots are cooked, remove the pan from the oven and add the remaining ingredients and the liquid the peppers have been soaking in. Chop the reconstituted peppers, add them to the pan, and spread the mixture out until the liquid is covering the barley. Cover the pan tightly with aluminum foil, place it in the oven, and bake until the barley is tender, about 45 minutes. Remove from the oven, fluff with a fork, and serve.

INGREDIENTS:

- 5 CARROTS, PEELED AND CUT INTO 3-INCH PIECES
- OLIVE OIL, TO TASTE
- SALT AND PEPPER, TO TASTE
- 6 DRIED PASILLA PEPPERS
- 2¼ CUPS BOILING WATER
- 1 CUP PEARL BARLEY
- 1 RED ONION, MINCED
- 2 TABLESPOONS ADOBO SEASONING
- 1 TABLESPOON SUGAR
- 1 TABLESPOON CHILI POWDER
- ¼ CUP FINELY CHOPPED FRESH OREGANO

THAI FRIED RICE

YIELD: 4 SERVINGS / **ACTIVE TIME:** 35 MINUTES / **TOTAL TIME:** 1 HOUR

The directions call for kohlrabi and peas, but you can include any vegetable you like, just cut it into very small cubes to give it equal footing with all the other ingredients and cook each one separately until done.

INGREDIENTS:

- 1 CUP JASMINE RICE
- 2 CUPS WATER
- 2 TABLESPOONS OLIVE OIL, PLUS MORE AS NEEDED
- 1 SHALLOT, DICED
- 1 KOHLRABI, PEELED AND DICED
- ½ CUP FROZEN PEAS
- 1-INCH PIECE FRESH GINGER, PEELED AND MINCED
- 1 TABLESPOON SOY SAUCE
- 1 TABLESPOON RICE VINEGAR
- ½ CUP DICED PINEAPPLE
- ¼ CUP CASHEWS
- ¼ CUP FINELY CHOPPED FRESH CILANTRO, FOR GARNISH

1. Place the rice and water in a saucepan and simmer for 20 minutes. Remove from heat, fluff with a fork, and let cool, uncovered, so that it dries out a little. Set aside.

2. Place 1 tablespoon of the oil in a large skillet and warm over medium-high heat. When it starts to shimmer, stir in the shallot, kohlrabi, peas, and ginger and sauté until the kohlrabi is tender and the peas are cooked through, about 8 minutes. Remove the mixture from the pan and set it aside.

3. Add the rice to the pan. It is very likely that the rice will stick to the bottom of the pan. Do your best to scrape it off with a spatula. Cook the rice until it starts to brown, about 5 to 10 minutes, taking care not to let it become too mushy. Add the soy sauce and rice vinegar and stir to incorporate.

4. Stir in the soy sauce, rice vinegar, pineapple, cashews, and the kohlrabi mixture. Gently fold to incorporate and cook for another minute to heat everything through. Season to taste, garnish with the cilantro, and serve.

SOUTHERN COLLARD GREENS

YIELD: 4 TO 6 SERVINGS / **ACTIVE TIME:** 30 MINUTES / **TOTAL TIME:** 2 HOURS AND 30 MINUTES

When you think these are done, just keep cooking them.

INGREDIENTS:

- 2 TABLESPOONS OLIVE OIL
- 1 ONION, DICED
- ½ LB. SMOKED HAM, DICED
- 4 GARLIC CLOVES, DICED
- 3 LBS. COLLARD GREENS, STEMS REMOVED, CHOPPED
- 2 CUPS VEGETABLE STOCK (SEE PAGE 664)
- ¼ CUP APPLE CIDER VINEGAR
- 1 TABLESPOON BROWN SUGAR
- 1 TEASPOON RED PEPPER FLAKES

1. Place the oil in a large saucepan and warm over medium-high heat. When the oil starts to shimmer, add the onion and sauté until translucent, about 3 minutes. Add the ham, reduce heat to medium, and cook until the ham starts to brown, about 5 minutes.

2. Add the remaining ingredients, stir to combine, and cover the pan. Braise the collard greens until they are very tender, about 2 hours. Check on the collards every so often and add water if all of the liquid has evaporated.

CARIBBEAN-STYLE PIGEON PEAS

YIELD: 4 SERVINGS / **ACTIVE TIME:** 30 MINUTES / **TOTAL TIME:** 1 HOUR

The sugar and the molasses temper the heat just enough to make the dish pleasant, rather than punishing.

INGREDIENTS:

- 2 TABLESPOONS COCONUT OIL
- 2 TABLESPOONS BROWN SUGAR
- 2 TEASPOONS MOLASSES
- 2 CUPS PIGEON PEAS
- 1 ONION, CHOPPED
- 2 GARLIC CLOVES, MINCED
- 2-3 PIMENTO PEPPERS, CHOPPED
- 1 TOMATO, CHOPPED
- 1 CUP PEELED AND CHOPPED PUMPKIN
- 2 SCALLIONS, TRIMMED AND CHOPPED
- 1 TEASPOON FINELY CHOPPED FRESH THYME
- ¼ CUP FINELY CHOPPED FRESH CILANTRO
- 1 CUP COCONUT MILK
- 1 CUP WATER
- 1 SCOTCH BONNET PEPPER, PIERCED
- SALT AND PEPPER, TO TASTE

1. Place the oil in a Dutch oven and warm over medium heat. When the oil starts to shimmer, add the brown sugar and cook until it is bubbling and starting to smoke, about 3 minutes.

2. Add the molasses and pigeon peas, being careful to avoid any splatter. Cover and let simmer for a 4 minutes, stirring and checking on the peas every so often. Uncover the pot, raise heat to high, and cook, stirring constantly, until a majority of the moisture has evaporated, 1 to 2 minutes.

3. Add the onion, garlic, pimiento peppers, tomato, pumpkin, green onion, thyme, and cilantro and sauté for 1 minute. Stir in the coconut milk, water, and Scotch bonnet pepper and bring the mixture to a boil. Reduce the heat to medium-low and simmer until the peas and pumpkin are tender, 20 to 30 minutes. Season with salt and pepper and ladle into warmed bowls.

HOT & GARLICKY EGGPLANT NOODLES

YIELD: 4 SERVINGS / **ACTIVE TIME:** 45 MINUTES / **TOTAL TIME:** 45 MINUTES

Eggplants make for good veggie noodles because of their fibrous nature. Use an Italian variety and make sure there is enough room in the pan to fry them; otherwise, they will steam instead of brown.

1. Trim the ends of each eggplant and peel them. Using the julienne attachment on a mandoline, carefully cut the eggplant into thin noodles. Alternatively, cut each eggplant into ¼-inch-thick slices, then cut each slice into ¼-inch-wide strips.

2. Place the chili garlic sauce and water in a small bowl and stir until thoroughly combined.

3. Warm a large nonstick skillet over medium heat for 1 minute. Add half of the olive oil, half of the sesame oil, and half of the chili-garlic mixture and raise heat to medium-high. When the oil begins to shimmer, add half of the eggplant noodles and a couple pinches of salt. Cook, stirring frequently, until the strands have softened and started turning golden brown, about 5 minutes. Transfer to a warmed serving platter and tent loosely with foil to keep warm. Wipe out the pan with a paper towel and repeat the process with the remaining eggplant, olive oil, sesame oil, and chili-garlic mixture. Garnish with the cilantro and almonds and serve immediately.

INGREDIENTS:

- 4 EGGPLANTS
- 2 TABLESPOONS CHILI GARLIC SAUCE, PLUS MORE TO TASTE
- 2 TEASPOONS WATER
- 3 TABLESPOONS OLIVE OIL
- 1 TABLESPOON TOASTED SESAME OIL
- SALT, TO TASTE
- 2 HANDFULS FRESH CILANTRO LEAVES, FINELY CHOPPED, FOR GARNISH
- ½ CUP TOASTED ALMONDS (TAMARI ALMONDS PREFERRED), CHOPPED, FOR GARNISH

STEAMED JAPANESE EGGPLANT WITH BLACK BEAN GARLIC SAUCE & BASIL

YIELD: 4 SERVINGS / **ACTIVE TIME:** 30 MINUTES / **TOTAL TIME:** 45 MINUTES

This recipe is a great way to showcase the lovely, delicate flavor of steamed Japanese eggplant. The sauce is made from fermented black beans and garlic and is intense and salty. You can find a jarred version in the Asian section of the supermarket. Thai basil is the best accompaniment for this dish, but if you can't find any, Italian basil will work fine.

INGREDIENTS:

- 1½ LBS. JAPANESE EGGPLANT, SLICED LENGTHWISE AND HALVED
- 1 GARLIC CLOVE, SLICED
- 1 TABLESPOON MINCED SHALLOT
- OLIVE OIL, AS NEEDED
- 2 TABLESPOONS BLACK BEAN GARLIC SAUCE
- 2 TEASPOONS SOY SAUCE
- 2 TEASPOONS RICE VINEGAR
- WATER, AS NEEDED
- 8 FRESH BASIL LEAVES, SHREDDED, FOR GARNISH

1. Place 1 inch of water in a saucepan, set a steaming tray above it, and bring the water to a boil.

2. Place the eggplant in the steaming tray and steam until tender, 5 to 8 minutes. Remove from heat and place on a serving plate.

3. Place the garlic and shallot in a small saucepan with enough oil to coat the bottom. Sauté over medium heat until the vegetables start to brown, about 5 minutes.

4. Add the black bean garlic sauce, soy sauce, and vinegar and stir until the sauce starts to thicken. If the sauce thickens so much that it becomes clumpy, add water 1 teaspoon at a time.

5. Taste, adjust the seasoning as needed, remove from heat, and pour over the eggplant. Garnish with the basil and serve.

DRY-FRIED BEANS

YIELD: 4 SERVINGS / **ACTIVE TIME:** 30 MINUTES / **TOTAL TIME:** 45 MINUTES

If you can find Chinese pickled vegetables, use them, but know that sauerkraut and kimchi will also work. This dish can accompany any and all meatballs, but prefers to be paired with those made with pork.

INGREDIENTS:

- 1 TABLESPOON OLIVE OIL, PLUS MORE AS NEEDED
- 1 LB. GREEN BEANS, TRIMMED
- 2 TABLESPOONS CHOPPED CHINESE PICKLED VEGETABLES, SAUERKRAUT, OR KIMCHI
- 1 GARLIC CLOVE, CHOPPED
- 2 TABLESPOONS SHERRY
- 2 TABLESPOONS SOY SAUCE
- 1 TABLESPOON FERMENTED BLACK BEAN GARLIC SAUCE
- 1 TEASPOON SUGAR

1. Place the oil in a large sauté pan and warm over high heat. When it starts to shimmer, add the green beans and cook, without stirring, under they are starting to char, about 6 minutes. Turn the beans over and cook until they are browned all over, about 5 minutes. Transfer to a bowl and set aside.

2. Add the pickled vegetables, sauerkraut, or kimchi and the garlic and sauté until the contents of the pan are fragrant, about 2 minutes. Stir in the sherry and cook until it has nearly evaporated. Add the soy sauce, fermented black bean garlic sauce, and sugar and stir to incorporate. Return the green beans to the pan, cook until heated through, and serve.

YU CHOY WITH GARLIC & SOY

YIELD: 4 SERVINGS / **ACTIVE TIME:** 10 MINUTES / **TOTAL TIME:** 15 MINUTES

Steaming yu choy keeps it tender and light. If the stalks are large, leave them to cook a little longer.

INGREDIENTS:

- 1½ LBS. YU CHOY (IF ESPECIALLY LONG, CUT THEM IN HALF)
- ¼ CUP WATER
- 1 TABLESPOON OLIVE OIL
- 2 GARLIC CLOVES, CHOPPED
- ½ TABLESPOON RICE VINEGAR
- 1 TABLESPOON SOY SAUCE

1. Place the yu choy in a sauté pan large enough to fit all of the stalks, cover with the water, cover the pan, and cook over high heat.

2. After about 5 minutes, check the thickest stalk to see if it is tender. If not, cook until it is. Once tender, add the oil and the garlic. Sauté until the garlic is fully cooked but not browned, about 2 minutes.

3. Add the vinegar and soy sauce, toss to combine, and serve.

SWEET POTATO HASH

YIELD: 6 SERVINGS / **ACTIVE TIME:** 20 MINUTES / **TOTAL TIME:** 45 MINUTES

This hash is positively lovely with both lamb- and chicken-based meatballs.

INGREDIENTS:

- 1 LB. SWEET POTATOES, PEELED AND MINCED
- 2 TABLESPOONS UNSALTED BUTTER
- 2 POBLANO PEPPERS, STEMMED, SEEDED, AND DICED
- 1 YELLOW ONION, MINCED
- 2 GARLIC CLOVES, MINCED
- 1 TABLESPOON CUMIN
- 1 TABLESPOON KOSHER SALT, PLUS MORE TO TASTE
- 1 TABLESPOON FINELY CHOPPED FRESH OREGANO
- BLACK PEPPER, TO TASTE

1. Fill a saucepan with water and bring it to a boil. Add the sweet potatoes and cook until they are just tender, about 7 minutes. Be careful not to overcook them, as you don't want to end up with mashed potatoes in the hash. Drain the sweet potatoes and set them aside.

2. Place the butter in a skillet and melt it over medium heat. Add the poblano peppers, onion, garlic, and cumin and sauté until the vegetables are soft, about 10 minutes.

3. Stir the sweet potatoes and salt into the skillet and cook for 15 minutes, stirring occasionally. Add the oregano, stir to incorporate, season with salt and pepper, and serve.

SAAG ALOO

YIELD: 2 TO 4 SERVINGS / **ACTIVE TIME:** 20 MINUTES / **TOTAL TIME:** 35 MINUTES

This spinach-and-potato dish goes particularly well with chicken and turkey meatballs. Though fresh spinach will work, use frozen to make sure it doesn't reduce down to a tiny portion.

INGREDIENTS:

- 1 TABLESPOON OLIVE OIL
- ½ LB. FINGERLING OR RED POTATOES, CHOPPED
- 1 SMALL ONION, DICED
- 1 TEASPOON MUSTARD SEEDS
- 1 TEASPOON CUMIN
- 1 GARLIC CLOVE, CHOPPED
- 1-INCH PIECE FRESH GINGER, PEELED AND MINCED
- 1 LB. FROZEN CHOPPED SPINACH
- 1 TEASPOON RED PEPPER FLAKES
- ½ CUP WATER
- SALT, TO TASTE
- 2 TABLESPOONS PLAIN YOGURT, OR TO TASTE

1. Place the oil and potatoes in a large skillet and cook over medium heat until the potatoes just start to brown, about 5 minutes.

2. Add the onion, mustard seeds, and cumin and cook for another 5 minutes, then add the garlic and ginger and cook, stirring constantly, for another 2 minutes.

3. Add the frozen spinach, the red pepper flakes, and water and cover the pan with a lid. Cook, stirring occasionally, until the spinach is heated through, about 10 minutes.

4. Remove the cover and cook until all of the liquid has evaporated. Season with salt, add the yogurt, and stir to incorporate. Add more yogurt if you prefer a creamier dish, stir to incorporate, and serve.

PATATAS BRAVAS

YIELD: 4 SERVINGS / **ACTIVE TIME:** 45 MINUTES / **TOTAL TIME:** 1 HOUR AND 15 MINUTES

Native to Spain, this smoky potato dish can be found in tapas bars all across that country.

INGREDIENTS:

- 4 POTATOES, CHOPPED
- 1 ONION, WITH SKIN AND ROOT, HALVED
- 3 TABLESPOONS OLIVE OIL
- 1 HEAD GARLIC, TOP ½ INCH REMOVED
- 1 (14 OZ.) CAN DICED TOMATOES, DRAINED
- 1 TABLESPOON SWEET PAPRIKA
- 1 TABLESPOON SHERRY VINEGAR
- SALT, TO TASTE

1. Place 2 cups of wood chips in a bowl of cold water and let them soak for 30 minutes.

2. Bring water to a boil in a large saucepan. Add the potatoes and boil for 4 minutes. Drain and run the potatoes under cold water.

3. Place the potatoes, onion, and 1 tablespoon of the olive oil in a mixing bowl and toss to coat.

4. Line a large wok with aluminum foil, making sure that the foil extends over the side of the pan. Add the soaked wood chips and place the wok over medium heat.

5. When the wood chips are smoking heavily, place a wire rack above them and place the potatoes, onion, and garlic on top. Cover the wok with a lid, fold the foil over the lid to seal the wok as best you can, and smoke the vegetables for 20 minutes. After 20 minutes, remove the pan from heat and keep the wok covered for another 20 minutes.

6. Place the tomatoes, paprika, vinegar, and remaining olive oil in a blender and puree until smooth. Set the mixture aside.

7. Remove the garlic and onion from the smoker. Peel and roughly chop. Add to the mixture in the blender and puree until smooth. Season the salsa brava with salt and serve alongside the potatoes.

HERBED POTATO SALAD

YIELD: 4 TO 6 SERVINGS / **ACTIVE TIME:** 10 MINUTES / **TOTAL TIME:** 40 MINUTES

The two most common potato salads have either a mayonnaise dressing or, in the German version, a sweet vinegar dressing. The French have a different approach with shallots and herbs and a tangy vinaigrette that lets the natural sweetness of the potatoes come through. The dressing is poured on the potatoes when they are still warm, letting them soak up the flavor.

1. Add the potatoes to a pot of water large enough to hold them all, bring to a boil, reduce heat, and simmer until tender, about 15 minutes.

2. While the potatoes are simmering, whisk together the oil, vinegar, wine, mustard, and teaspoon of salt.

3. When the potatoes are done, drain them and place them in a bowl. Add the vinaigrette and shallot immediately and gently toss, making sure to coat all of the potatoes. Let cool completely.

4. Taste and adjust seasoning as needed. Add the black pepper and fresh herbs, stir to incorporate, and serve.

INGREDIENTS:

- 1½ LBS. LOW-STARCH, NEW, OR RED POTATOES, CUBED
- ½ CUP OLIVE OIL
- 3 TABLESPOONS WHITE WINE VINEGAR
- 2 TABLESPOONS DRY WHITE WINE
- 1 TEASPOON GRAINY DIJON MUSTARD
- 1 TEASPOON KOSHER SALT, PLUS MORE TO TASTE
- 1 SHALLOT, MINCED
- BLACK PEPPER, TO TASTE
- 2 TABLESPOONS FINELY CHOPPED FRESH PARSLEY
- 2 TABLESPOONS FINELY CHOPPED FRESH CHIVES
- 2 TABLESPOONS FINELY CHOPPED FRESH DILL

FIVE-BEAN SALAD WITH GOOSEBERRY VINAIGRETTE

YIELD: 6 SERVINGS / **ACTIVE TIME:** 30 MINUTES / **TOTAL TIME:** 2 DAYS

Slow cooking the beans in chicken stock and cooling them overnight provides a lovely counter to the sweet and tangy dressing. This salad features the all-stars of the bean world, but you can use any bean you find appealing.

INGREDIENTS:

- ¼ LB. KIDNEY BEANS, SOAKED OVERNIGHT
- ¼ LB. CANNELLINI BEANS, SOAKED OVERNIGHT
- ¼ LB. PINK BEANS, SOAKED OVERNIGHT
- ¼ LB. PINTO BEANS, SOAKED OVERNIGHT
- ¼ LB. WHOLE DRIED GREEN PEAS, SOAKED OVERNIGHT
- 4-6 CUPS CHICKEN STOCK (SEE PAGE 660)
- 2 TABLESPOONS GRANULATED GARLIC
- 2 BAY LEAVES
- PINCH OF RED PEPPER FLAKES
- 3 TABLESPOONS KOSHER SALT
- 2 CUPS MINCED CELERY
- 2 LARGE RED RADISHES, GRATED
- 1 PARSNIP, PEELED AND MINCED
- ½ CUP CHOPPED FRESH PARSLEY
- 1 CUP CHOPPED SCALLION GREENS
- JUICE OF ½ LEMON
- GOOSEBERRY VINAIGRETTE (SEE RECIPE)

GOOSEBERRY VINAIGRETTE

- 3½ OZ. GOOSEBERRIES, WASHED
- ¼ CUP RED WINE VINEGAR
- ¼ CUP HONEY
- ½ CUP OLIVE OIL
- 1 TABLESPOON KOSHER SALT

1. Drain and rinse the beans and peas and transfer them to a slow cooker. Add the stock, granulated garlic, bay leaves, red pepper flakes, and salt and cook on low for 8 hours, or until the beans are tender. Turn off the slow cooker and let the beans come to room temperature. Place the beans in the refrigerator overnight.

2. Place all of the remaining ingredients, except for the dressing, in a large salad bowl. Stir until combined.

3. Drain the beans. Place the beans in the salad bowl, add half of the Gooseberry Vinaigrette, and toss to coat. Serve with the remaining dressing on the side.

TIP: Slow cooking the beans for this recipe imparts a far more complex flavor than using canned beans and is well worth the additional time.

GOOSEBERRY VINAIGRETTE

1. Place all of the ingredients in a blender and puree until the consistency is silky and the dressing is thick enough to coat a wooden spoon.

CHICKPEA SALAD

YIELD: 4 TO 6 SERVINGS / **ACTIVE TIME:** 10 MINUTES / **TOTAL TIME:** 10 MINUTES

The enigmatic flavor of saffron allows this salad to change with every bite.

INGREDIENTS:

- 1 (14 OZ.) CAN GARBANZO BEANS
- ½ ONION, DICED
- ½ CUP CHOPPED FRESH CILANTRO
- 2 RED CHILI PEPPERS, STEMMED, SEEDS AND RIBS REMOVED, AND SLICED
- 1 CUP HALVED CHERRY TOMATOES
- 2 TABLESPOONS OLIVE OIL
- JUICE OF 1 LEMON
- ¼ TEASPOON SAFFRON
- 1 TABLESPOON CUMIN
- 1 TEASPOON CINNAMON
- SALT AND PEPPER, TO TASTE

1. Place all of the ingredients in a salad bowl, toss until combined, and serve.

CHILLED CORN SALAD

YIELD: 4 TO 6 SERVINGS / **ACTIVE TIME:** 15 MINUTES / **TOTAL TIME:** 4 TO 24 HOURS

This recipe is a riff on the classic Mexican dish known as *esquites.*

INGREDIENTS:

- 2 CUPS CORN KERNELS
- 2 TABLESPOONS UNSALTED BUTTER
- 1 JALAPEÑO PEPPER, STEMMED, SEEDS AND RIBS REMOVED, AND DICED, PLUS MORE TO TASTE
- ½ TEASPOON KOSHER SALT, PLUS MORE TO TASTE
- 2 TABLESPOONS MAYONNAISE
- 2 TEASPOONS GARLIC POWDER
- 3 TABLESPOONS SOUR CREAM OR MEXICAN CREMA
- ¼ TEASPOON CAYENNE PEPPER
- ¼ TEASPOON CHILI POWDER
- 2 TABLESPOONS FETA CHEESE
- 2 TABLESPOONS COTIJA CHEESE
- 2 TEASPOONS FRESH LIME JUICE
- ½ CUP CHOPPED FRESH CILANTRO
- BLACK PEPPER, TO TASTE

1. Preheat the oven to 400°F.

2. Place the corn on a baking sheet and roast in the oven until it turns a light golden brown, about 35 minutes.

3. Remove the corn from the oven, let cool slightly, and then transfer to a large mixing bowl. Add the remaining ingredients and stir to combine.

4. Place the salad in the refrigerator for at least 3 hours, although letting it chill overnight is highly recommended.

TIP: The amount of jalapeño suggested in the ingredients is a safe amount of heat to serve to a broad spectrum of tastes. If you and yours like things spicier, feel free to include the seeds or another jalapeño.

COCONUT & CUCUMBER SALAD

YIELD: 6 SERVINGS / **ACTIVE TIME:** 30 MINUTES / **TOTAL TIME:** 40 MINUTES

A great way to cool down the spicier meatballs in this book.

1. Quarter each cucumber half and then cut the quarters into long, ⅛-inch-wide strips. Place the strips on paper towels to drain.

2. Place the coconut, lime juice, coconut milk, chili garlic sauce, ginger, sugar, cumin, and salt in a food processor and blitz until smooth.

3. Place the cucumbers in a large serving bowl. Top with the coconut mixture and toss to coat.

4. Sprinkle the lime zest, scallions, and peanuts on top of the dressed noodles, season to taste, and serve immediately.

INGREDIENTS:

- 5 LARGE CUCUMBERS, PEELED, HALVED LENGTHWISE, AND SEEDED
- ½ CUP SHREDDED UNSWEETENED COCONUT
- ZEST AND JUICE OF 2 LIMES
- ¼ CUP COCONUT MILK
- 1 TEASPOON CHILI GARLIC SAUCE, PLUS MORE AS NEEDED
- ½-INCH PIECE FRESH GINGER, PEELED AND GRATED
- 1 TEASPOON SUGAR
- 1 TEASPOON CUMIN
- 1 TEASPOON KOSHER SALT, PLUS MORE TO TASTE
- 6 SCALLIONS, TRIMMED AND SLICED THIN, FOR SERVING
- ½ CUP ROASTED PEANUTS, CHOPPED, FOR SERVING

CREAMED SPINACH

YIELD: 4 SERVINGS / **ACTIVE TIME:** 20 MINUTES / **TOTAL TIME:** 25 MINUTES

Definitely use frozen spinach for this one, especially if you are feeding a crowd.

1. Place the butter in a wide sauté pan and melt over medium heat. Add the onion and garlic and cook until the onion is just translucent, about 3 minutes.

2. Add the frozen spinach to the pan along with a few teaspoons water, cover the pan, and cook for a minute. Remove the lid, break the spinach up, and cook until it is completely thawed.

3. Add the cream cheese, nutmeg, and marjoram and stir to incorporate. Cook until the sauce has reduced and thickened, about 5 minutes. Season with salt and pepper and serve.

INGREDIENTS:

1 TABLESPOON UNSALTED BUTTER

1 YELLOW ONION, DICED

2 GARLIC CLOVES, CHOPPED

1 LB. FROZEN CHOPPED SPINACH

½ LB. CREAM CHEESE, AT ROOM TEMPERATURE

PINCH OF GROUND NUTMEG

1 TEASPOON DRIED MARJORAM

SALT AND PEPPER, TO TASTE

CAJUN OKRA & TOMATOES

YIELD: 4 SERVINGS / **ACTIVE TIME:** 15 MINUTES / **TOTAL TIME:** 20 MINUTES

This has enough punch to provide balance to some of the more subtly flavored preparations in this book.

INGREDIENTS:

- OLIVE OIL, AS NEEDED
- 1 ONION, CHOPPED
- 1 LB. OKRA, RINSED WELL AND CHOPPED
- 1 GARLIC CLOVE, CHOPPED
- 2 TOMATOES, CHOPPED
- 1 TEASPOON CAJUN SEASONING
- SALT, TO TASTE

1. Place the oil in a skillet and warm over medium heat. When the oil starts to shimmer, add the onion and sauté until it starts to brown, about 8 minutes. Add the okra and cook, stirring continuously, until it starts to brown, about 5 minutes.

2. Add the garlic and cook for 1 minute. Stir in the tomatoes and Cajun seasoning and cook until the tomatoes have collapsed and the okra is tender, about 8 minutes. Season with salt and serve.

MEATBALL LASAGNA

YIELD: 6 TO 8 SERVINGS / **ACTIVE TIME:** 15 MINUTES / **TOTAL TIME:** 1 HOUR AND 30 MINUTES

Once you have a cache of meatballs in the freezer, there's no end to how you can use them. This easy lasagna is one of the options, and maybe the very best of them.

INGREDIENTS:

- CLASSIC ITALIAN AMERICAN MEATBALLS (SEE PAGE 326)
- 1½ CUPS WATER
- 1 LB. OVEN-READY LASAGNA NOODLES
- 2 CUPS RICOTTA CHEESE
- ½ LB. FRESH MOZZARELLA CHEESE, GRATED
- 1 CUP GRATED PARMESAN CHEESE

1. Preheat the oven to 350°F and grease a 9 x 13–inch baking pan.

2. Remove the meatballs from the sauce, cut them in half, and set aside. Stir the water into sauce and then spread 1 cup of the mixture over the bottom of the baking pan. Arrange one-third of the noodles, overlapping if necessary, over the sauce, top with half of the ricotta, mozzarella, and meatballs, and ¼ cup of the Parmesan. Repeat the layering process, finishing with a layer of noodles on top. Spread the remaining sauce over the noodles and distribute the remaining Parmesan on top.

3. Cover the pan tightly with aluminum foil and place the pan on a baking sheet. Place the lasagna in the oven and bake for 1 hour, until the noodles are tender and filling is bubbly. Raise the oven temperature to 400°F, remove the foil, and bake for another 10 to 12 minutes, until the top is browned. Remove from the oven and let the lasagna rest for 10 minutes before slicing and serving.

VARIATION

- Use any other meatball recipe in this book that is finished in or dipped into a tomato sauce.

ROGAN JOSH

YIELD: 6 SERVINGS / **ACTIVE TIME:** 20 MINUTES / **TOTAL TIME:** 1 HOUR AND 30 MINUTES

This one-pot dish has a tendency to be even better the next day, so don't hesitate to make it a day ahead of time. A lamb or turkey meatball will work well in this dish.

1. Place the oil in a Dutch oven and warm over medium-high heat. When the oil starts to shimmer, add the meatballs and cook, turning them occasionally, until they are browned all over, about 8 minutes. Remove the meatballs with a slotted spoon and set aside.

2. Add the onions, ginger, garlic, curry, turmeric, cayenne, and garam masala to the Dutch oven and sauté for 2 minutes. Add the tomatoes, yogurt, and water and bring to a gentle boil. Return the meatballs to the pot, lower the heat, cover, and simmer for about 1 hour, stirring occasionally.

3. Season with salt, ladle into warmed bowls, and garnish with the cilantro and red onion.

INGREDIENTS:

1 BATCH MEATBALLS, FORMED AND UNCOOKED

2 TABLESPOONS OLIVE OIL

2 LARGE YELLOW ONIONS, SLICED THIN

2-INCH PIECE FRESH GINGER, PEELED AND MINCED

2 GARLIC CLOVES, MINCED

1 TABLESPOON CURRY POWDER, PLUS 1 TEASPOON

1 TEASPOON TURMERIC

1 TEASPOON CAYENNE PEPPER, OR TO TASTE

1 TEASPOON GARAM MASALA

1 (14 OZ.) CAN CRUSHED TOMATOES, PUREED

1 CUP PLAIN YOGURT

2 CUPS WATER

SALT, TO TASTE

FRESH CILANTRO, FINELY CHOPPED, FOR GARNISH

RED ONION, DICED, FOR GARNISH

RATATOUILLE

YIELD: 6 SERVINGS / **ACTIVE TIME:** 40 MINUTES / **TOTAL TIME:** 2 HOURS

Simply top this with the Beef & Sausage Meatballs (see page 330), and you've got an absolutely dynamite dinner.

INGREDIENTS:

- 1/3 CUP OLIVE OIL
- 6 GARLIC CLOVES, MINCED
- 1 EGGPLANT, CHOPPED
- 2 ZUCCHINI, SLICED INTO HALF-MOONS
- 2 BELL PEPPERS, STEMMED, SEEDS AND RIBS REMOVED, AND CHOPPED
- 4 TOMATOES, SEEDED AND CHOPPED
- SALT AND PEPPER, TO TASTE

1. Place a skillet over medium-high heat and add half of the olive oil. When the oil starts to shimmer, add the garlic and eggplant and cook, while stirring, until pieces are coated with oil and just starting to sizzle, about 2 minutes.

2. Reduce the heat to medium, add the zucchini, peppers, and remaining oil, and stir to combine. Cover the skillet and cook, while stirring occasionally, until the eggplant, zucchini, and peppers are almost tender, about 15 minutes.

3. Add the tomatoes, stir to combine, and cook until the eggplant, zucchini, and peppers are tender and the tomatoes have collapsed, about 25 minutes. Remove the skillet from heat, season with salt and pepper, and allow to sit for at least 1 hour. Reheat before serving.

SHAKSHUKA

YIELD: 4 SERVINGS / **ACTIVE TIME:** 20 MINUTES / **TOTAL TIME:** 30 MINUTES

You can serve this with or without the eggs, but the creamy quality and protein they'll add are great alongside the veggies and tender meatballs.

INGREDIENTS:

- 1 TABLESPOON OLIVE OIL
- 1 ONION, CHOPPED
- 2 GARLIC CLOVES, MINCED
- ½ LB. TOMATILLOS, HUSKED, RINSED, AND CHOPPED
- 1 (12 OZ.) PACKAGE FROZEN CHOPPED SPINACH
- 1 TEASPOON CORIANDER
- ¼ CUP WATER
- SALT AND PEPPER, TO TASTE
- 4 EGGS
- TABASCO, TO TASTE

1. Place the oil in a large skillet and warm over medium-high. When the oil starts to shimmer, add the onion and sauté until it just starts to soften, about 5 minutes. Add the garlic and cook until fragrant, about 2 minutes. Add the tomatillos and cook until they have collapsed, about 10 minutes.

2. Add the spinach, coriander, and water and cook, breaking up the spinach with a fork, until the spinach is completely defrosted and blended with the tomatillos. Season with salt and pepper.

3. Evenly spread the mixture in the pan and then make four indentations in the mixture. Crack an egg into each indentation. Reduce the heat to medium, cover the pan, and cook the eggs until the whites are set, 3 to 5 minutes. Season with Tabasco and serve.

DAL

YIELD: 4 SERVINGS / **ACTIVE TIME:** 20 MINUTES / **TOTAL TIME:** 1 HOUR AND 40 MINUTES

This stew could be a meal on its own, but ladling some over rice and topping it with a few meatballs is too good to leave it all by its lonesome.

INGREDIENTS:

- 2 TABLESPOONS OLIVE OIL
- 1 YELLOW ONION, CHOPPED
- 2 GARLIC CLOVES, MINCED
- 2 TEASPOONS RED PEPPER FLAKES, OR TO TASTE
- 2 CURRY LEAVES (OPTIONAL)
- 1 TEASPOON KOSHER SALT
- 1½ CUPS YELLOW SPLIT PEAS, SORTED AND RINSED
- 4 CUPS WATER
- 1 TEASPOON TURMERIC
- 1 CUP PEAS

1. Place the oil in a large saucepan and warm over medium-high heat. When the oil starts to shimmer, add the onion, garlic, red pepper flakes, curry leaves (if using), and salt and sauté until the onion is translucent, about 3 minutes.

2. Stir in the yellow split peas, water, and turmeric and bring to a simmer. Cover and gently simmer for 1 hour, removing the lid to stir the dal on occasion.

3. Remove the lid and simmer, while stirring occasionally, until the dal has thickened to the desired consistency, about 30 minutes. When the dal has the consistency of porridge, stir in the peas, cook until they are warmed through, and serve.

PEPPERS STUFFED WITH GREEK SALAD

YIELD: 4 SERVINGS / **ACTIVE TIME:** 10 MINUTES / **TOTAL TIME:** 25 MINUTES

The fresh crunch of the peppers and the salty feta will nicely complement many of the meatballs in this book.

1. Preheat the oven to 375°F and place the peppers on a parchment-lined baking sheet.

2. Place the cherry tomatoes, garlic, olive oil, feta, and black olives in a mixing bowl and stir to combine. Divide the mixture between the peppers, place them in the oven, and roast until the peppers start to collapse, 10 to 15 minutes.

3. Remove the peppers from the oven and let them cool slightly. Season with salt and pepper and top with the basil leaves before serving.

INGREDIENTS:

4 YELLOW BELL PEPPERS, STEMMED, SEEDS AND RIBS REMOVED, AND HALVED

12 CHERRY TOMATOES, HALVED

2 GARLIC CLOVES, MINCED

2 TABLESPOONS OLIVE OIL

½ CUP CRUMBLED FETA CHEESE

1 CUP BLACK OLIVES, PITTED

SALT AND PEPPER, TO TASTE

LEAVES FROM 1 BUNCH FRESH BASIL

MAC & CHEESE

YIELD: 6 SERVINGS / **ACTIVE TIME:** 15 MINUTES / **TOTAL TIME:** 1 HOUR

Reserve this dish for those nights when you're especially hungry and can afford to relax after the meal, as going back for seconds is a must.

INGREDIENTS:

- SALT, TO TASTE
- 1 LB. ELBOW MACARONI
- 7 TABLESPOONS UNSALTED BUTTER
- 2 CUPS PANKO
- ½ YELLOW ONION, MINCED
- 3 TABLESPOONS ALL-PURPOSE FLOUR
- 1 TABLESPOON YELLOW MUSTARD
- 1 TEASPOON TURMERIC
- 1 TEASPOON GRANULATED GARLIC
- 1 TEASPOON WHITE PEPPER
- 2 CUPS LIGHT CREAM
- 2 CUPS WHOLE MILK
- 1 LB. AMERICAN CHEESE, SLICED
- 10 OZ. BOURSIN CHEESE
- ½ LB. EXTRA-SHARP CHEDDAR CHEESE, SLICED
- 1 BATCH BEEF MEATBALLS

1. Preheat the oven to 400°F. Fill a Dutch oven with water, add salt to taste, and bring to a boil. Add the macaroni and cook until it is just shy of al dente, about 7 minutes. Drain and set aside.

2. Place the pot over medium heat and add 3 tablespoons of the butter. Cook until the butter starts to give off a nutty smell and brown. Add the panko, stir, and cook for 4 to 5 minutes, until the panko starts to look like wet sand. Remove from the pan and set aside.

3. Wipe the Dutch oven out, place it over medium-high heat, and add the onion and the remaining butter. Cook, while stirring, until the onion is soft, about 10 minutes. Gradually incorporate the flour, stirring constantly to prevent lumps from forming. Add the mustard, turmeric, granulated garlic, and white pepper and whisk until combined. Add the light cream and the milk and whisk until incorporated. Reduce heat to medium and bring the mixture to a simmer.

4. Once you start to see small bubbles forming around the outside of the mixture, add the cheeses one at a time, stirring to incorporate before adding the next one. When all of the cheeses have been incorporated and the mixture is smooth, cook until the flour taste is gone, about 10 minutes.

5. Add the meatballs, cover them with the macaroni, stir, and top with the bread crumbs.

6. Place the Dutch oven in the oven and bake until the bread crumbs are crispy, 10 to 15 minutes. Remove from the oven and serve immediately.

CALAMARI & MEATBALLS

YIELD: 2 SERVINGS / **ACTIVE TIME:** 15 MINUTES / **TOTAL TIME:** 30 MINUTES

A simple, but extremely fun take on spaghetti and meatballs for those who are trying to cut back on carbs, and are getting tired of zucchini noodles.

1. Place the sauce in a skillet and warm over medium-low heat. When the sauce starts to simmer, stir in the meatballs and cook, turning occasionally, until completely warmed through, about 4 minutes.

2. Add the calamari and cook until just cooked through, about 2 minutes. Remove the pan from heat, stir in the basil, and serve.

INGREDIENTS:

2 CUPS MARINARA SAUCE (SEE PAGE 674)

CLASSIC ITALIAN AMERICAN MEATBALLS (SEE PAGE 326)

½ LB. CALAMRI, CUT INTO LONG STRIPS

1 TABLESPOON FINELY CHOPPED FRESH BASIL

BEEF & CORN CASSEROLE

YIELD: 8 TO 10 SERVINGS / **ACTIVE TIME:** 30 MINUTES / **TOTAL TIME:** 1 HOUR AND 30 MINUTES

This homey layered pie is beloved in Chile, primarily because of the pino that forms the bottom layer: a liberally seasoned mixture of beef, olives, raisins, and hard-boiled eggs.

1. Preheat your oven to 350°F. Place the oil in a large cast-iron skillet and warm over medium-high heat. When the oil starts to simmer, add the onions and sauté until translucent, about 3 minutes. Stir in the cumin, paprika, half of the salt, the pepper, raisins, and olives, cook for 1 minute, and then remove the skillet from heat.

2. Place the corn, sugar, milk, cream, melted butter, and the remaining salt in a food processor and blitz until the mixture is a slightly chunky puree. Pour the puree into a bowl and stir in the basil.

3. Arrange the meatballs on top of the mixture in the skillet. Distribute the slices of egg on top and then pour the corn puree over everything. Place the skillet in the oven and bake until the top is golden brown, about 1 hour. If the top is not brown enough after 1 hour, place it under the broiler for approximately 1 minute. Remove from the oven and serve with Ensalada Chileana.

INGREDIENTS:

- 3 TABLESPOONS OLIVE OIL
- 4 YELLOW ONIONS, CHOPPED
- 1½ TABLESPOONS CUMIN
- 2 TEASPOONS SWEET PAPRIKA
- 2 TEASPOONS KOSHER SALT
- ½ TEASPOON BLACK PEPPER
- ¾ CUP GOLDEN RAISINS
- 1 CUP BLACK OLIVES, PITTED AND CHOPPED
- 3 CUPS COOKED CORN
- 1 TABLESPOON SUGAR
- ½ CUP MILK
- ½ CUP HEAVY CREAM
- ⅓ CUP BUTTER, MELTED AND SLIGHTLY COOLED
- 1 CUP BASIL LEAVES, CHOPPED
- 1 BATCH BEEF MEATBALLS, FORMED AND UNCOOKED
- 3 HARD-BOILED EGGS, SLICED
- ENSALADA CHILEANA (SEE PAGE 587), FOR SERVING

STOCKS AND SAUCES

Many of the individual recipes in this book include a stock or a sauce in which the meatballs are cooked or dipped in; the following recipes explain how to make all those stocks and sauces, and include some extras, as well.

CHICKEN STOCK

YIELD: 8 CUPS / **ACTIVE TIME:** 20 MINUTES / **TOTAL TIME:** 6 HOURS

A must for any homemade soup, this stock is also great when you need to deglaze a pan.

INGREDIENTS:

7 LBS. CHICKEN BONES, RINSED
4 CUPS CHOPPED YELLOW ONIONS
2 CUPS CHOPPED CARROTS
2 CUPS CHOPPED CELERY
3 GARLIC CLOVES, CRUSHED
3 SPRIGS FRESH THYME
1 TEASPOON BLACK PEPPERCORNS
1 BAY LEAF

1. Place the chicken bones in a stockpot and cover with cold water. Bring to a simmer over medium-high heat and use a ladle to skim off any impurities that float to the top. Add the vegetables, thyme, peppercorns, and bay leaf, reduce the heat to low, and simmer for 5 hours, while skimming to remove any impurities that rise to the surface.

2. Strain, allow to cool slightly, and transfer the stock to the refrigerator. Leave uncovered and allow to cool completely. Remove the layer of fat and cover. The stock will keep in the refrigerator for 3 to 5 days, and in the freezer for up to 3 months.

QUICK CHICKEN STOCK

YIELD: 8 CUPS / **ACTIVE TIME:** 10 MINUTES / **TOTAL TIME:** 30 MINUTES

It's happened to me more than I care to remember: I go to the freezer for some chicken stock but there is none to be found. Here's a way to make a reasonable facsimile in just a few minutes.

INGREDIENTS:

8 CUPS CANNED LOW-SODIUM CHICKEN STOCK
4 CELERY STALKS, MINCED
1 ONION, CHOPPED
2 CARROTS, PEELED AND MINCED
2 TABLESPOONS BLACK PEPPERCORNS
6 GARLIC CLOVES, CRUSHED
4 SPRIGS FRESH PARSLEY
4 SPRIGS FRESH THYME
2 BAY LEAVES

1. Place all of the ingredients in a large stockpot and bring to a boil over high heat. Reduce heat to low, cover the pan, and simmer for 20 minutes.

2. Strain the stock through a fine sieve and press down on the solids to remove as much liquid as possible. Discard the solids and use the stock immediately. It will keep in the refrigerator for up to 5 days, and in the freezer for up to 3 months.

BEEF STOCK

YIELD: 8 CUPS / **ACTIVE TIME:** 20 MINUTES / **TOTAL TIME:** 6 HOURS

If you want an extra-smooth stock, try using veal bones instead of beef bones, or use a combination of the two varieties.

INGREDIENTS:

- 7 LBS. BEEF BONES, RINSED
- 4 CUPS CHOPPED YELLOW ONIONS
- 2 CUPS CHOPPED CARROTS
- 2 CUPS CHOPPED CELERY
- 3 GARLIC CLOVES, CRUSHED
- 3 SPRIGS FRESH THYME
- 1 TEASPOON BLACK PEPPERCORNS
- 1 BAY LEAF

1. Place the beef bones in a stockpot and cover with cold water. Bring to a simmer over medium-high heat and use a ladle to skim off any impurities that float to the top. Add the vegetables, thyme, peppercorns, and bay leaf, reduce the heat to low, and simmer for 5 hours, while skimming to remove any impurities that rise to the surface.

2. Strain, allow to cool slightly, and transfer the stock to the refrigerator. Leave uncovered and allow to cool completely. Remove the layer of fat and cover. The stock will keep in the refrigerator for up to 5 days, and in the freezer for up to 3 months.

VEGETABLE STOCK

YIELD: 6 CUPS / **ACTIVE TIME:** 20 MINUTES / **TOTAL TIME:** 3 HOURS

A great way to make use of your vegetable trimmings. Just avoid starchy vegetables such as potatoes, as they will make the stock cloudy.

INGREDIENTS:

- 2 TABLESPOONS OLIVE OIL
- 2 LARGE LEEKS, TRIMMED AND RINSED WELL
- 2 LARGE CARROTS, PEELED AND SLICED
- 2 CELERY STALKS, SLICED
- 2 LARGE YELLOW ONIONS, SLICED
- 3 GARLIC CLOVES, UNPEELED AND CRUSHED
- 2 SPRIGS FRESH PARSLEY
- 2 SPRIGS FRESH THYME
- 1 BAY LEAF
- 8 CUPS WATER
- ½ TEASPOON BLACK PEPPERCORNS
- SALT, TO TASTE

1. Place the olive oil and the vegetables in a large stockpot and cook over low heat until the liquid the vegetables release has evaporated. This will allow the flavor of the vegetables to become concentrated.

2. Add the parsley, thyme, bay leaf, water, peppercorns, and salt. Raise the heat to high and bring to a boil. Reduce the heat so that the stock simmers and cook for 2 hours, while skimming to remove any impurities that rise to the surface.

3. Strain the stock through a fine sieve, let the stock cool slightly, and place it in the refrigerator, uncovered, to chill. Remove the fat layer and cover. The stock will keep in the refrigerator for up to 5 days, and in the freezer for up to 3 months.

CRAB STOCK

YIELD: 4 QUARTS / **ACTIVE TIME:** 30 MINUTES / **TOTAL TIME:** 2 TO 4 HOURS

This stock is made with cooked crab. If using raw crab, combine all the ingredients except for the crab in the stockpot and bring to a boil. Add the crab legs and cook for 8 minutes, remove, and submerge in ice water. Reduce the heat so that the stock simmers, remove the crab meat from the shells and return the shells to the stock.

INGREDIENTS:

- 2 TABLESPOONS OLIVE OIL
- 1 ONION, CHOPPED
- 1 CARROT, PEELED AND CHOPPED
- 1 CELERY STALK, CHOPPED
- 3 LBS. CRAB LEGS, COOKED IN THE SHELL, MEAT REMOVED AND RESERVED, SHELLS USED IN STOCK
- ½ CUP WHITE WINE
- ¼ CUP TOMATO PASTE
- 2 SPRIGS FRESH THYME
- 2 SPRIGS FRESH PARSLEY
- 3 SPRIGS FRESH TARRAGON
- 1 BAY LEAF
- ½ TEASPOON BLACK PEPPERCORNS
- 1 TEASPOON KOSHER SALT
- 8 CARDAMOM PODS

1. In a large stockpot, add the oil and warm over low heat. Add the vegetables and cook until any additional moisture has evaporated. This will allow the flavor of the vegetables to become concentrated.

2. Add the crab shells, the remaining ingredients, and enough water to cover the shells by 1 inch.

3. Raise heat to high and bring to a boil. Reduce heat so that the stock simmers and cook for a minimum of 2 hours. Skim fat and impurities from the surface as the stock cooks. As for when to stop cooking the stock, let the flavor be the judge.

4. When the stock is finished cooking, strain through a fine strainer or cheesecloth. Place stock in refrigerator to chill.

5. Once cool, skim the fat layer from the top and discard. Use immediately, refrigerate, or freeze.

MUSHROOM STOCK

YIELD: 6 CUPS / **ACTIVE TIME:** 20 MINUTES / **TOTAL TIME:** 3 HOURS AND 20 MINUTES

Any mushroom is perfect for this stock, so try to find the most affordable option. The trick to a great mushroom stock is cooking out as much of the mushroom's natural liquid prior to adding the water. This will speed up the cooking time and make for a more concentrated, flavorful stock.

INGREDIENTS:

- 2 TABLESPOONS OLIVE OIL
- 3 LBS. MUSHROOMS
- 1 ONION, CHOPPED
- 1 GARLIC CLOVE, MINCED
- 2 BAY LEAVES
- 1 TABLESPOON BLACK PEPPERCORNS
- 2 SPRIGS FRESH THYME
- 1 CUP WHITE WINE
- 8 CUPS WATER

1. In a large stockpot, add the oil and mushrooms and cook over low heat for 30 to 40 minutes. The longer you cook the mushrooms, the better.

2. Add onion, garlic, bay leaves, peppercorns, and thyme and cook for 5 minutes.

3. Add the white wine, cook 5 minutes, and then add the water.

4. Bring to a boil, reduce heat so that stock simmers, and cook for 2 to 3 hours, until you are pleased with the taste. Strain, chill the stock in the refrigerator, and remove the fat layer from the top before using.

THAI FISH BROTH

YIELD: 4 SERVINGS / **ACTIVE TIME:** 20 MINUTES / **TOTAL TIME:** 45 MINUTES

This is a very fragrant broth thanks to the lemongrass, chilies, galangal root, lime juice, and lime leaf. It's meant to be very sour, which makes it perfect as a palate cleanser.

INGREDIENTS:

- 4 CUPS FISH STOCK (SEE PAGE 672)
- 2 LEMONGRASS STALKS, BRUISED
- ZEST AND JUICE OF 2 LIMES
- 1-INCH PIECE GALANGAL ROOT, PEELED AND SLICED THIN
- 6 SPRIGS FRESH CILANTRO
- 1 KAFFIR LIME LEAF
- 2 MONKFISH FILLETS, SKINNED AND CUT INTO 1-INCH PIECES
- 12 SMALL SHRIMP
- 2 THAI CHILI PEPPERS, STEMMED, SEEDS AND RIBS REMOVED, AND SLICED THIN
- 1 TABLESPOON RICE VINEGAR
- ¼ CUP FISH SAUCE

1. In a medium saucepan, add the stock, lemongrass, lime zest, galangal root, cilantro, and lime leaf and bring to a boil. Reduce the heat so that the broth simmers and cook for 5 minutes.

2. Turn off the heat and let the broth stand for 15 minutes.

3. Strain the broth through a fine sieve. Place it in a clean pan and bring to a boil.

4. Reduce heat so that the broth simmers. Add the lime juice, monkfish, shrimp, Thai chilies, rice vinegar, and fish sauce. Simmer for 3 to 4 minutes, or until the fish is cooked.

5. Either strain and use the broth to poach your favorite meatballs, or leave everything and simply stir the meatballs in.

FISH STOCK

YIELD: 6 CUPS / **ACTIVE TIME:** 20 MINUTES / **TOTAL TIME:** 4 HOURS

If you buy whole fish, be sure to save the heads and bones in the freezer so you can make this stock when you need it.

INGREDIENTS:

- ¼ CUP OLIVE OIL
- 1 LEEK, TRIMMED, RINSED WELL, AND CHOPPED
- 1 LARGE YELLOW ONION, UNPEELED, ROOT CLEANED, CHOPPED
- 2 LARGE CARROTS, CHOPPED
- 1 CELERY STALK, CHOPPED
- ¾ LB. WHITEFISH BODIES
- 4 SPRIGS FRESH PARSLEY
- 3 SPRIGS FRESH THYME
- 2 BAY LEAVES
- 1 TEASPOON BLACK PEPPERCORNS
- 1 TEASPOON KOSHER SALT
- 8 CUPS WATER

1. Place the olive oil in a stockpot and warm over low heat. Add the vegetables and cook until the liquid they release has evaporated. Add the whitefish bodies, the aromatics, the salt, and the water to the pot, raise the heat to high, and bring to a boil. Reduce heat so that the stock simmers and cook for 3 hours, while skimming to remove any impurities that rise to the surface.

2. Strain the stock through a fine sieve, let it cool slightly, and place in the refrigerator, uncovered, to chill. When the stock is completely cool, remove the fat layer from the top and cover. The stock will keep in the refrigerator for 3 to 5 days, and in the freezer for up to 3 months.

SEAFOOD STOCK

YIELD: 8 CUPS / **ACTIVE TIME:** 15 MINUTES / **TOTAL TIME:** 1 HOUR AND 45 MINUTES

If your local seafood market sells cooked lobster meat or shrimp, chances are they will give you the shells necessary for this stock either for free or at a very reasonable cost.

INGREDIENTS:

- 2 LOBSTER CARCASSES
- SHELLS FROM 2 LBS. RAW SHRIMP
- 8 CUPS WATER
- 1 CUP DRY WHITE WINE
- 1 CARROT, PEELED AND CHOPPED
- 1 ONION, SLICED
- 1 CELERY STALK, SLICED
- 1 TABLESPOON BLACK PEPPERCORNS
- 3 SPRIGS FRESH PARSLEY
- 3 SPRIGS FRESH THYME
- 2 GARLIC CLOVES
- 1 BAY LEAF

1. Pull the top shell off of a lobster carcass, scrape off the feathery gills, discard them, and then break the body into small pieces. Place the pieces into a large saucepan or stockpot and repeat with the remaining lobster carcass.

2. Add the remaining ingredients and bring to a boil over high heat. Reduce the heat to low and simmer the stock for 1½ hours, skimming to remove any impurities that rise to the surface.

3. Strain the stock through a fine sieve, let it cool slightly, and place it in the refrigerator, uncovered, to chill. Remove the fat layer and cover. The stock will keep in the refrigerator for up to 5 days, and in the freezer for up to 3 months.

This stock will be hard to make if you don't live near the ocean. A good substitute is bottled clam juice. Use it in place of the water and simmer it with the wine and vegetables to intensify its flavor.

MARINARA SAUCE

YIELD: 8 CUPS / **ACTIVE TIME:** 20 MINUTES / **TOTAL TIME:** 2 HOURS

Every great cook needs a foolproof marinara sauce, as there remains no better method to capture the flavor of fresh tomatoes, and no better partner for classic meatballs.

INGREDIENTS:

4 LBS. TOMATOES, QUARTERED

1 LARGE YELLOW ONION, SLICED

15 GARLIC CLOVES, CRUSHED

2 TEASPOONS FINELY CHOPPED FRESH THYME

2 TEASPOONS FINELY CHOPPED FRESH OREGANO

2 TABLESPOONS OLIVE OIL

1½ TABLESPOONS KOSHER SALT

1 TEASPOON BLACK PEPPER

2 TABLESPOONS FINELY CHOPPED FRESH BASIL

1 TABLESPOON FINELY CHOPPED FRESH PARSLEY

1. Place all of the ingredients, except for the basil and parsley, in a Dutch oven and cook, stirring constantly, over medium heat until the tomatoes begin to break down, about 10 minutes. Reduce the heat to low and cook, stirring occasionally, for about 1½ hours, or until the flavor is to your liking.

2. Stir in the basil and parsley and season to taste. The sauce will be chunky. If you prefer a smoother texture, transfer the sauce to a blender and puree before serving.

SPICY TOMATO SAUCE

YIELD: 1 CUP / **ACTIVE TIME:** 15 MINUTES / **TOTAL TIME:** 30 MINUTES

A recipe for those times when you want a little more spice alongside the sweetness of tomatoes.

INGREDIENTS:

2 SPICY CHILI PEPPERS

2 TABLESPOONS OLIVE OIL

1 SMALL SHALLOT, MINCED

2 GARLIC CLOVES, MINCED

2 LBS. TOMATOES, CRUSHED

¼ CUP FINELY CHOPPED FRESH CILANTRO

1 TABLESPOON FINELY CHOPPED PARSLEY

2 TABLESPOONS FINELY CHOPPED FRESH CHIVES

SALT AND PEPPER, TO TASTE

1. Preheat the broiler to high and place the chilies on a baking sheet. Broil, turning the peppers occasionally, until they are charred and blistered all over. Remove from the oven and let cool. When the chilies are cool enough to handle, remove the stems and seeds, mince the flesh, and set aside.

2. Place the olive oil in a saucepan and warm over medium heat. When the oil starts to shimmer, add the shallot and garlic and sauté for 2 minutes. Stir in the chilies, add the tomatoes, and cook until they start to break down, about 10 minutes.

3. Stir in the cilantro, parsley, and chives and cook until the flavor has developed to your liking. Season with salt and pepper and serve.

SOFRITO

YIELD: 2 CUPS / **ACTIVE TIME:** 10 MINUTES / **TOTAL TIME:** 10 MINUTES

The strong aromatic qualities of this incredible versatile sauce is key to a number of beloved dishes in the Caribbean, and it also works well as a condiment.

1. Dice 1 of the poblanos, half of the onion, and half of each of the bell peppers. Set them aside.

2. Place the rest of the ingredients in a blender or food processor and blitz until smooth. Transfer the puree to a bowl, stir in the diced vegetables, and serve.

INGREDIENTS:

- 2 POBLANO PEPPERS, STEMMED AND SEEDS AND RIBS REMOVED
- 1 RED ONION, PEELED AND CUT INTO QUARTERS
- 1 RED BELL PEPPER, STEMMED AND SEEDS AND RIBS REMOVED
- 1 GREEN BELL PEPPER, STEMMED AND SEEDS AND RIBS REMOVED
- 3 PLUM TOMATOES
- 2 GARLIC CLOVES
- 1 TABLESPOON CUMIN
- 2 TABLESPOONS ADOBO SEASONING
- ¼ CUP FINELY CHOPPED FRESH PARSLEY
- ¼ CUP FINELY CHOPPED FRESH CILANTRO

MEXICAN TOMATO SAUCE

YIELD: 2 CUPS / **ACTIVE TIME:** 15 MINUTES / **TOTAL TIME:** 40 MINUTES

Not as spicy as you might imagine from the name. Instead, this sauce offers the earthy flavors that make Mexican cuisine beloved by so many.

INGREDIENTS:

- 3 TABLESPOONS OLIVE OIL
- 1 SMALL ONION, MINCED
- 3 GARLIC CLOVES, MINCED
- 3 TABLESPOONS CHILI POWDER
- 1 TABLESPOON CUMIN
- 1 TABLESPOON DRIED OREGANO
- ¾ CUP CHICKEN OR VEGETABLE STOCK (SEE PAGES 660 OR 664, RESPECTIVELY)
- 2 CUPS TOMATO SAUCE
- 1 (4 OZ.) CAN DICED MILD GREEN CHILIES, DRAINED
- ¼ CUP CHOPPED FRESH CILANTRO
- SALT AND PEPPER, TO TASTE

1. Place the olive oil in a saucepan and warm over medium-high heat. When it starts to shimmer, add the onion and garlic and sauté until the onion is translucent, about 3 minutes. Reduce the heat to low, stir in the chili powder, cumin, and oregano and cook for 1 minute.

2. Stir in the stock, tomato sauce, and green chilies. Bring to a boil, reduce the heat to low, and simmer until the sauce has reduced by one-quarter, about 15 minutes.

3. Stir in the cilantro, season with salt and pepper, and use as desired.

VARIATIONS

- For a spicier sauce, substitute 2 minced chipotle chili peppers in adobo for the green chilies.
- Substitute red or white wine for the stock.

SUN-DRIED TOMATO SAUCE

YIELD: 2 CUPS / **ACTIVE TIME:** 15 MINUTES / **TOTAL TIME:** 15 MINUTES

This sauce is on the sweeter side, making it a wonderful foil for the savory-leaning preparations in this book.

INGREDIENTS:

- ½ LB. CREAM CHEESE, AT ROOM TEMPERATURE
- ½ CUP MAYONNAISE
- ½ CUP SOUR CREAM
- 3 GARLIC CLOVES
- 2 TEASPOONS HERBES DE PROVENCE
- ½ CUP SUN-DRIED TOMATOES IN OLIVE OIL, DRAINED AND CHOPPED
- 4 SCALLIONS, TRIMMED AND CHOPPED
- SALT AND PEPPER, TO TASTE

1. Place the cream cheese, mayonnaise, sour cream, garlic, and Herbes de Provence in a food processor and puree until smooth.

2. Add the sun-dried tomatoes and scallions and pulse until they are minced and evenly distributed. Season with salt and pepper and use as desired.

If your sun-dried tomatoes are not packed in olive oil, rehydrate them in boiling water for 10 minutes, drain, and continue with the recipe.

ROMESCO SAUCE

YIELD: 1 CUP / **ACTIVE TIME:** 5 MINUTES / **TOTAL TIME:** 5 MINUTES

This red pepper–based sauce originated in the fishing communities of Catalonia, but its bold, zippy flavor has since carried it onto tables across the globe.

INGREDIENTS:

- 2 LARGE ROASTED RED BELL PEPPERS, STEMMED AND SEEDED
- 1 GARLIC CLOVE, SMASHED
- ½ CUP SLIVERED ALMONDS, TOASTED
- ¼ CUP TOMATO PUREE
- 2 TABLESPOONS FINELY CHOPPED FRESH PARSLEY
- 2 TABLESPOONS SHERRY VINEGAR
- 1 TEASPOON SMOKED PAPRIKA
- SALT AND PEPPER, TO TASTE
- ½ CUP OLIVE OIL

1. Place all of the ingredients, except for the olive oil, in a blender or food processor and pulse until the mixture is combined.

2. Add the olive oil in a steady stream and blitz until emulsified. Season with salt and pepper and use immediately.

GINGERY RED PEPPER SAUCE

YIELD: 1 CUP / **ACTIVE TIME:** 5 MINUTES / **TOTAL TIME:** 25 MINUTES

The sweet and velvety appearance of this sauce belies the kick provided by the ginger.

1. Place all of the ingredients in a food processor and blitz until smooth.

2. Place the puree in a saucepan and cook, stirring occasionally, over medium heat until the sauce has achieved the desired consistency and flavor, about 20 minutes. Strain before using or storing.

INGREDIENTS:

- 3 RED BELL PEPPERS, STEMMED, SEEDS AND RIBS REMOVED, AND CHOPPED
- 2-INCH PIECE FRESH GINGER, PEELED AND CHOPPED
- 4 GARLIC CLOVES
- ¼ CUP SUGAR
- 3 TABLESPOONS TOMATO PASTE
- 2 TABLESPOONS OLIVE OIL
- 2 TABLESPOONS APPLE CIDER VINEGAR
- 2 TABLESPOONS SOY SAUCE

SOUTHERN BARBECUE SAUCE

YIELD: 2 CUPS / **ACTIVE TIME:** 10 MINUTES / **TOTAL TIME:** 40 MINUTES

A vinegar-based BBQ sauce that is sure to provide the sweet, smoky, and slightly tart complexity you crave.

INGREDIENTS:

- 1⅓ CUPS KETCHUP
- ½ CUP APPLE CIDER VINEGAR
- ¼ CUP FIRMLY PACKED DARK BROWN SUGAR
- 3 TABLESPOONS WORCESTERSHIRE SAUCE
- 3-INCH PIECE FRESH GINGER, PEELED AND GRATED
- 2 TABLESPOONS OLIVE OIL
- 1 TABLESPOON MUSTARD POWDER
- 2 GARLIC CLOVES, MINCED
- 1 LEMON, SLICED THIN
- ½ TEASPOON HOT SAUCE, OR TO TASTE

1. Place all of the ingredients in a saucepan and bring to a boil over medium heat, stirring occasionally. Reduce the heat to low and simmer the sauce until it has thickened to the desired consistency, about 30 minutes.

2. Strain the sauce before using or storing in the refrigerator.

SOUTHWESTERN BARBECUE SAUCE

YIELD: 3 CUPS / **ACTIVE TIME:** 15 MINUTES / **TOTAL TIME:** 25 MINUTES

The chipotles and adobo sauce provide the subtle heat and deep flavor that one associates with Southwestern cuisine.

INGREDIENTS:

- 2 TABLESPOONS OLIVE OIL
- 1 LARGE ONION, CHOPPED
- 2 GARLIC CLOVES, MINCED
- 2 CHIPOTLE CHILI PEPPERS IN ADOBO, MINCED
- 2 CUPS CRUSHED TOMATOES
- ½ CUP FIRMLY PACKED DARK BROWN SUGAR
- ¼ CUP APPLE CIDER VINEGAR
- 3 TABLESPOONS FRESH LIME JUICE
- 2 TEASPOONS MUSTARD POWDER
- SALT, TO TASTE
- HOT SAUCE, TO TASTE

1. Place the oil in a saucepan and warm over medium-high heat. When it starts to shimmer, add the onion, garlic, and chilies and sauté until the onion starts to soften, about 5 minutes. Stir in the tomatoes, sugar, vinegar, lime juice, and mustard powder and bring the sauce to a boil over medium heat, stirring frequently.

2. Reduce the heat to low and simmer the sauce until it has thickened slightly, about 15 minutes. Season with salt and hot sauce, transfer to a food processor, puree until smooth, and serve or store in the refrigerator.

COFFEE & BOURBON BARBECUE SAUCE

YIELD: 2 CUPS / **ACTIVE TIME:** 10 MINUTES / **TOTAL TIME:** 20 MINUTES

A marriage of the Texan and Southern BBQ traditions, where the slight bitterness of the coffee and sweet bourbon work in perfect harmony.

INGREDIENTS:

- 2 CUPS BREWED COFFEE
- ¼ CUP DARK BROWN SUGAR
- ¾ CUP BOURBON
- 3 TABLESPOONS MOLASSES
- ¼ CUP RAW APPLE CIDER VINEGAR
- 2 TABLESPOONS WORCESTERSHIRE SAUCE
- ¼ CUP KETCHUP
- 1 TABLESPOON GRANULATED GARLIC
- ½ TABLESPOON BLACK PEPPER
- 1 TABLESPOON CORNSTARCH

1. Place all of the ingredients in a saucepan, stir to combine, and bring to a boil over medium-high heat.

2. Reduce the heat to medium, cook until the sauce has reduced to the desired consistency, and remove the pan from heat. Taste, adjust the seasoning as necessary, and use as desired.

SPICY PEACH BARBECUE SAUCE

YIELD: 1 CUP / **ACTIVE TIME:** 15 MINUTES / **TOTAL TIME:** 25 MINUTES

Another way to salvage some of the fleeting glory peach season contains.

INGREDIENTS:

- 2 TABLESPOONS OLIVE OIL
- 4 GARLIC CLOVES, MINCED
- 1 SMALL ONION, MINCED
- 1 CUP PUREED TOMATOES
- ½ CUP KETCHUP
- ¼ CUP FIRMLY PACKED LIGHT BROWN SUGAR
- ¼ CUP MOLASSES
- 2 TABLESPOONS HONEY
- 1 TABLESPOON WORCESTERSHIRE SAUCE
- 4 PEACHES, PEELED, PITTED, AND CHOPPED
- 2 TABLESPOONS PEACH PRESERVES
- JUICE OF ½ LEMON
- 1 TEASPOON BLACK PEPPER
- 1 TEASPOON KOSHER SALT

1. Place the olive oil in a saucepan and warm over medium-high heat. When the oil starts to shimmer, add the garlic and onion and sauté for 2 minutes. Add the remaining ingredients, bring to a boil, and then reduce the heat to medium. Simmer, stirring occasionally, until the sauce has reduced by half, about 20 minutes.

2. Remove the pan from heat, let it rest for 10 minutes, and strain before using or storing.

BASIL & CILANTRO PUREE

YIELD: 1 CUP / **ACTIVE TIME:** 5 MINUTES / **TOTAL TIME:** 5 MINUTES

A tremendous, and tremendously easy, way to infuse any preparation in this book with some fresh flavor and vibrant color.

1. Place the cilantro, basil, parsley, garlic, and jalepeño in a food processor and puree until smooth. Gradually add the lime juice and olive oil and blitz until the puree has the desired consistency. Season with salt and pepper and use or store in the refrigerator, where it will keep for up to 1 week.

INGREDIENTS:

- ½ CUP FRESH CILANTRO LEAVES
- ½ CUP FRESH BASIL LEAVES
- 2 TABLESPOONS FINELY CHOPPED FRESH PARSLEY
- 2 GARLIC CLOVES, MINCED
- 1 JALAPEÑO PEPPER, STEMMED, SEEDS AND RIBS REMOVED, AND MINCED
- 1 TABLESPOON FRESH LIME JUICE
- ¼ CUP OLIVE OIL
- SALT AND PEPPER, TO TASTE

GREEN CHILI CHOW CHOW

YIELD: 8 CUPS / **ACTIVE TIME:** 5 MINUTES / **TOTAL TIME:** 40 MINUTES

The Hatch chilies define this condiment.

1. Combine vinegar, mustard powder, mustard seeds, sugar, bay leaves, and cilantro in a medium saucepan. Cook over medium heat until reduced by one-third. Add the chilies and cook for another 5 minutes.

2. Add the Dijon mustard. Season with salt and chili powder and remove the pan from heat. Let cool until the mixture is gelatinous. Use immediately or store in the refrigerator, where it will keep for up to 1 week.

INGREDIENTS:

- 4 CUPS DISTILLED VINEGAR
- 1 TABLESPOON MUSTARD POWDER
- ½ CUP YELLOW MUSTARD SEEDS
- 1 CUP SUGAR
- 2 BAY LEAVES
- 1 BUNCH FRESH CILANTRO, STEMS ONLY, CHOPPED
- 2 (27 OZ.) CANS HATCH GREEN CHILIES, DRAINED
- ½ CUP DIJON MUSTARD
- SALT, TO TASTE
- HATCH CHILI POWDER, TO TASTE

BEER MUSTARD

YIELD: 4 CUPS / **ACTIVE TIME:** 5 MINUTES / **TOTAL TIME:** 1 HOUR

Simple to prepare, this dip is impossible to forget.

INGREDIENTS:

- 2 CUPS YELLOW MUSTARD SEEDS
- ½ CUP BROWN MUSTARD SEEDS
- 3 CUPS MALT VINEGAR
- 4 CUPS BEER
- ¾ CUP HONEY
- 1 CUP GENTLY PACKED BROWN SUGAR
- 1 TABLESPOON KOSHER SALT
- ½ CUP MUSTARD POWDER
- 5 ALLSPICE BERRIES, GROUND
- ½ CUP MUNICH MALT, GROUND

1. Place all ingredients in a large saucepan and cook over medium heat until the seeds are soft.

2. Transfer to a food processor and puree until it achieves the desired texture. Let cool completely before serving.

CILANTRO & MINT CHUTNEY

YIELD: 2 CUPS / **ACTIVE TIME:** 5 MINUTES / **TOTAL TIME:** 5 MINUTES

Typically served with Indian food, this chutney would be perfect alongside any of the spicy meatballs in this book.

INGREDIENTS:

- 2 CUPS PACKED FRESH CILANTRO SPRIGS
- 1 CUP PACKED FRESH MINT LEAVES
- ½ CUP CHOPPED WHITE ONION
- ⅓ CUP WATER
- 1 TABLESPOON FRESH LIME JUICE
- 1 TEASPOON MINCED GREEN CHILI PEPPER
- 1 TEASPOON SUGAR
- ¾ TEASPOON KOSHER SALT, OR TO TASTE

1. Place all ingredients in a blender and puree. Take care not to over-puree the mixture, as you want the chutney to have some texture.

TOMATO CHUTNEY

YIELD: 1 CUP / **ACTIVE TIME:** 10 MINUTES / **TOTAL TIME:** 25 MINUTES

If you have especially ripe tomatoes, go easy on the amount of sugar you add to this chutney.

1. Place the oil in a saucepan and warm over medium-high heat. When the oil starts to shimmer, add the onion and sauté until translucent, about 3 minutes. Stir in the curry powder, cumin, and ginger and cook until fragrant, about 2 minutes.

2. Add the tomatoes, vinegar, sugar, and salt, raise the heat to high, and bring to a boil. Reduce the heat and let the mixture simmer until it has reduced by about two-thirds, about 15 minutes.

3. Transfer the mixture to a food processor and pulse until it is a slightly chunky puree. Let cool before using or storing in the refrigerator, where it will keep for up to 1 week.

INGREDIENTS:

- 1 TABLESPOON OLIVE OIL
- ½ CUP MINCED ONION
- ½ TEASPOON CURRY POWDER
- ½ TEASPOON CUMIN
- ½-INCH PIECE FRESH GINGER, PEELED AND GRATED
- 2 LARGE RED TOMATOES, SEEDED AND DICED
- ½ CUP APPLE CIDER VINEGAR
- ¼ CUP SUGAR
- ½ TEASPOON KOSHER SALT

ATJAR CHUTNEY

YIELD: 1½ CUPS / **ACTIVE TIME:** 15 MINUTES / **TOTAL TIME:** 30 MINUTES

A beautiful balance of sweetness and spice that will serve you well with any of the meatballs that look to India or the Caribbean for inspiration.

1. Place all of the ingredients in a saucepan and stir to combine. Bring to a boil over medium-high heat, reduce the heat to medium, and simmer until the mixture acquires a jam-like consistency, about 20 minutes. If a smoother consistency is desired, mash the mangoes as they cook.

2. Remove the pan from heat and let the chutney cool. Use as desired or store in the refrigerator, where it will keep for up to 1 week.

INGREDIENTS:

2 LARGE MANGOES, PEELED, PITTED, AND DICED

1 CUP WHITE VINEGAR

¾ CUP SUGAR

1 LARGE RED ONION, CHOPPED

2-INCH PIECE FRESH GINGER, PEELED AND MINCED

1 TEASPOON CAYENNE PEPPER

1 TEASPOON MUSTARD SEEDS

2 GARLIC CLOVES, CHOPPED

1 TEASPOON KOSHER SALT

MOSTARDO

YIELD: 1 CUP / **ACTIVE TIME:** 5 MINUTES / **TOTAL TIME:** 15 MINUTES

This northern Italian condiment is made from candied fruit and a thick, mustard-flavored syrup.

1. In a small saucepan, combine the apricots, cherries, shallot, ginger, wine, vinegar, water, and sugar and bring to a boil. Cover and cook over medium heat until all of the liquid is absorbed and the fruit has softened, about 10 minutes.

2. Stir in the mustard powder, Dijon mustard, and butter. Simmer until the mixture is jam-like, about 2 to 3 minutes.

3. Remove from heat. Serve warm or at room temperature, or store in the refrigerator for up to 1 week.

INGREDIENTS:

- ¼ LB. DRIED APRICOTS, CHOPPED
- ¼ CUP DRIED CHERRIES, CHOPPED
- 1 SHALLOT, MINCED
- 1½ TEASPOONS MINCED CRYSTALLIZED GINGER
- ½ CUP DRY WHITE WINE
- 3 TABLESPOONS WHITE WINE VINEGAR
- 3 TABLESPOONS WATER
- 3 TABLESPOONS SUGAR
- 1 TEASPOON MUSTARD POWDER
- 1 TEASPOON DIJON MUSTARD
- 1 TABLESPOON UNSALTED BUTTER

GREEN TOMATO JAM

YIELD: 6 CUPS / **ACTIVE TIME:** 20 MINUTES / **TOTAL TIME:** 24 HOURS

This jam is a great way to utilize an overabundance of green tomatoes and allow tomato season to be enjoyed any time of the year.

INGREDIENTS:

- 3 LBS. GREEN TOMATOES
- 1 LEMON
- 1 LB. SUGAR

1. Wash the tomatoes and pat them dry. Remove the core, chop the tomatoes into small pieces, and remove the seeds. Place the tomato pieces in a large saucepan.

2. Zest the lemon. Keep the zest refrigerated in a small bowl with a small amount of lemon juice to keep it hydrated. Add the sugar and the juice of half of the lemon to the pot. Toss, cover, and place in the refrigerator to macerate overnight.

3. In the morning, place the pot over medium-high heat. The tomatoes should have given off a fair amount of liquid overnight. Bring to a boil, stirring occasionally.

4. Reduce the heat so that the tomatoes are gently boiling, and cook for about an hour, stirring occasionally. Once the mixture pulls away from the pot's walls when stirred, remove from the heat and stir in the lemon zest.

5. Transfer the mixture to a food processor and puree until smooth.

6. Pour the jam into clean jars and allow to cool to room temperature before using or storing in the refrigerator, where it will keep for up to 2 weeks.

FIG JAM

YIELD: 3 TO 4 CUPS / **ACTIVE TIME:** 30 MINUTES / **TOTAL TIME:** 1 HOUR AND 15 MINUTES

Yes, the store has some decent options, but this fig jam is easy to make at home and you'll certainly taste the difference.

INGREDIENTS:

- 2 LBS. FIGS, STEMMED AND CUT INTO ½-INCH PIECES
- 1½ CUPS GRANULATED SUGAR
- ¼ CUP WATER
- ¼ CUP FRESH LEMON JUICE
- PINCH OF KOSHER SALT
- 1 VANILLA BEAN, SPLIT AND SEEDED (OPTIONAL)
- 1 CINNAMON STICK (OPTIONAL)

1. Place all of the ingredients in a medium saucepan and bring to a boil. Stir occasionally until the sugar is dissolved. If you include the vanilla bean in your preparation, add the seeds and the pod.

2. Reduce heat to low. Cook, stirring occasionally, until the liquid is thick, sticky, and falls heavily from the spoon, about 30 to 45 minutes.

3. Remove pan from heat and, if using, discard the vanilla pod and cinnamon stick.

4. For a chunky jam, gently mash the large pieces of fig with a fork or potato masher. For a smoother jam, process the mixture in a food processor.

5. Spoon the jam into jars, leaving ¼-inch space at the top. Let cool completely before using or storing in the refrigerator, where the jam will keep for up to 2 weeks.

CRANBERRY SAUCE

YIELD: 6 TO 8 SERVINGS / **ACTIVE TIME:** 5 MINUTES / **TOTAL TIME:** 20 MINUTES

Ladle some of this over any of the meatballs made with turkey and transport yourself to the Thanksgiving table in a flash.

INGREDIENTS:

- 2 CUPS FRESH CRANBERRIES
- 1 CUP SUGAR, PLUS MORE TO TASTE
- 1 CUP WATER
- 1 TABLESPOON ORANGE ZEST

1. Place all of the ingredients in a saucepan and stir to combine. Bring to a simmer over medium heat and cook, while stirring occasionally, until the cranberries start to break down and the mixture thickens, about 15 minutes.

2. Taste the sauce and add more sugar if desired. Serve warm or chilled.

JALAPEÑO PEPPER JAM

YIELD: 6 CUPS / **ACTIVE TIME:** 20 MINUTES / **TOTAL TIME:** 12 TO 24 HOURS

If jalapeños aren't your favorite, feel free to substitute your preferred chili pepper. Should you want a milder jam, Anaheim peppers are a good choice.

INGREDIENTS:

- 1 CUP MINCED GREEN BELL PEPPER
- ¼ CUP MINCED JALAPEÑO PEPPER
- 4 CUPS SUGAR
- 1 CUP APPLE CIDER VINEGAR
- 1 (6 OZ.) PACKET OF LIQUID FRUIT PECTIN
- 4 DROPS OF GREEN FOOD COLORING (OPTIONAL)

1. Place the peppers, sugar, and vinegar in a large saucepan. Bring to a boil and cook for 5 minutes.

2. Remove from heat and let cool for 1 hour.

3. Add the pectin and the food coloring, if using. Return the saucepan to the stove, bring to a rolling boil over medium-high heat, and cook for 1 minute. Pour the mixture into jars. Let cool completely before using or storing in the refrigerator, where the jam will keep for up to 2 weeks.

GARLIC & DILL MUSTARD

YIELD: 1½ CUPS / **ACTIVE TIME:** 5 MINUTES / **TOTAL TIME:** 2 TO 3 DAYS

This mustard can dress up any meatballs, but works particularly well with ones made of chicken or turkey.

INGREDIENTS:

FOR BROWN MUSTARD

- ½ CUP MUSTARD SEEDS
- ½ CUP BEER
- ⅓ CUP WATER
- 1 TABLESPOON MINCED GARLIC
- 1 TABLESPOON MINCED DILL
- 3 TABLESPOONS APPLE CIDER VINEGAR
- 1 TABLESPOON MAPLE SYRUP

FOR YELLOW MUSTARD

- ½ CUP MUSTARD SEEDS
- ½ CUP WHITE WINE
- 2 GARLIC CLOVES, MINCED
- 1 TABLESPOON FINELY CHOPPED FRESH DILL
- ⅓ CUP WHITE WINE VINEGAR
- 1 TABLESPOON SUGAR

1. Combine the ingredients for the chosen mustard in a stainless steel bowl. Cover and let stand for 2 to 3 days.

2. Pour the mixture in a blender and puree until it is just slightly grainy.

3. If the mustard is too thick, incorporate water until you reach your desired consistency.

TIP: This mustard will keep for up to 6 months if refrigerated in an airtight container.

TRADITIONAL HUMMUS

YIELD: 1⅓ CUPS / **ACTIVE TIME:** 15 MINUTES / **TOTAL TIME:** 15 MINUTES

Hummus is easy to make, especially when using canned chickpeas. So make this hummus.

INGREDIENTS:

- 1 (14 OZ.) CAN CHICKPEAS OR 2 CUPS COOKED, DRIED CHICKPEAS
- 3 TABLESPOONS OLIVE OIL
- 3 TABLESPOONS TAHINI
- 1½ TABLESPOONS FRESH LEMON JUICE
- 1 SMALL GARLIC CLOVE, CHOPPED
- 1 TEASPOON KOSHER SALT
- ½ TEASPOON BLACK PEPPER

1. If using canned chickpeas, drain them and reserve the liquid. If time allows, remove the skins from each of the chickpeas. This will make your hummus much smoother.

2. Place the chickpeas, olive oil, tahini, lemon juice, garlic, salt, and pepper in a food processor.

3. Puree hummus until it is very smooth, about 5 to 10 minutes. Scrape down the sides of the bowl as needed and make sure to break up any large chunks.

4. Taste and adjust the seasoning as necessary. If your hummus is stiffer than you'd like, add 2 to 3 tablespoons of the reserved chickpea liquid and blend until desired consistency is achieved.

5. Scrape the hummus into a bowl and serve.

VARIATIONS

- Add 1 to 3 teaspoons of spices like cumin, sumac, harissa, or smoked paprika.
- Drizzle a little pomegranate molasses on top.
- For a roasted vegetable hummus, blend in 1 cup of roasted eggplant, zucchini, bell peppers, or garlic.
- For an olive hummus, fold in ¾ cup of chopped green or black olives.
- For a nutty hummus, blend in some lightly toasted walnuts, almonds, or pine nuts.
- For a lemony hummus, add ¼ cup of chopped preserved lemons.

RAITA

YIELD: 1 CUP / **ACTIVE TIME:** 5 MINUTES / **TOTAL TIME:** 5 MINUTES

This refreshing Indian specialty would be perfect beside the Bombay Turkey Meatballs (see page 311).

1. Place all of the ingredients in a bowl and stir until well combined. Refrigerate for 1 hour before serving.

INGREDIENTS:

½ CUP PLAIN YOGURT

½ ENGLISH CUCUMBER, SEEDED AND DICED

¼ CUP CHOPPED FRESH CILANTRO

2 SCALLIONS, TRIMMED AND MINCED

¼ TEASPOON CORIANDER

½ TEASPOON SEA SALT

½ TEASPOON BLACK PEPPER

PEANUT SATAY DIP

YIELD: 1 CUP / **ACTIVE TIME:** 10 MINUTES / **TOTAL TIME:** 10 MINUTES

This Thai specialty will go perfectly with a number of the meatballs using chicken as the protein.

INGREDIENTS:

- 1 CUP CREAMY PEANUT BUTTER
- 2 TABLESPOONS RICE VINEGAR
- ¼ CUP SOY SAUCE
- 1 TABLESPOON HONEY
- ¼ CUP BOILING WATER
- JUICE OF 2 LIMES
- 1 TEASPOON HOT SAUCE
- 1 TEASPOON BLACK PEPPER

1. Place all of the ingredients in a bowl, stir until thoroughly combined, and use as desired.

BABA GANOUSH

YIELD: 2 CUPS / **ACTIVE TIME:** 25 MINUTES / **TOTAL TIME:** 45 MINUTES

Roasting the eggplants is a must for this spread, as it draws out their meaty flavor.

1. Preheat the oven to 375°F. Cut the eggplants in half and poke holes in them with a fork. Drizzle the olive oil over the eggplants and sprinkle the salt on top. Place the eggplants, cut-side up, on a baking sheet and roast for 15 to 20 minutes, until lightly brown and tender all the way through.

2. Remove the eggplants from the oven and let them cool slightly. Once cool enough to handle, remove the skins and discard.

3. Place the eggplant in a food processor with the remaining ingredients and pulse until the mixture is a chunky puree.

4. Serve immediately or refrigerate until ready to use.

INGREDIENTS:

3 EGGPLANTS

½ CUP OLIVE OIL

1 TEASPOON SEA SALT

1 TABLESPOON TAHINI

½ TEASPOON CHILI POWDER

JUICE OF 2 LEMONS

1 GARLIC CLOVE, GRATED

1 TEASPOON BLACK PEPPER

BLUE CHEESE SAUCE

YIELD: 2 CUPS / **ACTIVE TIME:** 10 MINUTES / **TOTAL TIME:** 10 MINUTES

Any blue cheese will do here, but don't be afraid to switch it up and try different varieties with the various meatballs, as that process will lead to some perfect pairings.

INGREDIENTS:

- ¾ CUP MAYONNAISE
- ½ CUP SOUR CREAM
- 2 TABLESPOONS WHITE WINE VINEGAR
- ½ LB. BLUE CHEESE, CRUMBLED
- 3 TABLESPOONS FINELY CHOPPED FRESH CHIVES
- SALT AND PEPPER, TO TASTE

1. Place the mayonnaise, sour cream, and vinegar in a mixing bowl and stir until combined. Stir in the blue cheese and chives, season with salt and pepper, and either use or store in the refrigerator.

VARIATIONS

- For a low-fat version, substitute nonfat yogurt for both the mayonnaise and sour cream.
- Minced scallion greens can be substituted for the chives in this or any recipe.

DILL & SCALLION SAUCE

YIELD: 2 CUPS / **ACTIVE TIME:** 10 MINUTES / **TOTAL TIME:** 10 MINUTES

The subtle flavors of these two aromatics will make everyone stand at attention when combined, with an assist from a healthy amount of lemon juice.

INGREDIENTS:

- 1 CUP SOUR CREAM
- ¾ CUP MAYONNAISE
- ¼ CUP FRESH LEMON JUICE
- ⅓ CUP MINCED SCALLIONS
- ¼ CUP CHOPPED FRESH DILL
- 2 GARLIC CLOVES, MINCED
- SALT AND PEPPER, TO TASTE

1. Place the sour cream, mayonnaise, and lemon juice in a mixing bowl and stir until combined. Stir in the scallions, dill, and garlic, season with salt and pepper, and either use or store in the refrigerator, where it will keep for up to 4 days.

VARIATION

- For a low-fat version, substitute nonfat yogurt for both the mayonnaise and sour cream.

GREEN GODDESS SAUCE

YIELD: 1½ CUPS / **ACTIVE TIME:** 5 MINUTES / **TOTAL TIME:** 5 MINUTES

The divine moniker is no accident—this sauce is robust but also delicate enough to keep you mindful of the fresh herbs that produced it.

INGREDIENTS:

- ½ CUP MAYONNAISE
- ⅔ CUP BUTTERMILK
- 1 TABLESPOON FRESH LEMON JUICE
- 2 TABLESPOONS CHOPPED CELERY LEAVES
- 2 TABLESPOONS CHOPPED FRESH PARSLEY LEAVES
- 2 TABLESPOONS CHOPPED FRESH TARRAGON
- 2 TABLESPOONS CHOPPED FRESH CHIVES
- 2 TEASPOONS KOSHER SALT
- 1 TEASPOON BLACK PEPPER

1. Place all of the ingredients in a food processor and blitz until thoroughly combined. Transfer to a container and use as desired.

TARTAR SAUCE

YIELD: 2 CUPS / **ACTIVE TIME:** 10 MINUTES / **TOTAL TIME:** 10 MINUTES

Quite simply, the undisputed champion of seafood-related sauces.

INGREDIENTS:

- 1½ CUPS MAYONNAISE
- 3 SCALLION WHITES, CHOPPED
- ¼ CUP MINCED CORNICHONS
- 3 TABLESPOONS CAPERS, DRAINED AND RINSED
- 2 TABLESPOONS WHITE WINE VINEGAR
- 2 TABLESPOONS FINELY CHOPPED FRESH PARSLEY
- 1 TABLESPOON SMOOTH DIJON MUSTARD
- 1 TABLESPOON FINELY CHOPPED FRESH TARRAGON
- SALT AND PEPPER, TO TASTE

1. Place all of the ingredients in a mixing bowl and stir to combine. Adjust the seasoning as needed and either use or store in the refrigerator.

REMOULADE SAUCE

YIELD: 2 CUPS / **ACTIVE TIME:** 10 MINUTES / **TOTAL TIME:** 10 MINUTES

In the same family as tartar sauce, but with a little more of a kick thanks to the horseradish.

INGREDIENTS:

- 1⅓ CUPS MAYONNAISE
- 6 SCALLIONS, TRIMMED AND CHOPPED
- 3 GARLIC CLOVES, MINCED
- ¼ CUP FRESH LEMON JUICE
- 3 TABLESPOONS WHOLE GRAIN MUSTARD
- 3 TABLESPOONS FINELY CHOPPED FRESH PARSLEY
- 3 TABLESPOONS PREPARED HORSERADISH
- 2 TABLESPOONS CHILI SAUCE
- SALT AND PEPPER, TO TASTE

1. Place all of the ingredients in a mixing bowl and stir to combine. Adjust the seasoning as necessary and either use or store in the refrigerator.

VARIATIONS

- Grate 1 or 2 hard-boiled eggs into the sauce.
- Add 2 tablespoons Worcestershire sauce.

Cornichon is the French word for gherkin, and these sweet-tart pickles are frequently served with pâtés or smoked meats. Small gherkin pickles can be substituted, but don't use commercial pickle relish. It just doesn't have the requisite depth of flavor.

EASY AIOLI

YIELD: 2 CUPS / **ACTIVE TIME:** 10 MINUTES / **TOTAL TIME:** 10 MINUTES

An aioli is just mayonnaise flavored with garlic, and that delicious, simple base has the ability to accommodate an unthinkable amount of other ingredients.

INGREDIENTS:

1½ CUPS MAYONNAISE

6 GARLIC CLOVES, MINCED

3 TABLESPOONS FRESH LEMON JUICE

2 TABLESPOONS SMOOTH DIJON MUSTARD

SALT AND PEPPER, TO TASTE

1. Place all of the ingredients in a mixing bowl and stir to combine. Adjust the seasoning as necessary and either use or store in the refrigerator.

VARIATIONS

- Add 2 tablespoons chili powder.
- Add ¼ cup pureed roasted red bell peppers.

HOLLANDAISE SAUCE

YIELD: 2 CUPS / **ACTIVE TIME:** 15 MINUTES / **TOTAL TIME:** 15 MINUTES

As you'll discover after you try it with your favorite meatballs, this classic sauce isn't strictly for eggs Benedict.

1. Bring an inch of water to a gentle simmer in a saucepan. Place the butter and egg yolks in a heatproof mixing bowl, set the bowl over the simmering water, and whisk until the mixture is smooth and combined.

2. Add the boiling water in a slow stream, whisking constantly. Continue to whisk until the sauce has thickened to the desired consistency, about 7 minutes. Remove from heat, stir in the lemon juice, and use as desired.

INGREDIENTS:

- 1½ STICKS OF UNSALTED BUTTER, AT ROOM TEMPERATURE
- 6 LARGE EGG YOLKS
- ½ CUP BOILING WATER
- 2 TEASPOONS FRESH LEMON JUICE

CREAMY CHIPOTLE SAUCE

YIELD: 2 CUPS / **ACTIVE TIME:** 10 MINUTES / **TOTAL TIME:** 10 MINUTES

The mayonnaise and sour cream provide a soft landing spot for the bold flavor of the chipotles.

INGREDIENTS:

- 1 CUP MAYONNAISE
- ⅔ CUP SOUR CREAM
- 3 TABLESPOONS FRESH LIME JUICE
- 3 SCALLIONS, TRIMMED AND CHOPPED
- 3 GARLIC CLOVES, MINCED
- 3 CHIPOTLE CHILI PEPPERS IN ADOBO, MINCED
- 1 TEASPOON ADOBO SAUCE
- SALT, TO TASTE

1. Place all of the ingredients in a mixing bowl and stir to combine. Adjust the seasoning as necessary and either use or store in the refrigerator.

VARIATION

- To make a low-fat version, substitute nonfat yogurt for both the mayonnaise and sour cream.

GREEK FETA SAUCE

YIELD: 1½ CUPS / **ACTIVE TIME:** 10 MINUTES / **TOTAL TIME:** 10 MINUTES

Cutting the savory nature of feta with lemon juice and yogurt allows this sauce to work well beside a surprising number of dishes.

INGREDIENTS:

- ½ LB. FETA CHEESE, CRUMBLED
- ½ CUP SOUR CREAM
- ¼ CUP PLAIN GREEK YOGURT
- ¼ CUP OLIVE OIL
- 2 TABLESPOONS FRESH LEMON JUICE
- 2 GARLIC CLOVES
- ¼ CUP CHOPPED FRESH DILL
- SALT AND PEPPER, TO TASTE

1. Place the feta, sour cream, yogurt, olive oil, lemon juice, and garlic in a food processor and puree until smooth.

2. Place the mixture in a mixing bowl, stir in the dill, season with salt and pepper, and use as desired.

TAHINI

YIELD: 2 CUPS / **ACTIVE TIME:** 10 MINUTES / **TOTAL TIME:** 20 MINUTES

You can use this as the base of a creamy hummus, or as a stand-alone, nutty dip.

1. Place the unpeeled garlic cloves and the lemon juice in the blender. Add a pinch of the salt and blitz until the mixture is a coarse puree. Let the mixture stand for 10 minutes.

2. Working over a large mixing bowl, strain the puree through a fine sieve and press down on the solids to remove as much liquid as possible. Discard the solids and add the tahini, cumin, and remaining salt to the mixing bowl. Whisk until smooth and creamy, adding water as needed if the mixture needs thinning out. Use immediately or store in the refrigerator for up to 1 week.

INGREDIENTS:

- ½ HEAD GARLIC
- 6 TABLESPOONS FRESH LEMON JUICE
- 1 TEASPOON KOSHER SALT
- 1 CUP TAHINI
- ½ TEASPOON CUMIN
- ICE WATER, AS NEEDED

MIDDLE EASTERN YOGURT SAUCE

YIELD: 2 CUPS / **ACTIVE TIME:** 10 MINUTES / **TOTAL TIME:** 40 MINUTES

Mint's ability to lift everything around it is never more evident than in this sauce.

INGREDIENTS:

- 2 CUPS PLAIN YOGURT
- 1 SCALLION, TRIMMED AND CHOPPED
- 3 GARLIC CLOVES, MINCED
- 2 TABLESPOONS FINELY CHOPPED FRESH MINT
- 1 TABLESPOON OLIVE OIL
- SALT AND PEPPER, TO TASTE

1. Place the yogurt in a fine sieve and drain over a mixing bowl for 30 minutes.

2. Discard the whey and place the yogurt in the bowl. Stir in the scallions, garlic, mint, and olive oil, season with salt and pepper, and either use or store in the refrigerator.

VARIATION

• Add ¼ cup minced tomato.

CILANTRO & LIME YOGURT

YIELD: 2½ CUPS / **ACTIVE TIME:** 10 MINUTES / **TOTAL TIME:** 10 MINUTES

The vegetal tanginess of this creamy dip pairs well with any meatballs in this book that aren't prepared with a sauce.

INGREDIENTS:

- 1 CUP FRESH CILANTRO LEAVES
- 1 CUP BABY SPINACH
- ¼ CUP COLD WATER
- 2 CUPS PLAIN YOGURT
- 1 GARLIC CLOVE, CHOPPED
- JUICE OF ½ LIME
- PINCH OF CAYENNE PEPPER

1. Bring water to a boil in a saucepan and prepare an ice bath. Add the cilantro and spinach to the boiling water, cook for 1 minute, drain, and transfer them to the ice bath. Drain, squeeze to remove as much liquid from the mixture as possible, and transfer the mixture to a food processor.

2. Add the water, half of the yogurt, the garlic, and lime juice to the food processor and blitz until smooth. Place this mixture, the cayenne pepper, and the remaining yogurt in a bowl, stir to combine, and serve.

SESAME & HONEY MUSTARD SAUCE

YIELD: 2 CUPS / **ACTIVE TIME:** 10 MINUTES / **TOTAL TIME:** 10 MINUTES

Honey and mustard is a lauded pair, but the nutty aroma and flavor of the sesame oil let you know that something's been missing all this time.

INGREDIENTS:

- 1 CUP DIJON MUSTARD
- ⅔ CUP HONEY
- ⅓ CUP SESAME OIL
- ½ CUP CHOPPED FRESH CILANTRO
- SALT AND PEPPER, TO TASTE

1. Place all of the ingredients in a mixing bowl and stir to combine. Adjust the seasoning as needed and either use or store in the refrigerator.

HOT HONEY MUSTARD

YIELD: ¾ CUP / **ACTIVE TIME:** 2 MINUTES / **TOTAL TIME:** 2 MINUTES

If you like honey mustard, you'll love this, and you'll be well served to double up on the Hot Honey so you can use it on everything.

INGREDIENTS:

- ½ CUP MAYONNAISE
- 2 TABLESPOONS DIJON MUSTARD
- 2 TABLESPOONS HOT HONEY (SEE RECIPE)
- 1 TABLESPOON FRESH LEMON JUICE
- SALT, TO TASTE

1. Place all of the ingredients in a mixing bowl, stir until combined, and use as desired.

HOT HONEY

HOT HONEY

- 4 HOT CHILI PEPPERS
- 1 CUP HONEY

1. Place the chili peppers and honey in a saucepan and bring to a very gentle simmer over medium-low heat. Reduce the heat to its lowest possible setting and cook for 1 hour.

2. Remove the saucepan from heat and let the mixture infuse for another hour.

3. Remove the peppers. Transfer the honey to a container, cover, and store in the refrigerator.

TIP: Fresno and cayenne peppers produce the best results. If you're after additional heat, use habanero peppers.

APPLE & HOISIN DIPPING SAUCE

YIELD: 2 CUPS / **ACTIVE TIME:** 10 MINUTES / **TOTAL TIME:** 10 MINUTES

This sauce goes particularly well with grilled meatballs.

INGREDIENTS:

- ¾ CUP UNSWEETENED APPLESAUCE
- ½ CUP HOISIN SAUCE
- ¼ CUP FIRMLY PACKED DARK BROWN SUGAR
- 6 TABLESPOONS KETCHUP
- 2 TABLESPOONS HONEY
- 2 TABLESPOONS RICE VINEGAR
- 1 TABLESPOON SOY SAUCE
- 1 TABLESPOON CHILI GARLIC SAUCE, OR TO TASTE

1. Place all of the ingredients in a mixing bowl and stir to combine. Adjust the seasoning as needed and either use or store in the refrigerator.

SPICY THAI PEANUT SAUCE

YIELD: 2 CUPS / **ACTIVE TIME:** 10 MINUTES / **TOTAL TIME:** 10 MINUTES

The recommendation for chunky peanut butter is purely personal preference—if you're a devotee of smooth PB, by all means use it here.

INGREDIENTS:

- 1 CUP CHUNKY PEANUT BUTTER
- ½ CUP HOT WATER (125°F)
- ½ CUP FIRMLY PACKED DARK BROWN SUGAR
- ⅓ CUP FRESH LIME JUICE
- ¼ CUP SOY SAUCE
- 2 TABLESPOONS SESAME OIL
- 2 TABLESPOONS CHILI GARLIC SAUCE
- 6 GARLIC CLOVES, MINCED
- 3 SCALLIONS, TRIMMED AND CHOPPED
- ¼ CUP CHOPPED FRESH CILANTRO

1. Place the peanut butter, water, brown sugar, lime juice, soy sauce, sesame oil, and chili garlic sauce in a mixing bowl and stir to combine. Stir in the garlic, scallions, and cilantro and either use or store in the refrigerator.

SWEET & SOUR DIPPING SAUCE

YIELD: 1½ CUPS / **ACTIVE TIME:** 15 MINUTES / **TOTAL TIME:** 20 MINUTES

While the ingredients lean toward the flavors Asian cuisine is known for, you'll be surprised at how many other preparations this sauce fits beside.

INGREDIENTS:

- 2 TABLESPOONS OLIVE OIL
- 4 SCALLIONS, TRIMMED AND CHOPPED
- 2 GARLIC CLOVES, MINCED
- 2-INCH PIECE FRESH GINGER, PEELED AND GRATED
- ½ CUP MINCED FRESH PINEAPPLE
- ½ CUP RICE VINEGAR
- ⅓ CUP KETCHUP
- ¼ CUP FIRMLY PACKED DARK BROWN SUGAR
- 2 TABLESPOONS CHILI GARLIC SAUCE
- 1 TABLESPOON SOY SAUCE
- 1 TABLESPOON CORNSTARCH
- 1 TABLESPOON WATER

1. Place the oil in a small saucepan and warm over medium-high heat. When it starts to shimmer, add the scallions, garlic, and ginger and sauté until the scallions are translucent, about 3 minutes.

2. Stir in the pineapple, vinegar, ketchup, sugar, chili garlic sauce, and soy sauce and bring to a boil, stirring occasionally. Reduce the heat to low and simmer the sauce for 5 minutes.

3. Combine the cornstarch and water, stir the slurry into the sauce, and cook until it thickens slightly, about 2 minutes. Remove from heat and let the sauce cool to room temperature before using or storing.

VARIATIONS

- Substitute mango or papaya for the pineapple.
- Omit the chili garlic sauce if you want a sauce that isn't spicy.

Mirin is a sweet Japanese wine made from glutinous rice, and it's part of many classic dishes. You can substitute sweet sherry for it, adding 1 tablespoon of sugar for each ¼ cup of sherry.

SWEET & SPICY DIPPING SAUCE

YIELD: 2 CUPS / **ACTIVE TIME:** 10 MINUTES / **TOTAL TIME:** 10 MINUTES

The deep flavors Thai cuisine is renowned for inform this wonderful sauce.

INGREDIENTS:

- 1 CUP RICE VINEGAR
- ⅔ CUP FISH SAUCE
- ⅓ CUP FIRMLY PACKED DARK BROWN SUGAR
- 6 GARLIC CLOVES, MINCED
- 1½ TEASPOONS RED PEPPER FLAKES, OR TO TASTE

1. Place all of the ingredients in a jar and stir until the sugar has dissolved. Adjust the seasoning as needed and either use or store in the refrigerator.

PONZU SAUCE

YIELD: 2 CUPS / **ACTIVE TIME:** 10 MINUTES / **TOTAL TIME:** 10 MINUTES

A classic Japanese condiment with a tangy flavor that goes well with meatballs made from seafood or poultry.

INGREDIENTS:

- ½ CUP SOY SAUCE
- ½ CUP MIRIN
- ½ CUP FRESH LEMON JUICE
- ¼ CUP SESAME OIL
- 3-INCH PIECE FRESH GINGER, PEELED AND GRATED
- 1 TABLESPOON LEMON ZEST

1. Place all of the ingredients in a jar and stir until the sugar has dissolved. Adjust the seasoning as needed and either use or store in the refrigerator.

TARE SAUCE

YIELD: 2 CUPS / **ACTIVE TIME:** 10 MINUTES / **TOTAL TIME:** 25 MINUTES

Unfamiliar with tare? Think sweet, thickened soy sauce that in Japan is used for everything from dumplings to grilled meat.

INGREDIENTS:

- ½ CUP CHICKEN STOCK (SEE PAGE 660)
- ½ CUP SOY SAUCE
- ½ CUP MIRIN
- ¼ CUP SAKE
- ½ CUP BROWN SUGAR
- 2 GARLIC CLOVES, SMASHED
- 1-INCH PIECE FRESH GINGER, PEELED AND SLICED
- 1½ SCALLIONS, SLICED

1. Place the ingredients in a small saucepan and bring to a simmer over medium heat. Reduce heat to medium-low and simmer, stirring once or twice, until the sauce has reduced slightly, about 10 minutes.

2. Remove from heat, let the sauce cool, and strain before using.

TAKOYAKI SAUCE

YIELD: 1½ CUPS / **ACTIVE TIME:** 2 MINUTES / **TOTAL TIME:** 2 MINUTES

An easy-to-prepare sauce that is absolutely marvelous beside any of the seafood-based meatballs in the book.

INGREDIENTS:

- 1 CUP WORCESTERSHIRE SAUCE
- 2 TABLESPOONS MENTSUYU
- 1½ TABLESPOONS SUGAR
- 1 TABLESPOON KETCHUP

1. Place all of the ingredients in a small bowl and whisk to combine. Taste, adjust the seasoning as needed, and serve.

FERMENTED HOT SAUCE

YIELD: 2 CUPS / **ACTIVE TIME:** 10 MINUTES / **TOTAL TIME:** 30 DAYS TO 6 MONTHS

If you're addicted to hot sauce, fermented hot sauce will take that addiction to the next level.

INGREDIENTS:

2 LBS. CAYENNE PEPPERS

1 LB. JALAPEÑO PEPPERS

5 GARLIC CLOVES

1 RED ONION, QUARTERED

3 TABLESPOONS KOSHER SALT, PLUS MORE TO TASTE

FILTERED WATER, AS NEEDED

1. Remove the tops of the peppers and split them down the middle.

2. Place the split peppers and the garlic, onion, and salt in a mason jar and cover with water. Seal the jar and shake well.

3. Place the jar away from direct sunlight and let stand for at least 30 days and up to 6 months. Occasionally unscrew the lid to release some of the gases that build up. The flavor will improve the longer you let the mixture ferment.

4. Once you are ready to make the sauce, reserve most of the brine, transfer the mixture to a blender, and puree to desired thickness. If you want the sauce to be on the thin side, keep adding brine until you reach the desired consistency. Season with salt, transfer to a container, cover, and store in the refrigerator for up to 3 months.

GRILLED PEACH & CORN SALSA

YIELD: 6 SERVINGS / **ACTIVE TIME:** 15 MINUTES / **TOTAL TIME:** 20 MINUTES

The juicy peaches complement the natural sweetness of the grilled corn in a salsa that is hard to resist. A couple meatballs served over Spanish Rice (see page 552) and topped with this salsa make for an excellent meal.

INGREDIENTS:

- 1 TABLESPOON OLIVE OIL
- 2 EARS OF SWEET CORN
- 3 PEACHES, PEELED, PITTED, AND CHOPPED
- 1 CUP CHERRY OR GRAPE TOMATOES, HALVED
- ⅓ CUP DICED RED ONION
- 1 JALAPEÑO PEPPER, STEMMED, SEEDS AND RIBS REMOVED, AND MINCED
- ¼ CUP CHOPPED FRESH CILANTRO
- 1 LARGE AVOCADO, PITTED AND DICED
- 2 TABLESPOONS FRESH LIME JUICE
- SALT AND PEPPER, TO TASTE

1. Preheat a gas or charcoal grill to medium heat (400°F). Brush olive oil onto the ears of corn and grill for about 5 minutes, turning throughout. Remove from heat once grill marks appear.

2. Cut the kernels from the cobs and place them in a large bowl. Add the chopped peaches, tomatoes, onion, jalapeño, and cilantro. Stir to combine and then fold in the avocado.

3. Add the lime juice, salt, and pepper. Stir gently and either serve or store in the refrigerator.

HOMEMADE TOMATO SALSA

YIELD: 6 SERVINGS / **ACTIVE TIME:** 35 MINUTES / **TOTAL TIME:** 2 HOURS AND 35 MINUTES

While you can easily buy your own salsa at the store, nothing beats the fresh zing of homemade salsa. This recipe calls for cherry tomatoes. They are slightly more tart than other tomatoes, depending on the type you purchase, but you can use whatever tomatoes you have on hand.

INGREDIENTS:

2 TABLESPOONS OLIVE OIL

2 CUPS CHERRY TOMATOES

1 YELLOW ONION, CHOPPED

6 GARLIC CLOVES, CRUSHED

2 JALAPEÑO PEPPERS, STEMMED, SEEDS AND RIBS REMOVED, AND DICED

½ CUP FRESH CILANTRO LEAVES

JUICE FROM 1 LIME

1 TEASPOON GROUND CUMIN

SALT AND PEPPER, TO TASTE

1. Place a cast-iron skillet on a grill at medium-low heat. Combine the oil, tomatoes, onion, garlic, and jalapeño in a bowl. Next, transfer the mixture to the heated cast-iron skillet and grill for about 20 minutes, stirring every now and then until the tomatoes are charred.

2. Once charred, transfer the contents of the skillet to a food processor along with the remaining ingredients. Pulse until the salsa is the desired texture and then cover for at least 2 hours before serving.

TOMATILLO SALSA

YIELD: 6 SERVINGS / **ACTIVE TIME:** 15 MINUTES / **TOTAL TIME:** 15 MINUTES

The tomatillos provide a bright, acidic, fruity flavor to this salsa that is unmatched.

INGREDIENTS:

- 10 TOMATILLOS, HUSKED AND RINSED
- 1 SMALL ONION, CHOPPED
- 2 GARLIC CLOVES, MINCED
- ¼ CUP CHOPPED FRESH CILANTRO
- 1 JALAPEÑO PEPPER, STEMMED, SEEDS AND RIBS REMOVED, AND CHOPPED
- SALT AND PEPPER, TO TASTE

1. Place the tomatillos in a saucepan and cover with water. Place over medium-high heat on the stovetop, bring to a boil, and cook for 10 minutes.

2. After 10 minutes, remove the tomatillos from the saucepan and place in a food processor along with the remaining ingredients. Pulse until smooth.

TROPICAL SALSA

YIELD: 2 CUPS / **ACTIVE TIME:** 10 MINUTES / **TOTAL TIME:** 10 MINUTES

Between the mango, pineapple, and lime juice, this salsa tastes so good that you could serve it for dessert.

INGREDIENTS:

- 1 CUP MINCED PINEAPPLE
- ¼ CUCUMBER, MINCED
- ¼ CUP MINCED MANGO
- 1 SMALL SHALLOT, MINCED
- 2 TABLESPOONS MINCED RED BELL PEPPER
- 1 TABLESPOON FINELY CHOPPED FRESH CILANTRO
- 2 TABLESPOONS FRESH LIME JUICE
- HOT SAUCE, TO TASTE
- 1 TEASPOON BLACK PEPPER
- 1 TEASPOON KOSHER SALT

1. Place all of the ingredients in a small bowl, whisk until combined, and serve.

GUACAMOLE

YIELD: 2 CUPS / **ACTIVE TIME:** 5 MINUTES / **TOTAL TIME:** 5 MINUTES

The rich texture and taste of avocados were made to accompany the savory meatballs in this book.

1. Place the onion, lime zest and juice, salt, and jalapeño in a mixing bowl and stir to combine.

2. Add the avocados and work the mixture with a fork until the desired consistency has been reached. Add the cilantro and tomato, stir to incorporate, and taste. Taste, adjust the seasoning if necessary, and serve.

INGREDIENTS:

- 2 TABLESPOONS MINCED RED ONION
- ZEST AND JUICE OF 1 LIME
- SALT, TO TASTE
- 1 JALAPEÑO PEPPER, STEMMED, SEEDS AND RIBS REMOVED, AND MINCED
- FLESH FROM 3 AVOCADOS, CHOPPED
- 2 TABLESPOONS FINELY CHOPPED FRESH CILANTRO
- 1 PLUM TOMATO, SEEDED AND CHOPPED

CHIMICHURRI REDUX

YIELD: 1 CUP / **ACTIVE TIME:** 5 MINUTES / **TOTAL TIME:** 5 MINUTES

The one variable in this recipe is the herb other than parsley. Thyme, rosemary, and oregano have strong flavors, so use them sparingly, but basil, cilantro, and dill can be tossed in liberally.

INGREDIENTS:

- 1 CUP FRESH PARSLEY LEAVES
- 1 GARLIC CLOVE
- JUICE OF ¼ LEMON
- LEAVES FROM 1 SPRIG FRESH ROSEMARY OR PREFERRED HERB
- 1 TEASPOON KOSHER SALT
- 1 STRIP LEMON ZEST
- 1 TABLESPOON CAPERS
- ½ TEASPOON RED PEPPER FLAKES
- BLACK PEPPER, TO TASTE
- ¼ CUP OLIVE OIL

1. Place all of the ingredients, except for the oil, in a food processor and puree until it is nearly smooth, scraping down the work bowl as needed.

2. With the food processor running, slowly add the oil and blitz until emulsified.

3. If not using immediately, refrigerate the sauce and allow it to come to room temperature before serving.

CARAMEL

YIELD: 3 CUPS / **ACTIVE TIME:** 15 MINUTES / **TOTAL TIME:** 15 MINUTES

Take great care when adding the butter and cream, as the very hot syrup will splatter.

INGREDIENTS:

- 3 CUPS SUGAR
- 1 CUP WATER
- 6 TABLESPOONS UNSALTED BUTTER, CUT INTO SMALL PIECES
- 2 CUPS HEAVY CREAM
- 2 TEASPOONS PURE VANILLA EXTRACT

1. Place the sugar and water in a saucepan and bring to a boil over medium-high heat. Swirl the pan as it cooks, but do not stir. Raise the heat to high and cook until the syrup is a nut-brown color.

2. Remove the pan from the heat and stir in the butter and cream with a long-handled wooden spoon to avoid any splatter, as the mixture will bubble furiously at first. Place the pan over low heat and stir until the caramel is smooth. Stir in the vanilla, transfer to a jar, and serve hot or at room temperature.

VARIATION

- Decrease the amount of vanilla to ½ teaspoon and add 2 tablespoons brandy, rum, or a liqueur.

CHOCOLATE SAUCE

YIELD: 3 CUPS / **ACTIVE TIME:** 15 MINUTES / **TOTAL TIME:** 15 MINUTES

Delicious over ice cream, of course, but also over any of the desserts in this book.

INGREDIENTS:

- 10 OZ. QUALITY BITTERSWEET CHOCOLATE
- 1 CUP HEAVY CREAM
- ¼ CUP UNSWEETENED COCOA POWDER
- ½ TEASPOON PURE VANILLA EXTRACT
- PINCH OF KOSHER SALT

1. Place the chocolate in a food processor and pulse until chopped. Set it aside.

2. Place the cream in a saucepan and warm it over medium heat. Stir in the cocoa powder, vanilla, and salt and bring the mixture to a boil, stirring frequently. Remove the pan from heat, add the chocolate, cover the pan, and let it sit for 5 minutes. Stir until smooth, transfer to a jar, and either use immediately or store in the refrigerator, where it will keep for up to 1 week.

VARIATIONS

- Add 2 tablespoons instant coffee powder along with the cocoa for mocha sauce.
- Add 2 tablespoons of your favorite liqueur.
- Add ½ cup chopped toasted nuts.

APPENDIX

SAFETY FIRST

The first—and most important—requirement for good cooking, whether the food is a few meatballs or a whole roast, is knowing the basic rules of food safety. This begins with trips to the supermarket and ends after leftovers are refrigerated or frozen at the end of a meal.

This may seem like common sense, but after many decades as a food writer I've heard horror stories about very sick people who did not follow basic food safety rules.

If you have any questions about food safety, the U.S. Department of Agriculture is the place to go. The Food Safety Inspection Service was designed to help you. The website, fsis.usda.gov, provides a wealth of information in a very user-friendly format.

SHOP SAFELY

Most supermarkets are designed to funnel you into the produce section first. But that's not the best place to start. Begin your shopping with the shelf-stable items in the store's center, proceed to the produce section, and end with the other refrigerated and frozen food sections.

Never buy meat or poultry that is in a torn and leaking package. It's also a good idea to place all meats and poultry in the disposable plastic bags made available in each department. Check the sell-by and use-by dates, and never purchase food that is past either one.

The case is usually stocked with the least fresh offerings on top, so dig down a few layers and you'll probably find options with a few more days of life in them.

For the trip home, it's a good idea to keep an insulated cooler in the back of your car if it's hot outside or if the perishable items will be out of refrigeration for more than 1 hour. In hot weather, many seafood departments will provide crushed ice in a separate bag for your fish.

BANISH BACTERIA

Fruits and vegetables can contain some bacteria, but it's far more likely that it will grow on meat, poultry, and seafood. Store these foods on the bottom shelves of your refrigerator so their juices cannot accidentally drip down onto other foods. And keep these foods refrigerated as long as you can before they go into the pan, as bacteria multiply at room temperature. The so-called "danger zone" is between 40°F and 140°F. As food cooks, it's important for it to pass through this zone as quickly as possible.

AVOID CROSS-CONTAMINATION

Cleanliness is not only next to godliness; it's also the key to food safety. Wash your hands often while you're cooking, and never touch cooked food if you haven't washed your hands after handling raw food. The "cooked food and raw food shall never meet" precept extends beyond the cook's hands. Clean cutting boards, knives, and kitchen counters often. If you have the space, section off your countertops for raw foods and cooked foods, as many restaurant kitchens do.

As bacteria from raw animal proteins can contaminate other foods, don't place cooked foods or raw foods that will remain uncooked (i.e. salad greens) on cutting boards that have been used to cut any raw meat.

CHOOSE THE RIGHT CUTTING BOARD

A good way to prevent foodborne illness is by selecting the right cutting board. Wooden boards might be attractive, but you can never get them as clean as plastic boards that can be run through the dishwasher. Even with plastic boards, it's best to designate one for cooked food and foods such as vegetables that are not prone to contain bacteria, and have another one devoted to raw meats.

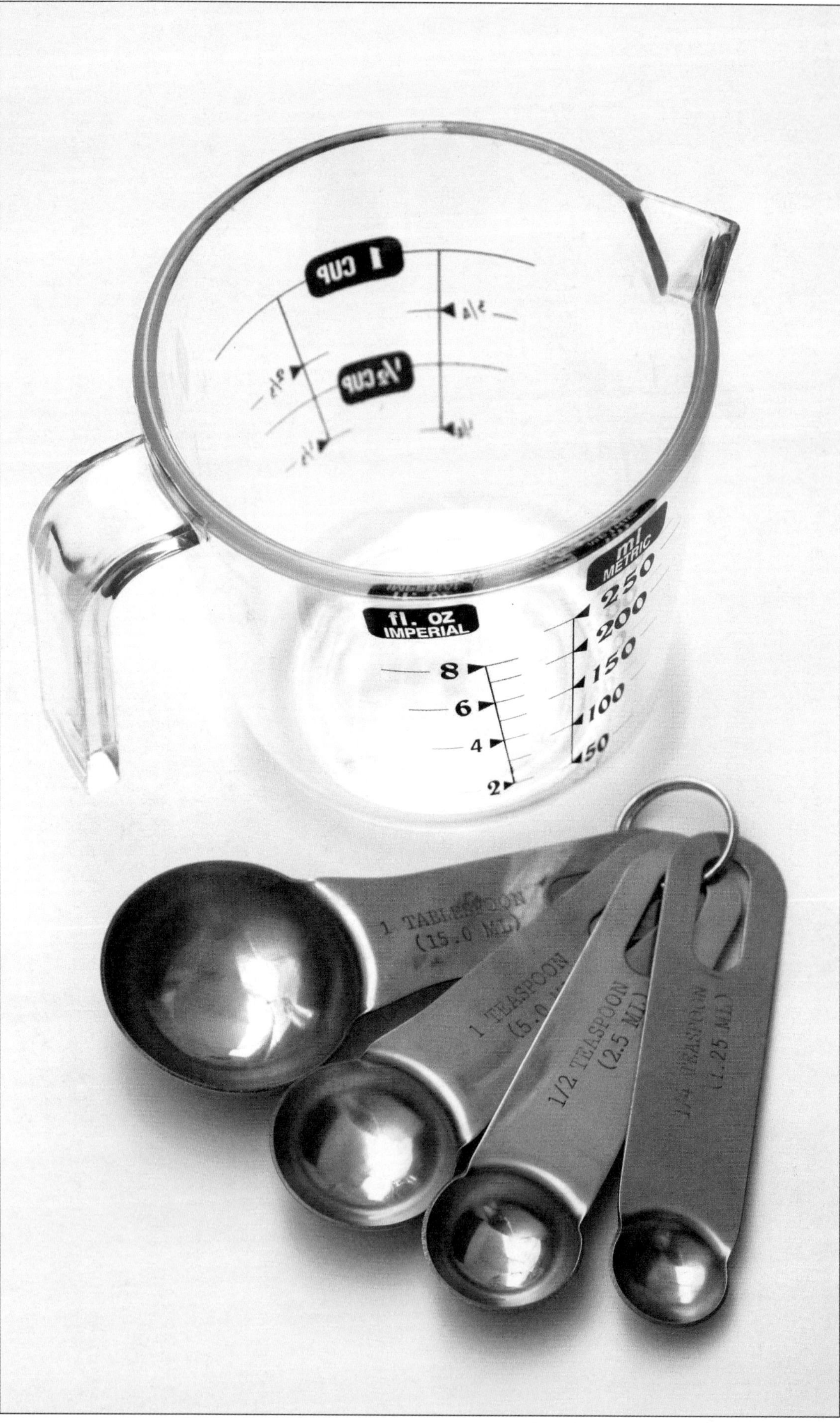
fl. oz
IMPERIAL
8
6
4
2
ml
METRIC
250
200
150
100
50
(15.0 ML)
1/2 TEASPOON (2.5 ML)
1/4 TEASPOON

METRIC CONVERSIONS

WEIGHTS

1 oz. = 28 grams
2 oz. = 57 grams
4 oz. (¼ lb.) = 113 grams
8 oz. (½ lb.) = 227 grams
16 oz. (1 lb.) = 454 grams

VOLUME MEASURES

⅛ teaspoon = 0.6 ml
¼ teaspoon = 1.23 ml
½ teaspoon = 2.5 ml
1 teaspoon = 5 ml
1 tablespoon (3 teaspoons) = ½ fluid oz. = 15 ml
2 tablespoons = 1 fluid oz. = 29.5 ml
¼ cup (4 tablespoons) = 2 fluid oz. = 59 ml
⅓ cup (5 ⅓ tablespoons) = 2.7 fluid oz. = 80 ml
½ cup (8 tablespoons) = 4 fluid oz. = 120 ml
⅔ cup (10 ⅔ tablespoons) = 5.4 fluid oz. = 160 ml
¾ cup (12 tablespoons) = 6 fluid oz. = 180 ml
1 cup (16 tablespoons) = 8 fluid oz. = 240 ml

TEMPERATURE EQUIVALENTS

°F	°C	Gas Mark
225	110	¼
250	130	½
275	140	1
300	150	2
325	170	3
350	180	4
375	190	5
400	200	6
425	220	7
450	230	8
475	240	9
500	250	10

LENGTH MEASURES

1⁄16 inch = 1.6 mm
⅛ inch = 3 mm
¼ inch = 1.35 mm
½ inch = 1.25 cm
¾ inch = 2 cm
1 inch = 2.5 cm

ABOUT THE AUTHOR

Ellen Brown is a 30-year veteran foodie and the founding food editor of *USA Today*. She is the author of more than 30 cookbooks, including several Complete Idiot's guides. Her writing has been featured in major publications including *The Washington Post, The Los Angeles Times, Bon Appétit, Art Culinaire,* and *The San Francisco Chronicle*, and she has a weekly column in the *Providence Journal*. She lives in Providence, Rhode Island.

IMAGE CREDITS

Images on pages 39, 41, 52, 56, 68, 71, 74, 77-78, 81, 85, 90, 93, 115-116, 119, 124, 128, 602, 630, and 652 courtesy of Cider Mill Press.

All other images used under official license from Shutterstock.com and StockFood.com.

INDEX

C

D

H

I

K

L

P

Q

R

S

T

ABOUT CIDER MILL PRESS BOOK PUBLISHERS

Good ideas ripen with time. From seed to harvest, Cider Mill Press brings fine reading, information, and entertainment together between the covers of its creatively crafted books. Our Cider Mill bears fruit twice a year, publishing a new crop of titles each spring and fall.

"Where Good Books Are Ready for Press"

Visit us on the Web at

cidermillpress.com

or write to us at

PO Box 454
12 Spring St.
Kennebunkport, Maine 04046